PRICING
STRATEGIES

edited by Z. John Zhang, Ph.D.

The Wharton School, The University of Pennsylvania

 **Custom Publishing**

Boston   Burr Ridge, IL   Dubuque, IA   Madison, WI   New York   San Francisco   St. Louis
Bangkok   Bogotá   Caracas   Kuala Lumpur   Lisbon   London   Madrid   Mexico City   Milan
Montreal   New Delhi   Santiago   Seoul   Singapore   Sydney   Taipei   Toronto

Pricing Strategies

McGraw-Hill's Primis Custom Publishing consists of products that are produced from camera-ready copy. Peer review, class testing, and accuracy are primarily the responsibility of the author(s).

    4 5 6 7 8 9 0   QSR QSR 0 9 8

ISBN-13: 978-0-256-39631-7
ISBN-10: 0-256-39631-0

Editor: Elaine Manke
Production Editor: Susan Culbertson
Cover Photo: David Reibstein
Cover Design: Maggie Lytle
Printer/Binder: Quebecor World

Contents

How Manufacturers Price Products

Companies continue to practice full-cost pricing, but there is a shift toward target costing.

BY EUNSUP SHIM, CMA, AND
EPHRAIM F. SUDIT

Certificate of Merit, 1993-94

In 1983, V. Govindarajan and R.N. Anthony (G & A) surveyed Fortune 1,000 companies, finding that most large companies price their products based on full cost rather than variable cost.[1] Full-cost pricing is based on variable costs plus allocated fixed costs.

In 1993, Eunsup Shim conducted a similar survey of pricing practices in U.S. manufacturing companies.[2] These results are compared with the 1983 survey by G & A and are used to assess the relationship between ABC implementation by U.S. manufacturers and their pricing practices. In addition, the rationale for choosing certain product pricing methods is discussed.

Why are pricing practices important? In a new manufacturing environment, managers are faced with global competition and increased productivity. Companies have become customer driven, focusing on delivering quality products at competitive prices. In many areas of manufacturing, domestic and foreign competition demand well-defined pricing strategies. Comprehensive product-cost systems should provide increased accuracy for managerial decisions concerning new products, pricing, and discontinuing and/or reengineering existing products.[3] Some evidence suggests that the distortion in reported product costs and, in turn, product pricing could be reduced by using activity-based costing (ABC).[4]

The use of costing information for pricing decisions has generated considerable debate over the years among economists, accounting researchers, and practitioners. Economists argue that, in order to maximize profits, prices should be set at the level of production where marginal cost intersects marginal revenue. In other words, pricing is based on marginal cost and marginal revenue; fixed charges for associated services are not used. The "profit maximization model" advocates the use of variable-cost pricing.

G & A drew on Herbert Simon's "satisficing" model, which states that the primary objective for companies is to seek a satisfactory return, as opposed to the "profit maximization" model. The "satisficing" model leads companies to use full-cost pricing and provides a possible rationale for the prevalent use of this method. Practitioners cite savings in gathering cost information as well as its simplicity.

1993 PRICING PRACTICES

In the Shim survey, data were gathered across U.S. industries garnering 141 usable responses, a response rate of 23.5%. The majority of the respondents (81.5%) were in top management including controllers, vice presidents, general managers, or chief financial officers. Most of the responding companies (91%) were in the multi-products environment, averaging 75 products. The reported high product diversification is a phenomenon consistent with companies being more flexible in response to the new manufacturing environment.

The survey showed that full-cost pricing dominated pricing practices (69.5%), with slightly more than 10% (12.1%) of the respondents using a variable-cost method (see Table 1). Full-cost pricing determines the selling prices based on full cost plus a certain percentage of profit. The full-cost pricing method is further broken into "percentage of manufacturing costs" and "percentage of all costs." Of the 98 full-cost pricing companies, 48 (49%) are reported to determine the prices based on percentage of manufacturing costs, and 50 (51%) used percentage of all costs in deriving product prices.

Variable-cost pricing follows similar procedures in arriving at product prices except for the use of "percentage of variable manufacturing costs" and "percentage of all variable costs."

Full-cost pricing, the predominant method, is used especially in the chemicals (80%) and

TABLE 1 / COMPARISON OF PRODUCT PRICING METHODS

Pricing Method		Shim (1993)		G & A (1983)	
		Frequency	Percent	Frequency	Percent
Full-Cost Pricing	Percent of Manufacturing Costs	48	34.0	209	41.0
	Percent of All Costs	50	35.5	208	41.0
	Subtotal	50	59.5	417	82.0
Variable-Cost Pricing	Percent of Variable Manufacturing Costs	8	5.7	54	11.0
	Percent of All Variable Costs	9	6.4	30	6.0
	Subtotal	17	12.1	84	17.0
Market-Based Pricing (Competitive Pricing)		25	17.7	Not Surveyed	Not Surveyed
Other		1	0.7	4	1.0
Total Respondents		141	100	505	100

TABLE 2 / PRODUCT PRICING METHODS BY:

A / INDUSTRY

	Full-Cost Pricing	Variable-Cost Pricing	Market-Based Pricing	Total (%)
Chemicals	4	0	1	5 (3%)
Machining	17	4	6	27 (19%)
Electronics	27	4	6	37 (26%)
Transportation	2	0	1	3 (2%)
Medical	34	7	9	50 (36%)
Others	14	2	3	19 (14%)
Total (%)	98 (70%)	17 (12%)	26 (18%)	141 (100%)

B / SIZE (ANNUAL SALES) OF COMPANY

	Full-Cost Pricing	Variable-Cost Pricing	Market-Based Pricing	Total (%)
Under $10 Million	11	0	3	14 (10%)
$11–100 Million	59	11	19	89 (63%)
$101–500 Million	25	6	4	35 (25%)
$501 Million– 1 Billion	1	0	0	1 (0.7%)
$1–5 Billion	2	0	0	2 (1.3%)
Total (%)	98 (70%)	17 (12%)	26 (18%)	141 (100%)

C / ABC IMPLEMENTATION

	Full-Cost Pricing	Variable-Cost Pricing	Market-Based Pricing	Total (%)
Fully or Partially Implemented	26	6	6	38 (26.9%)
Plan to Implement	33	7	13	53 (37.6%)
Not Plan to Implement	39	4	7	50 (35.5%)
Total (%)	98 (70%)	17 (12%)	26 (18%)	141 (100%)

electronics (72%) industries (see Table 2A). The prevalence of full-cost pricing, which requires considerable overhead cost allocation, underscores the importance of rational cost allocation. ABC tends to offer a better allocation scheme with activity analysis.

The 1993 survey reported that almost 20% of the respondents' companies use market-based (competitive) pricing. This result seems to indicate a movement to market or "target cost" pricing from cost-based pricing. Target costing is the long-run cost that a customer will bear or a market-based cost that is calculated using a sales price necessary to capture a predetermined market share.[5]

Full-cost pricing is the most popular method in companies of all sizes. Of the 14 small companies (sales under $10 million), 11 use full-cost pricing. For mid-sized companies ($11 million-$500 million in sales) there was a higher incidence of variable-cost pricing and competitive pricing (Table 2B).

The relationship between pricing method and stages of ABC implementation is highlighted in Table 2C. Companies that do not plan to implement ABC show the highest use of full-cost pricing (78%). Companies that have implemented or plan to implement ABC systems exhibit a slightly higher percentage of variable-cost pricing or market-based pricing methods (32% and 39%) than companies that do not plan to implement ABC systems (22%). The majority of companies, however, adhere to full-cost pricing.

The 1983 G & A survey showed similar results to the 1993 Shim survey, with 82% of the responding companies using full-cost pricing and 17% using variable-cost pricing. Thus, both surveys reveal the continuously prevailing use of full-cost pricing from 1983 to 1993. The consistent practice of full-cost pricing underscores the importance of proper cost allocation and product costing.

An interesting result of the 1993 survey is that 25 companies (18%) reported using market-based (competitive) pricing, which was not reported in the 1983 survey. This result indicates an important change in arriving at prices, one that is based on competitive market conditions rather than cost structures.

RATIONALE FOR FULL COST

There are a number of plausible reasons for the continuing use of full-cost pricing. First, increased implementation of ABC systems is likely to rationalize the allocation of fixed costs and makes more seemingly fixed costs variable or semi-variable. ABC systems enhance ways of tracing fixed costs to a specific product and lead to a better allocation of these costs. ABC systems provide more accurate product cost estimates that serve as a basis of determining full-cost price. The rapid implementation of ABC systems, therefore, tends to supply a support for the prevalent use of full-cost pricing practice.

Second, full-cost pricing provides a motivation to control fixed costs. For example, allocation of fixed costs to profit centers affects the performance of those centers. Accordingly, the profit center managers, whose performance varies with the amount of allocated fixed costs, can raise questions about the amount of corporate overhead (that is, fixed costs) and, as a result, may reduce the "empire building" phenomenon.[6] The use of fully allocated fixed costs in determining price could provide an alternative risk-sharing arrangement between profit center managers and top managers.

Finally, the difficulty in estimating marginal cost and marginal revenue for various products may prevent companies from using the marginal-cost approach. With manufacturing companies producing an average of 75 products, estimating marginal cost and marginal revenue may not be feasible or economical.

The majority of companies in the new manufacturing environment continue to practice full-cost pricing. The possible reasons for this practice are: "satisficing" behavior, availability of finer product costing information with implementation of ABC systems, possibility of controlling fixed costs, and difficulty in estimating marginal cost and marginal revenue in a multiproduct environment.

THE FUTURE?

Full-cost pricing continues to be the most popular product pricing method, but there is a shift toward variable-cost pricing or market-based (competitive) pricing. The 1993 survey exhibits only a very slow trend in this direction. The fierce domestic and foreign competition in the new manufacturing environment may bolster the use of some form of competitive pricing in the future. ∎

Eunsup Shim, CMA, CPA, Ph.D., is assistant professor of accounting at Saint Joseph's University, Philadelphia, Pa. He is a member of the Philadelphia Chapter, through which this article was submitted, and can be reached at (610) 660-1660.

Ephraim F. Sudit, Ph.D., is a professor of accounting and Information systems at the Graduate School of Management, Rutgers University, Newark, N.J. He is a member of the IMA and can be reached at (201) 648-5241.

[1]V. Govindarajan and R.N. Anthony, "How Firms Use Cost Data in Pricing Decisions," MANAGEMENT ACCOUNTING, July 1983, p. 30-37.

[2]Eunsup Shim, "Cost Management and Activity-based Cost Allocation in a New Manufacturing Environment," Unpublished Dissertation, Rutgers University, Newark, N.J., January 1993.

[3]R. Cooper and R.S. Kaplan, "How Cost Accounting Systematically Distorts Product Costs," *Accounting and Management: Field Study Perspective*, Harvard Business School Press, Boston, Mass., 1987, p. 226.

[4]R. Cooper, "Implementing an Activity-Based Cost System," *Emerging Practices in Cost Management*, Warren, Gorham & Lamont, Inc., Boston, Mass., 1990, p. 69.

[5]C. Berliner, and J. A. Brimson, *Cost Management for Today's Advanced Manufacturing: The CAM-I Conceptual Design*, Harvard Business School Press, Boston, Mass., 1988.

[6]Anthony, Dearden, and Govindarajan, *Management Control Systems*, 7th ed., Irwin, Homewood, Ill., 1992, p. 184.

4

Harvard Business School

584-149
Rev. September 29, 1986

Basic Quantitative Analysis for Marketing

Simple calculations often help in making quality marketing decisions. To do good "numbers work," one needs only a calculator, familiarity with a few key constructs, and some intuition about what numbers to look at. This note has as its primary purpose the introduction of key constructs. The development of intuition about what quantities to compute can begin with this note, but is best accomplished by repeated analyses of marketing situations and application of the concepts and techniques presented here. Case study analysis provides that opportunity.

The organization of the note is as follows. First we define key constructs such as variable cost, fixed cost, contribution and margin. Following definition of these basic constructs, we discuss a most useful quantity: the "break-even" volume. We show how to calculate and use this quantity in marketing decision making.

Basic Terminology

As marketers, we are usually concerned with understanding the market or demand for the product or service in question. However, if we are to assess the likely profit consequences of alternative actions, we must understand the cost associated with doing business as well. For example, consider a firm choosing a price for its new videocassette tape. The manager estimates weekly sales for different prices to be

Weekly Sales Estimate		Price
600	Units	$7.50
700	Units	6.00
1,000	Units	5.00

Which price is best for the firm? From the data given so far, we cannot answer the question. We can calculate the expected revenue generated by each pricing strategy, but without cost information, it is not possible to determine the preferred price. This is the reason we begin this marketing note by considering key cost concepts.

The cost concepts we introduce are variable cost, fixed cost, and total cost. Second, we combine the cost information with price information to determine unit contribution and total contribution. **Figure A** shows the relationship between a typical firm's unit output and total cost of producing that output.

Associate Professor Robert J. Dolan prepared this note.

The first important feature of **Figure A** is that the total cost line (the solid line) does not go through the origin, i.e., for a zero output level, total cost is not zero. Rather, total cost is OA dollars as shown by the length of the double headed arrow in **Figure A**. We call OA the firm's "fixed costs." Fixed costs are those costs which do not vary with the level of output. An example of a fixed cost is the lease cost of a plant. The monthly lease fee is set and would be incurred even if the firm temporarily suspended production.

Figure A   Total Cost as Function of Output

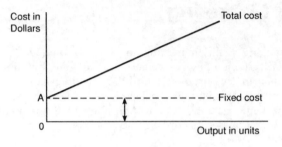

Although OA dollars are fixed, a second component of cost, called "variable cost," increases as output increases. As we have drawn **Figure A**, total costs increase in a linear fashion with output produced. In reality, it is possible for the total cost curve to be as shown in either **Figure B** or **Figure C**. **Figure B** represents a situation where each unit is cheaper to produce than the previous one. This would occur, for example, if the firm could buy raw material at lower unit prices as the amount it bought increased. **Figure C** shows the opposite situation, i.e., each unit is more expensive to produce than the previous one. This might happen if the firm faced limited supply of inputs and had to pay higher unit prices as its demand increased.

Figure B   Cost Increasing at Decreasing Rate

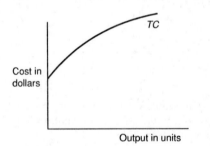

Figure C   Cost Increasing at Increasing Rate

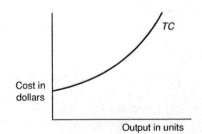

While many real world examples of **Figure B** and **C** type of situations exist, we will typically be making the assumption that **Figure A** is a good enough approximation of actual cost behavior. The total cost line drawn in **Figure A** is special, because it represents the case of each unit costing the same. Thus, for **Figure A**, we can write

$$
\begin{array}{l}
\text{Total cost} \\
\text{for output} \\
\text{level } V
\end{array}
\;=\;
\begin{array}{l}
\text{Fixed} \\
\text{cost}
\end{array}
\;+\;
\begin{array}{l}
\text{Total variable} \\
\text{cost for} \\
\text{output level } V
\end{array}
$$

$$
=\; \underset{\text{OA}}{\text{Fixed cost}} + [k \times V] \qquad (1)
$$

In Equation 1, k is the cost of producing one more unit of output. It is the slope of the total cost curve in **Figure A** and does not change over the range of output shown. In summary, one can divide the firm's total cost into two parts: fixed cost and variable cost. Second, we will frequently assume that the cost of producing an additional unit of output does not change, so we can write the variable cost as $k \times V$ where V is total output.

Having defined total, variable, and fixed cost, we can now introduce the concept of contribution. If k is the constant unit variable cost and P the price received for the good or service, then we define

$$
\begin{array}{l}
\text{Unit contribution} \\
\text{(in dollars)}
\end{array}
\;=\; P - k \qquad (2)
$$

If V is the total number of units the firm sells, then

$$
\text{Total contribution} \;=\; (P - k) \times V \qquad (3)
$$

That is total contribution equals unit contribution times unit volume sold.

If we take the V in Equation 3 inside the parentheses, we obtain

$$
\text{Total contribution} \;=\;
\underset{\substack{\text{Total} \\ \text{revenue}}}{PV} \;-\;
\underset{\substack{\text{Total} \\ \text{variable} \\ \text{cost}}}{kV} \qquad (4)
$$

Thus total contribution is the amount available to the firm to cover (or contribute to) fixed cost and profit after the variable cost has been deducted from total revenue.

Let's solidify our understanding of these definitions by working through the videocassette tape pricing problem. Suppose the unit variable cost k is \$4; then assuming the sales forecasts for each price level given above are correct:

Price = \$5

Unit contribution	=	$P - k = \$5 - \$4 = \$1$
Total contribution	=	$(P - k) \times V$
per week	=	\$1/unit × 1,000 × 1,000 units/week
	=	1,000/week

Price = \$6

Unit contribution	=	\$6 − \$4 = \$2
Total contribution	=	\$2/unit × 700 units/week
per week	=	\$1,400/week

Price = \$7.50

Unit contribution	=	\$7.50 − \$4 = \$3.50
Total contribution	=	\$3.50/unit × 600 units/week
per week	=	\$2.100/week

Since, by definition, the fixed cost associated with each output level is the same, the firm is best off by charging \$7.50 since of the three possible prices \$7.50 maximizes the total contribution. Demonstrate to yourself that if the unit variable cost were \$1, the firm would be better off at the \$5 price.

Margin Calculations

The term "margin" is sometimes used interchangeably with "unit contribution" for a manufacturer. Margin is also used to refer to the difference between the acquisition price and selling price of a good for a member of the channels of distribution. For example, consider **Figure D**, in which we have the videocassette tape manufacturer selling through a wholesaler, who in turn sells to retailers, who then sell to the public. Each of the three members of the channel of distribution (manufacturer, wholesaler, retailer) performs a function and is compensated for it by the margin it receives:

		Manufacturer's selling price to distributors	–	Manufacturing cost
Manufacturer's margin	=			
	=	$7.50	–	$4.00 = $3.50
Wholesaler's margin	=	Wholesaler's selling price to retailers	–	Price paid to manufacturer
	=	$8.70	–	$7.50 = $1.20
Retailer's margin	=	Retailer's selling price to consumers	–	Price paid to wholesaler
	=	$10.00	–	$8.70 = $1.30

So the dollar margin is a measure of how much each organization makes per unit of goods sold.

Figure D   Price and Cost at Levels in the Channel of Distribution

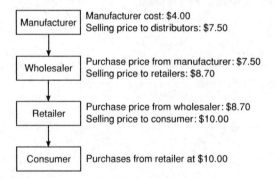

Manufacturer	Manufacturer cost: $4.00 / Selling price to distributors: $7.50
Wholesaler	Purchase price from manufacturer: $7.50 / Selling price to retailers: $8.70
Retailer	Purchase price from wholesaler: $8.70 / Selling price to consumer: $10.00
Consumer	Purchases from retailer at $10.00

The unit contributions and margins we have presented so far have all been in dollar terms. It is sometimes more useful to state margins in percentage terms. Consider the retailer in **Figure D**, who makes a $1.30 margin for videocassette tapes. Are all items offering the retailer a $1.30 margin equally attractive to the retailer? For example, would the retailer be interested in stocking a color television that retails for $300 if he or she has to pay $298.70 for it? The color TV offers the same $1.30 margin. Yet, intuitively, it seems the retailer would not view the $1.30 on the color TV as acceptable, whereas he or she might view the $1.30 on the tape as acceptable. In short, items offering the same dollar margin are not necessarily equally attractive. Often, margins in percentage terms are more useful.

We define the retailer's percent margin as

$$\text{Retailer's percent margin} = \frac{\text{Selling price to consumers} - \text{Purchase price from wholesaler}}{\text{Selling price to consumers}} \quad (5)$$

$$= \frac{\text{Retailer's dollar margin}}{\text{Selling price to consumers}}$$

Note that in the denominator of Equation 5, we have the selling price to consumers. It would have been as logical to put purchase price from wholesaler there instead. It is only by convention that we divide by the selling price. For any member of the channel, we will always compute "its percentage margin by dividing its dollar margin by the price at which it sells the goods. While this is the common definition and we 'will use it in all the cases and discussions, you should understand that this convention is not universal. Thus, you may encounter situations where an alternative convention is followed, and you must be alert to the distinction.

From Equation 5 and the numbers in **Figure D**, we see that

$$\text{Retailer's percent margin} = \frac{\$10.00 - \$8.70}{\$10.00}$$

$$= 13\%$$

Using similar logic, you should be able to show that manufacturer and wholesaler percent margins from **Figure D** are 46.67 percent and 13.79 percent respectively.

Break-Even Volume—Mechanics

Perhaps the single most useful summary statistic one can compute from quantities defined above is the break-even volume (BEV). The BEV is the volume at which the firm's total revenues equal total cost; below BEV, the firm has a loss; above BEV, the firm shows a profit. **Figure E** presents some example data. BEV calculation answers questions such as, if the firm charges $7.50, how many units must be sold to cover costs? We can obtain the answer by drawing a total revenue line as in **Figure F**. The point at which the total revenue line cuts the total cost is BEV. For volumes below BEV (to the left of BEV on **Figure F**), the firm runs a loss; for volumes above' (to the right on **Figure F**), the firm shows a profit.

Figure E   Total Cost Line with Fixed Cost = $2,000 and Unit Variable Cost = $4

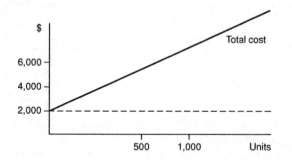

Figure F   Cost, Revenue, and Break-Even Volume

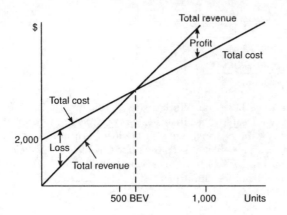

We can derive the BEV algebraically from the fact that at the BEV, total cost and total revenue are equal.

| Total revenue | = | Total cost | (6) |
| Price × BEV | = | Fixed cost + (k × BEV) | |

Solving Equation 6 for BEV, we obtain

$$BEV = \frac{\text{Fixed cost}}{\text{Price} - k}$$

$$= \frac{\text{Fixed cost}}{\text{Unit contribution}}$$

Hence, for the example of **Figure F**

$$BEV = \frac{\$2,000}{\$3.50/\text{unit}} = 571.43 \text{ units}$$

Break-Even Volume—Applications

So, the BEV calculation is simple. Simplicity plus relevance are the characteristics which make BEV so frequently warranted in case analysis. BEV can be of help in making decisions about unit contribution (through price or variable cost changes) or the appropriate level of fixed costs for a business. We now demonstrate each.

First, with respect to unit contribution, let us carry the videotape manufacturer example a little further. We have shown that at a price of $7.50, BEV is 571 units. Since

$$BEV = \frac{\text{Fixed cost}}{\text{Unit contribution}}$$

a price change impacts the BEV. For example, with price at $7, the BEV increases to 666.66 units. At $8, it decreases to 500 units. **Figure G** shows the BEV for various price levels. All price/volume combinations of the "iso-profit curve" offer the same profit, i.e., zero. From the perspective of a pricing decision, the decision maker may say: "Do I have a better chance of trying to sell 2,000 units at $5 or trying to sell 333.33 units at $10?" Notice that for our example cutting the price in half (from $10 to $5) would necessitate a six-fold increase in volume to be worthwhile for the firm. The reason for this, of course, is that this price cut would reduce the unit contribution from $6 ($10 − $4) to $1 ($5 − $4).

Taken with some sense of the market size and competitors' positions, this analysis can be very useful in narrowing the feasible price range for the product.

      Before considering fixed cost changes, we should note that this type of analysis can be done for any given level of profit as easily as the break-even level. For example, if the firm's goal is to make $1,000 per time period in addition to covering its fixed cost, then we can determine the volume required to achieve that goal given any particular price. All the points on the "isoprofit curve" in **Figure G** have the property that the (Price – V.C.) x Volume = $2,000, which is our fixed cost level. If the firm wants to make $1,000 per time period in addition to covering the $2,000 fixed cost, the relevant set of points becomes those satisfying (Price – V.C.) x Volume = $2,000 + $1,000 = $3,000. For any given price, the required volume is ($3,000)/(Price V.C.). **Figure H** shows these points along with the "break-even" curve of **Figure G**.

Figure G   Price and Associated Break-Even Volumes

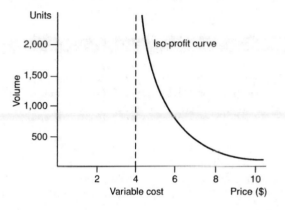

BEV is also useful in analysis of proposed changes in fixed costs. First, it can be used to aid in the decision of whether a new product should be marketed at all. For example, consider a firm which estimates the initial setup costs for plant and equipment and initial advertising outlays required to enter the market to be $3 million. The firm also believes that unit contribution from the product will be about $1,000. Should the firm enter the market? By BEV type of analysis, it is easy to see that the firm must sell 3,000 units just to cover its initial investment. Combined with some knowledge about total market size and competitive offerings, this analysis may suggest whether or not the $3 million investment should be made.

Figure H   Curves for Break-Even and $1,000 Profit

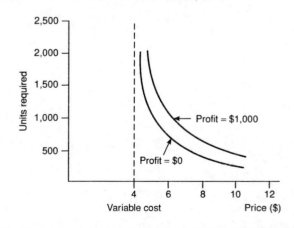

Second, the question of proposed changes in the fixed costs of marketing an existing product can be analyzed. For example, a proposition is made to the tape manufacturer that a $300,000 advertising campaign be undertaken. Should the firm do it? Following the BEV logic and assuming a $7.50 price, we can see

$$\text{Incremental volume required to justify expenditure} = \frac{\text{Incremental expenditure}}{\text{Unit contribution}}$$

$$= \frac{\$300,000}{\$3.50/\text{unit}}$$

$$85,714 \text{ units}$$

So for the $300,000 advertising expense to be justified, the decision maker would have to believe that the expenditure will generate incremental volume of almost 86,000 units.

Using the Numbers

In this note we have shown how one can calculate a quantity given other quantities. Essentially, we showed how to translate some facts or estimates into other facts/estimates. This translation process is useful if the end result is a fact/estimate which is suggestive of what one should do as the manager. For example, we put together a fixed cost of $2,000 (is this good, bad, or indifferent?) and a unit contribution of $3.50 (is this good, bad, or indifferent?) to come up with a break-even volume of 571 units (is this good, bad or indifferent?)—in the hope that the answer to the third question wouldn't be "indifferent" even though it's likely that's what the first two answers would be.

What makes one able to say if 571 units is good or bad? To be able to say it's good or bad, you have to have some other number in your head to compare it to. For example, if the total market for the product is estimated at 500 units, 571 is bad. If it's 50,000 units, 571 represents only a 1.14 percent share, so *maybe* 571 is good.

The key point is this: numbers have meaning only when there is some benchmark to compare them to. In marketing, such benchmarks are developed from understanding the market size, growth rate, and competitive activity. The finding BEV = 571 is, in and of itself, useless unless combined with other information to provide a meaningful context.

As noted at the outset, useful numbers work requires intuition about what quantities to calculate. This short note does little to develop that intuition. Our goals were more modest, i.e., to specify terminology, mechanics, and suggest potential applications. The goal of the quantitative analysis must always be kept clear: to help in making marketing policy decisions.

An eight-step process can help you make better decisions.

How Do You Know When the Price Is Right?

by Robert J. Dolan

Pricing is managers' biggest marketing headache. It's where they feel the most pressure to perform and the least certain that they are doing a good job. The pressure is intensified because, for the most part, managers believe that they don't have control over price: It is dictated by the market. Moreover, pricing is often seen as a difficult area in which to set objectives and measure results. Ask managers to define the objective for the company's manufacturing function, and they will cite a concrete goal, such as output and cost. Ask for a measure of productivity, and they will refer to cycle times. But pricing is difficult to pin down. High unit sales and increased market share sound promising but they may in fact mean that a price is too low. And forgone profits do not appear on anyone's scorecard. Indeed, judging pricing quality from outcomes reported on financial statements is perilous business.

Yet getting closer to the "right" price can have a tremendous impact. Even slight improvements can yield significant results. For example, for a company with 8% profit margins, a 1% improvement in price realization – assuming a steady unit sales volume – would boost the company's margin dollars by 12.5%.[1] For that reason, even one step toward better pricing can be worth a lot.

To improve a company's pricing capability, managers should begin by focusing on the process, not on the outcome. The first question to ask is not, What should the price be? but rather, Have we addressed all the considerations that will determine the correct price? Pricing is not simply a matter of getting one key thing right. Proper pricing comes from carefully and consistently managing a myriad of issues.

Based on observation and participation in setting prices in a wide variety of situations, I have identified two broad qualities of any effective pricing process and a "to do" list for improving that process. Not every point will apply to every business, and some managers will need to supplement the checklist with other actions that pertain to their specific situation. But in general, by using these criteria as a guide, managers will begin to set prices that earn the company measurably greater returns, and they will gain control over the pricing function.

Strategy and Coordination

All successful pricing efforts share two qualities: The policy complements the company's overall marketing strategy, and the process is coordinated and holistic.

Marketing Strategy. A company's pricing policy sends a message to the market – it gives customers an important sense of a company's philosophy. Consider Saturn Corporation (a wholly owned subsidiary of General Motors). The company wants to let consumers know that it is friendly and easy to do business with. Part of this concept is conveyed through initiatives such as inviting customers to the factory to see where the cars are made and sponsoring evenings at the dealership that combine a social event with training on car maintenance. But Saturn's pricing policy sends a strong message as well. Can a friendly, trusting relationship be established with customers if a salesperson uses all the negotiating ploys in the book to try to separate them from that last $100? Of course not. Saturn has a "no hassle, no haggle" policy (one price, no negotiations) which removes the possibility of adversarial discussions between dealer and po-

Robert J. Dolan is the Edward W. Carter Professor of Business Administration at the Harvard Business School in Boston, Massachusetts. His most recent book is Managing the New Product Development Process *(Addison-Wesley, 1993). He is currently writing a book on pricing strategy with Hermann Simon. It will be published by the Free Press in 1996.*

PAINTINGS BY JOHN T. O'CONNOR

tential customer. Customers have an easier time buying a car knowing that the next person in the door won't negotiate a better deal.

The pricing policy for Swatch watches illustrates the same point. The company's overall message is that a watch can be more than just functional; it can be fun as well – so much fun, in fact, that a customer ought to own several. The company's price, $40 for a basic model, has not changed in ten years. As Franco Bosisio, the head of the Swatch design lab, noted in William Taylor's interview "Message and Muscle: An Interview with Swatch Titan Nicholas Hayek" (HBR, March-April 1993): "Price has become a mirror for the other attributes we try to communicate.... A Swatch is not just affordable, it's approachable. Buying a Swatch is an easy decision to make, an easy decision to live with. It's provocative, but it doesn't make you think too much."

For Saturn and Swatch, the pricing policy flows directly from the overall marketing strategy. This consistency, or even synergy, of price and the rest of the marketing mix is a critical requirement for success.

Coordination. There are typically many participants in the pricing process: Accounting provides cost estimates; marketing communicates the pricing strategy; sales provides specific customer input; production sets supply boundaries; and finance establishes the requirements for the entire company's monetary health. Input from diverse sources is necessary. However, problems arise when the philosophy of wide participation is carried over to the price-setting process without strong coordinating mechanisms. For example, if the marketing department sets list prices, the salespeople negotiate discounts in the field, the legal department adjusts prices if necessary to prevent violation of laws or contractual agreements, and the people filling orders negotiate price adjustments for delays in shipment, everybody's best intentions usually end up bringing about less than the best results. In fact, the company may actually lose money on some orders, and some

specialty items positioned to earn high margins may end up returning margins in the commodity range.

Such was the case at a major truck manufacturer. Marketing set list

prices that were essentially meaningless because so many other functions then adjusted those prices for their own purposes. While salespeople chased volume incentives by offering the largest discounts they were allowed, finance and accounting were charged with making sure the company covered its variable costs on each order. In this case, the problem was exacerbated by shortcomings in the accounting systems, but the fundamental cause of the company's pricing dilemma was that the decision-making process involved people with different pricing objectives and different data. There was no coordinated process in place to resolve these conflicting objectives effectively. The company is still working on a long-term solution to the dilemma, but for the short term it has dealt with the problem by creating a separate pricing organization staffed by a group of senior executives that collectively acts as "pricing czar." The group is responsible for gathering input from everyone and then setting a price.

When considering the coordination of the pricing process, managers should ask the following questions:
☐ What is our pricing objective?
☐ Do all the participants in the process understand the objective?
☐ Do they all have an incentive to work in pursuit of the objective?

Proper pricing requires input from a number of people, but if there is no mechanism in place for creating

a unified whole from all the pieces, the overall pricing performance is likely to be dismal.

Eight Steps to Better Pricing

Fitting a pricing policy to a marketing strategy and considering the relevant information in a coordinated manner are broad goals. The following eight steps deal with the essentials of setting the right price and then monitoring that decision so that the benefits are sustainable.

1. Assess what value your customers place on a product or service. Surveys show that for most companies, the dominant factor in pricing is product cost. Determine the cost, apply the desired markup, and that's the price. The process begins inside the company and flows out to the marketplace. To establish an effective pricing policy, however, that process must be reversed. Before any price is determined, pricing managers must think about how customers will value the product.

Consider how Glaxo introduced its Zantac ulcer medication to the U.S. market in 1983 to compete with SmithKline Beecham Corporation's Tagamet. Tagamet had been introduced in 1977 and by 1983 was the number one ulcer medication and the number one selling drug in the world. Zantac, however, offered superior product performance: It had an easier schedule of doses, it had fewer side effects, and it could be taken safely with many other drugs that were not compatible with Tagamet. Thus, its perceived value to the customer was very high. If Glaxo had allowed product cost to drive the price of Zantac, it might have introduced the medication at a lower price than Tagamet; it might have used a "follow the leader" pricing strategy. But Glaxo instead relied on Zantac's perceived value to the customer, initially pricing the drug at a 50% premium over Tagamet. Within four years, Zantac became the market leader.

Northern Telecom's pricing of its highly successful Norstar telephone system demonstrates the same principle. In 1988, as Northern's senior managers developed the company's strategy for competing with Pacific

Rim suppliers, they realized that initially, the inherent superiority of their product didn't matter; resellers would value Norstar only at the market price then being charged by most of Northern's competitors. Therefore, rather than considering Norstar's cost and setting a price that might have been higher than competitors', Northern's managers decided to introduce the Norstar system at the prevailing market level and then look inward to determine how they could reduce costs in order to make money at that price.

Northern's managers knew that over time, they could convince consumers that their system was better than the competition's; in other words, they knew that Norstar's perceived value would increase as the system proved itself in the marketplace. Although the system entered the market at a price below what it was actually worth, eventually, as Northern's competitors began to fight the commodity battle and lower their prices, Northern was able to maintain its price level, secure a price premium, improve margins as its costs decreased, and increase its share of the market.

In Glaxo's case, a conventional "figure cost and take a markup" approach would have resulted in forgone profits; in Northern's case, the result would have been a noncompetitive price and no sales. By turning the process around and letting value as perceived by the customer be the driver, each company found a better initial price level and the foundation for its future growth.

There are several ways in which

Before determining a price, managers must think about how customers will value the product.

companies can assess what value customers perceive a product or service to have. Careful market research is one way; managers also should tap employees with direct customer contact, such as the sales force, for undiluted information from the outside.

2. Look for variation in the way customers value the product. By customizing prices, a company can earn much greater profits than it could expect with a single product/single price policy, yet many managers fail to recognize the benefits of customizing products and prices for different customer segments. A product will often have a much higher perceived value for an "ideal" customer than it will for an average prospect. If this is the case, a company would do well to separate the

markets or segments and charge different prices accordingly. For example, consider how Polaroid Corporation introduced its SX-70 instant photography camera. Polaroid knew that some consumers – such as people in the photo-identification card business – would place a high value on receiving pictures immediately and on knowing whether or not the shots had come out properly. So the company segmented the market over time. Initially, to target those customers who "couldn't wait" for the new product, Polaroid offered the SX-70 to dealers at a price of $120 per camera; end-user customers paid more than $200 on average. Two years later, to capture the wider market, Polaroid offered the SX-70 line at prices that were less than half the introductory level.

The same principle applies in any business. Airlines, for example, attempt to treat business and pleasure travelers differently by offering cheaper fares with Saturday-night stay requirements to the latter. By developing products with slightly different specifications from the same platform, companies can customize pricing for segments that value the product differently.

Customizing price not only is common; in some cases, it is the key to a company's financial health. Consider the magazine industry: The cost per copy of a magazine when a customer buys a subscription is dramatically less than the cost of a single copy purchased at a newsstand. Software manufacturers employ similar tactics: When they introduce a new version of a popular product, they offer discounted upgrade prices to customers who already use the old version. The manufacturers know that the users' ability to continue using the old version of the product makes them value the new product less than someone without the product altogether.

Simple differences in taste affect value variation to some extent – for instance, some people simply like Big Bertha golf clubs more than others. But managers will be able to spot value variation and opportunities for price customization by answering the following questions:

☐ Do customers vary in their intensity of use? Heavy users generally value a product more than light users, especially in the durable-product arena – golf clubs, television sets, cameras, and the like. Heavy users also may be more interested in added features or complementary products; a company can use ancillary products as a mechanism for differential pricing.

☐ Do customers use the product differently? Some customers will use a product differently from other customers, with a consequent difference in perceived value. For example, consider the coated air bubbles produced by Sealed Air Corporation, a supplier of protective packaging. The company recognized that for some applications of the product, viable substitutes were available in the market. But for other applications, Sealed Air had an immense advantage; for instance, its product offered superior cushioning for heavy items with long shipping cycles. Recognizing the extent of the advantages in various applications and understanding the value differential in each setting was the key to Sealed Air's product line expansion and pricing decisions. The insight helped

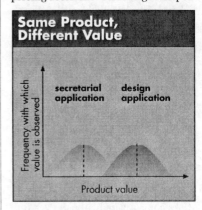

Same Product, Different Value

the company grow from $88 million in revenues in 1980 to more than $500 million 15 years later.

In many situations, companies find that a particular application for a product has a perceived value that is smoothly distributed around a mean. The mean for different applications, though, can be quite different. Take the case of a computer manufacturer offering similar workstations for two different applications: secretarial support and manufacturing design. (See the graph "Same Product, Different Value.") The mean value of the secretarial application is well above the company's costs – but also well below the value of the design application. In such a situation, customized pricing can be a great boost to profitability.

If markets are sufficiently large and show different means, a company should customize its prices. In some cases, customization can be accomplished without altering the product. This is possible if no information on the product can be exchanged and if the product cannot be resold between markets. For example, the computer won't be resold from the secretarial segment to the design segment. If information does flow between segments or if the product might be resold from one segment to another, product

customization obviously would be necessary before prices could be customized. However, such an investment – in different brand names, software preloads, or added features – can well be worth it.

☐ Does product performance matter more to some customers, even if the application is the same? Before its acquisition by S.C. Johnson Wax Company, "Bugs" Burger Bug Killers guaranteed total pest elimination and commanded a price ten times the industry norm because it focused on those customers, such as hotels and hospitals, for whom the cost of failure was extreme. "Bugs" Burger's guarantee of "zero pests" had much more perceived value for those customers than it did for other potential accounts.

3. Assess customers' price sensitivity. Price elasticity, a key concept in economics, is defined as the percent change in quantity sold given a 1% change in price. If a company raises its price on a given product or service by 1%, how will the quantity of sales be affected? On average, the answer is that the quantity will drop by about 2%, but an "on average" answer is not very useful for managers trying to set price. Elasticities vary widely across product categories and even across brands within a category. Therefore, companies should analyze each indi-

vidual situation. The most sophisticated pricing managers use market research procedures such as conjoint analysis to measure elasticities, but a good first step is simply to examine the important factors influencing price sensitivity in three broad areas: customer economics, customer search and usage, and the competitive situation.

First, consider customer economics. Price sensitivity increases – and a company's pricing latitude thus decreases – to the degree that:

☐ The end user bears the cost as opposed to a third party. For example, until recently pharmaceuticals manufacturers have had greater pricing latitude because neither the prescriber nor the patient paid the bulk of the charges.

☐ The cost of the item represents a

A product's different applications often have different perceived value.

substantial percentage of a customer's total expenditure.

☐ The buyer is not the end user, and sells his or her end product in a competitive market. Price pressure from further down a distribution channel ripples back up through the chain. For example, one steel producer was able to obtain good margins by selling a component to buyers who then

Factors Affecting Price Sensitivity

Customer Economics
☐ Will the decision maker pay for the product him or herself?
☐ Does the cost of this item represent a substantial percentage of the total expenditure?
☐ Is the buyer the end user? If not, will the buyer be competing on price in the end-user market?
☐ In this market, does a higher price signal higher quality?

Customer Search and Usage
☐ Is it costly for the buyer to shop around?
☐ Is the time of the purchase or the delivery significant to the buyer?
☐ Is the buyer able to compare the price and performance of alternatives?
☐ Is the buyer free to switch suppliers without incurring substantive costs?

Competition
☐ How is this offering different from competitors' offerings?
☐ Is the company's reputation a consideration? Are there other intangibles affecting the buyer's decision?

produced specialty items for end users. Selling that same component to buyers who made products for commodity-like markets meant lower realized prices: The buyers were more price sensitive.

☐ Buyers are able to judge quality without using price as an indicator. In hard-to-judge categories, such as perfume, price sometimes has little impact because the consumer's assumption is that high price and high quality go together.

Astute managers can gain a further advantage by considering proper product configurations.

The customer's search for and use of a product affect sensitivity to the degree that:

☐ Consumers can easily shop around and assess the relative performance and price of alternatives. Advances in information technology have enabled consumers to increase their awareness of prices and access to alternative options. Over time, this ability is likely to lead to increasing price sensitivity for a wide range of products and services. Currently, sophisticated companies are using information technology to track supplier prices on a worldwide basis. Soon, consumers shopping at home by computer or interactive TV will be able to check the prices of many different suppliers.

☐ The consumer can take the time he or she needs to locate and assess alternatives. For example, in an emergency, speed of delivery may be crucial: Price will not be the primary factor determining the purchase.

☐ The product is one for which it is easy to make comparisons. For example, it is easier to compare cameras than it is to compare computers.

☐ Buyers can switch from one supplier to another without incurring additional costs. For example, Borland International, in marketing its Quattro spreadsheet package, stressed its compatibility with and similarity to Lotus 1-2-3 in order to

position itself as an easy switch. This tactic put pressure on Lotus 1-2-3, increasing its price sensitivity.

Finally, regarding the competitive situation, a company's pricing latitude increases to the degree that.

☐ There is limited difference between the performance of products in the category.

☐ A long-term relationship with the company and its reputation are not important, and the consumer's focus is on minimizing the cost of this particular transaction. (See the table "Factors Affecting Price Sensitivity.")

4. Identify an optimal pricing structure. Determining whether the company should price the individual components of a product or service, or some "bundle," is critical. Should an amusement park operator charge admission to the park, a fee for each ride, or both? Should an entertainment service like HBO charge by what it makes available or by how much viewers "consume"? Answering these questions incorrectly can be very costly. The resources allocated to thinking about pricing are often misallocated; most companies invest too little time, money, and effort in determining a pricing structure, and too much in determining the pricing at different levels within a given structure.

Two important issues to consider when creating a pricing structure are whether to offer quantity discounts and whether to offer bundle pricing.

Quantity discounts are frequently offered in industrial selling situations. For example, consider a manufacturer that must create a pricing policy given Buyer A and Buyer B, who value successive units of the product differently:

Units	Buyer A	Buyer B
1	$70	$70
2	$20	$50
3	$20	$40
4	$20	$35
5	$20	$30

For simplicity, let's assume that the seller knows these valuations and that one buyer will not resell the product to the other. The naïve pricing manager would say, What is the optimal price to charge? If the producer's cost is $20 per unit, the answer is $70. At this price, the company would sell one unit to each buyer for a total profit of $100.

The astute pricing manager, on the other hand, asks, What is the optimal pricing schedule? The insight lies in asking the right question. With the given cost and value parameters, the optimal pricing schedule will be as follows:

buy 1-	$70
buy a second-	$50 additional
buy a third-	$40 additional
buy a fourth-	$35 additional
buy a fifth-	$30 additional

With this pricing schedule, buyer A would purchase one unit at $70, and buyer B would purchase five units – one at $70, one at $50, one at $40, one at $35, and one at $30, for total revenues of $295. Given the $20 cost to produce, the profits on those transactions would total $175 – a 75% greater margin than that generated by the naïve pricing manager's optimal price of $70.

Bundle pricing is the second factor managers should consider when creating a pricing structure. For a manufacturer providing complementary products, like cameras and film, for example, the strategy should be to give up some of the initial profit potential on the hardware to increase the volume sold and consequently increase the potential demand for software.

Astute managers can gain a further advantage by also considering proper product configurations. The two products need not have a camera-and-film-type relationship to be bundled. Movie distributors often sell packages of films rather than selling individual film rights because the package values vary less across buyers than do the individual film values. Take the following two movies and their corresponding value to buyers:

	Buyer A	Buyer B
Movie 1	$9,000	$5,000
Movie 2	$1,000	$5,000
Total	$10,000	$10,000

Both Buyer A and Buyer B value the package of Movie 1 and Movie 2 identically at $10,000. If the company offers a bundle of Movie 1 and Movie 2, it can charge $10,000, yielding a total revenue of $20,000. If the movies are priced à la carte, on the other hand, the distributor would maximize revenue by selling Movie 1 to both buyers at $5,000, and Movie 2 only to buyer B for $5,000. Thus, optimal à la carte pricing nets only $15,000. Asking the question Should we price the bundle or the individual components? generates a 33.3% profit improvement.

5. Consider competitors' reactions. Pricing is more like chess than like checkers. A seemingly brilliant pricing move can turn into a foolish one when competitors have had their chance to respond. Price wars, for example, can easily be set off by poorly designed pricing actions. The lens through which pricing decisions are considered must be broad enough to permit consideration of second- and third-order effects.

Managers should ask themselves how any change in price will affect competitors. What will the competitor's first thoughts be upon seeing the change? They also should ask themselves, What would I do if I were the competition? And, Do I have an effective response to that action? Finally, they should consider the overall impact of the new price on the industry's profitability.

Consider how Eastman Kodak Company addressed its continuing share loss in the U.S. film market. In 1994, Kodak's share – 70% – was still the largest among industry leaders, but it was declining. The company's flagship product, Kodak Gold, sold at a 17% premium over Fuji film. Kodak could have cut prices but that

would have been a very expensive move. What's more, it is unlikely that such an action would have achieved the purpose of reducing the price premium over Fuji. With a 55% gross margin on film, Fuji would almost surely have matched any straight price cut to maintain relative prices in the industry. Kodak instead introduced a low-priced brand, Funtime film, in larger package sizes and limited quantities – priced lower than Fuji film on a per roll basis.

Most often, any pricing action a company takes will provoke some response by major competitors. American Airlines' shift to value pricing, for example, elicited nearly identical programs from Delta and United within days. Philip Morris's price cut on Marlboro cigarettes was matched by R.J. Reynolds. But competitors' reactions may not be limited to price moves; one company's price cut may provoke a response in advertising or in another element of the marketing mix. Therefore, posing the question If I cut my price 5% in this product market, what price action will my competitor undertake? is only the beginning. A 5% price cut could provoke a response in any number of areas. Southwest Airlines, for example, responded to American's value-pricing move not with a price move of its own but rather with an advertising campaign proclaiming, "We'd like to

match their new fares, but we'd have to raise ours."

6. Monitor prices realized at the transaction level. The total set of pricing terms and conditions a company offers its various customers can be quite elaborate. They include discounts for early payment, rebates based on annual volume, rebates based on prices charged to others, and negotiated discounts. As M.V. Marn and R.L. Rosiello discuss in their article "Managing Price, Gaining Profits," (HBR, September-October 1992), while a product has one list price, it may have a wide array of final prices. The real net revenue earned by a product can also be heavily influenced by factors such as returns, damage claims, and special considerations given to certain customers. Yet although it is this "real" price (invoice plus any other factors) that ends up paying the bills, most companies spend 90% of their pricing efforts setting list figures. Treating the real price so casually can cost

> **If customers believe that a price is unfair, their negative reaction can be devastating for business.**

a company substantial forgone profits, especially in an intensely competitive marketplace.

Price setters must analyze the full impact of the pricing program, measuring and assessing the bottom-line impact. The interaction of the various pricing terms and conditions must be managed as a whole.

7. Assess customers' emotional response. When managers analyze how customers respond to a product's price, they must consider the long-term effects of the customers' emotional reaction as well as the short-term, economic outcome. Every transaction influences how a consumer thinks about a company and talks to others about it. Intuit prices its financial software Quicken at $35, and some believe that unit sales would be materially unaffected

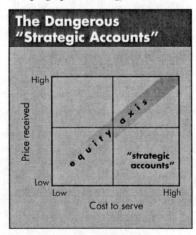

The Dangerous "Strategic Accounts"

High — Low : Price received (vertical axis)
Low — High : Cost to serve (horizontal axis)
equity axis
"strategic accounts"

in the short term by a moderate or even substantial price increase. However, Intuit holds to this price because the vast majority of consumers have come to view it as a "great deal." This perception has two valuable effects. One, it enhances Intuit's reputation with its customers, paving the way for the introduction and sale of future products. Two, the customers have become Intuit "apostles": They tell others about how good the company is and why they also should purchase the product. The pricing forgoes some profits now to create an important benefit down the road.

Of course, the same lesson cuts both ways. If customers believe that a company's product or service is unfairly priced (even if the price is, in fact, only slightly above cost), the negative message they send to other potential customers can be devastating for business. Some consumers have registered complaints with a company that offers database retrieval services, claiming that they were being "ripped off," even though the company was, in fact, saving them many hours in manual search time. The problem was communication: The company was not properly explaining how it justified its price. The solution was to increase aware-

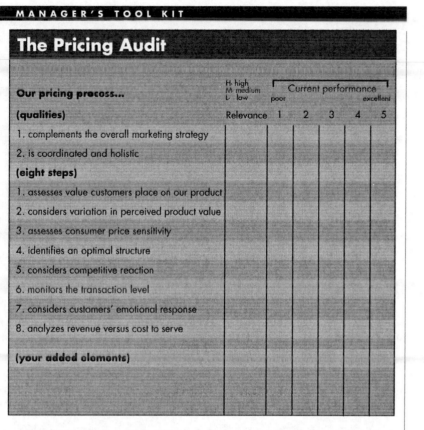

The Pricing Audit

Our pricing process... (qualities)	H: high M: medium L: low Relevance	Current performance poor 1	2	3	4	excellent 5
1. complements the overall marketing strategy						
2. is coordinated and holistic						
(eight steps)						
1. assesses value customers place on our product						
2. considers variation in perceived product value						
3. assesses consumer price sensitivity						
4. identifies an optimal structure						
5. considers competitive reaction						
6. monitors the transaction level						
7. considers customers' emotional response						
8. analyzes revenue versus cost to serve						
(your added elements)						

One automobile insurance company found that big risk offset by big price was a winning combination.

ness of the massive investment required in reformatting, indexing, and storing the data to make the service possible. Again, the key is understanding customers' perceptions. Simple market research procedures can be used to assess consumer reaction in terms of both perceived fairness and purchase intention.

8. Analyze whether the returns are worth the cost to serve. An article by B.P. Shapiro, V.K. Rangan, R.T. Moriarty, and E.B. Ross ("Manage Customers for Profits (Not Just Sales)," HBR, September-October 1987), in-

troduced the notion of the "customer grid," wherein each customer is plotted at the intersection of the revenue he or she generates and the company's cost to serve that customer. In a world of logic, fairness, and perfect information, one might expect customers to line up along an equity axis with a high correlation between cost to serve and price paid. In reality, though, this expectation is seldom met; indeed, the authors provided an example in which there was no correlation at all. Although customer value is crucial in pricing, managers also must consider the cost side, being certain to avoid the infamous "strategic accounts" zone. (See the graph "The Dangerous 'Strategic Accounts.'") These accounts – and they are typically very large – demand product customization, just-in-time delivery, small order quantities, training for operators, and installation support while at the same time negotiating price very aggressively, paying

late, and taking discounts that they have not earned. These accounts don't get what they pay for; they get a lot more. They are facetiously called strategic accounts because that's the justification given when account managers are confronted with the fact that the company is losing money on them.

High cost-to-serve accounts can be terrific – if the price they pay is high enough. One of the most profitable automobile insurance companies in the business specializes in high cost-to-serve customers (that is, people who have a high probability of being involved in an accident). While other insurance providers have shied away from these customers, this company has embraced them, but it also has made them pay rates commensurate with their costs and the fact that nobody else is willing to serve them. In terms of the map, this company was able to identify these accounts and push them well up into the top right. Big risk along with very big price can be a winning combination.

Similarly, a commodity parts distributor makes three times the industry average return on equity by focusing on accounts that order small quantities and have a proportionally high cost to serve. While competitors specify a minimum order of $400, this supplier accepts any size order – but its prices are 20% higher. Although this policy precludes getting the big buyers, the

The author wishes to acknowledge with thanks the comments of Professors Earl Sasser and Ben Shapiro of the Harvard Business School and discussions with participants in the Advanced Management Program.

company is extremely successful. It has lots of small accounts situated firmly in the top right portion of the industry price/cost map.

Judging a company's pricing activities against the qualities and actions I have outlined will give a good indication of the quality of the company's pricing process. "The Pricing Audit" scorecard should help. Consider the two preliminary qualities and eight action steps outlined above. Add any elements you feel appropriate for your situation. Rate each item for its relevance, and rank current performance on the

one through five scale.

An effective pricing process can't be created or implemented overnight. It is not a matter of making one or two sweeping changes in strategy or organization. Rather, it means getting lots of little things right and staying on top of the process to make sure that any improvements are sustainable.

1. M.V. Marn and R.L. Rosiello report in "Managing Price, Gaining Profits," HBR, September-October 1992, p. 85, that for the 2,463 companies in the Compustat aggregate, a 1% increase in price realization yields contribution improvement of 11.1% on average.

Reprint 95501

Customer Value Assessment in Business Markets: A State-of-Practice Study

James C. Anderson
Dipak C. Jain
Pradeep K. Chintagunta

ABSTRACT. The state-of-practice with respect to customer value assessment in business markets was studied. Familiarity with and usage of nine methods were investigated for a sample of 80 informants from the largest U.S. industrial firms and 20 informants from the largest U.S. market research firms that conduct studies in business markets. Focus group value assessments and importance ratings are the most widely-used methods, while conjoint analysis, though used less frequently, has the highest percentage of judged successful applications. Implications of the results for marketing practice are discussed and some worthwhile areas where academic research might advance the present state-of-practice are suggested.

In business markets, the value of a product offering in a given application can be thought of as the cornerstone of marketing strategy. Viewed in

James C. Anderson is the William L. Ford Distinguished Professor of Marketing and Wholesale Distribution and Professor of Behavioral Science in Management, and Dipak C. Jain is Associate Professor of Marketing, J. L. Kellogg Graduate School of Management, Northwestern University. Pradeep K. Chintagunta is Assistant Professor of Marketing, S. C. Johnson Graduate School of Management, Cornell University. The authors gratefully acknowledge the financial support of Penn State's Institute for the Study of Business Markets (ISBM) in sponsoring the research, and the many helpful comments and suggestions of a number of managers from ISBM member firms. The authors also gratefully acknowledge the able assistance of Jenny Lewelling and Steve Christiansen in the research.

Send correspondence to: James C. Anderson, Department of Marketing, Northwestern University, Evanston, IL 60208.

Journal of Business-to-Business Marketing, Vol. 1(1) 1993

this way, value is the underlying consideration that drives decisions about product development and modification, pricing, distribution alternatives and marketing communications. Given the fundamental nature of value in business markets, it is critical for managers to gain estimates of the value of their products in particular customer applications, and to learn how it can be enhanced (Wind 1990).

A number of methods for customer value assessment exist, but apart from knowledge about the commercial applications of conjoint analysis in business markets (Cattin and Wittink 1982; Wittink and Cattin 1989), little is known about the usage of these methods in practice. Specifically, greater knowledge and understanding of what the present awareness and usage of these methods by practitioners is, which of the methods practitioners consider appropriate for particular applications, and what the circumstances are under which practitioners would recommend, or not recommend, that each method be employed would be of considerable interest to both marketing academics and practitioners. A state-of-practice study would provide guidance on which methods are preferred for various business problems where knowledge of value is considered critical, and it also would provide direction on needed advancements in present methods.

In this paper, we examine the state-of-practice of customer value assessment in business markets, drawing upon a field research study of the present practices of the largest U.S. industrial firms. Our objective is to identify the set of methods used in assessing customer value and to determine the extent of their usage by industrial firms. Our interest is in gaining an understanding of present practice, not in developing theoretical aspects of value assessment or in deriving normative implications. Thus, the contribution of our study is that we examine a broad set of value assessment methods, focusing solely upon their usage in business markets, as contrasted with Wittink and Cattin (1989; Cattin and Wittink 1982), who focused solely on conjoint analysis, but more broadly considered its commercial applications in both consumer and business markets. In addition, we delineate the various business decisions that firms address with value assessment methods, and investigate the extent to which these firms judge the particular methods used to be successful. Finally, because our intent is to capture the "best" state-of-practice, rather than to be representative of all present practice, the research employs a purposive rather than a random sample.

An overview of the paper is as follows. First, we discuss the concept of value in business markets. Then, based upon exploratory field research, we briefly discuss the business decision areas for which knowledge of value is considered critical, followed by the methods that have been used to assess customer value. We next present our field study and its results, and discuss the implications of these results for marketing practice. We then suggest some worthwhile areas where academic research in marketing might advance the state-of-practice.

THE CONCEPT OF VALUE
IN BUSINESS MARKETS

A number of aspects need to be considered in defining the concept of value in business markets. Christopher (1982) considers value in terms of the price a customer is willing to pay for a product offering, and points out that willingness to pay needs to be understood in terms of the set of perceived benefits that the product offering provides to a customer firm. He relates this aspect of value to the notion of a customer surplus, which he expresses as the amount by which the monetary equivalent of the set of perceived benefits exceeds the price paid for it. Reuter (1986) introduces the notion of "usage value" which represents the value associated with the performance of the product in a given customer application. As Reuter (1986, p. 79) writes, "Especially in industrial products, the value analyst is primarily concerned with *use value* — the performance and reliability of the product — rather than its *existing* value (based on prestige or aesthetics, cost value, or exchange value)." Usage value appears to be closely related to the concept of a product offering's value-in-use (Wind 1990). Forbis and Mehta (1981) emphasize the aspect of competition in considering value. They introduce the concept of "economic value to the customer (EVC)," which refers to the maximum amount a customer firm would be willing to pay, given comprehensive knowledge of a focal product offering *and* the other, available competitive product offerings. This suggests that customer firms consider the value of a product offering relative to alternative offerings.

In sum, the concept of value in business markets: is perceptual in nature and should be expressed in monetary terms; needs to be viewed with respect to the set of benefits that the customer receives from usage of the product offering; and is inherently framed against a competitive backdrop. Thus, we define *value in business markets* as the perceived worth in monetary units of the set of economic, technical, service and social benefits received by a customer firm in exchange for the price paid for a product offering, taking into consideration the available alternative suppliers' offerings and prices.[1]

How does this definition of value in business markets relate to past work on value in consumer marketing? It appears to be consistent with the latter two alternate definitions of consumer perceived value reported by Zeithaml (1988, p. 13): "(3) value is the quality I get for the price I pay, and (4) value is what I get for what I give." In contrast, Monroe and Krishnan (1985) conceptualize a consumer's perceived value as the *difference* between the utility inferred from the perception of quality and utility (sacrifice) associated with the price to be paid, where perceived quality is "the perceived ability of a product to provide satisfaction 'relative' to the available alternatives" (p. 212). So, in their view, value captures the notion of the difference, or tradeoff (Dodds and Monroe 1985), between perceived worth and price paid. In the context of our definition, we might refer to this difference as "value surplus" or "incentive to purchase."[2]

Business Decision Areas Where Knowledge of Value Is Critical

We conducted in-depth field interviews with managers responsible for marketing research in nine large industrial firms, and with managers at three market research firms that conduct studies in business markets to gain an understanding of the business decisions that require an assessment of the value of a product offering to a customer firm and the methods that are used in these assessments. Each interview, lasting about an hour, started with the same set of questions, and depending on the interviewee's responses, we probed with follow-up questions. From these interviews, we identified a number of business decisions areas where knowledge of value is critical for supplier firms. We group these business decisions into three primary areas for expositional purposes, although some overlap exists among them.

The first area is *product development* which encompasses new product design and modification of existing product offerings. Decisions on modifications may involve either adding or deleting elements of a firm's offering. A second area can be termed *value audits*, where a supplier firm attempts to gain an estimate of the value of its present offering, or an estimate of the value of present augmenting services that "wrap" the core product. A final area is *competitive strategy*, where knowledge is sought on the value relationship of a firm's product offering to those of its competitors, with the results used to allocate resources to the various marketing mix variables.

Methods of Customer Value Assessment

Based on a review of the marketing literature and our exploratory field research, we identified nine methods that have been used to assess customer value, developed *operational definitions* for them for use in the research questionnaire, and elicited questions in the area of value assessment that were of particular interest to practitioners.

We elicited three methods surfaced during our field research that draw upon industrial engineering to provide estimates of customer value. The first method is *internal engineering assessment*, which requires little or no direct customer firm input. The operational definition of this method is:

> *Internal engineering assessment.* An estimate of the value for a product offering is obtained by laboratory tests conducted by scientists/engineers within the supplier's own firm.

Application of this method depends upon detailed knowledge of the usage of the supplier firm's product in the customer firm's product as well as the customer's production process. Assumptions are typically made about the way in which results from lab tests will generalize to the customer's actual usage of the product.

Field value-in-use assessments, by contrast, require considerable customer firm cooperation and active input to arrive at an estimate of customer value. The operational definition of this method is:

> *Field value-in-use assessment.* Interviews are conducted at customer firm(s) to determine a comprehensive listing of cost elements associated with the usage of a product offering compared with the incumbent product offering (e.g., life cycle cost). Making explicit assumptions, values are assigned to these cost elements to estimate the overall value-in-use of the product offering in that application. This value-in-use is typically expressed in cents per pound or dollars per unit.

In conducting a value-in-use analysis, all relevant costs associated with the product offering and its usage (e.g., life-cycle cost, Forbis and Mehta 1981) need to be considered, as well as any differential value due to the product offering that accrues downstream in the production-consumption value chain (Porter 1985). Customer firm reactions are typically sought to refine assumptions made about, or the initial values assigned to, particular cost elements.

The usage of *indirect survey questions* is the final industrial engineering based method, and it is intermediate to the previous two methods in the extent of customer firm cooperation or active input that is required to provide an estimate of value. The operational definition of this method is:

> *Indirect survey questions.* In a field research study, respondents are asked what the effects of one or more changes in the present product offering would be on certain aspects of their firm's operations. From these answers, typically combined in some way with other known information, estimates of the value or worth of each product offering change can be obtained.

Hence, this method can be used to fill in critical gaps in the supplier firm's knowledge of the customer firms' usage of its product offering, or to test whether assumptions made about this usage are reasonable.

Two methods provide overall estimates of customer value. The first, *focus group value assessment*, employs focus groups as a qualitative, phenomenological approach to gain a better understanding of the perceptions and reactions of participants to actual or potential product offerings (Calder 1977). In doing so, the researcher attempts to generate estimates of value. The operational definition of this method is:

> *Focus group value assessment.* Within a focus group setting, participants are exposed to potential product offerings or product concepts, and are then asked what the value or worth of them would be to their firms. As an example, this kind of value assessment might be made by asking them questions such as ''What would your boss be willing to pay for this?''

The participants are typically knowledgeable individuals within customer firms that are targets for the product offering, although the perceptions and reactions of industry consultants or pundits may also be studied.

The second method that generates an overall estimate of value is *direct survey questions*. This method, suggested by the managers we interviewed, was operationally defined as:

> *Direct survey questions.* In a field research survey, respondents are given a description of a potential product offering or product concept, and are then asked what the value or worth of it would be to their firms. As an example, this kind of value assessment might be made by asking them questions such as ''What would your firm be willing to pay for this?''

To obtain a dependable estimate of value, the respondents must be both willing and have the requisite knowledge to answer a direct question on the perceived worth of the product offering. To the extent that either of these conditions is not met, the validity of the obtained estimate will be problematic. A series of follow-up questions would be needed in either the focus group or direct survey question value assessment methods to gain an understanding of how the component parts of an offering contribute to its overall estimated value.

Two methods of customer value assessment can be grouped together as being decompositional in nature; that is, they enable a researcher to break down a respondent's overall perception of the value of a product offering into the elemental values contributed by its component parts. The first, *conjoint analysis*, has received the most research by marketing academics of any value assessment method (cf. Green and Srinivasan 1990; 1978). Its operational definition is:[3]

> *Conjoint or Tradeoff analysis.* In a field research survey, respondents are asked to evaluate a set of potential product offerings in terms of their firm's purchase preference for each of the offerings. Each offering consists of an array of attributes or features, and the levels of these attributes are systematically varied within the set of offerings. Respondents provide a purchase preference rating (or ranking) for the offerings. Statistical analysis is then used to "decompose" these ratings into the value ("part-worth") that the respondent places on each level of each attribute. The range of these values for the levels of each attribute determines the relative value of attributes themselves.

Wittink and Cattin (1989) have found that for the periods 1971-80 and 1981-85, industrial goods represented only 20% and 18% of the reported applications, respectively; in comparison, consumer goods respectively accounted for 61% and 59% of the reported applications for the same periods.[4] A potential explanation for this differential usage, drawing on our field interviews, is the greater perceived cost and complexity of conjoint analysis relative to other methods.[5]

Benchmarks, used by one of the firms we interviewed, represent a second decompositional method of customer value assessment. An operational definition of this method is:

> *Benchmarks.* In a field research survey, respondents are given a description of a product offering, typically representing the present

industry standard, that serves as a "benchmark" offering. They are then asked how much more their firm would be willing to pay for selected additions in product attributes or features to this "benchmark" offering. Likewise, they might be asked how much less their firm would expect to pay for selected reductions in attributes or features from the "benchmark" offering.

Thus, this method trades off some of the methodological rigor and breadth of value estimates provided by conjoint analysis in favor of lower cost and ease-of-use.

An opposite tack is taken with the *compositional approach*, also referred to as the self-explicated approach (Green and Srinivasan 1990). With this approach, an overall value estimate for an offering is built up from separate value estimates given by respondents for each of its elements. The operational definition of this method is:

> *Compositional approach.* In a field research survey, respondents are asked to directly give the value of selected levels of a set of attributes or features to their firm. For example, respondents might be asked to give the value in cents per pound or dollars per unit for each of three alternate levels of a given attribute, where all other attributes of the product offering were the same (held constant). The values given for the attribute levels can then be added to give estimates of the overall value of various product offerings to the respondent's firm.

Although the compositional approach has the strength of being relatively easy to use, particularly when the number of attributes studied is large, it does have some potential shortcomings, such as respondent unwillingness to reveal the true values for attribute levels (cf. Green and Srinivasan 1990).

Lastly, a method for assessing customer value that was given by a number of practitioners is *importance ratings* (Churchill 1987). An understanding of the value of a product offering, and where it can be strengthened, typically is gained by using the results from the importance ratings for a set of offering attributes in conjunction with the results for a corresponding set of performance ratings of the supplier on the offering attributes (e.g., Wilson, Corey and Ghingold 1990; Martilla and James 1977). The operational definition of this method is:

Importance ratings. In a field research survey, respondents are given a set of attributes or features of a product offering and are then asked to rate (or rank) them on importance to their firm. For the attributes or features that were rated, respondents are also asked to rate (or rank) the supplier firms with respect to their performance on them, thereby providing a competitor analysis of the value provided by each supplier's product offering.

A shortcoming of importance ratings as a method of customer value assessment is that they do not provide an estimate of the perceived worth in monetary units of the product offering or its elements. Related to this, importance ratings also do not provide an indication of a customer firm's relative value for a change in the level of performance on one attribute versus another (Montgomery 1986).

METHOD

Sampling Frame

The objective of the study was to gain an understanding of the state-of-practice with respect to the usage of customer value assessment methods. Further, in constructing our sampling frame, we purposively attempted to capture the "best" or most progressive state-of-practice. Our exploratory research indicated that only the largest industrial firms tend to have managers with market research responsibility, and that firms that do have in-house market research staffs are having a greater proportion of their market research studies being conducted by outside market research firms. These findings are consistent with the recent findings of Kinnear and Root (1989). Therefore, we limited our sampling frame to the 125 largest U.S. industrial firms (*Fortune* 1988) and supplemented it with the top 40 U.S. market research firms (*Advertising Age* 1988).

Seventy-seven of the *Fortune* 125 corporations serve business markets, while the remainder serve consumer product markets. We made this determination by referring to the *Business Week* 1000 Industry Classification (*Business Week* 1988).[6] To augment this list, we also consulted the Institute for the Study of Business Markets (ISBM) Contact Directory to include some firms in our study that are not included in the *Fortune* 125 list but are of comparable size and serve business markets. From this source, we added 3 member firms to our sampling frame: Dun & Bradstreet, GTE and United Telecom. Of the top 40 U.S. market research firms, only 24 conducted industrial marketing research studies. Thus, using a *purposive* or *judgment sampling* approach (Churchill 1987), our final sampling frame consisted of 80 of the largest industrial firms and 24 of the largest market research firms.

Fifty-eight of the 80 industrial firms and 16 of the 24 market research firms were able and willing to participate in the survey. The remaining 22 industrial firms either did not do any customer value assessment research (8 firms), were unable to participate because they were too busy (7 firms), were not interested in participating (5 firms), or could not get approval for senior management to participate in the survey (2 firms). The remaining eight market research firms either declined to participate (4 firms), participated in the pretest for market research firms (3 firms), or had headquarters located in England (1 firm: Research International Ltd.). Because of the large size of the firms studied and the diversity of experience that can occur within each firm, industrial firms were allowed to name up to three informants that were from different businesses and market research firms were allowed to name up to two informants that were from different offices.

We obtained the names of 122 participants from the industrial firms and 22 participants from the market research firms. Participants from the industrial firms had titles such as Manager of Marketing Research, Manager of Business Planning, and Manager of Marketing Planning and Development, while participants from the market research firms had titles such as Vice President, Senior Vice President, and Executive Vice President. We used this list of 144 potential participants as the target informants on the present state-of-practice for customer value assessment methods. Within the time frame of the study, interviews with 100 informants were able to be completed: 80 from industrial firms and 20 from market research firms. The busy schedules and frequent travel inherent to these informants' positions prohibited completing interviews with the remaining 44 informants (i.e., none of the informants refused to participate). A brief description of the informant sample appears in the Appendix.

Procedure

Survey Questionnaire Design. Based on our exploratory field research, we began the questionnaire with a brief overview of the study and as part of this provided some examples of research that we referred to as "*customer value studies*" (e.g., determining the value of potential changes in present product offerings). For each of the value assessment methods studied, its operational definition was first provided and then the same sequence of questions was asked. Briefly, the informants from industrial firms were asked:

"Are you familiar with this method?"
"Have you used this method in the past two years?"
"If you have used this method in the past, but no longer use it, what are the reasons for this?"

Informants who had used the method within the past two years were asked the remaining questions in the set:

"What business decision, or decisions, were addressed in the most recent application of this method?"
"In your judgment, how successful was this tool in answering the questions that you sought to answer with it?" [Not successful, Partly successful, Successful]
"Based upon your experience with it, under what circumstances would you recommend/not recommend usage of this method to assess customer value?"

The version of the questionnaire for market research firm informants was different in two respects. First, the internal engineering assessment method was not included as this method is applicable only to the industrial firms. Second, given that market research firms likely perform a greater number of value-assessment studies relative to industrial firms, we decided to shorten the time frame for the usage question and asked: "Have you used this method in the past twelve months?"

After the set of value assessment methods was covered, informants were asked about additional methods (up to two methods) that they had found most useful in assessing customer value. For each, they provided a brief description and answered the latter set of above questions. Finally, informants were asked:

"What, if any, problems in assessing customer value do you have that are not adequately addressed with the present methods?"

Each version of the questionnaire was pretested, and needed changes were made.

Data Collection Procedure. The data were collected from informants using a combination mail and telephone interview approach. The interviews were conducted by a market research firm, under the direction of the researchers. After our initial contact call to set up a time for the telephone interview, a copy of the questionnaire was mailed to each participant. Each participant then interviewed over the phone. This mail and telephone combined approach obviated having participants fill-out and return the questionnaire by mail, and enabled us to collect the data within the time frame set for the study.

Content analysis. To obtain a set of the kinds of business decisions that are addressed with value assessment methods, we content-coded the responses given by informants across the methods. A set of nine business decisions was defined from these responses, and then three judges assigned each business decision mentioned to one of the nine categories. As these categories were to be used in further analysis, we calculated the reliability index (I_r) recently developed by Perreault and Leigh (1989) to assess interjudge agreement. The I_r values (and 95% confidence intervals) for the three pairs of judges were .91 (± .03), .88 (± .03) and .86 (± .04), indicating significant and substantial reliability in the assignment judgments. The disagreements among judges in their initial assignments were resolved by discussion and then majority rule.

RESULTS AND DISCUSSION

Familiarity and Usage

The results for the informants' familiarity with and usage of the value assessment methods appear in Table 1. Although the pattern of results for informants from industrial firms and market research firms are similar, there are some significant differences. A greater percentage of industrial firm informants are familiar with field value-in-use assessments and report using it in the recent past. An explanation for this is that value-in-use assessments would either be performed by industrial firms themselves, or, when outside assistance is sought, they would typically go to engineering consulting firms rather than to market research firms.

A smaller percentage of industrial firm informants are familiar with conjoint analysis. Perhaps because of its greater complexity, a considerably smaller percentage of these informants have used conjoint analysis in the recent past, compared with market research firm informants. A general finding is that firms in business markets rely upon methods that have less complexity (or cost) associated with them. As support for this, note that focus group value assessments and importance ratings are the only methods that have 90% or greater familiarity and 60% or greater usage. Finally, informants report having the least familiarity with and usage of the compositional approach.[7]

TABLE 1

Familiarity With and Usage of Value Assessment Methods (%)

Method	Industrial Firms		Market Research Firms	
	Familiar With[a]	Usage[b]	Familiar With	Usage[c]
Internal engineering assessment	61.3	42.5	..[d]	..
Field value-in-use assessment	63.8	36.3	25.0	5.0
Focus group value assessment	92.5	60.0	90.0	60.0
Direct survey questions	91.3	48.8	85.0	55.0
Importance ratings	91.3	62.5	90.0	65.0
Benchmarks	83.8	27.5	80.0	25.0
Conjoint analysis	75.0	28.8	90.0	60.0
Compositional approach	45.0	10.0	40.0	5.0
Indirect survey questions	71.3	26.2	60.0	20.0
	(n = 80)		(n = 20)	

[a]After an operational definition was given for each method, informants from both industrial firms and market research firms were asked: "Are you familiar with this method?". The percentage of informants answering "yes" is presented.

[b]Informants from industrial firms were asked, "Have you used this method in the past two years?".

[c]Informants from market research firms were asked, "Have you used this method in the past twelve months?".

[d]Not asked for market research firm informants.

Business Decisions Addressed

The business decisions that are addressed with value assessment methods appear in Table 2. Of the nine business decisions, new product design or development and existing product modification or redesign represent slightly more than one-third of the business decisions mentioned. Obtaining an estimate of the value of the present offering and pricing decisions represent slightly less than another one-third of the business decisions.

TABLE 2

Business Decisions Addressed With Value Assessment Methods

Business Decision	Frequency of Mention		Number of Methods Used
	m	(%)	
New product design or development	67	20.2	8
Product modification or redesign	45	13.6	8
Value of present offering	50	15.1	9
Value of present or potential augmenting services	12	3.6	8
Design of marketing communications and sales tools	26	7.9	7
Determine pricing	52	15.7	9
Product positioning and competitive analysis	52	15.7	9
Demand analysis and forecasting	13	3.9	5
New investment or business entry	14	4.2	6
	331	99.9%	

It is interesting that only 15.1% of the mentioned applications were for assessment of the value of the present offering. Much discussion is taking place within industrial firms on becoming "customer-oriented" or "market-driven" (Gross and Kijewski 1988). It would seem that periodic assessments of the value provided by a firm's product offering in a given customer application would be an essential part of the firm truly becoming, and staying, "market-driven." Similarly, although there has been a recent emphasis on value-added services as a source of competitive advantage in business markets, assessment of the value of present or potential augmenting services receives just 3.6% of the mentions. It may be that for each of these situations, managers rely on other, more informal ways of obtaining value estimates from customers (and salespeople).

We observe from Table 2 that nearly all of the value assessment methods studied have been used to address each business decision. Although each method may have been mentioned at least once as being used to address a given business decision, some methods may be more widely used than others for given decision applications. To explore this possibility, a further analysis was conducted to determine the smallest subset of methods that would collectively account for 80% of the mentioned applications for each business decision. The results for this analysis appear in Table 3.

An interesting pattern of results emerges from Table 3. With the exceptions of obtaining the value of present or potential augmenting services and to determine pricing, a subset of five or fewer methods captures at least 80% of the reported value assessment applications for each business decision. Focus group value assessment is the only method that appears in each subset, with other methods being in the most-widely-used subset for only one or a few kinds of business decisions. As an instance of this, indirect survey questions appear in the subset for only one business decision—product modification or redesign, yet it is the most frequently mentioned method for addressing this decision. Similarly, while benchmarks appears in the most-widely-used subset for just three business decisions, it is the most frequently mentioned method for determining pricing, along with focus group value assessments.

Although importance ratings appear in the subset for only four business decisions, this method is the most widely used for three of them: obtaining the value of the present offering, designing marketing communications and sales tools, and product positioning. For this last decision, it accounted for 40.4% of the reported method applications, representing the largest "share" of reported method usage across any business decision.

TABLE 3

Value Assessment Methods Most Widely Used

For Each Business Decision Application[a]

Method	Business Decision Application[b]				
	New Product Design	Product Redesign	Value of Present Offering	Value of Augmenting Services	Design of Marketing Communications
Internal engineering assessment	20.9%[c]	15.6%			
Field value-in-use assessment	9.0	15.6	8.0%	33.3%	11.5%
Focus group value assessment	26.9[d]	17.8	16.0	16.7	26.9
Direct survey questions	19.4		14.0		11.5
Importance ratings		11.1	28.0		34.6
Benchmarks	7.5		16.0		
Conjoint analysis					
Compositional approach					
Indirect survey questions		20.0			
	———	———	———	———	———
	83.7%	80.1%	82.0%	50.0%[e]	84.5%
	(n = 67)	(n = 45)	(n = 50)	(n = 12)	(n = 26)

Method	Business Decision Application			
	Determine Pricing	Product Positioning	Demand Forecasting	New Investment
Internal engineering assessment	7.7%			14.3%
Field value-in-use assessment	7.7	7.7%		28.6
Focus group value assessment	21.2	17.3	23.1%	21.6
Direct survey questions	13.5	9.6	38.5	14.3
Importance ratings		40.4		
Benchmarks	21.2			

| Method | Business Decision Application | | | |
	Determine Pricing	Product Positioning	Demand Forecasting	New Investment
Conjoint analysis	15.4	7.7	23.1	14.3
Compositional approach				
Indirect survey questions				
	————	————	————	————
	86.7%	82.7%	84.7%	92.9%
	(m = 52)	(m = 52)	(m = 13)	(m = 14)

ᵃFor clarity, percentages are only given for the smallest subset of methods that collectively account for 80% of the mentioned applications (m) for each business decision.

ᵇTo conserve space, shortened headings for the business decisions given in Table 2 are employed.

ᶜTo be read as: "Internal engineering assessment was used for 20.9% of the 67 mentioned applications of value assessment methods for the new product design business decision".

ᵈUnderscored percentage indicates the most widely mentioned method used to address the given business decision.

ᵉAs each of the methods whose percentage is not listed for this application was mentioned only a single time (8.3%), only 50% of the mentioned applications are accounted for rather than 80%.

Further, consistent with the earlier results on familiarity and usage, the compositional approach did not appear in the most-widely-used subset for any business decision, the only method to not do so. We also note that the absence of conjoint analysis from the subset for new product design and product redesign reflects its lower usage *relative* to methods such as focus group value assessments and internal engineering assessments.

Judged Success

The judged success of the value assessment methods across business decisions addressed is presented in Table 4, and the judged success of value assessment methods in addressing each business decision appear in Table 5. It appears from these tables that even allowing for the subjective nature of judging success and the potential bias of the informants, applications of these methods are almost never "not successful." Out of 331 judgments, only three applications (.9%) were considered to be not successful. Further, by a considerable margin, applications of these methods

TABLE 4

Judged Success of Value Assessment Method (%)

Method	Partly Successful[a]	Successful
Internal engineering assessment (u — 34)[b]	44.1	55.9
Field value-in-use assessment (u — 32)	28.1	71.9
Focus group value assessment (u — 60)	30.0	70.0
Direct survey questions (u — 48)	33.3	66.7
Importance ratings (u — 62)	24.2	75.8
Benchmarks (u — 28)	32.1	67.9
Conjoint analysis (u — 34)	14.7	85.3
Compositional approach (u — 8)	25.0	75.0
Indirect survey questions (u — 25)	32.0	68.0

[a]Includes sparse informant reports of "not successful" (3 reports, .9%)

[b]The number of reported usages, u, is given in parens for each method.

are judged to be successful, rather than partly successful. Nonetheless, a substantial number of applications are judged to be only "partly successful," which also may represent a socially acceptable response for applications that have not worked out as planned (i.e., "not successful").

Considering specific results, conjoint analysis has the highest percentage of judged successful applications (85.3%). So, *when* informants use conjoint analysis, it successfully provides the answers to the value-related

TABLE 5

Judged Success of Value Assessment Methods in Addressing Each Business Decisions (%)

Decision	Partly Successful[a]	Successful
New product design or development (m = 67)[b]	33.3	66.7
Product modification or redesign (m = 45)	38.0	62.0
Value of present offering (m = 50)	32.0	68.0
Value of present or potential augmenting services (m = 12)	25.0	75.0
Design of marketing communications and sales tools (m = 26)	26.9	73.1
Determine pricing (m = 52)	25.0	75.0
Product positioning and competitive analysis (m = 52)	19.2	80.8
Demand analysis and forecasting (m = 13)	38.5	61.5
New investment or business entry (m = 14)	28.6	71.4

[a]Includes sparse informant reports of "not successful" (3 reports, .9%)

[b]The number of mentioned applications of value assessment methods, m, is given in parens for each business decision.

questions that they sought to address. Informant responses to the question on circumstances under which they would *not* recommend usage of conjoint analysis provide some insight on why it is not used more often in business markets. First, they do not recommend its usage for complicated or abstract product concepts, which tend to occur more frequently in business markets than consumer markets. Second, they do not recommend its usage "when the cost of the research is particularly an issue," which is consistent with our field depth interviews.[8]

Obversely, internal engineering assessment has the lowest percentage (55.9%) of judged success, perhaps because of the difficulties of internally having sufficient knowledge of the customer firm's actual usage of the product offering. Nonetheless, this method is used by 42.5% of the industrial firms in our sample. Further, the relatively greater usage of internal engineering assessment for new product development and product modification may explain the relatively lower percentages of judged success observed for these business decisions.

The most-widely-used methods, importance ratings, focus group value assessments and direct survey questions, are judged to be successful in 75.8%, 70.0% and 66.7% of their applications, respectively. However, the circumstances under which informants recommend and do *not* recommend usage of these methods suggest that these methods should not be used as "stand-alone" methods. To elaborate on this, focus group value assessments are perceived to be most useful as a preliminary value assessment method, particularly at the concept stage of product development, rather than as a method that can be used to conclusively determine value. Importance ratings can be used to identify key attributes of a product offering, but additional ratings of the relative performance of suppliers on the attributes of the product offering would be needed to obtain a ranking of the value provided by the alternate suppliers' offerings. Finally, informants recommend usage of direct survey questions when quick, quantitative information is needed and for familiar, simple, non-technical products, but recommend that in other settings it be used in conjunction with other methods.

With respect to business decisions, we see from Table 5 that product positioning and competitive analysis received the highest percentage of reported success for value assessment methods (80.8%). On the other hand, demand analysis and forecasting, and product modification or redesign received the lowest percentages of reported successes (61.5% and 62.0%, respectively).

Additional Methods Used to Assess Value

Three additional methods were mentioned by more than one informant: field-depth interviews, field tests, and opportunity analysis. Five informants have found field-depth interviews, conducted at either the customer firm, trade shows or industry meetings, to be useful. These informants recommend usage of field-depth interviews when the supplier firm has less information and expertise, for very technical products, and when the respondents are knowledgeable.

Five informants assess value with field tests of sample or prototype product offerings at selected customer firms. They recommend usage of field testing for customers with whom the firm has a good working relationship, for making go/no go decisions, and for assessing whether a higher performance product that improves upon the industry standard also meets customer requirements. Three informants use opportunity analysis, sometimes referred to as gap analysis, to identify specific ways to enhance the value of the firm's product offering, relative to either competitive offerings or presently unmet customer requirements, and recommend its usage for assessing the value of services or complicated industrial products.[9]

Problems Not Adequately Addressed by Present Methods

We limit our consideration of the problems not adequately addressed by present methods to those mentioned by more than one informant. Most-widely-mentioned was a concern about the validity of results obtained from present methods in that respondents may be unwilling or unable to reveal the "true" values. Next-most-mentioned problems were having the "right" individuals in the customer firms (i.e., ultimate decision-makers, end-users) as respondents, and that present methods are too costly. A final problem was that present methods work better with physical products than with services or "soft" attributes.

Implications for Research and Practice

Drawing upon the findings of our study, some areas for advancing the state-of-practice can be suggested. Our results indicate that practitioners presently rely upon simpler methods of customer value assessment, such as focus group assessments or importance ratings. A challenge for marketing academics is to identify the circumstances under which the risks of making incorrect inferences based on usage of a simpler method are acceptable. One useful research tack would be to conduct comparative studies where estimates of value are obtained using several methods of varying complexity and cost. This would enable triangulation of the methods under varying circumstances, to determine when the estimates from the simpler methods converge to those from more complex methods. Further, informants recommend that some of the simpler methods not be used as stand-alone methods. Thus, another potential result of this proposed research might be prescriptive guidance on the usage of particular methods in concert such that their potential liabilities would be off-setting.

The problem with customer value assessment methods most-widely-mentioned by informants in our study was concerns about the validity of results obtained. That is, do value estimates obtained via these methods actually predict customer firms' marketplace behavior? Concerns about the external or predictive validity of conjoint analysis have been expressed elsewhere (Green and Srinivasan 1990; Wittink and Cattin 1989), but our finding suggests that validity assessments need to be broadened to include the other value assessment methods as well.[10] Again, comparative validity studies are suggested, with marketing academics seeking the cooperative participation of industrial firms. After a suitable period of time, or sufficiently disguised, the relevant validity data (the value estimates and actual purchases) can be published.

Two related problems that have a direct bearing on validity of results from value assessment methods are having the "right" individual, or individuals, from a customer firm act as participants in the value assessment research, and the ability of present methods to effectively handle "soft" attributes. A critical issue in having the right individual participant is that for many product offerings in business markets, multiple individuals within a customer firm participate in the purchase decision process (Bonoma 1982; Montgomery 1986). Understanding which individual is the key decision-maker can be a difficult task. Although multiple participants from each customer firm can be asked to provide assessments of the value of the product offering, further research is needed to better understand how these multiple estimates can be meaningfully aggregated into a firm-level estimate (e.g., Wilson, Lilien and Wilson 1989).

Our exploratory research and the informant reports suggest that present methods have difficulty when the attributes being studied are "soft," such as services and less tangible performance attributes (e.g., perceived image quality for x-ray film). Further research is needed to suggest ways to effectively characterize or capture these kinds of attributes, such as alternative forms of stimulus presentation (Anderson 1987; Green and Srinivasan 1990). Research is also needed to devise methods for developing operational definitions that "tangibilize" these less tangible elements (e.g., attitude of customer service personnel) of the product offering (Levitt 1981).

SUMMARY

Everything is worth what its purchaser will pay for it.

— Publilius Syrus, First Century, B.C.

Although this maxim has existed for two millennia, gaining an understanding of what customers would be willing to pay for existing or potential product offerings remains a challenging task for business marketers. We have studied the state-of-practice with respect to the usage of value assessment methods by firms in business markets to gain estimates of the worth of their product offerings. We found that nine different kinds of business decisions are addressed with value assessment methods, and that researchers typically have preferences for a particular subset of the nine methods in addressing each business decision.

Focus group value assessments and importance ratings are presently the most-widely-used methods in business markets. Conjoint analysis, which is not as widely-used, has the highest judged success of the nine methods in addressing the questions that the informants sought to answer. Although most applications of these methods were judged to have been successful, nonetheless, a substantial percentage of applications were judged to be only partly successful. Thus, there remains considerable opportunity to advance the state-of-practice through research that focuses on conducting comparisons among methods and substantiating the validity of results obtained from these value assessment methods.

NOTES

1. Note that in this definition, we purposely have not specified the focal perspective from which the worth of the offering is perceived. Customer value assessment, by contrast, refers to the customer firm as the focal perspective on perceived worth. Further, in this definition, we regard benefits as "net" benefits that subsume costs other than acquisition price (e.g., life-cycle costs) and use "received" to reflect performance in a given usage application.

2. The concept of value, as we have discussed it, is quite different from the fundamental psychological concept of values, such as the terminal values and instrumental values discussed by Rokeach (1973). A method has been developed to study the linkages between the values that consumers hold and attributes possessed by product offerings (cf. Reynolds and Jamieson 1985). Although it would

be interesting to generalize this psychological concept of values to the organizational setting and consider how an individual's understanding of an organization's values affects his or her judgments of value for specific product offerings, this is beyond the scope of the present paper.

3. For clarity of understanding to the respondents and meaningful interpretation of the results, the operational definition focused on conjoint analysis as it is most often employed, the full-profile stimulus construction with a rating scale or rank order response (cf. Wittink and Cattin 1989). Provision was made for respondents to describe and evaluate other forms of conjoint analysis, such as hybrid models (Green 1984), as additional methods that they used to assess customer value.

4. Some proportion of the 18% (1981-1985) and 13% (1971-1980) applications reported by Wittink and Cattin (1989) as financial and other services could be considered business marketing applications, however.

5. Support for this explanation is provided by the recent finding of Kinnear and Root (1989) that industrial firms typically have much smaller marketing research budgets than consumer firms of equivalent size. Montgomery (1986) also discusses the relatively greater cost of conjoint analysis in business markets.

6. The classification of firms into those that serve business markets versus those that serve consumer markets is a difficult, if not an impossible, task. Ultimately, it becomes a matter of judgment. For example, although a number of firms in the *Business Week* Food Processing classification (e.g., Heinz, Kraft) have institutional sales, we considered these firms as primarily serving consumer markets. Our intent was to construct a sampling frame that was comprised of firms whose customers of *primary* interest were other firms or institutions, not consumers.

7. Relatively few informants report no longer using one or more of the value assessment methods that they have used in the past. Seven informants report no longer using benchmarks, four informants each no longer use focus groups and direct survey questions, and three informants each no longer use importance ratings, conjoint analysis and the compositional approach.

8. Two recent developments in conjoint analysis are the commercial availability of software packages and the usage of telephone-mail-telephone data collection approaches (Green and Srinivasan 1990; Wittink and Cattin 1989). The high judged success for conjoint analysis taken together with these developments suggest greater future usage of this method in business markets.

9. Of the remaining additional methods mentioned, the only noteworthy one was the usage of an experimental design method by one informant. Samples of the target audience were divided into two groups, with each shown the product at different prices, and then the purchase intent was assessed.

10. See Montgomery (1986) for a discussion of the empirical support for the external or predictive validity of conjoint analysis in business settings.

REFERENCES

Advertising Age (1988), "Top 50 U.S. Research Organizations," May 23, S-4.

Anderson, James C. (1987), "The Effect of Type of Representation on Judgments of New Product Acceptance," *Industrial Marketing and Purchasing*, 2(2), 29-46.

Bonoma, Thomas V. (1982), "Major sales: Who *Really* Does the Buying?," *Harvard Business Review*, 82 (May-June), 111-19.

Business Week (1988), "The Top 1000 U.S. Companies," April 15 special issue.

Calder, Bobby J. (1977), "Focus Groups and the Nature of Qualitative Marketing Research," *Journal of Marketing Research*, 14 (August), 353-364.

Cattin, Philippe and Dick R. Wittink (1982), "Commercial Use of Conjoint Analysis: A Survey," *Journal of Marketing*, 46 (Summer), 44-53.

Christopher, Martin (1982), "Value-In-Use Pricing," *European Journal of Marketing*, 16(5), 35-46.

Churchill, Gilbert A. (1987), *Marketing Research*, fourth edition. Chicago: The Dryden Press.

Dodds, William B. and Kent B. Monroe (1985), "The Effect of Brand and Price Information on Subjective Product Evaluations," in *Advances in Consumer Research*, vol. 12, Elizabeth Hirschman and Morris B. Holbrook, eds. Provo, UT: Association for Consumer Research, 85-90.

Forbis, John L. and Nitin T. Mehta (1981), "Value-Based Strategies for Industrial Products," *Business Horizons*, 24 (May-June), 32-42.

Fortune (1988), "The *Fortune* 500 Largest U.S. Industrial Corporations," April 25, D1-D54.

Green, Paul E. (1984), "Hybrid Models for Conjoint Analysis: An Expository Review," *Journal of Marketing Research*, 21 (May), 155-69.

Green, Paul E. and V. Srinivasan (1990), "Conjoint Analysis in Marketing Research: New Developments and Directions, " *Journal of Marketing*, 54 (October), 3-19.

Green, Paul E. and V. Srinivasan (1978), "Conjoint Analysis in Consumer Research: Issues and Outlook," *Journal of Consumer Research*, 5 (June), 103-123.

Gross, Irwin and Valerie Kijewski (1988), "Is Your Company 'Market Driven'?," *Marketplace: The ISBM Review*, Spring, 1-2.

Kinnear, Thomas C. and Ann R. Root, Eds. (1989), *1988 Survey of Marketing Research*. Chicago: American Marketing Association.

Levitt, Theodore (1981), "Marketing Intangible Products and Product Intangibles," *Harvard Business Review*, 81 (May-June), 94-102.

Martilla, John A. and John C. James (1977), "Importance-Performance Analysis," *Journal of Marketing*, 41 (January), 77-79.

Monroe, Kent B. and R. Krishnan (1985), "The Effect of Price on Subjective Product Evaluations," in *Perceived Quality*, Jacob Jacoby and Jerry C. Olson, eds. Lexington, MA: Lexington Books, 209-232.

Montgomery, David B. (1986), "Conjoint Calibration of the Customer/Competitor Interface in Industrial Markets,'' in *Industrial Marketing: A German-American Perspective*, Klaus Backhaus and David Wilson, eds. Berlin: Springer-Verlag, Inc., 297-319.

Perreault, William D., Jr. and Laurence E. Leigh (1989), ''Reliability of Nominal Data Based on Qualitative Judgments,'' *Journal of Marketing Research*, 26 (May), 135-48.

Porter, Michael E. (1985), *Competitive Advantage*, New York: Free Press.

Thomas J. Reynolds and Linda F. Jamieson (1985), ''Image Representations: An Analytic Framework,'' in *Perceived Quality*, Jacob Jacoby and Jerry C. Olson, eds. Lexington, MA: Lexington Books, 115-138.

Reuter, Vincent G. (1986), ''What Good Are Value Analysis Programs,'' *Business Horizons*, 29 (March-April), 73-79.

Rokeach, Milton (1973), *The Nature of Human Values*, New York: Free Press.

Wilson, David T., Robert J. Corey, and Morry Ghingold (1990), ''Beyond Cost-Plus: A Checklist for Pricing Under Pressure,'' *Journal of Pricing Management*, 1 (Winter), 41-49.

Wilson, Elizabeth J., Gary L. Lilien, and David T. Wilson (1989), ''Situational Factors and Formal Models of Group Choice in Organizational Buying: A Contingency Paradigm,'' ISBM Working Paper # 5-1989, Pennsylvania State University.

Wind, Yoram (1990), ''Getting a Read on Market-Defined 'Value','' *Journal of Pricing Management*, 1 (Winter), 5-14.

Wittink, Dick R. and Philippe Cattin (1989), ''Commercial Use of Conjoint Analysis: An Update,'' *Journal of Marketing*, 53 (July), 91-96.

Zeithaml, Valarie A. (1988), ''Consumer Perceptions of Price, Quality, and Value: A Means-End Model and Synthesis of Evidence,'' *Journal of Marketing*, 52 (July), 2-22.

Appendix

Informant Sample

Industrial Firms:

Industry	Number of Informants
Fuels	7
Office equipment	9
Conglomerate	13
Aerospace	3
Steel	3
Chemicals	6
Leisure	2
Machinery	3
Aluminum	4
Paper	9
Electrical products	6
Semi-conductors	1
Drug & research	6
Auto parts	5
Lumber	1
Service industry (business publishing)	1
Telecommunications	1
Total	**80**

Market Research Firms:

20 Informants representing 16 firms that do research on business markets. All firms were ranked in the top 40 market research firms in the U.S.

Augmenting Conjoint Analysis to Estimate Consumer Reservation Price

Kamel Jedidi • Z. John Zhang

Graduate School of Business, Columbia University, 3022 Broadway, New York, New York 10027
The Wharton School, 700 Jon M. Huntsman Hall, 3730 Walnut Street, Philadelphia, Pennsylvania 19104-6340
kj7@columbia.edu • zjzhang@wharton.upenn.edu

Consumer reservation price is a key concept in marketing and economics. Theoretically, this concept has been instrumental in studying consumer purchase decisions, competitive pricing strategies, and welfare economics. Managerially, knowledge of consumer reservation prices is critical for implementing many pricing tactics such as bundling, target promotions, nonlinear pricing, and one-to-one pricing, and for assessing the impact of marketing strategy on demand. Despite the practical and theoretical importance of this concept, its measurement at the individual level in a practical setting proves elusive.

We propose a conjoint-based approach to estimate consumer-level reservation prices. This approach integrates the preference estimation of traditional conjoint with the economic theory of consumer choice. This integration augments the capability of traditional conjoint such that consumers' reservation prices for a product can be derived directly from the individual-level estimates of conjoint coefficients. With this augmentation, we can model a consumer's decision of not only which product to buy, but also whether to buy at all in a category. Thus, we can simulate simultaneously three effects that a change in price or the introduction of a new product may generate in a market: the customer switching effect, the cannibalization effect, and the market expansion effect. We show in a pilot application how this approach can aid product and pricing decisions. We also demonstrate the predictive validity of our approach using data from a commercial study of automobile batteries.

(*Reservation Price; Conjoint Analysis; Pricing Strategy; Product Stratgy*)

---

1. Introduction

In making pricing and product decisions, a firm needs to gauge their effects not only on product demand, but also on market demand. Consider, for instance, the case in which a computer company, say Compaq, is deciding whether to enter the market of notebook computers with a low-end product at a low price to pursue a penetration strategy, or with a high-end product at a high price to pursue a skimming strategy, or with both high-end and low-end products to pursue a product line strategy. To make such a decision, Compaq needs to consider how its product or products may take customers away from its competition, say Dell, i.e. "the customer switching effect." It

must also assess how its high-end (low-end) product may suffer in sales because of its low-end (high-end) product, or "the cannibalization effect," and how its product or products may draw more customers into the market because of better functionality or affordability, or "the market expansion effect." In this paper, we propose a simple, conjoint-based approach to estimate all these three effects and further illustrate how this approach can facilitate such complex product and pricing decisions.

From the perspective of the standard economic theory of consumer choice, the key to assessing all these effects in a single model is knowledge of consumers' reservation prices for current and new product

MANAGEMENT SCIENCE © 2002 INFORMS
Vol. 48, No. 10, October 2002 pp. 1350–1368

0025-1909/02/4810/1350$5.00
1526-5501 electronic ISSN

offerings in a category. To continue with our notebook computer example, if a market researcher at Compaq knows how much each of the target consumers is willing to pay for its high-end and low-end products and for each of the Dell's products, she can then determine who will switch away from Dell to purchase a Compaq notebook (the customer switching effect), to what extent Compaq's one product may compete with the other (the cannibalization effect), and how category sales may expand (the market expansion effect) as a result of Compaq's new offering. Cannibalization (switching) results when consumers derive more surplus from a new offering than from the company's (competitor's) existing product. Market expansion results when noncategory buyers now derive positive surplus from a new offering.

The practical importance of estimating consumer reservation prices is not, of course, limited to assessing these three demand effects. Knowledge of consumer reservation prices aids market researchers in implementing many pricing tactics such as bundling (Jedidi et al. 2002), target promotions, nonlinear pricing, and one-to-one pricing (Shaffer and Zhang 1995, 2000). For instance, with no information on individual-level reservation prices, one-to-one pricing is largely a theoretical curiosity or an exercise of guesswork. Furthermore, such knowledge bridges the gap between economic theories and marketing practice and enables researchers to study a host of other issues related to competitive interactions, policy evaluations, welfare economics, and brand value. The importance of the reservation price concept is also shared by managers. In a survey conducted by Anderson et al. (1993), managers consider consumer reservation prices as "the cornerstone of marketing strategy," particularly in the areas of product development, value audits, and competitive strategy.

Despite the practical and theoretical importance of the concept of consumer reservation price, its measurement at the individual level in a practical setting proves elusive. Researchers most frequently elicit such information directly from consumers, although stated consumer reservation prices are known to be biased downward (Monroe 1990). Kohli and Mahajan (1991) first propose the use of conjoint analysis to estimate a consumer's willingness to pay for a product.

The reservation price they estimate measures, however, the differentiation value of a product relative to the status quo product. This definition of reservation price implies that all consumers are category buyers and hence it assumes away any market expansion effect. In this paper, we follow Kohli and Mahajan's approach to derive individual-level reservation prices directly from the estimates of conjoint coefficients. However, we depart from Kohli and Mahajan (1991) in two ways. First, we adopt the standard definition of consumer reservation price in economics. Second, we dismiss the assumption of unconditional category purchase.

Our approach integrates the preference estimation from conjoint with the standard economic theory of consumer utility maximization. Using the economic theory of consumer choice, namely consumers maximizing their utility by choosing a consumption bundle from their respective feasible consumption set, we show that a consumer's reservation price for a product can be generated from a rather simple transformation of attribute utilities estimated through conjoint. With this transformation, we can model a consumer's decision of not only which product to buy in a category of interest, but also whether to buy at all in that category. As a result, we can simultaneously simulate all three effects that a change in price or the introduction of a new product may generate in a market: the customer switching effect, the cannibalization effect, and the market expansion effect. Besides, we can do so while preserving the conceptual and operational simplicity of conjoint, which has contributed to its enduring popularity.[1]

As commonly used in practice, conjoint analysis captures only the customer switching and cannibalization effects. Many scholars have advanced the conjoint approach in the past to enable researchers to capture the market expansion effect. Louviere and Woodworth (1983) and later Desarbo et al. (1995) allow for a "no-choice" option in the conjoint design

---

[1] For survey articles of conjoint applications, see Green and Srinivasan (1990), Wittink and Cattin (1989), Anderson et al. (1993), and Wittink and Bergestuen (1999). For some specific conjoint applications, see Green and Wind (1975), Mahajan et al. (1982), and Page and Rosenbaum (1987).

to capture the market expansion effect. Mason (1990) suggests merging a preference model (conjoint) with a demand model based on the concept of the total product class attraction. More recently, Jedidi et al. (1996) model the market expansion effect by letting consumer consideration sets depend on the product offerings in a category. We show that our approach offers the distinct advantages of taking decision making from the "choice" arena to the "value" arena by estimating the reservation price at the individual level. However, it is reassuring, as we will demonstrate, that our approach does as well as a Tobit-based model such as that of Jedidi et al. (1996) in predicting consumer choices.

In the rest of the paper, we first discuss the concept of consumer reservation price and show how it can be estimated through conjoint analysis. Then, we illustrate how our approach can facilitate complex product and price decisions using a pilot application and demonstrate the predictive validity of our approach using data from a commercial study of automobile batteries. Finally, we conclude with some remarks on the advantages and limitations of our approach.

2. Consumption Utility and Reservation Price

A consumer's reservation price for a specific product is simply the price at which the consumer is indifferent between buying and not buying the product, given the consumption alternatives available to the consumer. Formally, let $\mathcal{P}$ denote a product profile, where $\mathcal{P} \in [\mathbf{P}^1, \ldots, \mathbf{P}^J]$. Assume that the utility function of consumer i is given by $U_i(\mathcal{P}, y_i)$, where y_i denotes the composite good consisting of all other goods the consumer purchases, measured in some individual-specific basket. Since each individual consumer has a different buying pattern, we allow the price of the composite good to differ across consumers and denote it by p_i^y. We further assume that consumer i has income m_i and consumes only one unit of the product in question. Therefore, the budget constraint facing consumer i is $p_i^y y_i + p = m_i$, where $p \in (p^1, \ldots, p^J)$ is the price the consumer pays to get product $\mathcal{P}$. This means that consumer i's indirect utility function is given by $U_i(\mathcal{P}, (m_i - p)/p_i^y)$ if the product $\mathcal{P}$ is purchased and by $U_i(0, m_i/p_i^y)$ if it is not.

Then, by definition, consumer i's reservation price for product profile $\mathcal{P}$, denoted by $r_i(\mathcal{P})$, is implicitly given by

$$U_i\left(\mathcal{P}, \frac{m_i - r_i(\mathcal{P})}{p_i^y}\right) - U_i\left(0, \frac{m_i}{p_i^y}\right) \equiv 0. \quad (1)$$

This definition of $r_i(\mathcal{P})$ in Equation (1) is quite different from that of Kohli and Mahajan (1991). They define reservation price for a product as the maximum price the consumer is willing to pay to switch away from the most preferred choice in her evoked set to the product in question. Thus, a consumer's reservation price for a product depends not only on the additional value the product provides, but also on how much the consumer pays for her most preferred choice. This definition, based on the differentiation value of a product, facilitates their discussion about the market share impact of a new product's price, one of the main thrusts of their paper. However, by explicitly assuming the existence of a status quo product for each consumer, their approach cannot assess whether the product and pricing decisions by firms can expand or contract a market, an issue of importance in this paper.

Our definition is a conventional one. It captures a consumer's valuation of a product's nonprice attributes given the consumption opportunities elsewhere and the budget constraint she faces. As we show in Appendix A, with some quite general assumptions about consumer utility function, $r_i(\mathcal{P})$ always exists such that for any $p \leq r_i(\mathcal{P})$, the consumer is better off purchasing the product $\mathcal{P}$. Otherwise, the consumer will not. Therefore, $r_i(\mathcal{P})$ is the maximum price the consumer is willing to pay for the product. This definition naturally allows us to determine whether a consumer purchases a product in question. Furthermore, with some additional restrictions on a consumer's utility function, a consumer's reservation price thus defined also allows us to examine the market share impact of a product's price in a straightforward manner. Specifically, if a consumer's utility function is of quasi-linear form, i.e., $U_i(\mathcal{P}, y_i) = u_i(\mathcal{P}) + \alpha y_i$, where $\alpha > 0$ is a scaling factor, a utility-maximizing consumer will only need to know her reservation prices for the product offerings and the corresponding prices for these products to make the optimal choice. For instance, if consumer i faces two alternative choices in the same product category, say some $\mathcal{P}$ and $\mathbf{P}^l (\mathcal{P} \neq \mathbf{P}^l)$, she will choose product $\mathcal{P}$ if $r_i(\mathcal{P}) - p \geq r_i(\mathbf{P}^l) - p^l$ and $r_i(\mathcal{P}) \geq p$. In other words, consumer i will purchase product $\mathcal{P}$, given that product $\mathbf{P}^l$ is also available, if consuming product $\mathcal{P}$ gives her more surplus and if her reservation price for the product is higher than the price she has to pay (see Appendix B for a proof).

In general, facing $j \leq J$ available choices in a product category, consumer i with a quasilinear utility function will purchase a product, say $\mathcal{P}$, in the category if the following two conditions are satisfied:

$$r_i(\mathcal{P}) - p \geq \max\{r_i(\mathbf{P}^1) - p^1, \dots, r_i(\mathbf{P}^l) - p^l\}, \quad (2)$$

$$r_i(\mathcal{P}) \geq p. \quad (3)$$

She will forego purchase in the category if

$$\max\{r_i(\mathbf{P}^1) - p^1, \dots, r_i(\mathbf{P}^l) - p^l\} < 0. \quad (4)$$

Equations (2)–(4) fully characterize a consumer's whether-to-buy and what-to-buy decisions.

3. Conjoint Analysis and Reservation Price

To estimate consumer reservation prices, it is natural to think of conjoint analysis, as the utility function specified for such analysis is quasilinear. In this section, we show how conjoint analysis can be augmented for that purpose.

Substituting in the individual-specific budget constraint, a quasi-linear utility function can be written as

$$U_i(\mathcal{P}) = u_i(\mathcal{P}) + \alpha \frac{m_i - p}{p_i^y}. \quad (5)$$

As in multiattribute utility models, we assume that the utility a consumer derives from consuming a product is the sum of utilities for its attributes or features. Specifically, we assume

$$u_i(\mathcal{P}) = \sum_{k=1}^{N} u_{ik}(\mathcal{P}) = \sum_{k=1}^{N} \beta_{ik} A_k, \quad (6)$$

where $u_{ik}(\mathcal{P}) = \beta_{ik} A_k$ is consumer i's utility from non-price attribute k of product profile $\mathcal{P}$, where $k = 1$,

$2, \dots, N$, and A_k is the value of the kth non-price attribute. Furthermore, let $\beta_{i0} = \alpha(m_i/p_i^y)$ and $\beta_{ip} = (\alpha/p_i^y)$. Then, Equation (5) can be written as

$$U_i(\mathcal{P}) = \beta_{i0} + \sum_{k=1}^{N} \beta_{ik} A_k - \beta_{ip} p. \quad (7)$$

Using the definition in Equation (1), it is straightforward to show that under this specification, a consumer's reservation price for product profile $\mathcal{P}$ is given by

$$r_i(\mathcal{P}) = \frac{1}{\beta_{ip}} \sum_{k=1}^{N} \beta_{ik} A_k. \quad (8)$$

Note that $r_i(\mathcal{P})$ does not depend on the intercept term β_{i0}.

As Equation (7) resembles the common specification of conjoint analysis, it is tempting to use a conjoint design to estimate the parameters in Equation (7) directly and then use Equation (8) to compute a consumer's reservation price. However, note that each product attribute in Equation (7) is measured by its actual level, rather than by an indicator variable as is commonly the case in conjoint analysis. We therefore need to transform Equation (7) further before we can use a conjoint design to estimate it.

Assume for now that each attribute has only two levels of realization, say $\underline{A}_k$ and $\overline{A}_k$ ($\underline{A}_k < \overline{A}_k$) for non-price attributes and $\underline{p}$ and $\bar{p}$ ($\underline{p} < \bar{p}$) for price. We use $\mathbf{P}^l$ to denote the product profile that has the lowest level of each attribute among all possible product choices, and the expression for $U_i(\mathbf{P}^l)$ can be found using Equation (7). By taking the difference between $U_i(\mathcal{P})$ and $U_i(\mathbf{P}^l)$ and applying some simple arithmetic manipulations, we have

$$U_i(\mathcal{P}) = \beta_{i0}^c + \sum_{k=1}^{N} \beta_{ik}^c d_k - \beta_{ip}^c d_p, \quad (9)$$

where the superscript c indicates conjoint parameters defined as

$$\beta_{i0}^c = U_i(\mathbf{P}^l), \quad \beta_{ik}^c = \beta_{ik} \Delta A_k, \quad \beta_{ip}^c = \beta_{ip} \Delta p, \quad (10)$$

$$d_k = \frac{A_k - \underline{A}_k}{\Delta A_k}, \quad \text{and} \quad d_p = \frac{p - \underline{p}}{\Delta p}. \quad (11)$$

Note that when each attribute has only two levels of realization in a conjoint design, d_k and d_p are actually dummy variables with a value of either 1 or 0. Equation (9) can be estimated as

$$U_i(\mathscr{P}) = \beta_{i0}^c + \sum_{k=1}^{N} \beta_{ik}^c d_k - \beta_{ip}^c d_p + \epsilon_i. \qquad (12)$$

A standard conjoint design can be used to estimate this equation. Once the estimates of β_{i0}^c, β_{ik}^c, and β_{ip}^c are obtained, we can easily use Equations (10)–(11) to find the corresponding utility parameters and derive the estimate of a consumer's reservation price for product $\mathscr{P}$ by using Equation (8). We have

$$r_i(\mathscr{P}) = \frac{\Delta p}{\beta_{ip}^c} \left(\sum_{k=1}^{N} \frac{\beta_{ik}^c}{\Delta A_k} A_k \right). \qquad (13)$$

Equation (13) has a nice interpretation: Δp is the change in price from the base level and β_{ip}^c is the corresponding change in consumer i's utility. Therefore, $\Delta p/\beta_{ip}^c$ is the dollar value that the consumer implicitly assigns to each unit of her utility ($ per utile). In other words, it is the "exchange rate" between utility and money for the consumer. Similarly, $\beta_{ik}^c/\Delta A_k$ indicates the worth of each unit of attribute k in utiles (e.g., utiles per GB hard drive). Since product $\mathscr{P}$ has A_k as its level of attribute k, $(\beta_{ik}^c/\Delta A_k)A_k$ is the utility consumer i derives from attribute k. Therefore, the summation over all attributes for product $\mathscr{P}$, excluding price, simply yields the total utility the consumer derives from all nonprice attributes of product $\mathscr{P}$. Thus, this total utility multiplied by the revealed exchange rate between utility and money for the consumer in Equation (13) gives the total dollar value the consumer places on product $\mathscr{P}$, which ought to be consumer i's reservation price for the product. Equation (13) is also empirically appealing. From this equation we note that all else being equal, more price-sensitive consumers, or those with a larger β_{ip}^c, will have smaller reservation prices. A larger magnitude of positive response to any nonprice attribute will, however, increase a consumer's reservation price.

As in Equation (8), note that a consumer's reservation price in Equation (13) does not depend on the intercept term β_{i0}^c. This feature reflects the fact that β_{i0}^c conveys no preference information and hence should

not play any role in a consumer's reservation price. This is true because β_{i0}^c does not survive a monotonic transformation of Equation (12). To see this, apply the following monotonic transformation to Equation (12): Multiply the right side of the equation by 1 and then subtract β_{i0}^c from the resulting expression. We see that β_{i0}^c disappears from the resulting utility function that represents the same preference ordering.[2]

From an empirical perspective this feature is quite valuable, as it removes the "scale effect" from our estimation of consumer reservation prices and creates a level playing field for interpersonal comparisons. The scale effect arises from the fact that subjects performing conjoint tasks may have different "internal scales" in measuring their utility. Because of these differences, a consumer who uses a large (small) number to convey her utility from a product may or may not be willing to pay a high (low) price for the product. Thus, no presumption should be made with regard to the relationship between a consumer's representation of her utility on the high or low end of an external scale and her willingness to pay for a product. Interestingly, our derivations show, as we can see from Equation (10), that this "scale effect" is indicated, in the case of two attribute levels, by a consumer's utility from consuming the product with the lowest level of all nonprice attributes.

With a consumer's reservation price for a product estimated, we can use Conditions (2)–(4) to predict whether a consumer will buy in a category and which product she will buy when different alternatives are present. However, we need to clarify three issues before we proceed to empirical applications. First, in many marketing applications a product attribute may simply be a nominal variable such as brand name. How should the transformation be carried out in this case? Second, the linearity of attribute utilities that we adopt through Equation (6) implicitly assumes that an attribute does not have any meaningful utility only when the measurement of that attribute is zero. However, in practical applications it may be desirable to allow a threshold value such that an attribute does not generate any utility unless it exceeds the threshold. For instance, in the case of cellular phones a consumer may attach zero value to "stand-by time" if it

[2] For details, see Varian (1992, p. 95).

is less than two hours. How should Equation (13) be adjusted to accommodate this threshold value? Third, a product attribute can have more than two levels of realization. How should the transformation be carried out then, especially when the attribute of price has multiple levels?

The answer to the first question is not difficult to find. As in conjoint analysis, a nominal variable such as brand name can enter in Equation (6) only as a dummy variable indicating its presence or absence. This means that if the kth attribute is a nominal variable, we must have $\Delta A_k = 1$ so that $\beta_{ik}^c = \beta_{ik}$ as one would expect. However, our approach to reservation prices is constructive. To generate a meaningful estimation of the value that a consumer places on an attribute, one needs to code a nominal variable in a way that can generate a meaningful measurement of the total, rather than relative, attribute utility from the variable. The key to coding a nominal variable is to select a proper reference point or a default. In the case of brand name, for instance, a default could be a *generic* brand from whose name alone consumers derive no meaningful utility.[3] Obviously, the choice of the default in this case does not affect comparisons among different brands, as the generic brand is now the common base for comparison.

Admittedly, for some other nominal attributes, it may not always be straightforward to find such a default. However, even in that case, we do not face any insurmountable obstacle in estimating consumer reservation prices. In §5, we show how one can use a Tobit approach to resolve such a problem. The catch is that a "no-buy" option is required in the conjoint design.

To address the second question, we note that the utility from an attribute that has a value below a threshold, say T_k, is zero. Yet, Equation (13) uses the

absolute level A_k in computing a consumer's reservation price, which will obviously inflate the estimate of a consumer's willingness to pay. However, this problem can be easily corrected in theory by subtracting the threshold value from A_k in Equation (13), i.e., $A_k - T_k$. Mathematically, this operation is equivalent to relocating the origin in the attribute space and Equation (13) is then modified as

$$r_i(\mathcal{P}) = \frac{\Delta p}{\beta_{ip}^c}\left(\sum_{k=1}^{N}\frac{\beta_{ik}^c}{\Delta A_k}A_k\right) - \frac{\Delta p}{\beta_{ip}^c}\left(\sum_{k=1}^{N}\frac{\beta_{ik}^c}{\Delta A_k}T_k\right). \quad (14)$$

The first term in Equation (14) is the gross value a consumer places on product $\mathcal{P}$. The second term is the implied value of dead-weight attributes, which cannot be appropriated by a firm. Note that the second term is constant for all $\mathcal{P} \in (P^1, P^2, \ldots, P^J)$.

In practice, the estimation of the thresholds can proceed in three possible ways. First, as in hybrid conjoint, the attribute thresholds T_ks can be directly elicited from subjects. Second, multiple levels of an attribute can be included in the conjoint design to identify the "jump" in part-worth estimates so that each T_k can be identified. Finally, as we will show in §5, if estimating individual T_ks is not critical, the second term of Equation (14) can be estimated as one parameter through a Tobit model. This option is possible only if each respondent's preferences are left-censored (i.e., we observe preferences only for the profiles that a respondent would consider buying).

When a product attribute has multiple levels, we can allow nonlinear effects of the attribute on a consumer's utility. In this case, the variable transformation is a bit more involved conceptually, but straightforward operationally. In Appendix C, we show that an attribute with three levels of realization, say attribute k, lends itself very well to conjoint estimation. What one needs to do is to specify two dummy variables for the attribute using the middle level as the default. Then, the attribute can be written as

$$u_{ik}(\mathcal{P}) = \underline{\beta}_{ik}^c \underline{d}_k + \bar{\beta}_{ik}^c \bar{d}_k + \underline{\beta}_{ik}\widetilde{A}_k, \quad (15)$$

where $\underline{d}_k = 1$ if the kth attribute is at the lowest level and $\underline{d}_k = 0$ if otherwise, and $\bar{d}_k = 1$ if the kth attribute is at the highest level and $\bar{d}_k = 0$ if otherwise. Then

---

[3] Note here that this way of coding a brand name does not imply that consumers will have a zero reservation price for the "generic" product. It merely means that consumers derive zero value from the generic brand name per se. From (13), we can readily see that a consumer's reservation price for a product, whether it is a branded or generic product, is positive as long as the consumer derives sufficient positive utilities from all of the product's attributes. Thus, the reservation price of a generic product will be a function of the nonbrand attributes only.

we can redefine $U_i(\mathbf{P}^l)$ as consumer i's utility from the product profile that has the lowest level of each two-level attribute and the intermediate level of each three-level attribute. By doing so, we can simply substitute in the first two terms of Equation (15) for any attribute that has three levels of realization in Equation (12), as the last term in Equation (15) is canceled out when we take the difference between $U_i(\mathcal{P})$ and $U_i(\mathbf{P}^l)$. Then, $\underline{\beta}^c_{ik}$ and $\bar{\beta}^c_{ik}$ can be estimated through conjoint analysis, which will in turn allow us to find the value that a consumer places on the attribute through a set of transformation formulas detailed in Appendix C. This kind of transformation can also be done, as we show in Appendix D, to deal with attributes that have four or more levels.

When price has three levels of realization, the transformation is not as straightforward as it may seem. If we were to follow the common practice of conjoint specifications, we can let price enter Equation (7) arbitrarily as a piecewise linear function $\delta_1(p)\beta_{ip}p + \delta_2(p)\bar{\beta}_{ip}p$, instead of $\beta_{ip}p$, where

$$\delta_1(p) = \begin{cases} 1 & \text{if } p \in [\underline{p}, \tilde{p}] \\ 0 & \text{if otherwise} \end{cases}$$

$$\delta_2(p) = \begin{cases} 1 & \text{if } p \in (\tilde{p}, \bar{p}] \\ 0 & \text{if otherwise.} \end{cases} \qquad (16)$$

Then, the transformation can proceed in the same way as a nonprice attribute. In this case, we need to replace $\beta^c_{ip}d_p$ in Equation (12) with $\underline{\beta}^c_{ip}\underline{d}_p + \bar{\beta}^c_{ip}\bar{d}_p$, where

$$\underline{\beta}^c_{ip} = \beta_{ip}(\underline{p} - \tilde{p}), \qquad \bar{\beta}^c_{ip} = \bar{\beta}_{ip}(\bar{p} - \tilde{p}), \qquad (17)$$

$$\underline{d}_p = \begin{cases} 1 & \text{if } p = \underline{p} \\ 0 & \text{otherwise,} \end{cases} \qquad \bar{d}_p = \begin{cases} 1 & \text{if } p = \bar{p} \\ 0 & \text{otherwise.} \end{cases} \qquad (18)$$

As a result, one can use conjoint analysis to estimate $\underline{\beta}^c_{ip}$ and $\bar{\beta}^c_{ip}$, and then substitute into Equation (13) the exchange rate specific to the price range of a product to compute a consumer's reservation price.

However, the economic theory of consumer choice does not treat price as any other attribute and it allows the price of a product to enter the utility function only through the budget constraint. This implies a linear price effect in the utility function. The key to

reconciling the difference between theory and practice and to preserving the operational simplicity is to introduce some additional, reasonable assumptions to our theoretical derivations. In Appendix E, we show that if we assume p_i^y to be different in a high-price vs. a low-price environment, we could reasonably use Equation (17) to recover from conjoint estimations the exchange rate for a specific price range.

In summary, to estimate a consumer's reservation price for a product, we can simply conduct a regular conjoint analysis and use Equation (13) to compute the reservation price when each product attribute has only two levels of realization. When a nonprice attribute has three levels of realization, the two dummy variables assigned to the attribute in conjoint analysis should use the intermediate level as the default. When price also has three levels of realization, we simply assign two dummy variables, again with the intermediate level as the default. Once the conjoint parameters for the dummy variables are estimated, we can use Equation (17) to find the exchange rate appropriate to the price range of the product in question and use Equation (13) to compute reservation price.

4. Application

In this section, we present a pilot application to illustrate our approach. The primary purpose of this application is to show how our approach allows a researcher to estimate consumer reservation prices at the individual level with ease. By analyzing the estimated reservation prices, a researcher can then make product and pricing decisions with the same analytical flexibility and simplicity as afforded by traditional conjoint. However, we show that the strategy prescriptions for product introduction and pricing based on our approach differ significantly from those based on traditional conjoint, as our approach takes into account the market expansion effect and does not presume unconditional purchase by the target market.

To continue with the Compaq example discussed in the introduction, suppose that Compaq's management has decided that processing speed, hard drive, memory, price, and brand name are the five attributes

Table 1   Aggregate Conjoint Results[1]

Brand	Level	Coefficient	Standardized coefficient
Price	—[2]	−0.0225	−0.252
Brand	Dell	17.36	0.259
	Generic	0[3]	0
	Compaq	12.04	0.207
Memory	32 MB	−9.67	−0.144
	64 MB	0	0
	96 MB	4.67	0.070
Speed	266 mHz	0	0
	300 mHz	7.89	0.136
Hard drive	3 GB	0	0
	4 GB	2.42	0.041

[1] All coefficients are significant at α 0.01.

[2] We used three price levels $1,999, $2,599, and $2,895. Using the Chow test, we failed to reject the null hypothesis that the price effect is linear ($p > 0.1$). We therefore report the results of the regression model with the linear price effect.

[3] 0 indicates the base level for dummy coding.

that consumers value.[4] The levels of each of these attributes are given in Table 1 (Columns 1 and 2). To simplify the application further, assume that Dell is already selling a notebook computer with 266 mHz in speed, 64 MB in memory, and 4 GB in hard drive at $2,599. We hereafter refer to this product as DELL. Compaq must decide whether to enter the market using a *penetration strategy*, introducing a low-end product (*CPQL*) with 266 mHz in speed, 32 MB in memory, and 3 GB in hard drive in the price range of ($1,999 \le p \le $2,599$); or a *skimming strategy*, introducing a high-end product (*CPQH*) in a high price range ($2,599 \le p \le $2,895$); or a *product line strategy*, introducing both *CPQL* and *CPQH* simultaneously in their respective price range.[5] The question is which strategy Compaq should pursue and at what price(s).

Conceptually, Compaq can answer this question by estimating the demand for *CPQL*, given that only *CPQL* and *DELL* are available in the market, the demand for *CPQH* when only *CPQH* and *DELL* are

[4] Our design of this application is adapted from Lehmann et al. (1997).

[5] Obviously, to narrow down to these three strategic options, many other factors such as market dynamics, consumer acceptance, brand positioning, etc., must be considered. However, using the procedure we describe here for all possible permutations of the product profiles can also help.

available, and the demand for both *CPQL* and *CPQH* when all three are available. It can then simulate the profit for the three different product introduction scenarios based on its own cost structure and choose the scenario and price that generate the most profit for the company. To add some realism to this application, we surveyed a random sample of MBA students in a major East Coast University to generate the demand information. For this survey, we used a 16-trial orthogonal design *à la* Addelman (1962) and asked each subject to rate each of these 16 notebook profiles on a 0 to 100 scale. The survey generated a total of 848 usable observations from 53 subjects. In addition, following Monroe (1990, p. 114), we asked each subject in three separate questions to indicate the acceptable price he or she would consider paying, respectively, for *CPQL*, *CPQH*, and *DELL*. We further asked each subject at the end of the survey to indicate whether or not she or he will purchase *CPQL* for $1,999 if that is the only choice available in the market, and the same question is repeated for *CPQH* at $2,895 and *DELL* at $2,599.

In Table 1, we report the raw and standardized conjoint coefficients for the whole sample. All coefficients are statistically significant with the expected signs. The standardized coefficients suggest that brand and price are the most important attributes, followed by memory and speed. Hard drive plays a minor role in consumer preference for notebooks, probably because of the small GB range we tested.

4.1.   A Tale of Two Models

Using the *individual-level* conjoint coefficients, we first conduct conventional market share simulations for different product introduction scenarios and price ranges. The results are summarized in Table 2 for each strategy scenario.

From Table 2, we can see that traditional conjoint simulations can generate several managerial insights. First, in terms of market shares, Dell is most vulnerable to Compaq's product introduction at the high end. At the $2,599 price, Compaq can steal 69.6% from Dell if it enters at the high end but only 7.7% at the low end. However, by giving consumers more options to choose from, a product line strategy by Compaq can

Table 2   Traditional Conjoint Market Share Simulation Results*

Strategy	Compaq pricing		Share		
	P_{CPQL}	P_{CPQH}	Q_{DELL}	Q_{CPQL}	Q_{CPQH}
Penetration	$1,999		51.7	48.3**	
(introduction at low end)	$2,599		92.3	7.7	
Skimming		$2,599	30.4		69.6
(introduction at high end)		$2,895	50.2		49.8
Product line	$1,999	$2,895	28.5	37.3	34.2
(introduction at both ends)	$1,999	$2,599	23.6	22.8	53.6
	$2,599	$2,895	46.9	5.1	48

*Simulations are conducted using the share of preference rule. The results are only slightly different when using the first choice rule. The quantity demanded is expressed as percentage of the target market. All numbers are rounded up. P_i and Q_i, where $i = DELL, CPQL, CPQH$, are price and sales for product profile i, respectively.

**To be read as follows: When Compaq enters with low-end notebook priced at $1,999, Dell's share is 51.7% and Compaq's share for CPQL is 48.3%

Table 3   Demand Estimates Based on Consumer Reservation Price*

Strategy	Compaq pricing		Share			No purchase
	P_{CPQL}	P_{CPQH}	Q_{DELL}	Q_{CPQL}	Q_{CPQH}	
Penetration	$1,999		38.9	11.1		50.0**
(introduction at low end)	$2,599		46.3	1.9		51.9
Skimming		$2,599	18.5		33.3	48.1
(introduction at high end)		$2,895	24.1		27.8	48.1
Product line	$1,999	$2,895	22.2	5.6	24.1	48.1
(introduction at both ends)	$1,999	$2,599	18.5	1.9	31.5	48.1
	$2,599	$2,895	24.1	0	27.8	48.1

*The quantity demanded is expressed as percentage of the target market. All numbers are rounded up. P_i and Q_i, where $i = DELL, CPQL, CPQH$, are price and sales for product profile i, respectively.

**With Dell only in market, the nonpurchase rate is 53%. Thus, the introduction of CPQL has expanded the market by 3%.

do significantly more damage to Dell than any single product strategy, rewarding it with up to 76.4% share. Second, the demand for the Compaq notebook is quite price elastic at the low end, with the arc price elasticity of demand $\epsilon = -5.6$, but much less so at the high end, with $\epsilon = -3.1$. Third, if Compaq introduces a product line and changes its prices from ($2,599; $2,895) to ($1,999; $2,895), i.e., lowering only the price for the low-end notebook, CPQL sales increase by about 32 percentage points in market share, about 18 percentage points coming from DELL (the customer switching effect) and about 14 points from CPQH (the cannibalization effect). If, on the other hand, Compaq changes its product line prices from ($1,999; $2,895) to ($1,999; $2,599), i.e., lowering only the price for the high-end notebook, CPQH will gain about 19 percentage points, with all but about 5 percentage points coming from CPQL. Overall, traditional conjoint simulations suggest an eager market that can perhaps be best exploited through a product line strategy.

The picture of the market changes quite substantially, however, if we examine the conjoint estimates through the lens of the approach we have proposed in this paper. We can apply Equation (13) to our individual-level conjoint estimates and then use Conditions (2)–(4) to assess the market demand for

different strategy scenarios while allowing for the market expansion effect. The results for each strategy scenario are summarized in Table 3. As a benchmark, our analysis shows that Dell's market penetration would be about 47% if its notebook is priced at $2,599 and is a monopoly. The untapped 53% of the market may decrease when Compaq enters the market, thus enabling us to gauge the market expansion effect.

From Table 3, we can see that a new product introduction at the low end has very limited market potential, capturing 11.1% of the target market at best. About eight percentage points of this demand come from Dell (Dell's share decreases from 47% in the benchmark case to 38.9% after Compaq enters with CPQL at $1,999). Three points result from market expansion (the category penetration increases from the benchmark case of 47% to the post-Compaq rate of 50%). Furthermore, the demand for CPQL is quite elastic, with the arc price elasticity $\epsilon = -5.42$. A price increase by Compaq from $1,999 to $2,599 for CPQL will reduce its share to a mere 2%. Thus, through the lens of the augmented approach, CPQL is drastically less attractive than what traditional conjoint suggests. This is because the traditional approach presumes full and unconditional market participation by all surveyed subjects and seriously inflates, in this application, the number of Compaq's customers. Once that presumption is dismissed, the augmented approach suggests a rather dismal prospect of profitability for Compaq at the low end of the market.

At the high end, the demand for *CPQH* is considerably less price sensitive with $\epsilon = -1.67$. At the high price of $2,895, Compaq can capture 27.8% of the target market, with about 23 percentage points from *DELL* and about 5 points from market expansion. A price decrease from $2,895 to $2,599 for *CPQH* will draw approximately 5 more percentage points from *DELL* without expanding the market. Thus, relative to the entry at the low end, the augmented approach suggests that the *CPQH* introduction has an immensely larger market share for Compaq.

Compaq can enhance its high-end entry by simultaneously introducing the low-end product. However, this product line strategy brings little additional gain to Compaq, although consumers have one more option. From Table 3, we can see that Compaq's share of the target market with the product line strategy is not significantly different from what the company would capture with the high-end product alone. This suggests that the customers in this target market are mostly high-end purchasers, a characterization that fits rather well with the profiles of the MBAs we have surveyed. In fact, Table 1 shows that brand is slightly more important than price for these students.

Since two different approaches paint two different pictures about the market, it is not surprising that we may come to a different decision with regard to Compaq's product introduction strategy and pricing if we use this augmented conjoint approach rather than traditional conjoint. To see this, note that Tables 2 and 3 contain sufficient information for us to fit a linear demand curve for each product in each strategy scenario in the given price range. With additional costs information, we can easily determine the optimal price(s) and payoffs for a specific strategy scenario and then proceed to determine the most profitable strategy for Compaq to pursue. To carry through with this application, let us assume that the target market has one million consumers. The variable costs for the low-end notebook are $1,400 and those for the high-end $1,600. Furthermore, for simplicity we assume that the fixed cost associated with producing, marketing, and distributing the low-end notebook alone is $300 million and that for the high-end notebook it is $310 million. The fixed costs for the whole product line are $330 million due to scale economies in marketing and distribution.

Under this cost structure, the traditional conjoint analysis suggests that Compaq should take the product line strategy, selling its high-end product for $2,895 and its low-end product for $2,324 to capitalize on the expected strong demands at both ends of the market. The estimated profit from the product line strategy are $393 million. The skimming strategy, selling *CPQH* for $2,619, is the second best, generating an estimated profit of $385.6 million.

However, our augmented conjoint suggests a strikingly different product introduction and pricing strategy for Compaq. As the high-end product generates a strong customer switching effect and the maximum market expansion effect, the skimming strategy is the best entry strategy for Compaq: entering the high end of the market at the price point of $2,895. The estimated profit from this strategy is $50 million, which is significantly higher than the profit from the product line strategy ($32.76 million). In this market, the product line strategy suffers from the fact that it generates little incremental sales while requiring additional development costs. It is interesting to note that traditional conjoint and our augmented approach make very different predictions about the maximum profits that Compaq can gain from the market. Traditional conjoint yields a high profit estimate in this application because it assumes full participation of all consumers in the target market.

This difference in strategy prescriptions means that Compaq would have to face a dire consequence if it makes the entry decision based on a wrong model. If, in fact, not every consumer in the target market will purchase unconditionally from one of the two brands and the market expansion effect is present, it would cost Compaq dearly if it were to pursue the wrong strategy of the product line, following the prescription from traditional conjoint, rather than the right strategy of skimming. The wrong choice of strategy in this case would mean a substantial amount of forgone profits for Compaq.

4.2. Prima Facie Validity
There are good reasons to believe that the augmented approach may produce a better strategic prescrip-

tion in this application. From a theoretical perspective, the validity of traditional conjoint rests on the assumption that all the consumers in the target market make a purchase in a product category regardless of what product and pricing strategies the firms take or whether all competing products and brands in a market are included in a research design. However, this assumption is quite problematic in the context of this application, and indeed it is unlikely to hold for most practical applications. From an empirical perspective, we can establish some face validity here for our model by comparing the reservation prices and choices predicted by our model with the self-stated reservation prices and choices from the subjects we have surveyed. We will further examine the predictive validity using holdout samples in the next section.

Recall that we have asked our subjects to state their reservation prices for *CPQL*, *CPQH*, and *DELL*. Although biased, these self-stated reservation prices should have some positive correlation with their corresponding "true" reservation prices. Thus, if our model has any validity in capturing actual consumer reservation prices, we would expect the reservation prices predicted by our model to correlate

Table 4 Correlation Between Predicted and Self-Stated Reservation Prices (Augmented Conjoint)

Predicted reservation price for	Mean reservation price (90% Confidence interval)	Correlation		
		Self-stated reservation price for		
		DELL	*CPQL*	*CPQH*
DELL	$2,705 ($330–$5,164)	0.43**		
CPQL	$1,926 ($0–$4,325)		0.15	
CPQH	$3,141 ($330–$7,300)			0.28*

**Significant at $\alpha = 0.0017$ level; *Significant at $\alpha = 0.0478$ level.

with the *self-stated* reservation prices. In Table 4, we report the results of this correlational analysis. The mean self-stated reservation prices for products *DELL*, *CPQL*, and *CPQH* are, respectively, $2,341, $1,854, and $2,643, and they are all lower than their corresponding predicted value (see Table 4). This outcome is rather expected, as subjects tend to understate their reservation prices (Monroe 1990, p. 107). This bias will, of course, exaggerate the demand at low prices and understate the demand at high prices, as we show in Figure 1 for *DELL*. However, what

Figure 1 Theoretical and Self-Stated Demands

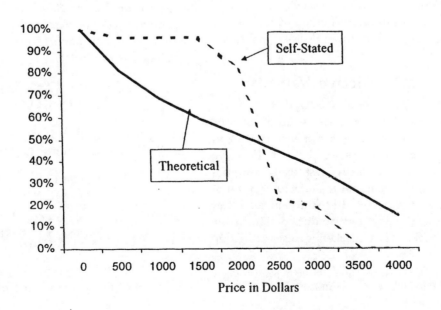

% of Respondents Willing to Buy

is revealing is the fact that our estimated reservation prices are positively correlated with the self-stated reservation prices in all three product scenarios, with the correlations for *DELL* and *CPQH* both being statistically significant. The correlation for *CPQL* is statistically insignificant. Perhaps this is because most of our subjects are high-end buyers and they may have a higher degree of uncertainty about what they are willing to pay for a low-end product.

The augmented conjoint can be put to a more stringent test by examining the quality of choice predictions by the model. We make choice predictions by comparing a product's estimated reservation price with its actual price (see Equation (3)). We then compare the predicted choices with the subjects' revealed choices. We conduct this analysis for *DELL*, *CPQL*, and *CPQH*. The hit rate for *DELL* is 60.4%, which is statistically significant at $\alpha = 0.10$, and the hit rate for *CPQH* is 62.3%, which is significant at $\alpha = 0.05$. However, the hit rate for *CPQL* is only 54.7% and is not significant. We performed the same predictions using the self-stated reservation prices. The results show that our approach performed better for *CPQH* and *DELL*, but worse for *CPQL*. This result is generally consistent with the finding in Kalish and Nelson (1991).

Overall, our model performs reasonably well in capturing subjects' reservation prices and predicting their choices, which offer prima facie evidence in support of our theory-based augmentation of conjoint as a useful tool in aiding managerial decision making.

5. Assessing Predictive Validity Through Holdout Samples

To further assess the predictive validity of our approach and to compare its performance relative to models that capture the market expansion effect, we use a dataset from a commercial study of automobile batteries.[6] A multinational manufacturer of automobile batteries sponsored this study in an effort to improve its marketing and product design in the replacement market. The marketing research group

[6] To maintain confidentiality, we disguised the type of batteries being studied and the identity of some attributes.

in charge of the project selected six attributes after in-depth consumer interviews. They are brand (four brands: A, B, C, D), price ($60, $75, $90), built-in charge meter (no, yes), environmental safety (no, yes), rapid recharge (no, yes), and battery life (standard, 50% longer). An orthogonal design of 32 profiles was used. Personal interviews were conducted at outlets where replacement car batteries were sold. Respondents were screened to be the key decision makers for car battery purchases. In exchange for a payment, each respondent evaluated 32 profiles descriptions. Each respondent first indicated if he or she would consider buying the described car battery and would then rate it on a 1–100 preference intensity scale only if the profile is considered (on average, 21.7% of the observations indicated no purchase). The order of profile presentations was randomized across respondents. In this study we use data from 169 respondents, totaling 5,408 observations (169 × 32 profiles) available to us. For validation purposes, we use 26 randomly drawn profiles for calibration and the remaining 6 profiles for holdout sample validation.

Unlike data typically collected in conjoint analysis studies, the car battery dataset is left-censored (i.e., preferences are observed only for products that are considered for purchase). As we show below, this left-censoring simplifies the estimation of reservation prices for product profiles. Recall that, by definition, consumer i will purchase product $\mathcal{P}$ if $r_i(\mathcal{P}) \geq p$. This means, from Equation (14), that the consumer will purchase the product if

$$\frac{\Delta p}{\beta_{ip}^c}\left(\sum_{k=1}^{N}\frac{\beta_{ik}^c}{\Delta A_k}A_k\right) - \frac{\Delta p}{\beta_{ip}^c}\left(\sum_{k=1}^{N}\frac{\beta_{ik}^c}{\Delta A_k}T_k\right) \geq p. \quad (19)$$

Letting $\beta_{ip} = \beta_{ip}^c/\Delta p$ and with some simple algebraic manipulations, Condition (19) can be written as

$$\beta_{i0} + \left(\sum_{k=1}^{N}\frac{\beta_{ik}^c}{\Delta A_k}(A_k - \underline{A}_k)\right) - \beta_{ip}p$$

$$\geq \beta_{i0} + \left(\sum_{k=1}^{N}\frac{\beta_{ik}^c}{\Delta A_k}(T_k - \underline{A}_k)\right). \quad (20)$$

Note that the expression $(A_k - \underline{A}_k)/\Delta A$ in the second term of the left-hand side of Equation (20) takes on the value of either 1 or 0 when the realization of the attribute has two levels and can be simplified as d_k.[7] The right-hand side of Equation (20) is constant over product profiles and we denote it by $\bar{c}_i$. Then, Condition (20) can be simplified as

$$\beta_{i0} + \sum_{k=1}^{N} \beta_{ik}^c d_k - \beta_{ip} p \geq \bar{c}_i. \tag{21}$$

To estimate the parameters in Equation (21) from censored preference data, define a partially latent utility variable

$$U_i^*(\mathcal{P}) = \beta_{i0} + \sum_{k=1}^{N} \beta_{ik}^c d_k - \beta_{ip} p + \epsilon_i. \tag{22}$$

$U_i^*(\mathcal{P})$ is related to the observed (left-censored) conjoint preferences $U_i(\mathcal{P})$ as follows:

$$U_i(\mathcal{P}) = \begin{cases} U_i^*(\mathcal{P}) & \text{if } U_i^*(\mathcal{P}) \geq \bar{c}_i, \\ 0 & \text{if otherwise,} \end{cases} \tag{23}$$

where ϵ_i is an error term independently and identically distributed as $N(0, \sigma_i^2)$. Note that as β_{i0}^c and $\bar{c}_i$ are both constant for respondent i, only their difference is estimable.

Once the parameters $\beta_{i0}^c - \bar{c}_i$, all β_{ik}^cs, and β_{ip} are estimated, it is easy to show that the consumer reservation price for profile $\mathcal{P}$ is recovered as

$$r_i(\mathcal{P}) = \frac{\beta_{i0}^c - \bar{c}_i}{\beta_{ip}} + \frac{1}{\beta_{ip}} \sum_{k=1}^{N} \beta_{ik}^c d_k. \tag{24}$$

It is important to point out that using the Tobit model specification in Equations (22) and (23) to estimate the consumer reservation price has two practical advantages. First, as T_ks are all absorbed in $\bar{c}_i$ in Equation (24), one need not estimate T_ks directly in order to estimate a consumer's reservation price. Second, one no longer needs to find a proper default in specifying a nominal variable. Take brand names, for instance. If there are three brand names, say Brands A, B, and C, and one generic name, one needs to specify three brand dummies using the generic name as

the default when we use traditional conjoint analysis (see §3). Then, these brand dummies enter into Equation (23) as $\beta_{iA} d_A + \beta_{iB} d_B + \beta_{iC} d_C$. However, in practice, it may be difficult to find a generic name from which a consumer derives zero attribute utility. Indeed, researchers typically code only two brand dummies, say, $\tilde{d}_B$ and $\tilde{d}_C$, using Brand A as the default. Fortunately, when using the Tobit model in Equation (23), a generic default is not necessary for estimating a consumer's reservation price.

To see this, note that given these two ways of specifying the dummy variables, we necessarily have $\beta_{iA} d_A + \beta_{iB} d_B + \beta_{iC} d_C \equiv \beta_{iA}(1 - \tilde{d}_B - \tilde{d}_B) + (\beta_{iB} + \beta_{iA})\tilde{d}_B + (\beta_{iC} + \beta_{iA})\tilde{d}_C$, which we can further simply as

$$\beta_{iA} d_A + \beta_{iB} d_B + \beta_{iC} d_C \equiv \beta_{iA} + \beta_{iB}\tilde{d}_B + \beta_{iC}\tilde{d}_C. \tag{25}$$

When the right-hand side of Equation (25) is used in Equation (23), β_{iA}, a constant, is absorbed into $\bar{c}_i$ and needs not be explicitly estimated to derive a consumer's reservation price. However, our derivation process shows that this advantage, along with the advantage of not estimating T_ks, comes at the cost of not being able to quantify specific attribute values. In other words, the gain in the ease of estimation comes at the expense of losing more detailed managerial insights.

We analyze the car battery data using our reservation price model (see Equations (22) and (24)) and compare our results to those from the consideration set approach proposed by Jedidi et al. (1996) which captures the market expansion effect through a Tobit model formulation (see also Malhotra 1986). Because our interest is in estimating individual-level reservation prices, we estimate both models using PROC LIFEREG in SAS for each respondent.[8] To conserve space we only report summary statistics for model fit and predictive validity for both models. We also report the distribution of consumer reservation prices and present the demand curves produced from both models.[9]

---

[7] When the realization has three or more levels, we can similarly write two or more dummies following the steps in Appendices D and E.

[8] The main difference between the two models lies in the way price enters the utility function. The reservation price approach treats price linearly (see equation (22)) whereas the consideration set approach treats price via two dummy variables. Note that the estimation in Jedidi et al. (1996) is performed at the segment level.

[9] Further detailed results can be obtained from the authors.

Figure 2   Estimated Demand for a Brand D's Product*

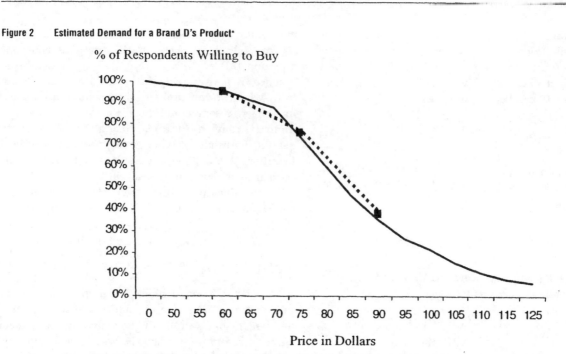

% of Respondents Willing to Buy

Price in Dollars

* The solid line is based on our approach. The dotted line is based on Jedidi, Kohli, and Desarbo (1996).

The goodness-of-fit statistics are excellent for both models. Using the same criteria as in Kalish and Nelson (1991), the average Spearman rank correlation between actual preference rankings and predicted surplus rankings is 0.834, and the average purchase incidence hit rate is 91.8% for our reservation price model. For the Jedidi et al. model, the average Spearman rank correlation between actual and predicted preference rankings is 0.85, while the average purchase incidence hit rate is 92.5%.

Figure 2 illustrates the differences between the demand curves obtained from our model and that of Jedidi et al (1996) for a Brand D battery with no built-in charge meter, no rapid recharge, no environmental safety, and standard battery life. This figure is constructed differently for each approach. For our approach, we first computed reservation prices for each respondent for the above product profile (see Figure 3). We then computed the percentage of respondents whose reservation price is greater than the actual price, which we varied from $0 to $125. For the Jedidi et al. approach we computed the percent of respondents whose utility exceeds the threshold for each price level (i.e., $60, $75, and $90).

To assess and compare predictive validity, we used the parameters from each model to predict purchase incidence, preference ranking, and choice for six hold-out profiles. Specifically, for our approach we computed the surplus (reservation price minus actual price) for each of these profiles. We predict purchase incidence if the surplus of the profile in question is positive. We predict choice of a profile if its surplus is the largest among the considered profiles. Similarly, for the Jedidi et al. approach, we predict purchase incidence if the utility of the profile is greater than the threshold and choice if its utility is maximum among the considered profiles. Using the same predictive validity statistics as in Kalish and Nelson (1991), the purchase incidence hit rate is 86.00% for our model and 86.25% for the Jedidi et al. model, whereas the choice hit rates are, respectively, 65.10% and 66.6%. For our model, the Spearman rank correlation between the actual preference rankings and the predicted surplus rankings is 0.836. For the Jedidi et al. model, the rank correlation between actual and predicted preferences is 0.834.

In sum, both approaches performed very well in predicting holdout profile preferences, and well

Figure 3   Distribution of Consumer Reservation Prices

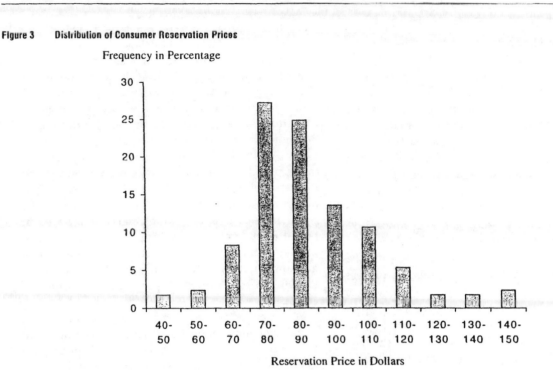

Reservation Price in Dollars

beyond chance. Obviously, the Jedidi et al. approach performed slightly better than our approach. This is rather expected because the Tobit model upon which Jedidi et al. is based allows for possible nonlinear price effect through multiple price dummies in utility equation (see Footnote 8), whereas our theory-based approach only let price enter a utility function through the budget constraint and hence allows for only a linear price effect. However, the advantages of our approach are equally obvious in that it generates consumer reservation prices at the individual level (see Figure 3) and allows for nonlinear demand estimation (see Figure 2).

6.   Conclusion
Our main contribution in this paper is to provide the proper transformation to estimate consumers' reservation prices from conjoint. We show how conjoint analysis can be integrated with the principles of economics to estimate consumers' reservation prices. This integration is possible fundamentally because a consumer's response to changes in price and other attributes for a product contains information about

her money's worth, or her internal exchange rate between money and the utility of consuming the product. This exchange rate allows us to gauge a consumer's willingness to pay for a specific bundle of nonprice attributes. Thus, we can determine how much a consumer is willing to pay for a product and how much surplus a consumer will obtain from a product at a given price.

Knowledge of consumer reservation prices in a practical setting offers a much-needed decision aid for managers. Such knowledge takes their decision making from the choice arena to the value arena and offers them a fresh, direct perspective on the economics of their strategic alternatives. By using our approach, managers can assess the value of an attribute, the value of a product offering, and the value of a customer. This value perspective bridges theory and practice, and enables managers to implement many marketing strategies and pricing tactics that hitherto remain mostly theoretical curiosities.

Specifically, our pilot application shows that this value perspective allows managers to study consumer purchase decisions and estimate the full impact of their decisions on demand, whether they are making product or pricing decisions. By assessing in a single model all three demand effects, namely customer switching, cannibalization, and market expansion, managers can then decide with some rigor and confidence whether to use a skimming, penetration, or product line strategy when entering a market. Our pilot application shows that our approach can provide a distinct perspective on a market and can help managers to make better strategic decisions.

Our theoretical derivations also validate a common conjoint practice of converting attribute utility changes to dollar values (see Dolan and Simon 1996, pp. 58–59 for an example). For instance, suppose a price decrease, say, from $2,599 to $1,999, produces the same increase in utility as a change in processing speed from 266mHz to 300mHz. Then, we can conclude that the improvement in processing speed is worth $600 for the consumer. With this and cost information, managers can decide whether it is more profitable to provide more processing speed or to reduce price. Our derivations confirm that this kind of analysis is theoretically sound. Equation (13) clearly assigns a dollar value to each nonprice attribute (exchange rate × attribute utility). Our derivations, however, clarify that it is inappropriate to multiply the exchange rate with the total utility from conjoint to estimate the consumer reservation price. The correct transformation must exclude the intercept and the price effect from total utility while properly scaling the attribute utilities.

It is important to emphasize that our approach provides a unique analytical apparatus that can estimate both consumer reservation prices and assess all three demand effects. It is also important to emphasize that our approach has two distinct advantages. First, our model is based on the standard economic theory of consumer choice, yet it retains the conceptual and operational simplicity of traditional conjoint. It entails no new data gathering or estimation techniques and imposes no expedient assumptions or any ad hoc rules to pin down consumer buy or no-buy decision. Any practitioner or student who knows how to use conjoint can easily use this augmented approach, all within the framework of utility theory.

Thus, this approach serves not only practical functions, but also pedagogical purposes. Second, the augmented conjoint estimates *individual-level* reservation prices for a specific product. Thus, it can potentially aid the implementation of one-to-one pricing.

In addition, we demonstrate, using commercial data, that our approach can be easily implemented through a Tobit model specification with a linear price effect. Although this specific way of implementing our approach has a more stringent data requirement, it offers the advantage of bypassing some conjoint design and estimation issues and is advisable when researchers care only about reservation prices but not attribute values. Our application to the automobile battery data shows that our approach has good predictive validity both by itself and relative to the utility-based approach proposed by Jedidi et al. (1996).

However, as our approach is dependent on traditional conjoint, it inherits all its shortcomings. Thus, the usual cautions associated with applying conjoint and making inferences from the analysis must be exercised in applying this approach. Specifically, it is worth noting that our model cannot capture any purchase dynamics or accommodate multiple-unit purchases. Furthermore, our model also relies on (piecewise) linear extrapolations and the additive nature of attribute utilities. Such linear approximations may not be accurate enough for some applications. Indeed, our model is not a statistical model and we do not quantify statistical errors inherent in our estimation of consumer reservation prices. Future research can extend our approach in that direction, perhaps following the approach proposed by Kohli and Mahajan (1991) or through a Bayesian approach. As the real test ground is in practical applications, this shortcoming can be minimized if every effort is made to validate and benchmark the results from the analysis. Like any other approach in marketing, the augmented conjoint can only aid, but not substitute for, sound managerial intuition and judgment.

Acknowledgments
The authors thank Rehana Farrell for her research assistance for this project. They are grateful to Rajeev Kohli for his generous encouragement and constructive comments throughout the different phases of this project. They also thank profusely two

Since $\widetilde{A}_k - \underline{A}_k \neq 0$ and $\overline{A}_k - \widetilde{A}_k \neq 0$, with some simple algebraic manipulations and using $\delta_1(A_k) + \delta_2(A_k) \equiv 1$, we can write Equation (C.3) as

$$u_{ik}(\mathcal{P}) = -\underline{\beta}_{ik}(\widetilde{A}_k - \underline{A}_k)\frac{(\widetilde{A}_k - A_k)\delta_1(A_k)}{(\widetilde{A}_k - \underline{A}_k)}$$
$$+ \bar{\beta}_{ik}(\overline{A}_k - \widetilde{A}_k)\frac{(A_k - \widetilde{A}_k)\delta_2(A_k)}{(\overline{A}_k - \widetilde{A}_k)} + \underline{\beta}_{ik}\widetilde{A}_k, \quad (C.4)$$

for all $A_k \in [\underline{A}_k, \overline{A}_k]$.

To simplify notation, we define the following two dummy variables:

$$\underline{d}_k = \begin{cases} 1 & \text{if } A_k = \underline{A}_k, \\ 0 & \text{otherwise;} \end{cases}$$

$$\bar{d}_k = \begin{cases} 1 & \text{if } A_k = \overline{A}_k, \\ 0 & \text{otherwise.} \end{cases} \quad (C.5)$$

We also let

$$\underline{\beta}_{ik}^c = -\underline{\beta}_{ik}(\widetilde{A}_k - \underline{A}_k) \quad \text{and} \quad \bar{\beta}_{ik}^c = \bar{\beta}_{ik}(\overline{A}_k - \widetilde{A}_k). \quad (C.6)$$

Then, when A_k has only three levels of realization, i.e., $A_k = \underline{A}_k, \widetilde{A}_k,$ or $\overline{A}_k$, it is straightforward to verify that for all A_k we have,

$$\underline{d}_k = \frac{(\widetilde{A}_k - A_k)\delta_1(A_k)}{(\widetilde{A}_k - \underline{A}_k)} \quad \text{and} \quad \bar{d}_k = \frac{(A_k - \widetilde{A}_k)\delta_2(A_k)}{(\overline{A}_k - \widetilde{A}_k)}. \quad (C.7)$$

Thus, Equation (C.4) can be simplified as

$$u_{ik}(\mathcal{P}) = \underline{\beta}_{ik}^c \underline{d}_k + \bar{\beta}_{ik}^c \bar{d}_k + \underline{\beta}_{ik}\widetilde{A}_k. \quad (C.8)$$

It is obvious from Equation (C.8) that an attribute with three levels of realization lends itself very well to conjoint estimation. All we need to do is to redefine $U_i(\mathbf{P}^l)$ as consumer i's utility from the product profile that has the lowest level of each two-level attribute and the intermediate level of each three-level attribute. Thus, we can simply substitute in the first two terms of Equation (C.8) for any attribute that has three levels of realization in Equation (12), as the last term in Equation (15) is canceled out when we take the difference between $U_i(\mathcal{P})$ and $U_i(\mathbf{P}^l)$. Once $\underline{\beta}_{ik}^c$ and $\bar{\beta}_{ik}^c$ are estimated through conjoint analysis, we can use Equation (C.6) to find $\underline{\beta}_{ik}$ and $\bar{\beta}_{ik}$. Then, Equation (C.1) will give us the estimate of $u_{ik}(\mathcal{P})$ that we need to calculate the consumer's reservation price using Equation (13).

Appendix D. Four or More Levels of Realization

We will focus on four levels of realization in our derivation. However, the same procedure can be applied to any higher levels of realization. For simplicity of notation, we omit the index number for the attribute and the consumer. Let A^i be the i's realization of a certain attribute, where $i = 1, 2, 3, 4$ and a larger i indicates a higher level of the attribute. To allow for diminishing utility, we can write

the utility from the attribute as a piecewise linear function below:

$$u(\mathcal{P}) = \begin{cases} \beta_1 A & \text{if } A \in [A^1, A^2] \\ \beta_1 A^2 + \beta^2(A - A^2) & \text{if } A \in (A^2, A^3] \\ \beta_1 A^2 + \beta^2(A^3 - A^2) + \beta^3(A - A^3) & \text{if } A \in (A^3, A^4]. \end{cases} \quad (D.1)$$

As in Appendix C, we define the following three switching functions:

$$\delta_3(A) = \begin{cases} 1 & \text{if } A \in [A^1, A^2], \\ 0 & \text{otherwise;} \end{cases}$$

$$\delta_4(A) = \begin{cases} 1 & \text{if } A \in (A^2, A^3], \\ 0 & \text{otherwise;} \end{cases}$$

$$\delta_5(A) = \begin{cases} 1 & \text{if } A \in (A^3, A^4], \\ 0 & \text{otherwise.} \end{cases}$$

By these three definitions, for all $A \in [A^1, A^4]$, we have

$$\delta_3(A) + \delta_4(A) + \delta_5(A) \equiv 1. \quad (D.2)$$

We can then write Equation (D.1) as

$$u(\mathcal{P}) = \delta_3(A)\beta_1 A + \delta_4(A)\{\beta_1 A^2 + \beta^2(A - A^2)\}$$
$$+ \delta_5(A)\{\beta_1 A^2 + \beta^2(A^3 - A^2) + \beta^3(A - A^3)\}.$$

With some simple algebraic manipulations and using the Identity (D.2), we can write the above equation as

$$u(\mathcal{P}) = \delta_3(A)\beta_1(A - A^1) + \delta_4(A)\beta_2(A - A^1)$$
$$+ \delta_5(A)\beta_3(A - A^1) + \beta_1 A^1 + \delta_4(\beta_1 - \beta_2)(A^2 - A^1)$$
$$+ \delta_5\{(\beta_1 - \beta_2)(A^2 - A^1) + (\beta_2 - \beta_3)(A^3 - A^1)\}. \quad (D.3)$$

Note that the second line in Equation (D.3) is approximately zero if $\beta_1 \approx \beta_2$ and $\beta_2 \approx \beta_3$, which we will assume. Then, we have

$$u(\mathcal{P}) \approx \delta_3(A)\beta_1(A - A^1) + \delta_4(A)\beta_2(A - A^1)$$
$$+ \delta_5(A)\beta_3(A - A^1) + \beta_1 A^1$$
$$= \delta_3(A)\beta_1(A^2 - A^1)\frac{(A - A^1)}{(A^2 - A^1)} + \delta_4(A)\beta_2(A^3 - A^1)\frac{(A - A^1)}{(A^3 - A^1)}$$
$$+ \delta_5(A)\beta_3(A^4 - A^1)\frac{(A - A^1)}{(A^4 - A^1)} + \beta_1 A^1. \quad (D.4)$$

To simplify our notation, let

$$d_i = \delta_{i+2}(A)(\frac{A - A^1}{A^{i+1} - A^1}),$$
$$\beta_i^c = \beta_i(A^{i+1} - A^1),$$

where $i = 1, 2, 3$. Then, we have from Equation (D.4)

$$u(\mathcal{P}) \approx \beta_1^c d_1 + \beta_2^c d_2 + \beta_3^c d_3 + \beta_1 A^1. \quad (D.5)$$

It is straightforward to show that d_i is simply a dummy variable indicating the $(i+1)$th level of realization with the lowest level of realization as the default. The last term will drop as we take the anonymous reviewers and the associate editor for their thoughtful comments. However, they are solely responsible for all the errors in the paper. The authors acknowledge the financial support for this project from the Eugene Lang Research Fellowship.

Appendix A. Existence of Consumer Reservation Price

We show that $r_i(\mathcal{P})$ as defined in Equation (1) always exists. To do so, we maintain the standard assumption that a consumer marginal utility from both "goods" is positive. Furthermore, we assume that it is never optimal for any consumer to purchase the product in question if the price for the product is as high as the consumer's income, or $U_i(\mathcal{P}, 0) < U_i(0, m_i/p_i^y)$. Define a consumer's utility gain function as

$$\mathcal{F}_i(p) = U_i\left(\mathcal{P}, \frac{m_i - p}{p_i^y}\right) - U_i\left(0, \frac{m_i}{p_i^y}\right). \tag{A.1}$$

Note that our two assumptions about a consumer's utility function imply $\mathcal{F}_i(0) > 0$ and $\mathcal{F}_i(m_i) < 0$. Since $\partial \mathcal{F}_i(p)/\partial p < 0$, there must always exist a $r_i(\mathcal{P}) \in (0, m_i)$ such that

$$\mathcal{F}_i(r_i(\mathcal{P})) = U_i\left(\mathcal{P}, \frac{m_i - r_i(\mathcal{P})}{p_i^y}\right) - U_i\left(0, \frac{m_i}{p_i^y}\right) \equiv 0. \tag{A.2}$$

Clearly, for any $p \le r_i(\mathcal{P})$, we must have $\mathcal{F}_i(p) \ge 0$ so that the consumer is better off purchasing the product. Otherwise, the consumer will not purchase the product as $\mathcal{F}_i(p) < 0$. Q.E.D

Appendix B. Equivalence between Utility Maximization and Surplus Maximization

We show that when a consumer's utility function is of the quasi-linear form, or $U_i(\mathcal{P}, y_i) = u_i(\mathcal{P}) + \alpha y_i$, where $\alpha > 0$, the consumer will choose Product A over Product B, given p_A and p_B, if and only if $s_A = [r_i(A) - p_A] \ge [r_i(B) - p_B] = s_B$.

For a consumer with income m_i and the price of consumption basket p_i^y, her utility from purchasing Product A at the price of p_A and that from purchasing Product B at p_B are respectively given by

$$U_i(A, p_A) = u_i(A) + \alpha \frac{m_i - p_A}{p_i^y}, \tag{B.1}$$

$$U_i(B, p_B) = u_i(B) + \alpha \frac{m_i - p_B}{p_i^y}. \tag{B.2}$$

Define $F(p_A, p_B) = U_i(A, p_A) - U_i(B, p_B)$. Then, consumer i will choose Product A over Product B if $F(p_A, p_B) \ge 0$ and choose Product B if otherwise. However, by definition, we have

$$
\begin{aligned}
F(p_A, p_B) = & \left\{ u_i(A) + \alpha \frac{m_i - r_i(A) + s_i(A)}{p_i^y} \right\} \\
& - \left\{ u_i(B) + \alpha \frac{m_i - r_i(B) + s_i(B)}{p_i^y} \right\} \\
= & \left\{ u_i(A) + \alpha \frac{m_i - r_i(A)}{p_i^y} - u_i(B) - \alpha \frac{m_i - r_i(B)}{p_i^y} \right\} \\
& + \alpha \frac{s_i(A) - s_i(B)}{p_i^y}.
\end{aligned}
\tag{B.3}
$$

Note that the first term in Equation (B.3) is, by the definitions of $r_i(A)$ and $r_i(B)$ in Equation (1), zero. Thus, we have

$$F(p_A, p_B) = \frac{\alpha}{p_i^y}\{s_i(A) - s_i(B)\}. \tag{B.4}$$

This implies that we have $F(p_A, p_B) \ge 0$ if and only if $s_i(A) \ge s_i(B)$.
Q.E.D

Appendix C. Three Levels of Realization

Suppose that the kth attribute has three levels of realization. As a continuous variable in the attribute space, we have $A_k \in [\underline{A}_k, \overline{A}_k]$. Since the level of this attribute can take on three values, it is desirable in our utility specification to account for possible diminishing or increasing utility from this attribute as the level of the attribute increases. This can be accomplished by specifying $u_{ik}(\mathcal{P})$ in Equation (6) not as proportional to, but as piecewise linear in, attribute k. Let $\widetilde{A}_k$ be an intermediate point in the range for A_k, or $\underline{A}_k < \widetilde{A}_k < \overline{A}_k$. In practice, we can take $\widetilde{A}_k$ as the intermediate level of realization for attribute k. We can specify

$$u_{ik}(\mathcal{P}) = \begin{cases} \underline{\beta}_{ik} A_k & \text{if } A_k \in [\underline{A}_k, \widetilde{A}_k] \\ \underline{\beta}_{ik}\widetilde{A}_k + \bar{\beta}_{ik}(A_k - \widetilde{A}_k) & \text{if } A_k \in (\widetilde{A}_k, \overline{A}_k]. \end{cases} \tag{C.1}$$

Equation (C.1) is illustrated in Figure 4. If $\underline{\beta}_{ik} = \bar{\beta}_{ik}$, we have a linear specification as in Equation (6). However, if $\underline{\beta}_{ik} > \bar{\beta}_{ik}$ ($\underline{\beta}_{ik} < \bar{\beta}_{ik}$), the consumer derives diminishing (increasing) utility from the attribute.

To facilitate our derivation, we define the following two switching functions:

$$\delta_1(A_k) = \begin{cases} 1 & \text{if } A_k \in [\underline{A}_k, \widetilde{A}_k], \\ 0 & \text{if otherwise;} \end{cases}$$

$$\delta_2(A_k) = \begin{cases} 1 & \text{if } A_k \in (\widetilde{A}_k, \overline{A}_k], \\ 0 & \text{if otherwise.} \end{cases} \tag{C.2}$$

By these two definitions, for all $A_k \in [\underline{A}_k, \overline{A}_k]$, we have $\delta_1(A_k) + \delta_2(A_k) \equiv 1$. Then, Equation (C.1) can be written compactly as

$$u_{ik}(\mathcal{P}) = \delta_1(A_k)\underline{\beta}_{ik}A_k + \delta_2(A_k)\{\underline{\beta}_{ik}\widetilde{A}_k + \bar{\beta}_{ik}(A_k - \widetilde{A}_k)\}. \tag{C.3}$$

Figure 4   Piece-Wise Linear Attribute Utility

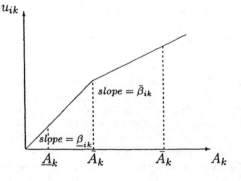

difference the way we do in the text for two levels of realization.
Q.E.D

Appendix E. Price Dependent Exchange Rate

To introduce price-dependent exchange rate in the context of our model, we need to assume that p_i^y is different in a high-price vs a low-price environment. Then we can write a consumer's utility function as

$$U_i(\mathscr{P}) = u_i(\mathscr{P}) + \delta_1(p)\left\{\frac{m_i}{p_i^y} - \frac{p}{p_i^y}\right\} + \delta_2(p)\left\{\frac{m_i}{\bar{p}_i^y} - \frac{p}{\bar{p}_i^y}\right\}, \qquad (E.1)$$

where $\delta_1(p)$ and $\delta_2(p)$ are as defined in Equation (16). With this specification, we have

$$U_i(\mathbf{P}^l) = u_i(\mathbf{P}^l) + \frac{m_i}{p_i^y} - \frac{\bar{p}}{p_i^y}. \qquad (E.2)$$

Taking the difference between Equations (E.1) and (E.2), we have

$$U_i(\mathscr{P}) - U_i(\mathbf{P}^l) = \{u_i(\mathscr{P}) - u_i(\mathbf{P}^l)\} + \delta_1(p)\left\{\frac{m_i}{p_i^y} - \frac{p}{p_i^y}\right\}$$

$$+ \delta_2(p)\left\{\frac{m_i}{\bar{p}_i^y} - \frac{p}{\bar{p}_i^y}\right\} - \frac{m_i}{p_i^y} + \frac{p}{p_i^y}. \qquad (E.3)$$

Let $\beta_{i0} = m_i/p_i^y$, $\beta_{ip} = 1/p_i^y$, $\bar{\beta}_{i0} = m_i/\bar{p}_i^y$, and $\bar{\beta}_{ip} = 1/\bar{p}_i^y$. We can write (E.3) as

$$U_i(\mathscr{P}) - U_i(\mathbf{P}^l) = \{u_i(\mathscr{P}) - u_i(\mathbf{P}^l)\} + \{\delta_1(p)\beta_{i0} + \delta_2(p)\bar{\beta}_{i0} - \beta_{i0}\}$$

$$- \{\delta_1(p)\beta_{ip} + \delta_2(p)\bar{\beta}_{ip} - \beta_{ip}\}\bar{p} - \delta_1(p)\beta_{ip}(p - \bar{p})$$

$$- \delta_2(p)\bar{\beta}_{ip}(p - \bar{p}) \qquad (E.4)$$

Note that if the difference between p_i^y and $\bar{p}_i^y$ is small, which we can reasonably assume, we must have $\beta_{i0} \approx \bar{\beta}_{i0}$ and $\beta_{ip} \approx \bar{\beta}_{ip}$. Then, since $\delta_1 + \delta_2$, we must also have

$$\delta_1(p)\beta_{i0} + \delta_2(p)\bar{\beta}_{i0} - \beta_{i0} \approx 0 \quad \text{and} \quad \delta_1(p)\beta_{ip} + \delta_2(p)\bar{\beta}_{ip} - \beta_{ip} \approx 0.$$
$$(E.5)$$

Thus, from Equations (E.4) and (E.5), we must have

$$U_i(\mathscr{P}) - U_i(\mathbf{P}^l)$$

$$\approx \{u_i(\mathscr{P}) - u_i(\mathbf{P}^l)\} - \delta_1(p)\beta_{ip}(p - \bar{p}) - \delta_2(p)\bar{\beta}_{ip}(p - \bar{p}). \qquad (E.6)$$

The process of transforming Equation (E.6) into conjoint analysis specification is the same as in the text. Q.E.D

References

Addelman, Sidney. 1962. Orthogonal main-effect plans for asymmetrical factorial experiments. *Technometrics.* **4** (February) 21–46.

Anderson, J. C., Dipak Jain, Pradeep K. Chintagunta. 1993. Understanding customer value in business markets: Methods of customer value assessment. *J. Bus.-to-Bus. Marketing.* 1(1) 3–30.

Desarbo, Wayne S., Venkatram Ramaswamy, Steven H. Cohen. 1995. Market segmentation with choice-based conjoint analysis. *Marketing Lett.* 6(2) 137–147.

Dolan, Robert J., Hermann Simon. 1996. *Power Pricing.* The Free Press, New York.

Green, Paul E., V. Srinivasan. 1990. Conjoint analysis in marketing research: New developments and directions. *J. Marketing.* **54** 3–19.

——, Yoram Wind. 1975. New way to measure consumers' judgments. *Harvard Bus. Rev.* 53 (July-August) 107–117.

Jedidi, Kamel, Rajeev Kohli, Wayne S. Desarbo. 1996. Consideration sets in conjoint analysis. *J. Marketing Res.* 33 (August) 364–372.

——, Sharan Jagpal, Puneet Manchanda. 2002. Measuring heterogeneous reservation prices for product bundles. *Marketing Sci.* Forthcoming.

Kalish, Shlomo, Paul Nelson. 1991. A comparison of ranking, rating and reservation price measure in conjoint analysis. *Marketing Lett.* 2(4) 327–335.

Kohli, Rajeev, Vijay Mahajan. 1991. A reservation-price model for optimal pricing of multiattribute products in conjoint analysis. *J. Marketing Res.* **28** (August) 347–354.

Lehmann, Donald R., Sunil Gupta, Joel H. Steckel. 1997. *Marketing Research.* Addison-Wesley, New York, 540–564.

Louviere, Jordan J., George Woodworth. 1983. Design and analysis of simulated consumer choice or allocation experiments: An approach based on aggregate data. *J. Marketing Res.* **20** 350–367.

Mahajan, Vijay, Paul E. Green, Stephen M. Goldberg. 1982. A conjoint model for measuring self- and cross-price/demand relationships. *J. Marketing Res.* **19** (August) 334–342.

Malhotra, Naresh K. 1986. An approach to the measurement of consumer preferences using limited information. *J. Marketing Res.* **23** 33–40.

Mason, Charlotte H. 1990. New product entries and product class demand. *Marketing Sci.* 9 (Winter) 58–73.

Monroe, Kent B. 1990. *Pricing: Making Profitable Decisions*, 2nd ed. McGraw-Hill, New York.

Page, Albert L., Harold F. Rosenbaum. 1987. Redesigning product lines with conjoint analysis: How Sunbeam does it. *J. Product Innovation Management.* 4 120–137.

Shaffer, G., Z. John Zhang. 1995. Competitive coupon targeting. *Marketing Sci.* 14 395–416.

——, ——. 2000. Pay to switch or pay not to switch: Third degree price discrimination in markets with switching costs. *J. Econom. and Management Strategy*, forthcoming.

Varian, Hal R. 1992. *Microeconomic Analysis*, 3rd ed. W.W. Norton & Company, New York.

Wittink, Dick R., Philippe Cattin. 1989. Commercial use of conjoint analysis: An update. *J. Marketing* 53 (July) 91–96.

——, Trond Bergestuen. 1999. Forecasting with conjoint analysis, J. Scott Armstrong, ed. *Principles of Forecasting: A Handbook for Researchers and Practitioners.* Kluwer Academic Publishers, Norwell, MA.

Accepted by Dipak C. Jain; received December 27, 2000. This paper was with the authors for 2 revisions.

MARKETING SCIENCE
Vol. 4, No. 3, Summer 1985
Printed in U.S.A

MENTAL ACCOUNTING AND CONSUMER CHOICE

RICHARD THALER

Cornell University

A new model of consumer behavior is developed using a hybrid of cognitive psychology and microeconomics. The development of the model starts with the mental coding of combinations of gains and losses using the prospect theory value function. Then the evaluation of purchases is modeled using the new concept of "transaction utility". The household budgeting process is also incorporated to complete the characterization of mental accounting. Several implications to marketing, particularly in the area of pricing, are developed.
(Mental Accounting; Consumer Choice; Pricing)

1. Introduction

Consider the following anecdotes:

1. Mr. and Mrs. L and Mr. and Mrs. H went on a fishing trip in the northwest and caught some salmon. They packed the fish and sent it home on an airline, but the fish were lost in transit. They received $300 from the airline. The couples take the money, go out to dinner and spend $225. They had never spent that much at a restaurant before.

2. Mr. X is up $50 in a monthly poker game. He has a queen high flush and calls a $10 bet. Mr. Y owns 100 shares of IBM which went up $\frac{1}{2}$ today and is even in the poker game. He has a king high flush but he folds. When X wins, Y thinks to himself, "If I had been up $50 I would have called too."

3. Mr. and Mrs. J have saved $15,000 toward their dream vacation home. They hope to buy the home in five years. The money earns 10% in a money market account. They just bought a new car for $11,000 which they financed with a three-year car loan at 15%.

4. Mr. S admires a $125 cashmere sweater at the department store. He declines to buy it, feeling that it is too extravagant. Later that month he receives the same sweater from his wife for a birthday present. He is very happy. Mr. and Mrs. S have only joint bank accounts.

All organizations, from General Motors down to single person households, have explicit and/or implicit accounting systems. The accounting systems often influence decisions in unexpected ways. This paper characterizes some aspects of the implicit mental accounting system used by individuals and households. The goal of the paper is to develop a richer theory of consumer behavior than standard economic theory. The new theory is capable of explaining (and predicting) the kinds of behavior illustrated by the four

0732-2399/85/0404/0199/$01.25

anecdotes above. Each of these anecdotes illustrate a type of behavior where a mental accounting system induces an individual to violate a simple economic principle. Example 1 violates the principle of fungibility. Money is not supposed to have labels attached to it. Yet the couples behaved the way they did because the $300 was put into both "windfall gain" and "food" accounts. The extravagant dinner would not have occurred had each couple received a yearly salary increase of $150, even though that would have been worth more in present value terms. Example 2 illustrates that accounts may be both topically and temporally specific. A player's behavior in a poker game is altered by his current position in that evening's game, but not by either his lifetime winnings or losings nor by some event allocated to a different account altogether such as a paper gain in the stock market. In example 3 the violation of fungibility (at obvious economic costs) is caused by the household's appreciation for their own self-control problems. They are afraid that if the vacation home account is drawn down it will not be repaid, while the bank will see to it that the car loan is paid off on schedule. Example 4 illustrates the curious fact that people tend to give as gifts items that the recipients would not buy for themselves, and that the recipients by and large approve of the strategy. As is shown in §4.3, this also violates a microeconomic principle.

The theory of consumer behavior to which the current theory is offered as a substitute is the standard economic theory of the consumer. That theory, of course, is based on normative principles. In fact, the paradigm of economic theory is to first characterize the solution to some problem, and then to assume the relevant agents (on average) act accordingly.

The decision problem which consumers are supposed to solve can be characterized in a simple fashion. Let $z = \{z_1, \ldots, z_i, \ldots, z_n\}$ be the vector of goods available in the economy at prices given by the corresponding vector $p = \{p_1, \cdots p_i, \cdots p_n\}$. Let the consumer's utility function be defined as $U(z)$ and his income (or wealth) be given as I. Then the consumer should try to solve the following problem:

$$\max_z U(z) \quad \text{s.t.} \quad \sum p_i z_i \leq I.$$

Or, using Lagrange multipliers

$$\max_z U(z) - \lambda(\sum p_i z_i - I). \tag{1}$$

The first order conditions to this problem are, in essence, the economic theory of the consumer. Lancaster (1971) has extended the model by having utility depend on the characteristics of the goods. Similarly, Becker (1965) has introduced the role of time and other factors using the concept of household production. These extended theories are richer than the original model, and, as a result, have more to offer marketing. Nevertheless, the economic theory of the consumer, even so extended, has not found widespread application in marketing. Why not? One reason is that all such models omit virtually all marketing variables except price and product characteristics. Many marketing variables fall into the category that Tversky and Kahneman (1981) refer to as *framing*. These authors have shown that often choices depend on the way a problem is posed as much as on the objective features of a problem. Yet within economic theory, framing cannot alter behavior.

To help describe individual choice under uncertainty in a way capable of capturing "mere" framing effects as well as other anomalies, Kahneman and Tversky (1979) have developed "prospect theory" as an alternative to expected utility theory. Prospect theory's sole aim is to describe or predict behavior, not to characterize optimal behavior. Elsewhere (Thaler 1980), I have begun to develop a similar descriptive alternative to the deterministic economic theory of consumer choice. There I argue that consumers often fail to behave in accordance with the normative prescriptions of economic theory. For example, consumers often pay attention to sunk costs when they shouldn't, and underweight opportunity costs as compared to out-of-pocket costs.[1]

This paper uses the concept of mental accounting to move further toward a behaviorally based theory of consumer choice. Compared to the model in equation (1) the alternative theory has three key features. First, the utility function $U(x)$ is replaced with the *value function* $v(\cdot)$ from prospect theory. The characteristics of this value function are described and then extended to apply to compound outcomes. Second, price is introduced directly into the value function using the concept of a *reference* price. The new concept of *transaction utility* is developed as a result. Third, the normative principle of *fungibility* is relaxed. Numerous marketing implications of the theory are derived. The theory is also used to explain some empirical puzzles.

2. Mental Arithmetic

2.1. *The Value Function*

The first step in describing the behavior of the representative consumer is to replace the utility function from economic theory with the psychologically richer *value function* used by Kahneman and Tversky. The assumed shape of the value function incorporates three important behavioral principles that are used repeatedly in what follows. First, the function $v(\cdot)$ is defined over perceived gains and losses relative to some natural reference point, rather than wealth or consumption as in the standard theory. This feature reflects the fact that people appear to respond more to perceived changes than to absolute levels. (The individual in this model can be thought of as a pleasure machine with gains yielding pleasure and losses yielding pain.) By using a reference point the theory also permits framing effects to affect choices. The framing of a problem often involves the suggestion of a particular reference point. Second, the value function is assumed to be concave for gains and convex for losses. ($v''(x) < 0$, $x > 0$; $v''(x) > 0$, $x < 0$.) This feature captures the basic psychophysics of quantity. The difference between \$10 and \$20 seems greater than the difference between \$110 and \$120, irrespective of the signs of the amounts in question. Third, the loss function is steeper than the gain function ($v(x) < -v(-x)$, $x > 0$). This notion that losses loom larger than gains captures what I have elsewhere called the endowment effect: people generally will demand more to sell an item they own than they would be willing to pay to acquire the same item (Thaler 1980).

2.2. *Coding Gains and Losses*

The prospect theory value function is defined over single, unidimensional outcomes. For the present analysis it is useful to extend the analysis to incorporate compound outcomes where each outcome is measured along the same dimension (say dollars).[2]

The question is how does the joint outcome (x, y) get coded? Two possibilities are considered. The outcomes could be valued jointly as $v(x + y)$ in which case they will be said to be *integrated*. Alternatively they may be valued separately as $v(x) + v(y)$ in which case they are said to be *segregated*. The issue to be investigated is whether segregation or integration produces greater utility. The issue is interesting from three different perspectives. First, if a situation is sufficiently ambiguous how will individuals choose to

---

[1] These propositions have recently been tested and confirmed in extensive studies by Arkes and Hackett (1985), Gregory (1982) and Knetch and Sinden (1984).

[2] Kahneman and Tversky are currently working on the single outcome, multi-attribute case. It is also possible to deal with the compound multi-attribute case but things get very messy. Since this paper is trying to extend economic theory which assumes that all outcomes can be collapsed into a single index (utils or money) sticking to the one-dimensional case seems like a reasonable first step.

code outcomes? To some extent people try to frame outcomes in whatever way makes them happiest.[3] Second, individuals may have preferences about how their life is organized. Would most people rather have a salary of $30,000 and a (certain) bonus of $5,000 or a salary of $35,000? Third, and most relevant to marketing, how would a seller want to describe (frame) the characteristics of a transaction? Which attributes should be combined and which should be separated? The analysis which follows can be applied to any of these perspectives.

For the joint outcome (x, y) there are four possible combinations to consider:

1. Multiple Gains. Let $x > 0$ and $y > 0$.[4] Since v is concave $v(x) + v(y) > v(x + y)$, so segregation is preferred. Moral: don't wrap all the Christmas presents in one box.

2. Multiple Losses. Let the outcomes be $-x$ and $-y$ where x and y are still positive. Then since $v(-x) + v(-y) < v(-(x + y))$ integration is preferred. For example, one desirable feature of credit cards is that they pool many small losses into one larger loss and in so doing reduce the total value lost.

3. Mixed Gain. Consider the outcome $(x, -y)$ where $x > y$ so there is a net gain. Here $v(x) + v(-y) < v(x - y)$ so integration is preferred. In fact, since the loss function is steeper than the gain function, it is possible that $v(x) + v(-y) < 0$ while $v(x - y)$ must be positive since $x > y$ by assumption. Thus, for mixed gains integration amounts to *cancellation*. Notice that all voluntarily executed trades fall into this category.

4. Mixed Loss. Consider the outcome $(x, -y)$ where $x < y$, a net loss. In this case we cannot determine without further information whether $v(x) + v(-y) \gtrless v(x - y)$. This is illustrated in Figure 1. Segregation is preferred if $v(x) > v(x - y) - v(-y)$. This is more likely the smaller is x relative to y. Intuitively, with a large loss and a small gain, e.g., ($40, -$6000) segregation is preferred since v is relatively flat near -6000. This will be referred to as the "silver lining" principle. On the other hand, for ($40, -$50) integration is probably preferred since the gain of the $40 is likely to be valued less than the reduction of the loss from $50 to $10, nearly a case of cancellation.

2.3. *Evidence on Segregation and Integration*

The previous analysis can be summarized by four principles: (a) segregate gains, (b) integrate losses, (c) cancel losses against larger gains, (d) segregate "silver linings". To see whether these principles coincided with the intuition of others, a small experiment was conducted using 87 students in an undergraduate statistics class at Cornell University. The idea was to present subjects with pairs of outcomes either segregated or integrated and to ask them which frame was preferable. Four scenarios were used, one corresponding to each of the above principles.

The instructions given to the students were:

> Below you will find four pairs of scenarios. In each case two events occur in Mr. A's life and one event occurs in Mr. B's life. You are asked to judge whether Mr. A or Mr. B is happier. Would most people rather be A or B? If you think the two scenarios are emotionally equivalent, check "no difference." In all cases the events are intended to be financially equivalent.

The four items used and the number of responses of each type follow.

---

[3] This is illustrated by the following true story. A group of friends who play poker together regularly had an outing in which they played poker in a large recreational vehicle while going to and from a race track. There were significant asymmetries in the way people (honestly) reported their winnings and losings from the two poker games and racetrack bets. Whether the outcomes were reported together or separately could largely be explained by the analysis that follows.

[4] For simplicity I will deal only with two-outcome events, but the principles generalize to cases with several outcomes.

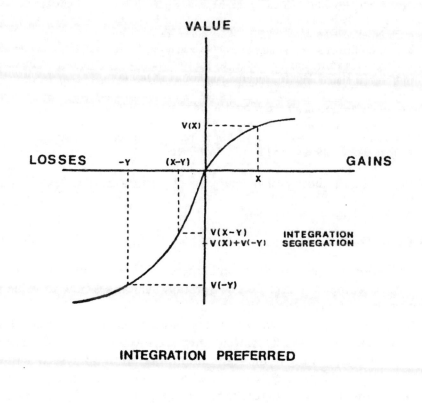

INTEGRATION PREFERRED

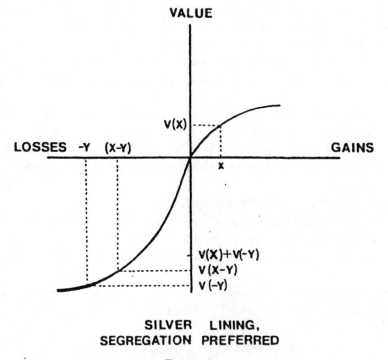

SILVER LINING,
SEGREGATION PREFERRED

FIGURE 1

1. Mr. A was given tickets to lotteries involving the World Series. He won $50 in one lottery and $25 in the other.

Mr. B was given a ticket to a single, larger World Series lottery. He won $75.

Who was happier?   56 A   16 B   15 no difference

2. Mr. A received a letter from the IRS saying that he made a minor arithmetical mistake on his tax return and owed $100. He received a similar letter the same day from his state income tax authority saying he owed $50. There were no other repercussions from either mistake.

Mr. B received a letter from the IRS saying that he made a minor arithmetical mistake on his tax return and owed $150. There were no other repercussions from his mistake.

Who was more upset?   66 A   14 B   7 no difference

3. Mr. A bought his first New York State lottery ticket and won $100. Also, in a freak accident, he damaged the rug in his apartment and had to pay the landlord $80.

Mr. B bought his first New York State lottery ticket and won $20.

Who was happier?   22 A   61 B   4 no difference

4. Mr. A's car was damaged in a parking lot. He had to spend $200 to repair the damage. The same day the car was damaged, he won $25 in the office football pool.

Mr. B's car was damaged in a parking lot. He had to spend $175 to repair the damage.

Who was more upset?   19 A   63 B   5 no difference

For each item, a large majority of the subjects chose in a manner predicted by the theory.[5]

2.4. *Reference Outcomes*

Suppose an individual is expecting some outcome x and instead obtains $x + \Delta x$. Define this as a reference outcome $(x + \Delta x: x)$. The question then arises how to value such an outcome. Assume that the expected outcome was fully anticipated and assimilated. This implies that $v(x: x) = 0$. A person who opens his monthly pay envelope and finds it to be the usual amount is unaffected. However, when $\Delta x \neq 0$ there is a choice of ways to frame the outcome corresponding to the segregation/integration analysis of simple compound outcomes. With reference outcomes the choice involves whether to value the unexpected component Δx alone (segregation) or in conjunction with the expected component (integration). An example, similar to those above, illustrates the difference:

• Mr. A expected a Christmas bonus of $300. He received his check and the amount was indeed $300. A week later he received a note saying that there had been an error in this bonus check. The check was $50 too high. He must return the $50.

• Mr. B expected a Christmas bonus of $300. He received his check and found it was for $250.

It is clear who is more upset in this story. Mr. A had his loss segregated and it would inevitably be coded as a loss of $50. Mr. B's outcome can be integrated by viewing the news as a reduction in a gain $-[v(300) - v(250)]$. When the situation is structured in a neutral or ambiguous manner then the same four principles determine whether segregation or integration is preferred:

(1) An increase in a gain should be segregated.

(2) An increase in (the absolute value of) a loss should be integrated.

(3) A decrease in a gain should be integrated (cancellation).

(4) A small reduction in (the absolute value of) a loss should be segregated (silver lining).

The concept of a reference outcome is used below to model a buyer's reaction to a market price that differs from the price he expected.

3. Transaction Utility Theory

In the context of the pleasure machine metaphor suggested earlier, the previous section can be thought of as a description of the hard wiring. The machine responds to perceived gains and losses in the way described. The next step in the analysis is to use this structure to analyze transactions. A two-stage process is proposed. First, individuals evaluate po-

---

[5] Two caveats must be noted here. First, the analysis does not extend directly to the multi-attribute (or multiple account) case. It is often cognitively impossible to integrate across accounts. Thus winning $100 does not cancel a toothache. Second, even within the same account, individuals may be unable to integrate two losses that are framed separately. See Johnson and Thaler (1985).

tential transactions. Second, they approve or disapprove of each potential transaction. The first stage is a judgment process while the second is a decision process. They are analyzed in turn.

3.1. *Evaluating Transactions*

Consider the following excerpt from a movie review:

> My sister just found out that for a $235 per month sublet she shares with another woman, she pays $185 per month. The other woman justifies her $50 per month rent two ways: one, she is doing my sister a favor letting her live there given the housing situation in New York City, and, two, everyone with a room to sublet in NYC will cheat her at least as badly. Her reasons are undeniably true, and that makes them quadruply disgusting.

(Cornell Daily Sun, Feb. 21, 1983)

Notice that the writer's sister is presumably getting a good value for her money (the room is worth $185 per month) but is still unhappy. To incorporate this aspect of the psychology of buying into the model, two kinds of utility are postulated: *acquisition utility* and *transaction utility*. The former depends on the value of the good received compared to the outlay, the latter depends solely on the perceived merits of the "deal".

For the analysis that follows, three price concepts are used. First, define p as the actual price charged for some good z. Then for some individual, define $\bar{p}$ as the *value equivalent* of z, that is, the amount of money which would leave the individual indifferent between receiving $\bar{p}$ or z as a gift.[6] Finally, let p^* be called the *reference* price for z. The reference price is an expected or "just" price for z. (More on p^* momentarily.)

Now define acquisition utility as the value of the compound outcome $(z, -p) = (\bar{p}, -p)$. This is designated as $v(\bar{p}, -p)$. Acquisition utility is the net utility that accrues from the trade of p to obtain z (which is valued at $\bar{p}$). Since $v(\bar{p}, -p)$ will generally be coded as the integrated outcome $v(\bar{p} - p)$, the cost of the good is not treated as a loss. Given the steepness of the loss function near the reference point, it is hedonically inefficient to code costs as losses, especially for routine transactions.

The measure of transaction utility depends on the price the individual pays compared to some reference price, p^*. Formally, it is defined as the reference outcome $v(-p: -p^*)$, that is, the value of paying p when the expected or reference price is p^*. Total utility from a purchase is just the sum of acquisition utility and transaction utility.[7] Thus the value of buying good z at price p with reference price p^* is defined as $w(z, p, p^*)$ where:

$$w(z, p, p^*) = v(\bar{p}, -p) + v(-p: -p^*) . \tag{2}$$

Little has been said as to the determinants of p^*. The most important factor in determining p^* is fairness. Fairness, in turn, depends in large part on cost to the seller. This is illustrated by the following three questionnaires administered to first-year MBA students. (The phrases in brackets differed across the three groups.)

> Imagine that you are going to a sold-out Cornell hockey playoff game, and you have an extra ticket to sell or give away. The price marked on the ticket is $5 (but you were given your tickets for

---

[6] In the standard theory, p equals the reservation price, the maximum the individual would pay. In this theory, p can differ from the reservation price because of positive or negative transaction utility. Acquisition utility is comparable in principle to consumer surplus.

[7] A more general formulation would be to allow differing weights on the two terms in (2). For example, equation (2) could be written as

$$w(z, p, p^*) = v(p, -p) + \beta v(-p: -p^*),$$

where β is the weight given to transaction utility. If $\beta = 0$ then the standard theory applies. Pathological bargain hunters would have $\beta > 1$. This generalization was suggested by Jonathan Baron.

free by a friend) [which is what you paid for each ticket] {but you paid $10 each for your tickets when you bought them from another student}. You get to the game early to make sure you get rid of the ticket. An informal survey of people selling tickets indicates that the going price is $5. You find someone who wants the ticket and takes out his wallet to pay you. He asks how much you want for the ticket. Assume that there is no law against charging a price higher than that marked on the ticket. What price do you ask for if

1. he is a friend   ————
2. he is a stranger   —— —

What would you have said if instead you found the going market price was $10?

3. friend   ————
4. stranger   ————

The idea behind the questionnaire was that the price people would charge a friend would be a good proxy for their estimate of a fair price. For each question, three prices were available as possible anchors upon which people could base their answers: the price marked on the ticket, the market price, and the price paid by the seller, i.e., cost. As can be seen in Table 1, the modal answers in the friend condition are equal to the seller's costs except in the unusual case where seller's cost was above market price. In contrast, the modal answers in the stranger condition are equal to market price with the same lone exception. The implication of this is that buyers' perceptions of a seller's costs will strongly influence their judgments about what price is fair, and this in turn influences their value for p^*.

The next questionnaire, given to those participants in an executive development program who said they were regular beer drinkers, shows how transaction utility can influence willingness to pay (and therefore demand).

Consider the following scenario:

> You are lying on the beach on a hot day. All you have to drink is ice water. For the last hour you have been thinking about how much you would enjoy a nice cold bottle of your favorite brand of beer. A companion gets up to go make a phone call and offers to bring back a beer from the only nearby place where beer is sold (a fancy resort hotel) [a small, run-down grocery store]. He says that the beer might be expensive and so asks how much you are willing to pay for the beer. He says that he will buy the beer if it costs as much or less than the price you state. But if it costs more than the price you state he will not buy it. You trust your friend, and there is no possibility of bargaining with (the bartender) [store owner]. What price do you tell him?

The results from this survey were dramatic. The median price given in the fancy resort hotel version was $2.65 while the median for the small run-down grocery store version was $1.50. This difference occurs despite the following three features of this example:

1. In both versions the ultimate consumption act is the same—drinking one beer on the beach. The beer is the same in each case.

TABLE 1

Percent of Subjects Giving Common Answers to Hockey Ticket Question

Cost	Market Value	Friend				Stranger			
		0	5	10	Other	0	5	10	Other
0	5 N = 31	68	26	3	3	6	77	10	6
0	10	65	26	6	3	6	16	58	19
5	5 N = 28	14	79	0	7	0	79	7	14
5	10	7	79	4	9	0	14	57	29
10	5 N = 26	0	69	23	8	0	42	46	12
10	10	0	15	69	15	0	0	73	27

Note: Modal answer is underlined.

2. There is no possibility of strategic behavior in stating the reservation price.[8]

3. No "atmosphere" is consumed by the respondent.

The explanation offered for these choices is based on the concept of transaction utility. (Acquisition utility is constant between the two cases.) While paying $2.50 for a beer is an expected annoyance at the resort hotel, it would be considered an outrageous "rip-off" in a grocery store. Paying $2.50 a bottle is $15.00 a six-pack, considerably above the reference price.

3.2. Purchase Decisions—Multiple Accounts

The introduction of $w(\cdot)$ as the purchase evaluation device requires additional changes to the standard theory described in the introduction. Since $w(\cdot)$ is defined over individual transactions it is convenient to give each unit of a specific good its own label. Optimization would then require the individual to select the set of purchases that would maximize $\Sigma \, w(\cdot)$ subject to the budget constraint $\Sigma \, p_i z_i \leq I$ where I is income. A solution to this integer programming problem would be to make purchases if and only if

$$w(z_i, p_i, p_i^*)/p_i \geq k \tag{3}$$

where k is a constant that serves a role similar to that of the Lagrange multiplier in the standard formulation.

Notice that if k is selected optimally then (3) can be applied sequentially without any explicit consideration of opportunity costs. This sort of sequential analysis seems to be a good description of behavior.[9] First, the consumer responds to local temporal budget constraints. That is, the budget constraint that most influences behavior is the current income flow rather than the present value of lifetime wealth. For many families, the most relevant time horizon is the month since many regular bills tend to be monthly. Thus, the budgeting process, either implicit or explicit, tends to occur on a month-to-month basis. Second, expenditures tend to be grouped into categories. Potential expenditures are then considered within their category. (Families that take their monthly pay and put it into various use-specific envelopes to be allocated during the month are explicitly behaving in the manner described here. Most families simply use a less explicit procedure.) The tendency to group purchases by category can violate the economic principle of fungibility.

Given the existence of time and category specific budget constraints, the consumer evaluates purchases as situations arise. For example, suppose a couple is called by friends who suggest going out to dinner on Saturday night at a particular restaurant. The couple would have to decide whether such an expenditure would violate either the monthly or the entertainment constraints. Formally, the decision process can be modelled by saying the consumer will buy a good z at price p if

$$\frac{w(z, p, p^*)}{p} > k_{it}$$

where k_{it} is the budget constraint for category i in time period t.

Of course, global optimization would lead all the k_{it}'s to be equal which would render irrelevant the budgeting process described here. However, there is evidence that individuals do not act as if all the k's were equal. As discussed elsewhere (Thaler and Shefrin 1981), individuals face self-control problems in regulating eating, drinking, smoking, and con-

---

[8] The question is what economists would call "incentive compatable". The respondent's best strategy is to state his or her true reservation price. Subjects given extensive explanations of this feature nevertheless still display a large disparity in answers to the two versions of the problem.

[9] The model that follows is based, in part, on some extensive, open-ended interviews of families conducted in 1982. The families were asked detailed questions about how they regulate their day-to-day expenditures, and what they have done in various specific situations such as those involving a large windfall gain or loss.

sumption generally. The whole mental accounting apparatus being presented here can be thought of as part of an individual's solution to these problems. For example, the rule of thumb to restrict monthly expenditures to no more than monthly income is clearly nonoptimal. Yet, when borrowing is permitted as a method of smoothing out monthly k's, some families find themselves heavily in debt. Restrictions on borrowing are then adopted as a second-best strategy. The technology of self-control often implies outright prohibitions because allowing a little bit eventually leads to excesses. (Although smoking cigarettes is undoubtedly subject to diminishing marginal utility, almost no one smokes between 1 and 5 cigarettes a day. That level, while probably preferred by many smokers and former smokers to either zero or 20, is just unattainable.)

Unusually high category specific k's are most likely to be observed for goods that are particularly seductive or addictive. Unusually low k's are observed for goods viewed to be particularly desirable in the long run such as exercise or education. Application of these ideas to gift giving behavior is discussed below.

4. Marketing Implications

The previous sections have outlined a theory and presented some survey evidence to support its various components. The following sections discuss the implications of this theory to marketing. There are two types of implications presented here. First, the theory is used to explain some empirical puzzles such as why some markets fail to clear. Second, some advice for sellers is derived, based on the presumption that buyers behave according to the theory. This advice is illustrated with actual examples. The implications are derived from each of the three main components of the theory: compounding principles, transaction utility, and budgetary rules.

4.1. *Compounding Rule Implications*

This section will illustrate how the results from the analysis of mental arithmetic can influence marketing decisions either in the design or products or in the choice of how products are described. The results of §2.2 can be summarized by two principles: segregate gains and integrate losses. Each principle also has a corollary: segregate "silver linings" (small gains combined with large losses) and integrate (or cancel) losses when combined with larger gains.

Segregate gains. The basic principle of segregating gains is simple and needs little elaboration or illustration. When a seller has a product with more than one dimension it is desirable to have each dimension evaluated separately. The most vivid examples of this are the late-night television advertisements for kitchen utensils. The principle is used at two levels. First, each of the items sold is said to have a multitude of uses, each of which is demonstrated. Second, several "bonus" items are included "if you call right now." These ads all seem to use the same basic format and are almost a caricature of the segregation principle.

The silver lining principle can be used to understand the widespread use of rebates as a form of price promotion. It is generally believed that rebates were first widely used because of the threat of government price controls. By having an explicitly temporary rebate it was hoped that the old price would be the one for which new regulations might apply. Rebates for small items have the additional feature that not all consumers send in the form to collect the rebate. However, rebates continue to be widely used in the automobile industry in spite of the following considerations:

(1) Price controls seem very unlikely during the Reagan administration, especially with inflation receding.

(2) All purchasers claim the rebate since it is processed by the dealer and is worth several hundred dollars.

(3) Consumers must pay sales tax on the rebate. This can raise the cost of the purchase by 8% of the rebate in New York City. While this is not a large amount of money relative to the price of the car, it nonetheless provides an incentive to adopt the seemingly equivalent procedure of announcing a temporary sale.

Why then are rebates used in the automobile industry? The silver lining principle suggest one reason. A rebate strongly suggests segregating the saving. This can be further strengthened for those consumers who elect to have the rebate mailed to them from the corporate headquarters rather than applied to the down payment.[10]

Integrate losses. When possible, consumers would prefer to integrate losses. The concavity of the loss function implies that adding $50 less to an existing $1000 loss will have little impact if it is integrated. This means that sellers have a distinct advantage in selling something if its cost can be added on to another larger purchase. Adding options to an automobile or house purchase are classic, well-known examples. More generally, whenever a seller is dealing with an expensive item the seller should consider whether additional options can be created since the buyers will have temporarily inelastic demands for these options. The principle also applies to insurance purchases. Insurance companies frequently sell riders to home or car insurance policies that are attractive (I believe) only because of this principle. One company has been advertising a "paint spill" rider for its homeowner policy. (This is apparently designed for do-it-yourselfers who have not yet discovered drop cloths.) Another example is credit card insurance which pays for the first $50 of charges against a credit card if it is lost or stolen. (Claims over $50 are absorbed by the credit card company.)

The principle of cancellation states that losses will be integrated with larger gains where plausible. The best example of this is withholding from paychecks. In the present framework the least aversive type of loss is the reduction of a large gain. This concept seems to have been widely applied by governments. Income taxes would be perceived as much more aversive (in addition to being harder to collect) if the whole tax bill were due in April. The implication for sellers is that every effort should be made to set up a payroll withdrawal payment option. Probably the best way to market dental insurance, for example, would be to sell it as an option to group health insurance through employers. If the employee already pays for some share of the health insurance then the extra premium would be framed as an increase in an existing deduction; this is the ultimate arrangement for a seller.

4.2. *Transaction Utility Implications*

Sellouts and scalping. The tool in the economist's bag in which most economists place the greatest trust is the supply and demand analysis of simple commodity markets. The theory stipulates that prices adjust over time until supply equals demand. While the confidence put in that analysis is generally well founded, there are some markets which consistently fail to clear. One widely discussed example is labor markets where large numbers of unemployed workers coexist with wages that are not falling. Unemployment occurs because a price (the wage) is too high. Another set of markets features the opposite problem, prices that are too low. I refer to the class of goods and services for which demand exceeds supply: Cabbage Patch dolls in December 1983 and 1984, tickets to any Super Bowl, World Series, World Cup Final, Vladimir Horowitz or Rolling Stones concert, or even dinner reservations for 8:00 p.m. Saturday evening at the most popular restaurant in any major city. Why are these prices too low? Once the Cabbage Patch rage started, the going black market price for a doll was over $100. Why did Coleco continue to sell

---

[10] In the first year that rebates were widely used, one manufacturer reported (to me in personal communication) that about one-third of the customers receiving rebates chose the option of having the check sent separately. My impression is that this has become less common as rebates have become widespread.

the dolls it had at list price? Why did some discount stores sell their allotted number at less than list price? Tickets for the 1984 Super Bowl were selling on the black market for $300 and up. Seats on the 50-yard line were worth considerably more. Why did the National Football League sell all of the tickets at the same $60 price?

There are no satisfactory answers to these questions within the confines of standard microeconomic theory. In the case of the Super Bowl, the league surely does not need the extra publicity generated by the ticket scarcity. (The argument that long lines create publicity is sometimes given for why prices aren't higher during first week's showing of the latest *Star Wars* epic.) The ticket scarcity occurs every year so (unlike the Cabbage Patch Doll case) there is no possible surprise factor. Rather, it is quite clear that the league *knowingly* sets the prices "too low". Why?

The concept of transaction utility provides a coherent, parsimonious answer. The key to understanding the puzzle is to note that the under-pricing only occurs when two conditions are present. First, the market clearing price is much higher than some well-established normal (reference) price. Second, there is an ongoing pecuniary relationship between the buyer and the seller. Pure scarcity is not enough. Rare art works, beachfront property, and 25-carat diamonds all sell at (very high) market clearing prices.

Once the notion of transaction (dis)utility is introduced, then the role of the normal or reference price becomes transparent. The goods and services listed earlier all have such norms: prices of other dolls similar to Cabbage Patch dolls, regular season ticket prices, prices of other concerts, dinner prices at other times or on other days, etc. These well-established reference prices create significant transaction disutility if a much higher price is charged.

The ongoing relationship between the buyer and the seller is necessary (unless the seller is altruistic), else the seller would not care if transaction disutility were generated. Again that ongoing relationship is present in all the cases described. Coleco couldn't charge more for the dolls because it had plans for future sales to doll customers and even nondoll buyers who would simply be offended by an unusually high price. Musical performers want to sell record albums. Restaurants want to sell dinners at other times and days. When a well-established reference price exists, a seller has to weigh the short-run gain associated with a higher price against the long-run loss of good will and thus sales.

The pricing of sporting events provides a simple test of this analysis. For major sporting events, the price of tickets should be closer to the market clearing price, the larger is the share of total revenues the seller captures from the event in question. At one extreme are league championships such as the World Series and the Super Bowl. Ticket sales for these events are a tiny share of total league revenue. An intermediate case is the Indianapolis 500. This is an annual event, and is the sponsor's major revenue source, but racegoers frequently come year after year so some ongoing relationship exists. At the other extreme is a major championship fight. A boxing championship is a one-time affair involving a promoter and two fighters. Those three parties are unlikely to be a partnership again. (Even a rematch is usually held in a different city.) There is no significant long-run relationship between the sellers and boxing fans.

While it is impossible to say what the actual market clearing prices would be, the figures in Table 2 indicate that the predictions are pretty well confirmed. Good seats for

TABLE 2

Recent Prices for Major Sporting Events

1983 World Series	$25–30
1984 Super Bowl	all seats $60
1984 Indianapolis 500	top price $75
1981 Holmes–Cooney fight	top price $600

the Super Bowl are probably the single item in greatest demand and are obviously underpriced since even the worst seats sell out at $60.

Of course, some Super Bowl tickets and Cabbage Patch dolls do change hands at high prices through scalpers. Since the black market price does rise to the market clearing level, why do the sellers permit the scalpers to appropriate these revenues? There are two reasons. First, the transaction disutility generated by a high black market price is not attributed to the original seller. The NFL sets a "fair" price; it is the scalper who is obtaining the immoral rents.[11] Second, in many cases the seller is really getting more than the face value of the tickets. Tickets to the Super Bowl are distributed to team owners in large numbers. Many of these tickets are resold to tour operators (see the next section) at prices which are not made public. Similarly, tickets to the NCAA basketball tournament finals are distributed in part to the qualifying teams. These tickets are sold or given to loyal alumni. The implicit price for such tickets is probably in the thousands of dollars.

Methods of raising price. A seller who has a monopoly over some popular product may find that the price being charged is substantially less than the market clearing price. How can price be raised without generating excessive negative transaction utility (and thus loss of good will)? The theory provides three kinds of strategies that can be tried. First, steps can be taken to increase the perceived reference price. This can be done in several ways. One way is to explicitly suggest a high reference price (see next section). Another way is to increase the perceived costs of the product, perhaps by providing excessive luxury. As the hockey question showed, perceptions of fairness are affected by costs. In the beer on the beach example, the owner of the run-down grocery store could install a fancy bar. Notice that the extra luxury need not increase the value of the product to the buyer; as long as p^* is increased then demand will increase holding acquisition utility constant. An illustration of this principle is that short best-selling books tend to have fewer words per page (i.e., larger type and wider margins) than longer books. This helps to raise p^*.

A second general strategy is to increase the minimum purchase required and/or to tie the sale of the product to something else. Because of the shape of the value function in the domain of losses, a given price movement seems smaller the larger is the quantity with which it is being integrated. The Super Bowl provides two illustrations of this phenomenon. Tickets are usually sold by tour operators who sell a package including air fare, hotel and game ticket. Thus the premium price for the ticket is attached to a considerably larger purchase. Also, hotels in the city of the Super Bowl (and in college towns on graduation weekend) usually impose a three-night minimum. Since the peak demand is for only one or two nights this allows the hotel to spread the premium room rate over a larger purchase.

The third strategy is to try to obscure p^* and thus make the transaction disutility less salient. One simple way to do this is to sell the product in an unusual size or format, one for which no well-established p^* exists. Both of the last two strategies are used by candy counters in movie theaters. Candy is typically sold only in large containers rarely seen in other circumstances.

Suggested retail price.[12] Many manufacturers offer a "suggested retail price" (SRP) for their products. In the absence of fair trade laws, SRP's must be only suggestions, but there are distinct differences across products in the relationship between market prices and SRPs. In some cases the SRP is usually equal to the market price. In other cases the

---

[11] Transferring the transaction disutility is often a good strategy. One way this can be done is to turn over an item for sale to an agent who will sell it at auction. The seller then bears less responsibility for the price.

[12] This paragraph was motivated by a discussion with Dan Horsky several years ago.

SRP exceeds the market price by as much as 100% or more. What is the role of an SRP that is twice the typical retail price? One possibility is that the SRP is being offered by the seller as a "suggested reference price." Then a lower selling price will provide positive transaction utility. In addition, inexperienced buyers may use the SRP as an index of quality. We would expect to observe a large differential between price and the SRP when both factors are present. The SRP will be more successful as a reference price the less often the good is purchased. The SRP is most likely to serve as a proxy for quality when the consumer has trouble determining quality in other ways (such as by inspection). Thus, deep discounting relative to SRP should usually be observed for infrequently purchased goods whose quality is hard to judge. Some examples include phonograph cartridges which usually sell at discounts of at least 50%, home furniture which is almost always "on sale", and silver flatware where "deep discounting—selling merchandise to consumers at 40% to 85% below the manufacturer's 'suggested retail price' has become widespread in the industry".[13]

4.3. *Budgeting Implications: A Theory of Gift Giving*

The analysis of budgeting rules suggests that category and time specific shadow prices can vary. This implies that individuals fail to undertake some internal arbitrage operations that in principle could increase utility. In contrast, the standard theory implies that all goods that are consumed in positive quantities have the same marginal utility per dollar, and in the absence of capital market constraints, variations over time are limited by real interest rates. Observed patterns of gift giving lend support to the current theory. Suppose an individual G wants to give some recipient R a gift. Assume that G would like to choose that gift which would yield the highest level of utility to R for a given expenditure. (Other nonaltruistic motives are possible, but it seems reasonable to start with this case.) Then the standard theory implies that G should choose something that is already being consumed in positive quantities by R.

How does this compare with common practice? Casual observation and some informal survey evidence suggest that many people try to do just the opposite, namely buy something R would not buy for himself. Flowers and boxed candy are items that are primarily purchased as gifts. "Gift shops" are filled with items that are purchased almost exclusively as gifts. Did anyone buy a pet rock for himself?

Once the restriction that all shadow prices be equal is relaxed, the apparent anomaly is easily understood. Categories that are viewed as luxuries will tend to have high k's. An individual would like to have a small portion of the forbidden fruit, but self-control problems prevent that. The gift of a small portion solves the problem neatly.

A simple test of the model can be conducted by the reader via the following thought experiment. Suppose you have collected $100 for a group gift to a departing employee. It is decided to give the employee some wine since that is something the employee enjoys. Suppose the employee typically spends $5 per bottle on wine. How expensive should the gift wine be? The standard theory says you should buy the same type of wine currently being purchased. The current theory says you should buy fewer bottles of more expensive wine, the kind of wine the employee wouldn't usually treat himself to.

One implication of this analysis is that goods which are priced at the high end of the market should be marketed in part as potential gifts. This suggests aiming the advertising at the giver rather than the receiver. "Promise her anything but give her Arpege."

The gift-giving anomaly refers to those goods in categories with high k's. Individuals may also have categories with low k's. Suppose I like to drink expensive imported beer but feel it is too costly to buy on a regular basis. I might then adopt the rule of drinking

[13] See *Business Week*, March 29, 1982. This example was suggested by Leigh McAlister.

the expensive beer only on specific occasions, such as at restaurants or while on vacation.[14] Advertisers may wish to suggest other occasions that should qualify as legitimate excuses for indulgence. One example is Michelob's theme: "Weekends are made for Michelob." However, their follow-up campaign may have taken a good idea too far: "Put a little weekend in your week." Lowenbrau's ads stress a different category, namely, what beer to serve to company. "Here's too good friends, tonight is something special. . . ." While impressing your friends is also involved here, again the theme is to designate specific occasions when the beer k should be relaxed enough to purchase a high cost beer.

Another result of this analysis is that people may sometimes prefer to receive a gift in kind over a gift in cash, again violating a simple principle of microeconomic theory. This can happen if the gift is on a "forbidden list". One implication is that employers might want to use gifts as part of their incentive packages. Some organizations (e.g., Tupperware) rely on this type of compensation very heavily. Dealers are paid both in cash and with a multitude of gift-type items: trips, furniture, appliances, kitchen utensils, etc. Since most Tupperware dealers are women who are second-income earners, the gifts may be a way for a dealer to:

(1) mentally segregate her earnings from total family income;
(2) direct the extra income toward luxuries; and
(3) increase her control over the spending of the extra income.[15]

Another similar example comes from the National Football League. For years the league had trouble getting players to come to the year-end All-Star game. Many players would beg off, reporting injuries. A few years ago the game was switched to Hawaii and a free trip for the player's wife or girlfriend was included. Since then, no-shows have been rare.

Conclusion. This paper has developed new concepts in three distinct areas: coding gains and losses, evaluating purchases (transaction utility), and budgetary rules. In this section I will review the evidence presented for each, describe some research in progress, and suggest where additional evidence might be found.

The evidence on the coding of gains and losses comes from two kinds of sources. The "who is happier" questions presented here are a rather direct test, though of a somewhat soft variety. More research along these lines is under way using slightly different questions such as "two events are going to happen to you, would you rather they occurred on the same day or two weeks apart?" The two paradigms do not always lead to the same results, particularly in the domain of losses (Johnson and Thaler 1985). The reasons for the differences are interesting and subtle, and need further investigation. The other source for data on these issues comes from the investigation of choices under uncertainty. Kahneman and Tversky originally formulated their value function based on such choices. In Johnson and Thaler (1985) we investigate how choices under uncertainty are influenced by very recent previous gains or losses. We find that previous gains and losses do influence subsequent choices in ways that complicate any interpretation of the loss function. Some of our data comes from experiments with real money and so are in some sense "harder" than the who is happier data. Kahneman and Tversky are also investigating the multi-attribute extension of prospect theory, and their results suggest caution in extending the single attribute results.

The evidence presented on transaction utility was the beer on the beach and hockey ticket questionnaires, and the data on sports pricing. The role of fairness is obviously quite important in determining reference prices. A large-scale telephone survey undertaken

[14] One bit of evidence that people on vacation adopt temporarily low k's is that all resorts seem to have an abundance of gift and candy shops. Some of their business, of course, is for gifts to bring home, but while on vacation, people also seem to buy for themselves at these shops.

[15] Tax evasion may be another incentive if recipients (illegally) fail to declare these gifts as income.

by Daniel Kahneman, Jack Knetch and myself is under way and we hope it will provide additional evidence on two important issues in this area. First, what are the determinants of people's perceptions of fairness? Second, how are market prices influenced by these perceptions? Evidence on the former comes directly from the survery research, while evidence on the latter must come from aggregate economic data. The latter evidence is much more difficult to obtain.

Both the theory and the evidence on the budgetary processes are less well developed than the other topics presented here. The evidence comes from a small sample of households that will not support statistical tests. A more systematic study of household decision making, perhaps utilizing UPC scanner data, should be a high priority.

More generally, the theory presented here represents a hybrid of economics and psychology that has heretofore seen little attention. I feel that marketing is the most logical field for this combination to be developed. Aside from those topics just mentioned there are other extensions that seem promising. On the theory side, adding uncertainty and multiple attributes are obviously worth pursuing. Regarding empirical tests, I would personally like to see some field experiments which attempt to implement the ideas suggested here in an actual marketing environment.[17]

Acknowledgement. An earlier version of a portion of this paper was presented at the Association for Consumer Research conference in San Francisco, October 1982, and is published in the proceedings of that meeting. The author wishes to thank Hersh Shefrin, Daniel Kahneman and Amos Tversky for many useful discussions. Financial support from the Alfred P. Sloan Foundation is gratefully acknowledged.

[17] This paper was received June 1983 and has been with the author for 2 revisions.

References

Arkes, Hal R. and Catherine Blumer (1985), "The Psychology of Sunk Cost," *Organizational Behavior and Human Decision Processes*, 35, 1, 124–140.

Becker, Gary S. (1965), "A Theory of the Allocation of Time," *Economic Journal*, 75 (September).

Gregory, Robin (1982), "Valuing Non-Market Goods: An Analysis of Alternative Approaches," unpublished dissertation, University of British Columbia.

Johnson, Eric and Richard Thaler (1985), "Hedonic Framing and the Break-Even Effect," Cornell University, Working Paper.

Kahneman, Daniel and Amos Tversky (1979), "Prospect Theory: An Analysis of Decision Under Risk," *Econometrica*, 47 (March), 263–291.

Knetch, Jack L. and J. A. Sinden (1984), "Willingness to Pay and Compensation Demanded: Experimental Evidence of an Unexpected Disparity in Measures of Value," *Quarterly Journal of Economics*, 99.

Lancaster, Kelvin J. (1971), *Consumer Demand, A New Approach*, New York: Columbia University Press.

Thaler, Richard (1980), "Toward a Positive Theory of Consumer Choice," *Journal of Economic Behavior and Organization*, 1 (March), 39–60.

——— and H. M. Shefrin (1981), "An Economic Theory of Self-Control," *Journal of Political Economy*, 39 (April), 392–406.

Tversky, Amos and Daniel Kahneman (1981), "The Framing of Decisions and the Rationality of Choice," *Science*, 211 453–458.

Tweeter etc.

On August 16, 1996, Sandy Bloomberg, founder and CEO of Tweeter etc., reflected on the recent history of his small, upscale New England retailer of consumer electronics. Tweeter had grown from a 13-store chain with $35 million in annual sales in 1991 to a 21-store chain with $82 million in annual sales in 1996. Bloomberg had always attributed part of this growth to Tweeter's "Automatic Price Protection" policy, which had been implemented in 1993. Under Automatic Price Protection (APP), Tweeter monitored local newspaper ads and automatically mailed a refund check to a consumer if an item purchased at Tweeter during the past 30 days was advertised for a lower price by a competitor.

Two recent developments in the marketplace gave Bloomberg reason to reflect on APP, however. First, on May 16, 1996, Tweeter ventured outside its traditional New England base and purchased a controlling interest in Bryn Mawr Stereo, another small, high-end consumer electronics chain based in suburban Philadelphia. One year earlier, Bryn Mawr had adopted Tweeter's "Automatic Price Protection" policy, but up to the time of Tweeter's purchase, had failed to see any significant impact on sales. Second, on June 16, 1996, Nobody Beats the Wiz ("The Wiz") opened a 50,000 square foot electronics retail outlet in suburban Boston, the second of ten outlets planned for the New England market and the first in Greater Boston. The Wiz, a nationally recognized New Jersey-based discount retailer, threatened to change the playing field in the already highly competitive New England audio and video consumer electronics market.

Three years earlier, Tweeter's introduction of APP had received national press coverage in *The Wall Street Journal* (see **Exhibit 1**). Now, Bryn Mawr's seeming lack of success with the policy gave Bloomberg cause to question the impact of APP. Moreover, whatever its past impact, Bloomberg wondered how effective the policy would be in a market increasingly dominated by large discount retailers such as The Wiz.

The Consumer Electronics Industry

The United States Market

In 1995, consumer electronics was a $30 billion industry in the United States, as measured by manufacturer sales (see **Exhibit 2**). The previous ten years had seen the market grow at a 5.6% compound annual rate, with future growth projected to be strong through 1998. While industry data on retail sales was unavailable, it was widely believed that retail margins averaged about 30% across product categories.

Professors John Gourville and George Wu prepared this case with research assistance from James Evans as the basis for class discussion rather than to illustrate either effective or ineffective handling of an administrative situation. Some nonpublic data have been disguised.

At the retail level, consumer electronics were distributed through a variety of channels, including specialty electronics stores (e.g., Tweeter), electronics/appliance superstores (e.g., Circuit City), mass merchants (e.g., Wal-Mart), warehouse clubs (e.g., Sam's Club), department stores (e.g., Macy's) and mail order houses (e.g., Sound City). **Exhibit 3** provides an overview of these channels. **Exhibit 4** shows the distribution of sales across channels for select categories of consumer electronics.

The New England Market

With a population of 13.2 million, New England represented 5% of the U.S. consumer electronics market. In 1996, there were 8 retailers in this region with market shares in excess of 2% (see **Exhibit 5**). By far the two largest were Lechmere (35% share) and Circuit City (19%).

For decades, Lechmere had been the region's most popular retailer of consumer electronics and home appliances, growing to 28 stores (averaging 50,000 square feet) throughout New England and northern New York by 1995. Selling televisions and stereos since the 1960s, Lechmere had become, for many New Englanders, the only place to consider when buying video and audio equipment. Historically, such attitudes had been reinforced with well-informed salespeople, good customer service and fair pricing on a wide variety of entry and middle-level products. In 1994, Lechmere was purchased for $200 million by Montgomery Ward, a privately-owned, national mass merchant with approximately $6 billion in annual sales. While Lechmere stores continued to operate under the Lechmere name, many consumers believed that the level of customer service and salesperson knowledge had decreased appreciably under Montgomery Ward's control.

In contrast to the regional legacy of Lechmere, Circuit City, the nation's largest consumer electronics retailer, only arrived to the New England market in early 1993. However, their New England presence quickly grew to 15 full-sized stores (approximately 30,000 square feet) and 6 smaller "Circuit City Express" stores (approximately 3,000 square feet). With a reputation for knowledgeable salespeople and good service, Circuit City topped $5.5 billion in sales across more than 350 stores nationwide in 1995. Although Circuit City's offerings included personal computers, medium to large home appliances, audio tapes and compact discs, approximately 60% of their total sales were derived from the sale of video and audio equipment.

At the other end of the spectrum was Cambridge Soundworks, with less than a 1% share of the New England market. Founded in 1988, Cambridge Soundworks specialized in the design, manufacture and sale of their exclusive line of medium to high-end stereo and home theater speakers. Accounting for 69% of their total revenues in 1995, these speakers regularly received positive reviews in the audio and consumer electronic magazines and were often rated as a good value for their $200 to $600 per set price tags. The bulk of Cambridge Soundworks' remaining sales consisted of popular brand-name audio electronics, such as receivers by Harman Kardon and CD players by Sony, which complemented the sale of their private label speakers. While still only a niche player in the region, Cambridge Soundworks had grown appreciably in recent years, with revenues increasing from $14.3 million in 1993 to $26.9 million in 1995. Having traditionally relied on catalog sales (67% of total sales in 1993), much of this growth was due to the opening of a series of small retail outlets in 1994 and 1995. By the end of 1995, Cambridge Soundworks had 23 retail locations throughout New England (15 stores) and Northern California (8 stores), and revenues were divided between catalog (32%), wholesale (13%) and retail sales (55%).

Tweeter etc. Company History

The Formative Years: 1972 to the Mid-1980s

The competitive environment was quite different when Tweeter first arrived upon the consumer electronics scene in 1972. In the early-1970s, 21-year old Sandy Bloomberg had been working at Audio Lab, a hi-fi repair shop and components dealer located in Harvard Square in Cambridge, Massachusetts. While at Audio Lab, Bloomberg became entranced by high quality audio components.[1] At that time, the high-end stereo market was only just developing in the United States, with few consumers beyond the hobbyists and avid audiophiles even aware of the increasingly high quality of stereo components available to the general public. In 1972, Bloomberg traveled to Europe where he witnessed and was encouraged by a more mainstream acceptance of high-end stereo components. Shortly afterward, Bloomberg opened his first Tweeter etc. in the storefront of his cousin's industrial music business located near Boston University.

Within a few years of Tweeter's founding, the U.S. stereo components market tripled and the Boston market became littered with a number of small independent retailers, of which Tweeter was only one. At the time, there were two major stereo retailers in the Boston—Tech Hi-fi, started in 1963 by two MIT dropouts, and Lechmere. Tweeter avoided direct confrontation with either retailer by initially focusing on the student market, serving their more sophisticated tastes for higher quality stereo components. Bloomberg's business philosophy was built on a commitment to value, quality, and service.

By 1979, Tweeter had expanded to six stores in the Boston area and one in Rhode Island (see **Exhibit 6** for a chronology of Tweeter's expansion). These stores averaged 6,000 square feet in space, although some, such as the Harvard Square store at 2,000 square feet, were significantly smaller. At about this time, Tweeter expanded its product line to take on high-end video equipment, principally in the form of color televisions.

Much as Bloomberg had anticipated, the general population's knowledge of and demand for high-end stereo and video equipment continued to grow through the mid-1980s. This growth was aided by strong regional and national economies and by the introduction of new technologies (e.g., Video Cassette Recorders [VCRs], Compact Disc [CD] Players). These conditions helped to solidify Tweeter's positioning at the high-end of the audio and video market.

By the end of 1986, Tweeter had grown to 13 stores throughout eastern Massachusetts and Rhode Island and by the late-1980s, Tweeter's share of the New England consumer electronics market had grown to almost 2% overall, and close to 5% in the Boston area.

During this period, Tweeter continued to be recognized as a retailer of high quality, high-end audio components and video equipment, with knowledgeable salespeople who offered high levels of customer service. Two of their advertising slogans during this period were, "We don't carry all the brands, only the ones that count" and "Some hi-fi salesman can sell you anything, and often do." Tweeter customers generally perceived that they were paying a premium price for the products they purchased, but were receiving the best customer service in the region for that premium.

---

[1] Stereo components are separate audio devices that can be combined to form a single a stereo system. For example, a component system might consist of a receiver, a CD player, a cassette deck, and one or two pairs of speakers, all separately purchased to obtain the best of what each manufacturer has to offer. Typically, component systems are more flexible (components can be added or upgraded with ease) and capable of higher quality sound than "rack systems" or "compact systems," which offer prepackaged componentry.

The Shake-Out Years: Mid-1980s to 1993

The euphoria of the mid-1980s was short lived, however, as three factors contributed to an overall decline in the New England electronics market in the late-1980s and early-1990s.

First, the market growth of the mid-1980s led to new competitive entrants, especially at the lower end of the retail market. In 1985, for instance, two Michigan-based chains, Fretter Superstores and Highland Superstores, both warehouse-like electronics chains, opened four stores each in the Boston area. Second, by the late-1980s, household penetration for color televisions, VCRs and many other home electronics had grown appreciably, thereby limiting future growth in those product categories. Third, the once growing U.S. economy came to a screeching halt in 1987 and 1988, with New England among those geographic regions hardest hit.

These factors combined to have two major consequences. First, not all retailers survived. The first to falter was Tech Hi-fi, which found itself financially overextended just as competition was heating up. In 1985, it declared bankruptcy and closed its 11 Massachusetts stores. The demise of Tech Hi-fi was followed six years later by Highland Superstores (10 New England stores) and in 1995 by Fretter (15 stores), both of whom also suffered from being financially overextended.

The second major result of the increasingly competitive environment of the late-1980s was increased price promotion. Traditionally, the New England electronics market had been characterized by four major "Sale" periods during which retailers discounted certain products to draw consumers into their stores—a Presidents' Day Sale in mid-February, a Father's Day Sale in June, a "Back to School" Sale in early-September, and a "Wrap it up Early" or "Pre-Holiday" Sale in mid-November. For the remainder of the year, product prices remained relatively steady, with only limited advertised price discounting.

Beginning in 1988, however, as the Boston economy bottomed out and consumer electronics sales growth flattened, Lechmere initiated an ongoing series of weekend "Sale" campaigns in which they would cut prices on select items on Friday, Saturday and Sunday. In order to retain their market shares, Tweeter and most other major retailers followed suit. As a result, the weekend "Sale" became a commonplace event, and consumers began to expect price discounts when purchasing audio and video equipment. In some cases, sales people would even tell customers not to buy on Wednesday, but rather to wait until Saturday when the desired item would be 20% off. During this period, it was not uncommon for 60% to 80% of a retailer's sales to occur on Saturday and Sunday.

As consumers increasingly focused on price in their purchasing process, Tweeter's profitability suffered. Noah Herschman, Tweeter's vice president of Marketing, described the problem in the following fashion:

> The consumers just wanted price, price, price. But, we didn't carry entry-level products, like a $139 VCR or a $399 camcorder. We carried the middle and high-end stuff. So people would look at our ads and they would look at Lechmere's ads. Lechmere would advertise a $139 VCR, and we would advertise a $199 VCR. They'd have a $399 camcorder, and we'd have a $599 camcorder. Even though their middle and high-end equipment sold for the same price as ours, we seemed to be more expensive to the inexperienced consumer. Our print advertising was actually driving people away—doing more damage to our business than if we never ran it.

In response to the profitability downturn, Tweeter attempted to compete on price as well as product quality and customer service. For instance, Tweeter began to carry Sherwood audio components, an entry-level brand comparable in price to the low-end offerings of Lechmere, Fretter and others. In addition, Tweeter began to stock the lower-end models of brands it had been carrying only at the middle and high-end, such as Sony. Nevertheless, the majority of Tweeter's product line was still in the middle to high-end and included brands such as Denon, Alpine, Kenwood, Klipsch and Boston Acoustics.

To further aid in this price-based competition, Tweeter joined the Progressive Retailers Organization in 1988, a buying consortium founded in 1986 that consisted of small high-end consumer electronics retailers throughout the United States which combined for over $1 billion in annual sales. As a result, Tweeter was able to obtain prices from manufacturers that were comparable with those obtained by its larger competitors.

Despite these efforts, the public perception of Tweeter remained unchanged. Customers continued to view Tweeter as more specialized and more expensive than Lechmere and the other New England retailers. While most consumers still recognized the high level of service Tweeter provided, many believed that such service came at the expense of higher prices, something they were increasingly less willing to accept. As a result, Tweeter's sales and profitability began to deteriorate starting in the early-1990s (see **Exhibit 7**). Tweeter's plight was exacerbated by Circuit City's entrance into the New England market in the spring of 1993. Circuit City's media-blitz advertising and fierce price competition further focused consumers attention on price as the primary determinant of product choice.

A Change in Strategy: August 16, 1993

Frustrated by Tweeter's financial performance, Sandy Bloomberg, Jeff Stone (Tweeter's recently hired president and COO), Noah Herschman and the rest of the Tweeter management hashed out possible competitive responses at a management retreat in the spring of 1993.

In preparation for this retreat, Tweeter had conducted a number of focus groups in the months leading up to the retreat. Herschman boiled down the results of these focus groups into the two sets of insights.

First, individuals shopping for consumer electronics in the New England area displayed the following general characteristics and behavior:

- On average, consumers actively thought about purchasing a new product one to two months before actually making the purchase.

- On average, consumers visited two to three retailers prior to purchasing a desired product. The factors most cited by consumers in their selection of stores to visit include newspaper advertisements (cited by 70% of consumers), past experience with the store (50%) and recommendations of friends and family (40%).

- Eight out of ten consumers checked newspaper advertisements for product availability and price information when in the market for consumer electronic equipment. Virtually all of these consumers delayed purchase until they saw the desired product or class of product advertised in a newspaper circular.

Second, individuals who were familiar with or considered purchasing at Tweeter displayed the following specific characteristics and behavior:

- Four out of five consumers viewed Tweeter as being more expensive than the major competitors in the market (i.e., Lechmere, Fretter). However, most of these consumers reported that if price were not an issue, they would prefer to purchase their desired product from Tweeter.

- Of all consumers who visited Tweeter in search of a product, 60% also visited Lechmere, 45% also visited Fretter and 20% also visited Sears in the course of their product search.

- One in three consumers specifically came to Tweeter to figure out what to buy and then went to Lechmere or Fretter, believing they could get a better price there.

These focus groups also allowed Tweeter to characterize four types of electronics consumers in the New England market: the "entry-level customer", the "price biter", the "convenience customer", and the "quality/service customer":

Entry-Level Customers   The *entry level customer* was interested in buying the cheapest item in a given category and was relatively indifferent to product quality and customer service.

The Price Biter   The *price biter* was very cognizant of price, but was also concerned with product quality and customer service. Price biters were more focused on getting the "absolute best deal" than on getting the "absolute lowest price" in a particular category.

The Convenience Customer   For the *convenience customer*, price, service and product quality were of secondary importance to shopping convenience. A convenience customer tended to shop in a store such as Lechmere or Sears because it was familiar and/or because they could purchase products in many different categories (e.g., luggage, jewelry, camera equipment, housewares, etc.) on the same shopping trip.

The Quality/Service Customer   For the *quality/service customer*, high levels of product quality and customer service were of primary concern and price, while still important, was of secondary concern. Some retailers referred to these consumers as "BBCOs"—"Buy the Best and Cry Once".

Herschman estimated that while this final group represented only 10% of the total New England customer base, it accounted for 70% of Tweeter's clientele. **Exhibit 8** provides Herschman's estimates for the distribution of customers for Tweeter as well as for the other major competitors in the New England market.

Armed with these insights, Bloomberg and his team used the spring management retreat to completely revamp the marketing strategy for Tweeter etc. This new strategy was announced to the public on August 16, 1993 and was referred to by Herschman as a "three-pronged attack" to restore price credibility at Tweeter.

Abandonment of the "Sale"

First, in a radical departure from the practices of its competitors and from their own historic behavior, Tweeter eliminated the use of the "Sale" to build store traffic and promote consumer spending. Herschman explained:

> We were getting killed by the big players—Lechmere, Circuit City and Fretter. Every weekend, everyone was having a sale, but on different makes and models of product. This made it almost impossible to compare prices across retailers. This worked in favor of the big stores, who were already perceived as low priced, but it was killing us. Even though we were competitively priced, because of our high-price image, no one was listening. And even more frustrating was the fact that our

increasing reliance on the weekend "Sale" drew attention away from our unique selling proposition—high quality products and great customer service.

Thus, as part of Tweeter's new strategy, Sandy Bloomberg and Jeff Stone decided to do away with the weekend "Sale" and move to an "Every Day Fair Pricing" strategy. They vowed to set Tweeter's prices competitively and to look to policies other than the "Sale" to communicate its price competitiveness to potential customers.

Automatic Price Protection

As the primary means to communicate their price competitiveness, Tweeter instituted "Automatic Price Protection" as the second prong of their "three-pronged" strategy. "Price Protection" or "Price Guarantees" were an oft-used retailing tactic intended to assure customers that they were receiving the best price available on any given product. In its typical form, if a consumer purchased a product at one store and later found it for a lower price at another store, the consumer could return to the first store with proof of that lower price and get reimbursed for the difference. Typically, these price protection policies were in effect for 30 days from the time of purchase and promised to refund 100% of the price difference, although some retailers promise refunds of 110%, 150% or even 200% of the price difference.

Over the years, this form of price protection had led to some interesting battles amongst retailers. In New York City, for instance, the consumer electronics retailer Crazy Eddie advertised "We will not be undersold. Our prices are the lowest—guaranteed. Our prices are insane." At the same time, its primary competitor, Newmark and Lewis, advertised a "Lifetime low-price guarantee" which promised to rebate 200% of the price difference if a consumer found a lower price at any time during the life of the product. Both stores declared bankruptcy in the 1980s.

As of 1993, most of the major consumer electronics retailers in New England practiced some form of price protection. For instance, Lechmere, Circuit City and Fretter all offered a 110% refund for a period of 30 days. In contrast, Tweeter offered a 100% refund for 30 days. Jeff Stone, president of Tweeter, estimated that Tweeter refunded $3,000 to $4,000 per month to its customers under this price protection strategy. One industry expert estimated that across all price protection programs, only about 5% of consumers entitled to a rebate actually followed through and redeemed that rebate.[2] Often cited reasons for this low rebate redemption included the effort needed to physically track newspaper ads and to travel back to the retailer to obtain the refund.

On August 16, 1993, Tweeter took price protection one step further. Under Automatic Price Protection, Tweeter took it upon itself to track the local newspapers and send out rebates. If a consumer purchased an item at Tweeter and it was advertised for less in a major local newspaper within 30 days, Tweeter automatically mailed that consumer a check for the difference. Tweeter's APP covered individual items priced at $50 or more and applied to price differences of $2 and greater (see **Exhibit 9** for Tweeter's advertised explanation of their policy). In addition to APP, Tweeter retained and extended their former price protection policy to 60 days and renamed it "Regular Price Protection."

Operationally, APP was administered by a specialized department at Tweeter's corporate headquarters in Canton, Massachusetts. A staff member would physically check every issue of eight major newspapers in the New England area for price advertisements from Tweeter's competitors. These papers included *The Boston Globe, The Boston Herald, The Cape Cod Times, The Danbury News Times, The Hartford Courant, The New Haven Register, The New London Day* and *The Providence Journal*. If any product carried by Tweeter was advertised by a competitor, the price and model number of that product and the date of the advertisement were entered into the Tweeter database. This

---

[2] *The Wall Street Journal*, August 17, 1993, p. B6.

information was then cross matched against Tweeter sales data to check for purchases of that product at a higher price within the past thirty days. If any such purchase was found, the computer generated a check for the difference and automatically mailed it to the purchaser within five days.

A Change in the Marketing Mix

The third prong of Tweeter's "three-pronged" strategy to restore price credibility was a shift in their marketing mix away from print advertising and toward television and radio advertising as well as direct mail and product catalogs.

Over the years, Tweeter's marketing budget had typically run at about 8% of gross sales. Under their old "Sale" based promotional strategy, the vast majority of this marketing budget was dedicated to newspaper advertising in the form of weekly "Sale" announcements. In FY 1993, for example, 80% of their $3.1 million marketing budget was spent on newspaper advertising, with the remaining 20% split between radio advertising, direct mail, market research and in-store promotions.

With the elimination of their Sale-based strategy, the Tweeter marketing mix changed significantly (see **Exhibit 10**). Most noticeably, the choice of media and message shifted from newspaper advertising which focused on "Sale" prices to radio and television advertising which focused on Tweeter's price competitiveness and Automatic Price Protection policy.

In conjunction, Tweeter instituted a direct marketing campaign which revolved around a 50- to 100-page seasonal "Buyer's Guide", which provided product descriptions and prices for all of Tweeter's major products. Produced four times per year, by 1996 this guide was mailed to approximately 325,000 individuals. Herschman estimated that of these 325,000 recipients, 270,000 had made a purchase at Tweeter within the past 18 months. It was believed that 90% of those who purchased some item at Tweeter ended up on this catalog mailing list for at least a period of two years. Buyer's Guides were also made available to consumers at each of Tweeter's retail locations as well as at various musical events sponsored by Tweeter, such as the summer outdoor concert series at Great Woods in Mansfield, Massachusetts.

August 1996

By most accounts, Tweeter's shift in strategy had a positive effect on financial performance. Sales almost doubled in the three years since the institution of the new strategy, from $43.7 million in FY 1993 to a projected $82.3 million in FY 1996. A breakdown of 1996 sales across major product categories, by percentage, is shown in **Exhibit 11.** Part of this recent growth could be attributed to an increase in sales per store, with same-store sales increasing by 50% between 1993 and 1996, and part could be attributed to an increase in the number of stores from 14 to 21 over the same period.

The Impact of Automatic Price Protection

Immediately after the announcement of Tweeter's new strategy, the media response to APP was extremely positive, with articles in *The Wall Street Journal*, *The Boston Globe* and *The Boston Herald* all extolling the virtues of the Tweeter's unique price guarantee. There were a few skeptics, however:

> . . . most suppliers sell retailers products that are not available elsewhere in the market. Thus, there is little chance that many items will qualify for the refunds.[3]

---

[3] *The Boston Globe*, August 17, 1993, p. 35

... the impact will be more one of perception than of massive price refunds, in part because Tweeter's moderate to high-end products don't overlap with many other retailers.[4]

Other observers disagreed. Edgar Dworsky, the Massachusetts assistant attorney general for consumer protection commented:

> It's a brilliant idea. The problem with price protection guarantees has been that it's the consumer's burden to find a lower price somewhere else. Tweeter's going to do the watching for you. I just hope they don't lose their shirts.[5]

By the end of 1995, Tweeter had mailed a total of 29,526 APP checks totaling over $780,000 (see **Exhibit 12**). It was not clear to Sandy Bloomberg what to make of this number, however. For instance, if Tweeter's prices were competitive, why were they sending out any checks?

An added concern for Bloomberg and his management team was whether Tweeter's message of price competitiveness was reaching potential customers. While routine price comparisons suggested that Tweeter was competitive on price relative to its major competitors (**Exhibit 13**), some recent surveys indicated that many customers still perceived Tweeter as being more expensive (see **Exhibit 14**). In addition, few consumers seemed to understand the essence of APP and most were unaware of that it was Tweeter who offered it (see **Exhibit 14**). In looking at this data, Herschman noted the difference in customer attitudes between those who were aware of Tweeter's APP policy and those who were not.

The Purchase of Bryn Mawr Stereo and Video

APP was only one of the things on the mind of Tweeter management in spring and summer of 1996. On May 16, after several years of friendly discussions, Tweeter finalized the purchase of Bryn Mawr Stereo and Video, a privately-owned consumer electronics chain headquartered outside of Philadelphia, in King of Prussia, Pennsylvania. Using a similar high-end, high-service strategy as Tweeter, Bryn Mawr had grown to approximately $35 million in annual sales over 13 stores located in eastern Pennsylvania, New Jersey, Delaware and Maryland. Tweeter planned to retain the Bryn Mawr name to capitalize on its brand recognition, while merging management across the two chains.

Not surprisingly, Bryn Mawr faced many of the same competitive challenges as Tweeter. Long known for its high-end merchandise and superior service quality, many consumers held the perception that Bryn Mawr was not price competitive with the large electronic superstores operating in the Mid-Atlantic region, such as Circuit City, Best Buy and Nobody Beats the Wiz. To fight this perception, at Bloomberg's urging, Bryn Mawr adopted Tweeter's Automatic Price Protection in September of 1995. Unlike Tweeter, however, Bryn Mawr failed to see any appreciable increase in sales through the time of their purchase by Tweeter. While some at Tweeter attributed this shortcoming to Bryn Mawr's less aggressive campaign to advertise APP and its features, it gave others cause to question the role of APP in building sales.

Nobody Beats the Wiz

Another issue that concerned Tweeter management in the summer of 1996 was the recent entry of Nobody Beats the Wiz into the local market. On June 16th, The Wiz opened a sleek new 50,000 square foot retail outlet in Saugus, Massachusetts, their first store in the Greater Boston area and their second in Massachusetts. In total, The Wiz had plans to open ten stores in the New

---

[4] *The Boston Herald*, August 17, 1993, p. 1
[5] *The Wall Street Journal*, August 17, 1993, p. B6

England market over the next several years. Lon Rebackin, vice president of real estate for The Wiz, noted:

> This is a priority market for us. In the short term and the long term, we will be a player in New England.[6]

A privately held company with over $900 million in sales in 1994, the Wiz was the third largest consumer electronics retailer chain in the United States, offering a wide selection of audio and video electronics, as well as personal computer hardware and software. The Wiz operated a total of over 50 stores in New York, New Jersey, Connecticut, Pennsylvania and most recently, Massachusetts.

The Wiz was known for its monstrous marketing campaigns touting rock bottom prices, a strategy they had used with great effectiveness in the New York metropolitan market. These campaigns often included noted sports stars as football's Joe Namath and basketball's Julius Irving. In addition, The Wiz was generally recognized as offering intensive customer service. They also offered 110% price protection for 30 days on all items except camcorders and cellular telephones.

Publicly, the competitive reaction to the entry of The Wiz was understated. Harlan Platt, a professor of finance at Northeastern University commented:

> They're marvelous at creating the perception that they're giving customers the best deal of all. But the New England consumer is more worldly and wise. I wouldn't be surprised to see The Wiz withdraw and seek greener pastures.[7]

In commenting for Tweeter, Noah Herschman claimed:

> It's a great time to be in Boston when The Wiz comes in. They only generate interest in the product category. But the people we sell to are enthusiastic about what we have. Our niche is more the personal touch.[8]

Privately, however, Tweeter's management was concerned that the entry of The Wiz could lead to a new round of price wars, much like those of the late 1980s and early 1990s. Bloomberg could not help but wonder whether APP would continue to be an effective policy under those circumstances.

The Future

Having reviewed the events of the recent past, Sandy Bloomberg found himself back where he had started. He had always believed that Automatic Price Protection had played a major role in Tweeter's growth, but now Bryn Mawr gave him reason to question that belief. Even if he could attribute Tweeter's recent success to APP, however, the entry of The Wiz had the potential to reshape the competitive playing field in the increasingly crowded New England market. Sandy wondered what role Automatic Price Protection would play in Tweeter's future competitive positioning.

---

[6] *The Boston Globe*, June 7, 1996, p. 38
[7] *The Boston Globe*, March 1, 1996, p. 65
[8] Ibid.

Exhibit 1   *The Wall Street Journal* Article, August 17, 1993

Tweeter's Customers Told: 'Your Check Is in the Mail'

* * *

New England Retailer Says Its Computers Shop the Ads Of Rivals to Ensure Refunds

---

By WILLIAM M. BULKELEY
Staff Reporter of THE WALL STREET JOURNAL

Tweeter etc., a New England stereo and television retailer, is going a step beyond its rivals by promising to automatically mail customers a refund check anytime a competitor advertises a lower price.

Most companies in the competitive electronics field will give refunds to customers who buy a product, then see it advertised for less and bring in the ad within 30 days. Tweeter says it will save customers the trouble of monitoring ads and returning to the store.

"In electronics, everyone has a low-price guarantee. But then, it's try and catch them," said Jeffrey Stone, president of Tweeter. "This time, the check really is in the mail."

Nothing Under $50

Based in Canton, Mass., Tweeter, a unit of closely held New England Audio Co., sets some limits. It said it will monitor one or two daily newspapers in each of its markets. Any time a competitor within 25 miles of one of its stores advertises a lower price, the "automatic price protection" program goes into effect. Radio, television and direct mail ads don't count. And the guarantee applies only to items over $50.

When Tweeter's competitive marketing staffers see a rival's ad quoting a price, they enter it in Tweeter's computer. A program then checks to see if anybody has bought that item from Tweeter for a higher price in the past 30 days. If so, the computer spits out a check for the difference.

Edgar Dworsky, Massachusetts assistant attorney general for consumer protection, said: "It's a brilliant idea. The problem with price protection guarantees has been that it's the consumer's burden to find a lower price somewhere else. Tweeter's going to do the watching for you. I just hope they don't lose their shirts."

Volume Discounts Available

Tweeter, with $40 million a year in sales at 14 stores, is a medium-sized player in the increasingly competitive New England market. It sells name-brand stereos, televisions, car radios and car phones. It doesn't compete at the very low end of the market. However, Tweeter says that because it is part of the Progressive Retailers Organization Inc., a Palm Springs, Calif., buying group, it can get the same volume discounts available to national chains.

Mr. Stone of Tweeter estimates that the company mails $3,000 to $4,000 a month in refund checks to sharp-eyed customers. He says the amount could double under the new program.

Retail consultants say the total may be far higher. "I'd guess 5%" of customers actually check competitors' ads, says Robert Kahn, a retail consultant in Lafayette, Calif. But he says, "This will build customers because somebody who gets a check will say something exceptional about Tweeter to his friends."

Banking on 'Incremental Sales'

That's what Tweeter is counting on. "A few incremental sales will more than pay for the program," said Sandy Bloomberg, chief executive and founder of Tweeter.

Tweeter officials said the company worked to build a high-price, high-quality image during the 1980s. But focus group research showed it needed to reverse that image for the '90s. "People used to boast about how much they paid for something. Now they boast about how much they saved on it," said Mr. Stone.

Exhibit 2 Annual Domestic and Import Manufacturer Sales of Consumer Electronics in the United States by Category [a] (in millions of dollars)

		1990	1991	1992	1993	1994	1995	1996 (est.)
Video:								
Direct view color TV		$ 6,247	$ 6,035	$ 6,651	$ 7,376	$ 7,285	$ 6,969	$ 7,100
Projection TV		626	683	714	841	1,117	1,398	1,720
Monochrome TV		132	92	79	73	70	65	62
TV/VCR combo		178	265	375	599	710	729	816
VCRs		2,504	2,525	2,996	2,912	2,933	2,859	2,716
Camcorders		2,269	2,013	1,841	1,958	1,985	2,160	2,183
Laserdisc players		72	81	93	123	123	105	92
Home satellite		421	370	379	408	900	1,265	1,479
	Sub-Total	$12,449	$12,064	$13,128	$14,290	$15,123	$15,550	$16,168
Audio:								
Rack systems		$ 804	$ 667	$ 614	$ 545	$ 595	$ 537	$ 507
Compact systems		466	597	756	919	1,108	1,242	1,335
Separate components		1,935	1,805	1,586	1,635	1,686	1,940	2,100
Portable equipment		1,645	1,780	2,096	2,187	2,495	2,749	2,724
Home radios		360	310	324	307	306	298	298
	Sub-Total	$5,210	$5,159	$5,376	$5,593	$6,190	$6,766	$6,964
Mobile Electronics:								
Car stereo equipment [b]		1,192	1,232	1,467	1,604	1,898	1,935	1,975
Cellular telephones		1,133	962	1,146	1,257	1,275	1,431	1,620
	Sub-Total	$2,325	$2,194	$2,613	$2,861	$3,173	$3,366	$3,595
Blank Media:		$1,638	$1,661	$1,568	$1,486	$1,436	$1,413	$1,442
Accessories & Batteries:		$2,167	$2,145	$2,253	$2,974	$3,286	$3,475	$3,745
	Total	$23,789	$23,223	$24,938	$27,204	$29,208	$30,570	$31,914

Sources: *U.S. Consumer Electronics Sales & Forecasts 1991-1996*; Consumer Electronics Manufacturers Associations, January 1996

[a] Excludes home office equipment (e.g., telephones, fax machines, personal computers), and electronic gaming equipment.

[b] Excludes factory installed car stereo equipment.

Exhibit 3   Channels of Distribution for Consumer Electronics

Specialty Stores and Boutiques

Characterized by good to excellent customer service, high salesperson knowledge and moderate selling pressure. Medium- to high-end product lines, especially in terms of audio components (e.g., Sony, . . .). Limited use of promotional sales. Typically smaller in size with good facilities (e.g., sound-proof listening rooms). Examples include Tweeter, Cambridge Sound Works, and Bryn Mawr Stereo.

Electronic/Appliance Superstores

Hectic, high-volume selling machines. Moderate to good customer service, varied salesperson knowledge, and strong selling pressure. Carry a wide selection of all the major product lines (e.g., Sony, Pioneer, JVC, . . .). Heavy use of promotional sales. Large, open facilities with listening rooms common, but not a certainty. Examples include Circuit City, Best Buy, Nobody Beats the Wiz and Lechmere.

Department Stores

Poor to moderate customer service, limited salesperson knowledge and low to moderate selling pressure. Carry a more limited product line, mainly entry and middle level products. Prone to promotional sales. Examples include Sears and Macy's.

Mass Merchants

Little to no customer service, little salesperson knowledge and little selling pressure. Limited product line, geared toward "value" brands, such as Sound Design and Yorx. Unlikely to find audio components at these stores. Examples include Wal-mart and K-Mart.

Warehouse Clubs

No customer service and no selling pressure. Price, not service or ambiance, is the reason people shop at warehouse clubs. Product selection is varies and limited and selection changes all the time. On occasion, good values on good quality equipment can be found. Examples include Costco and Sam's Club.

Mail Order Houses

Advertise in stereo and video magazines as well as via their own catalogs. No service and no selling pressure. No ability to sample equipment. Prices are sometimes attractive, but shipping can be expensive. Returns are difficult. Examples include Crutchfield and Sound City.

Source: *Consumer Reports*, February, 1996, pp. 18-27.

Exhibit 4   1995 Market Share by Channel for Select Consumer Electronics Categories

	Direct View Color TV's	Video Camcorders	Portable Audio[a]	Audio Components	Blank Media[b]
Specialty Stores/Electronic Superstores	49.0%	46.0%	37.0%	64.0%	17.0%
Mass Merchants/Warehouse Clubs	25.0%	25.0%	32.0%	14.0%	45.0%
Department Stores	6.5%	7.5%	17.0%	6.5%	16.0%
Mail Order Houses	3.0%	6.5%	5.0%	3.5%	2.0%
Other	15.0%	15.0%	9.0%	12.0%	20.0%
Total	100.0%	100.0%	100.0%	100.0%	100.0%

Source: *Dealerscope Merchandising,* July 1996, p.46-50

[a] Portable Audio includes Walkman and Discman-type portable systems

[b] Blank Media includes bland audio cassettes, VCR cassettes and Camcorder cassettes

Exhibit 5   New England Market Share—1992 to 1996[a]

	1992	1994	1996
Lechmere	33.0%	36.0%	35.6%
Circuit City	0.0%	7.4%	18.6%
Sears	7.8%	7.4%	8.7%
Radio Shack	4.9%	5.8%	3.9%
Wal-Mart	n/a[b]	n/a[b]	3.9%
Tweeter	2.8%	2.7%	3.6%
Bradlee's	2.2%	2.5%	2.4%
Service Merchandise	4.1%	3.0%	2.1%
Fretter	5.0%	4.9%	1.7%
BJ's Wholesale Club	2.5%	2.3%	1.2%
K-Mart	0.6%	0.4%	1.2%
Costco	n/a[b]	0.7%	0.6%
Jordan Marsh	1.3%	0.4%	0.6%
Cambridge Sound Works	n/a[b]	n/a[b]	0.6%
Other	35.8%	26.5%	15.3%

Source: Company records; Based on research conducted by WCVB-TV, Boston, MA.

[a] Based on an annual telephone survey of approximately 1,000 adults in the New England market in response to the question, "In the past 2 years, at which store did you make your LAST purchase of home electronics equipment?".

[b] Market share not reported separately, but included in "Other".

Exhibit 6   Tweeter Store Openings

1972	Commonwealth Avenue, Boston, MA
1973	Harvard Square, MA
1974	Newton, MA
1976	Burlington, MA
1977	Framingham, MA
1979	Dedham, MA; Warwick, RI
1982	Peabody, MA
1984	Hyannis, MA
1985	Waterford, CT; Hanover, MA
1986	Danbury, CT; Seekonk, MA
1990	Newington, CT
1993	Avon, CT
1994	Manchester, CT; Salem, NH
1995	Boylston Street, Boston, MA; Milford, CT
1996	Holyoke, MA; Nashua, NH

Source: Company records

Exhibit 7   Tweeter etc. Income Statement: FY 1990 to FY 1996[a]

	FY 1990	FY 1991	FY 1992	FY 1993	FY 1994	FY 1995	FY 1996 (est.)[b]
Gross Revenues	$39,500	$35,660	$41,140	$43,714	$55,164	$70,305	$82,400
Cost of Goods Sold	26,228	23,586	27,209	28,485	35,739	45,299	52,300
Total Gross Margin	$13,272	$ 12,074	$13,931	$15,229	$19,425	$25,006	$30,100
Total Expenses	15,146	14,085	13,894	15,890	18,038	22,304	26,500
Net Income	($1,874)	($2,011)	$ 37	($661)	$ 1,387	$ 2,702	$ 3,600

Source: Company Records

[a]Fiscal Years are from October 1 of the previous year through September 30 of the year indicated.

[b]Figures for FY 1996 are based on midyear projections and do not include the purchase of Bryn Mawr Stereo and Video.

Exhibit 8   Makeup of Customer Bases Across New England Retailers

Customer Segment	Total Market	Tweeter	Lechmere	Circuit City
Entry Level	50%[a]	5%[b]	40%	35%
Price-Biter	15%	20%	10%	35%
Convenience	25%	5%	40%	15%
Quality/Service	10%	70%	10%	15%
	100%	100%	100%	100%

Source: Tweeter Company Estimates

[a]To be read, 50% of all New England consumer electronics customers are Entry-level customers.

[b]To be read, 5% of all Tweeter customers are Entry-level customers.

Exhibit 9   Tweeter Automatic Price Protection

Only Tweeter Automatically Mails You A Check For The Difference!

If you buy something at Tweeter and it's advertised for less in a major local newspaper within 30 days, we'll automatically mail you a check for the difference!

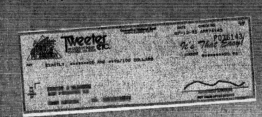

It's been more than two full years since we introduced Automatic Price Protection℠. And to date, Tweeter remains the only retailer in the country (world?) to provide such a service.

Needless to say, customers who have received APP℠ checks in the mail have been delighted by the fact that they didn't have to shop around for a better price. INSTEAD, TWEETER DID THE PRICE SHOPPING FOR THEM AFTER THE SALE!

Here's How APP™

Step 1

Staff members in the Automatic Price Protection Department go through each consumer electronics ad in every edition of the major local newspaper. When we find an item advertised that Tweeter sells, we record the model#, price, and date of the ad in our computer.

Step 2

Our Management Information Department then finds every customer who purchased that item from Tweeter within the 30-day period preceding the ad.

Step 3

The names and addresses of customers who paid more than the advertised prices are separated and spooled.

Step 4

Checks are cut for the difference between what the customer paid and the price advertised. They are mailed within five days.

Common Myths about Automatic Price Protection℠

Myth: That APP doesn't work because most retailers have model numbers that are unique to them, so we can't compare prices.

Reality: The truth is, that Tweeter has no unique model numbers. In fact, we share all of our TV, VCR, Camcorder, and Portable Audio models with the other big retailers like Lechmere, Circuit City, and the Wiz. And we share most of our Car Stereo models, and many of our Home Stereo models with them as well.

Myth: That Tweeter only mails out checks for large amounts and that small price protection amounts are omitted.

Reality: Tweeter mails out APP checks for amounts of $2 and over.

Myth: That Tweeter only Price Protects items that are high-priced.

Reality: Tweeter Price Protects items priced $50 and over.

Myth: That the APP checks Tweeter mails out are only redeemable for merchandise at Tweeter.

Reality: The APP refunds that Tweeter mails out are bonafide checks. You can cash them anywhere.

Source: Company Records

Exhibit 10   Tweeter Marketing Mix

	FY 1993		FY 1996	
	$ (000s)	As % of Sales	$ (000s)	As % of Sales
Print	$2,500	7.1%	$ 300	0.3%
Television	0	0.0	1,150	1.4
Radio	375	1.1	2,750	3.3
Direct Mail[a]	125	0.3	1,000	1.2
Music Series[b]	0	0.0	225	0.3
Pre-Openings[c]	0	0.0	275	0.3
Other[d]	125	0.3	1000	1.2
Total	$3,125	8.9%	$6,700	8.0%

Source: Company Records

[a] Includes quarterly Buyers Guides and other one-time only direct mail campaigns

[b] Includes sponsorship of Great Woods Concert Series

[c] Includes promotional efforts related to new store openings

[d] Includes Marketing Research, Public Relations and Cellular Telephone Promotions

Exhibit 11   Tweeter Product Mix: 1996

Product Category		% of Dollar Sales
Video:		
TV's 40" and Under		14%
TV's Over 40"		10%
Video Cassette Recorders (VCRs)		6%
Camcorders		4%
Direct Satellite Systems (DSS)		1%
	Sub-Total	35%
Audio:		
Speakers		14%
Receivers		9%
CD Players		7%
Personal Portable		4%
Tape Decks		2%
Other Audio Electronics[a]		5%
	Sub-Total	41%
Car Stereo:		14%
Other:[b]		10%
	Total	100%

Source: Company Records

[a] Includes Amplifiers, Preamplifiers, Boom Boxes and Compact Systems

[b] Includes Cellular Phones, Cables, Bland Tapes, Warranties and Labor

Exhibit 12   Automatic Price Protection Rebates by Month (in dollars)

		Number of Checks		$ Value of Checks	
		Month	Cumulative	Month	Cumulative
1993	August	89	89	$ 1,816	$ 1,816
	September	268	356	5,105	6,921
	October	549	905	15,718	22,639
	November	843	1,748	25,595	48,234
	December	1,571	3,319	31,229	79,463
1994	January	433	3,751	10,295	89,758
	February	341	4,093	9,188	98,945
	March	403	4,495	12,410	111,355
	April	475	4,970	10,600	121,955
	May	591	5,561	13,714	135,669
	June	690	6,251	14,331	150,000
	July	483	6,734	11,350	161,350
	August	529	7,263	12,014	173,364
	September	581	7,844	9,354	182,718
	October	681	8,525	14,949	197,666
	November	1,594	10,119	39,003	236,669
	December	4,249	14,368	104,260	340,929
1995	January	1,528	15,895	36,389	377,318
	February	849	16,744	17,751	395,069
	March	850	17,594	20,154	415,223
	April	561	18,155	12,656	427,879
	May	610	18,765	12,636	440,515
	June	1,108	19,873	25,583	466,098
	July	160	20,033	3,236	469,334
	August	675	20,708	16,614	485,948
	September	628	21,335	16,498	502,445
	October	1,078	22,413	27,881	530,326
	November	2,403	24,815	72,038	602,364
	December	4,711	29,526	181,499	783,863

Source: Company records

Exhibit 13   Product Line and Price Comparisons Across Major New England Retailers—27″ Color Televisions

Model	Lechmere	Circuit City	Wiz	Tweeter
GE-27GT600	320 (Sale)			
GE-27GT616	280 (Ad)			
Hitachi-27CX1B		450		
Hitachi-27CX5B	480 (Sale)	500 (Ad)		
Hitachi-27CXSB		440		
JVC-AV27720	450	430		
Magnavox-TP2770	500			
Magnavox-TP2782C	500	450		
Magnavox-TS2743			400	
Magnavox-TS2752C	350 (Sale)	350 (Ad)		
Magnavox-TS2753C	370			
Magnavox-TS2775C		380 (Sale)		
Magnavox-TS2779			400 (Ad)	
Mitsubishi-CS27205	500 (Ad)		479	500
Mitsubishi-CS27305	670		598	600
Mitsubishi-CS27407	920		850	850
Panasonic-CT27G11	400 (Sale)	430	430	
Panasonic-CT27G21	430 (Sale)	480	497	480
Panasonic-CT27SF12	650 (Sale)	630		
Panasonic-CT27SF21	700 (Sale)			650
Panasonic-CT27SF22	700 (Sale)			
Panasonic-CT27SF23	750		750	750
Panasonic-CT27SF33	900			
ProScan-PS27108		600 (Ad)	548	600

Model	Lechmere	Circuit City	Wiz	Tweeter
ProScan-PS27113		630 (Sale)	578	
ProScan-PS27123				750
ProScan-PS27160		870		
RCA-F27204BC	530 (Ad)			
RCA-F27240WT	350 (Sale)		380	
RCA-F27638BC				400
RCA-F27675BC		450	395 (Ad)	
RCA-F2767BC	430 (Sale)			
Sharp-27GS60	330 (Ad)			
Sharp-27HS120			330 (Ad)	
Sony-KV27S20	500 (Ad)	500		550
Sony-KV27S25	550 (Sale)	550	550	550
Sony-KV27V20	590	550 (Sale)	550	550
Sony-KV27V25				650
Sony-KV27V35	840		750	750
Sony-KV27V55	800		750	
Sony-KV27XBR45	900 (Sale)		970	1000
Toshiba-CF27E30	400 (Ad)			
Toshiba-CF27F50	470 (Sale)		497	
Toshiba-CF27F55	500 (Ad)	500		
Zenith-SM2789BT	650	500		
Zenith-SR2787DT	650 (Sale)			
Zenith-SR2787DT	550 (Sale)			
Zenith-SY2772DT	480			
Zenith-SY2773DT		450 (Ad)		

Source: Comparison of products and prices in the week of September 16, 1996

Notes: (Ad) indicates a price advertised in the local paper; (Sale) indicates an unadvertised, in-store markdown.

Exhibit 13 (continued) Product Line and Price Comparisons Across Major New England Retailers—Multiple CD Players

Model	Lechmere	Circuit City	Wiz	Tweeter
Adcom-GCD700				700
Admiral-MWDK1	90 (Sale)			
Denon-DCM360				330
Denon-DCM460				400
Fisher-DAC503			158	
Fisher-DAC6005			219 (Ad)	
Harmon-Kar.-FL8300		300 (Sale)	299 (Ad)	
JVC-XLF108BK	120 (Ad)	120		
JVC-XLF152BK		180 (Sale)	180	
JVC-XLF252BK		200 (Ad)	180 (Sale)	
JVC-XLM418BK			220 (Sale)	300
Kenwood-DPJ1070		300 (Ad)		
Kenwood-DPJ2071		500		
Kenwood-DPR3080	200	170	199	180
Kenwood-DPR4070		180 (Ad)	188	
Kenwood-DPR4080	220		230	200
Kenwood-DPR5080		220		
Kenwood-DPR6080				300
Onkyo-DXC320	350			
Onkyo-DXC330	270	300	280	
Onkyo-DXC530	330			
Onkyo-DXC606	400 (Sale)			
Pioneer-PD65				800
Pioneer-PDF59				300
Pioneer-PDF79				400

Model	Lechmere	Circuit City	Wiz	Tweeter
Pioneer-PDF109				800
Pioneer-PDF505	220	200 (Ad)	200	
Pioneer-PDF605	200 (Sale)		220	
Pioneer-PDF705		240		
Pioneer-PDF901		300 (Ad)		
Sony-CDPC425		180		
Sony-CDPC445	200 (Ad)			
Sony-CDPC545			279	
Sony-CDPCA7ES				350
Sony-CDPCA8ES				550
Sony-CDPCE405		200 (Sale)	200	200
Sony-CDPCE505		250	270	
Sony-CDPCX153	350 (Ad)	300	377	
Sony-CDPCX200		350 (Sale)		350
Sony-CDPCX270				450
Sony-CDPXE500	160			160
Technics-SLMC400			299 (Ad)	
Technics-SLMC50	230 (Ad)		248 (Ad)	
Technics-SLPD687	150 (Sale)	170 (Sale)		
Technics-SLPD787			168	
Technics-SLPD887	170 (Ad)	140	168 (Sale)	
Yamaha-CDC555			230 (Ad)	220
Yamaha-CDC755				350
Yamaha-CDC845				450

Source: Comparison of products and prices in the week of September 16, 1996

Notes: (Ad) indicates a price advertised in the local paper; (Sale) indicates an unadvertised, in-store markdown.

Exhibit 13 (continued) Product Line and Price Comparisons Across Major New England Retailers—Camcorders

Model	Lechmere	Circuit City	Wiz	Tweeter
Canon-ES80		470		
Canon-ES90		560		
Canon-ES100		500		
Canon-ES200		600	598	
Canon-ES900		800	898	
Hitachi-VM1900A		500		
Hitachi-VM2900A		600		
Hitachi-VMH710A		800		
Hitachi-VMH720A		800 (Ad)		
Hitachi-VMH825LA		1200		
JVC-GRAX310			498 (Ad)	
JVC-GRAX350		550 (Ad)	648	
JVC-GRAX410U	500	550 (Ad)	498 (Ad)	
JVC-GRAX510U	500			
JVC-GRAX710U	600 (Ad)	630 (Sale)	648	
JVC-GRAX810U		700 (Sale)		
JVC-GRAX910U	730 (Ad)	800	798	
JVC-GRAX1010U		900		
Panasonic-PVA206	550 (Ad)	570	528 (Ad)	
Panasonic-PVA306	600 (Sale)	680		700
Panasonic-PVD406	800	800	800	800
Panasonic-PVD506	900	900 (Ad)	900	900
Panasonic-PVL606	1000 (Ad)	1000 (Sale)	998 (Ad)	1000
Panasonic-PVIQ295			600	
Panasonic-PVIQ305		600		
Panasonic-PVIQ475		630 (Sale)		
Panasonic-PVIQ505			798	
RCA-CC431	500 (Ad)			
RCA-CC436	600			
RCA-CC616	700 (Sale)			

Model	Lechmere	Circuit City	Wiz	Tweeter
RCA-PRO800	300 (Ad)	300 (Ad)	370	
RCA-PRO844		500		
RCA-PRO847		600		
RCA-PROV712		600 (Ad)	648 (Ad)	
RCA-PROV714		850 (Ad)	798 (Sale)	
RCA-PROV949HB		800 (Ad)		
Sharp-VLE37U	600 (Ad)	580		
Sharp-VLE39U	600 (Sale)		700	
Sharp-VLE47U	800 (Ad)	850	998	
Sharp-VLL65U	450 (Ad)			
Sony-CCDFX730		900 (Sale)		
Sony-CCDTR44	500 (Ad)	500 (Ad)		
Sony-CCDTR54		500 (Ad)		500
Sony-CCDTR64	600 (Ad)	600 (Ad)	598	
Sony-CCDTR74	650	650 (Sale)	648	650
Sony-CCDTR78			650	
Sony-CCDTR82	650 (Ad)			
Sony-CCDTR83	850 (Ad)	750 (Sale)		
Sony-CCDTR84	770		700	700
Sony-CCDTR88			748	
Sony-CCDTR94	800	800 (Ad)	800 (Sale)	800
Sony-CCDTR600	1150 (Sale)	1100 (Ad)		
Sony-CCDTR910				1300
Sony-CCDTRV11	700 (Ad)	700 (Ad)	698 (Sale)	700
Sony-CCDTRV21	900 (Ad)	900 (Ad)	898	900
Sony-CCDTRV29		1000 (Ad)		
Sony-CCDTRV30		800	998	
Sony-CCDTRV40	1190 (Sale)	1100	1198	
Sony-CCDTRV41	1200	1200 (Ad)		1200
Sony-CCDTRV81	1500 (Ad)	1500 (Ad)		1500

Source: Comparison of products and prices in the week of September 16, 1996

Notes: (Ad) indicates a price advertised in the local paper; (Sale) indicates an unadvertised, in-store markdown.

Exhibit 13 (continued) Product Line and Price Comparisons Across Major New England Retailers—Full-Sized Speakers

Model	Lechmere	Circuit City	Wiz	Tweeter
Advent-ADVAmber			299	
Advent-ADVHeritage			350	
Advent-ADVLaureate			250	
BOSE-100		75		
BOSE-151		120		
BOSE-201 Series 1VB	100 (Ad)	100 (Ad)		
BOSE-301 Series 1VB	160 (Ad)	159 (Ad)		
Compact Reference-CR6				200
Compact Reference-CR7				260
Compact Reference-CR8				340
Compact Reference-CR9				420
Infinity-REF20001		100		
Infinity-REF20003		160		
Infinity-REF20004		200		
Infinity-REF20005		280 (Ad)		
Infinity-REF20006		350		
Infinity-RS20002C	280			
Infinity-RS20003C	330			
Infinity-RS200SL	300			
Infinity-RS225BL	220			
Infinity-RS325	200 (Sale)			
Infinity-RS625	250			
JBL-ARC30		130		
JBL-ARC50		170 (Sale)		
JBL-CM42		130		
JBL-L1		260 (Ad)		
JBL-L3		400		
JBL-L5		500		
KEF-Q10				250
KEF-Q30				400

Model	Lechmere	Circuit City	Wiz	Tweeter
KEF-Q50				600
KEF-Q70				900
Klipsch-Heritage				1000
Klipsch-KG.5			198 (Ad)	200
Klipsch-KG1.5				300
Klipsch-KG2.5				400
Klipsch-KG3.5V				500
Klipsch-KG4.5V				600
Klipsch-KG5.5V			800	800
Klipsch-KLPKSS3				
Klipsch-Series				1300
Lerwin-VS80	130			
Lerwin-VS100	180			
Lerwin-VS120	200			
Lerwin-VS150	370			
Lerwin -CVEAT10BK			230	
Lerwin -CVEAT12BK			250	
Lerwin -CVEAT1SBK			400	
Lynnfield -VR20				550
Lynnfield -VR30				500
Lynnfield -VR40				1400
Mirage-M90IS				200
Mirage-M290IS				450
Mirage-M5901				600
Mirage-M8901				700
Mirage-M10901				1200
Mission -731	180			
Mission -732	300			
Mission -735	450			
Polk-M3IIB			250	
Polk-S8B			200	

Source: Comparison of products and prices in the week of September 16, 1996

Notes: (Ad) indicates a price advertised in the local paper; (Sale) indicates an unadvertised, in-store markdown.

Exhibit 14   1995 Customer Survey Data[a]

Q1: Home electronic stores are offering price protection plans. What is AUTOMATIC PRICE PROTECTION?

Response	% of Responders (n=1286)
Buy item/Receive a Refund by Mail *	17.8%
Guaranteed Lowest Price *	14.2%
Buy item/ Pickup Refund Check	9.7%
Item Covered under Warranty	8.9%
Buy Item/Pickup Refund Check + 10%	4.4%
Other	4.4%
Don't Know	40.6%

*Considered a correct response to the question.

Q2: Automatic Price Protection is after you buy an item, if the store sees the item advertised for less, the store mails you a refund check. Which one store sells home electronics and offers the Automatic Price Protection plan?

Response	% of Responders (n=1286)
Tweeter etc.	22.1%
Circuit City	13.4%
Lechmere	10.3%
Fretter	5.8%
Radio Shack	1.2%
Sears	1.0%
Other	4.6%
Don't Know	37.9%
None	3.9%

Q3: Compared to the big chains, like Lechmere and Circuit City, do you think that Tweeter's prices are. . .

Tweeter Prices are ...	% of Responders (n=1286)	Aware of Tweeter's APP Policy (n=284)	Unaware of Tweeter's APP Policy (n=1002)
Lower	4.7%	5.1%	4.6%
About the Same	25.3%	36.1%	22.2%
Higher	16.0%	14.5%	16.4%
Don't Know	54.0%	44.3%	56.8%

Source: Company records; Based on research conducted by WCVB-TV, Boston, MA.

[a]Data are based on a random telephone survey conducted in the Greater Boston area.

THE JOURNAL OF INDUSTRIAL ECONOMICS
Volume XLIII   September 1995

0022-1821 $2.00

No. 3

PRICE-MATCHING POLICY AND THE PRINCIPLE
OF MINIMUM DIFFERENTIATION*

Z. John Zhang

This paper shows that if duopolists are allowed to choose their product locations, a price-matching policy, and their prices sequentially and independently, both tacit collusion and minimum differentiation occur.

I. INTRODUCTION

IN MANY industries, firms publicly commit themselves to match or beat the prices of their competitors—i.e., to charge prices that are always equal to or less than those of their rivals. For the purpose of this paper I describe this property as "price-matching". This practice has been widely recognized in theory as a device that can facilitate tacit collusion among competing firms either through consumer-enforced information exchange or through incentive management (Salop [1986]).[1] Empirical testing also suggests that a price-matching policy coordinates firms' pricing and supports a higher market price (Hess and Gerstner [1991]).

However, there are other likely consequences from the adoption of a price-matching policy. As this paper demonstrates, there may be a reduction in product differentiation as a result of the adoption of the price-matching policy.[2] Intuitively, since the policy moderates price competition, firms might be less compelled to create their own market niches and may find it

---

* I would like to thank Chakravarthi Narasimhan, Mike Orszag, Steve Salant, Greg Shaffer, Hal Varian, and Michelle White for their comments. I am also grateful to Lawrence J. White and two anonymous referees for their insightful suggestions. However, I am solely responsible for all the remaining errors in the paper.

[1] The price-matching policy in the context of duopoly with differentiated products is studied by Belton [1987]; in the context of Bertrand oligopoly by Doyle [1988] and by Logan and Lutter [1989]; and in the context of imperfect information by Png and Hirshleifer [1987] and by Lin [1988].

[2] Salop [1986] has suggested three ways in which price matching might benefit consumers: First, individual consumers may value the policy for insurance reasons. Second, consumers' search processes can be shortened as a result, which may benefit both consumers and producers. Third, the price-matching policy allows a firm to indulge in price discrimination, which can benefit some consumers while harming the others. This paper suggests an additional potential benefit: a reduction in product differentiation, which might be excessive. In the context of this model, if consumers are concentrated toward the middle point, minimum differentiation still occurs. In this case, social welfare improves due to reduced transportation costs. However, a general discussion on social welfare in the context of product differentiation is beyond the scope of this paper (see Spence [1976], Dixit and Stiglitz [1977], and Beckmann [1976]).

advantageous to pursue a "me too" strategy to reduce product differentiation. I will address this question here by using the Hotelling [1929] location model.

Hotelling [1929] first proposed what was subsequently termed as the principle of minimum differentiation: two competing firms may have incentives to choose their product locations arbitrarily close to each other in order to secure maximum market shares. The proposition has been challenged on technical grounds since, with the original Hotelling specifications, equilibrium in pure strategies fails to exist as the two firms locate close to each other (D'Aspremont, Gabszewicz, and Thisse [1979]). Indeed, under quite general specifications in accordance with the spirit of the Hotelling model, maximum differentiation prevails (Economides [1986], Neven [1985, 1986]). This has prompted many efforts to restore the validity of this principle: by specifying a hidden dimension of product differentiation (De Palma, Ginsburgh, Papageorgiou, and Thisse [1985]), by fixing the market price exogenously and imposing some harmonious conjectural variations (Stahl [1982], Hauser [1988]), or, most recently, by introducing unobservable attributes in consumers' brand choice (Rhee, De Palma, Fornell, and Thisse [1993]) or explicit collusion on price (Jehiel [1992] and Friedman and Thisse [1993]). These efforts have generated many insights; however, they have not been able to show that the principle of minimum differentiation holds, as originally suggested by Hotelling, in the case of one-dimensional product space where purchasing decisions by consumers and location decisions by the competing firms are based on the same attribute and where pricing decisions are independent and not in unison.

In this paper, I will show that if the duopolists are allowed to choose their product locations, a price-matching policy, and their prices sequentially and independently, both tacit collusion and minimum differentiation occur. Minimum differentiation occurs due to the fact that price competition is relegated to a secondary effect by both firms' independent decisions to adopt the price-matching policy, and market expansion or competition for market shares thereby becomes a predominant concern for the competing firms in their location decisions. While setting their prices independently, both firms gravitate toward the middle of the product space to prevent the rival firm from leapfrogging in its pursuit for maximal market share.

Section II sets up the model. Sections III and IV develop the simple case of a uniform distribution of consumers over product space, in order to establish the basic intuition and driving force of the model. Section V concludes.

II. NOTATIONS AND THE MODEL

The model in this paper follows closely the D'Aspremont, Gabszewicz, and Thisse [1979] paper where maximum differentiation is the subgame perfect equilibrium in their two stage game. Consumers are uniformly distributed along a unit line with the quadratic transportation cost td^2, where d is the

Euclidean distance traveled by a consumer to the firm from which a purchase is made and t is a constant. The number of consumers in the market is, without loss of generality, normalized to one. As in the Hotelling model, each consumer is assumed to have a unit demand with reservation price V and buys from the firm that offers the lowest hedonic price $P + td^2$. Furthermore, consumers are assumed to have perfect information about the prices and locations of the two firms, denoted as A and B respectively. This assumption is restrictive, but not unconventional or unduly unrealistic in a market where aggressive marketing by firms is a norm.

Both firms are assumed to produce with an identical and constant unit cost. That is, without loss of generality, normalized to zero. The game is played in three stages. In the first stage, both firms simultaneously choose their product locations, a and b respectively. In the second stage, the product locations are known, and the two firms choose simultaneously whether or not to adopt a price-matching ("meet or beat the rival's prices") policy. In the third stage, the previous choices by both firms are known, and the firms choose their prices P_A and P_B independently. If firm i has adopted the price-matching policy in the previous stage, then the price a consumer pays at the firm is given by $\min\{P_A, P_B\}$.

The three-stage setup reflects the fact that it is typically harder for a firm to change its product location than to implement the price-matching policy, which in turn is harder to change than the price.[3] The concept of subgame perfect equilibrium is used in this paper so that, as a firm changes its product location, for instance, it takes into account the fact that the market will develop a new equilibrium for the other variables.

III. CONTINGENT PRICING STRATEGIES

We can now solve the game backwards. In the third stage of the game, there are four subgames in which a firm has to make pricing decisions for given locations, a and b. They are $G_A G_B$, $G_A \bar{G}_B$, $\bar{G}_A G_B$, and $\bar{G}_A \bar{G}_B$, where G_i ($\bar{G}_i$) refers to firm i having (not) adopted a price-matching policy. Without loss of generality, I assume $a \leqslant b$ throughout the following intermediate derivations. In the case $a \geqslant b$, one can simply exchange firm A with firm B and interchange a with b.

Subgame 1 $(G_A G_B)$:

In this subgame, since both firms have adopted the price-matching policy, consumers pay identical prices to both firms, $\min\{P_A, P_B\}$. In determining a

---

[3] Although the setup adds realism to the model, the results in the paper remain the same as long as the price is the last decision variable to be set in the game.

firm's pricing strategy, we first notice that none of the firms will ever choose its price to be below zero. Furthermore, with the assumption of perfect information and binding commitment, each firm expects that a unilateral price cut below the rival's price will be matched by its competitor. This expectation engendered by the price-matching policy reduces a firm's incentives to undercut its competitor's price. However, the incentives do exist if a firm can, by undercutting, create sufficient incremental sales to compensate for the lost revenues from its intramarginal consumers even though price-matching is expected from its rival. This is the case, given a sufficiently large V, when the market is not covered at one or both margins of a firm's market. This means that, as a firm strives to expand its market, its choice of price in this subgame has a non-trivial upper bound, H_i, to ensure that both margins of its market are covered if the price ends up being the lowest in the market. Therefore, $P_i \in [0 \quad H_i]$. The following lemma formalizes the analysis:

Lemma 1. Given $0 \leqslant a \leqslant b \leqslant 1$ and $V > 5t,$[4] $P_A \in [0 \quad H_A]$ and $P_B \in [0 \quad H_B]$, where $H_A = \min\left\{V - a^2 t, \ V - \left(\dfrac{t-a}{2}\right)^2 t\right\}$ and $H_B = \min\left\{V - (1-b)^2 t, \ V - \left(\dfrac{b-a}{2}\right)^2 t\right\}$.

Proof: see appendix (1).

By lemma 1, the market is necessarily covered in any equilibrium of the subgame. However, the consequences of the price-matching policy take effect once the market is covered, since no further incremental sales can be created by either firm through independent price-cutting. With the price-cutting incentives removed, the equilibrium price in this subgame is expected to stay at the ceiling. The following lemma formally states the result.

Lemma 2. Given $0 \leqslant a \leqslant b \leqslant 1$ and $V > 5t$, there exists a unique Nash equilibrium in the subgame $\tilde{P}_A = H_A$ and $\tilde{P}_B = H_B$ that satisfies the iterative dominance criterion.

Proof: see appendix (2).

Since consumers pay the identical price $\min\{H_A, H_B\}$ at both firms, the payoffs for both firms in this subgame are given by:

$$\pi_A^1 = \begin{cases} \min\{H_A, H_B\} \dfrac{a+b}{2} & \text{if } a < b \\ \min\{H_A, H_B\} \dfrac{1}{2} & \text{if } a = b \end{cases}$$

---

[4] The condition $V > 5t$ is a sufficient, overly strong condition assumed to simplify the notation.

$$\pi_B^1 = \begin{cases} \min\{H_A, H_B\}\left(1 - \dfrac{a+b}{2}\right) & \text{if } a < b \\ \min\{H_A, H_B\}\dfrac{1}{2} & \text{if } a = b \end{cases}$$

where the superscript indicates the subgame associated with the payoffs. Clearly, when both firms adopt the price-matching policy, tacit collusion on price ensues.

Subgame 2 $(G_A \bar{G}_B)$:

In this subgame, firm A has adopted a price-matching policy, but firm B has not. Firm A has a zero conjecture about firm B's pricing since the latter firm has not related its pricing to firm A's. However, firm B expects price-matching if it tries to undercut firm A's price, since firm A has committed to the price-matching policy. Formally, consumers pay $\min\{P_A, P_B\}$ at firm A and P_B at firm B. Since the market is again covered in any equilibrium for a sufficiently large V, the firms' payoffs are given below for any equilibrium prices $\tilde{P}_A$ and $\tilde{P}_B$:

$$\pi_A = \min\{\tilde{P}_A, \tilde{P}_B\}\frac{\max\{\tilde{P}_B - \tilde{P}_A, 0\} + (b^2 - a^2)t}{2(b - a)t}$$

$$\pi_B = \tilde{P}_B\left(1 - \frac{\max\{\tilde{P}_B - \tilde{P}_A, 0\} + (b^2 - a^2)t}{2(b - a)t}\right).$$

We can now proceed to characterize the equilibrium conditions in this subgame.

Note that in any equilibrium of the subgame, we necessarily have $\tilde{P}_A \leqslant \tilde{P}_B$ for a sufficiently large V. Otherwise, firm B, as the price setter in the market, can always raise its price profitably.[5] This implies that, in any equilibrium of the subgame, either $\tilde{P}_A < \tilde{P}_B$ or $\tilde{P}_A = \tilde{P}_B$. For $a + b < 1$—i.e., if firm A is located closer to the left end than firm B to the right end, or stated differently, there are less hinterland consumers for firm A than for firm B—we have a unique Nash equilibrium where $\tilde{P}_A < \tilde{P}_B$ and the two equilibrium prices are given by:

$$\tilde{P}_A = \frac{(b + a + 2)(b - a)t}{3}, \qquad \tilde{P}_B = \frac{(4 - b - a)(b - a)t}{3}.$$

---

[5] If, to the contrary, $\tilde{P}_A > \tilde{P}_B$ in equilibrium, firm A will refrain from undercutting firm B only if $\tilde{P}_A \leqslant (b^2 - a^2)t$. Since, in equilibrium, $\pi_B = \tilde{P}_B\left(1 - \dfrac{a+b}{2}\right)$, firm B can profitably increase $\tilde{P}_B$ so long as $\min\left\{V - (1 - b)^2 t, V - \left(\dfrac{b - a}{2}\right)^2 t\right\} > (b^2 - a^2)t$—i.e., the increase in firm B's price will not lead to the market being uncovered at B's margins, which is the case given our assumption that $V > 5t$.

This is the regular Nash equilibrium prices without any policy constraint. The price-matching policy adopted by firm A has no bearing on the equilibrium outcome. In this case, firm A, having less hinterland consumers, worries less about the loss of revenues from its intramarginal consumers when it tries to create incremental sales by undercutting firm B's price. This fact encourages firm A to price aggressively to gain market share even though firm B has little incentive to undercut firm A's price. In the case $a + b \geqslant 1$ — i.e., firm A is located further away from the left end (more hinterland customers) than firm B from the right end — we have multiple equilibria in the subgame.

Lemma 3.   For $a + b \geqslant 1$, the equilibria of the subgame are characterized by $(b - a)(2 - b - a)t \leqslant \tilde{P}_A = \tilde{P}_B \leqslant (b^2 - a^2)t$.

Proof: see appendix (3).

To shrink the set of Nash equilibria in the case where $a + b \geqslant 1$, we notice that firm A, having adopted the price-matching policy, desires to set $P_A = (b^2 - a^2)t$ and to be a price follower in this subgame. This is so since firm A has a more favorable market location except when $a = b$. Having more hinterland consumers, firm A loses relatively more revenues from its intramarginal consumers in its pursuit for more market share by undercutting firm B's price. Firm A can reason as follows: For any $P_B \in [(b - a)(2 - b - a)t, (b^2 - a^2)t]$, setting $P_A = (b^2 - a^2)t$ is always the best response since consumers pay P_B at firm A. However, the choice of $P_A < (b^2 - a^2)t$ is not the best response to firm B if the latter ever charges a price $P_B \in [P_A, (b^2 - a^2)t]$. Having adopted the price-matching policy, $P_A = (b^2 - a^2)t$ weakly dominates any other equilibrium strategies for firm A.[6]

The equilibrium payoffs for both firms in this subgame are given below:

$$\pi_A^2 = \begin{cases} \dfrac{(b + a + 2)^2 (b - a)t}{18} & \text{if } a + b < 1 \\[2mm] \dfrac{(b + a)^2 (b - a)t}{2} & \text{if } a + b \geqslant 1 \end{cases}$$

$$\pi_B^2 = \begin{cases} \dfrac{(4 - b - a)^2 (b - a)t}{18} & \text{if } a + b < 1 \\[2mm] \dfrac{(2 - a - b)(b + a)(b - a)t}{2} & \text{if } a + b \geqslant 1. \end{cases}$$

Note that, in this subgame, if $a = b$, $\tilde{P}_A = \tilde{P}_B = 0$ and $\pi_A = \pi_B = 0$ as

---

[6] This is, in essence, the same kind of argument that Logan [1989] has used when he considers the trembles on firm B's price to refine the multiple equilibria commonly encountered in a game involving the price-matching policy.

expected, since firm A has a zero conjecture about firm B. Furthermore, firm A in this subgame will never get a payoff less than that of the regular Nash equilibrium without any policy constraint, a fact critical to firm A's choice in the second stage.

Subgame 3 $(\bar{G}_A G_B)$

In this subgame, firm B has adopted the price-matching policy while firm A has not. Since the analysis here is essentially the same as in the last case, I state the equilibrium payoffs below without proof:

$$
\pi_A^3 = \begin{cases} \dfrac{(2 - a - b)(a + b)(b - a)t}{2} & \text{if } a + b \leqslant 1 \\[2ex] \dfrac{(b + a + 2)^2(b - a)t}{18} & \text{if } a + b > 1. \end{cases}
$$

$$
\pi_B^3 = \begin{cases} \dfrac{(2 - a - b)^2(b - a)t}{2} & \text{if } a + b \leqslant 1 \\[2ex] \dfrac{(4 - b - a)^2(b - a)t}{18} & \text{if } a + b > 1. \end{cases}
$$

Note also that firm B in this subgame will get a payoff at least as large as that of the regular Nash equilibrium without any policy constraint.

Subgame 4 $(\bar{G}_A \bar{G}_B)$

In this subgame, both firms have a zero conjecture about each other. It is well-known that a unique equilibrium exists for any given a and b in this subgame and the payoffs are given by:[7]

$$
\pi_A^4 = \frac{(b + a + 2)^2(b - a)t}{18}, \quad \pi_B^4 = \frac{(4 - b - a)^2(b - a)t}{18}.
$$

IV. COLLUSIVE PRICING AND MINIMUM DIFFERENTIATION

In the second stage of the game, both firms, anticipating the subsequent price competition, simultaneously choose whether or not to adopt the price-matching policy. The normal form of the game in the second stage is given in figure 1. By inspection, it is seen that G_A and G_B are dominant strategies for each firm.[8] This outcome is quite natural. First, a firm can remove its

---

[7] See, for instance, De Palma, et al. [1985].
[8] It can be easily verified that $\pi_A^1 > \pi_A^3$, $\pi_A^2 \geqslant \pi_A^4$, $\pi_B^1 > \pi_B^2$, and $\pi_B^3 \geqslant \pi_B^4$.

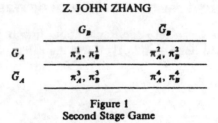

	G_B	$\bar{G}_B$
G_A	$\pi_A^1,\,\pi_B^1$	$\pi_A^2,\,\pi_B^2$
$\bar{G}_A$	$\pi_A^3,\,\pi_B^3$	$\pi_A^4,\,\pi_B^4$

Figure 1
Second Stage Game

rival's incentives to price aggressively by adopting the price-matching policy itself if the rival has already adopted such a policy. Further, if the rival has not adopted the policy, a unilateral adoption by the firm is desirable since, in the Hotelling model, a firm prefers to be a price follower and the price-matching policy has the effect of placing the rival in the position of the price leader.[9] This result confirms, in the Hotelling model, that the price-matching policy facilitates tacit collusion.

In the first stage, both firms choose their product locations independently. Firm A chooses a to maximize its payoff given below:

$$\pi_A = \begin{cases} \min\left\{V - a^2t, V - \left(\dfrac{b-a}{2}\right)^2 t,\, V - (1-b)^2 t\right\}\dfrac{a+b}{2} & \text{if } a < b \\[3mm] \min\left\{V - a^2t, V - (1-b)^2 t\right\}\dfrac{1}{2} & \text{if } a = b \\[3mm] \min\left\{V - b^2t,\, V - \left(\dfrac{b-a}{2}\right)^2 t, V - (1-a)^2 t\right\}\left(1 - \dfrac{a+b}{2}\right) & \text{if } a > b. \end{cases}$$

Here, we allow firm A to locate on either side of firm B. Similarly, firm B chooses b to maximize its payoff given below:

$$\pi_B = \begin{cases} \min\left\{V - a^2t, V - \left(\dfrac{b-a}{2}\right)^2 t,\, V - (1-b)^2 t\right\}\left(1 - \dfrac{a+b}{2}\right) & \text{if } a < b \\[3mm] \min\left\{V - a^2t, V - (1-b)^2 t\right\}\dfrac{1}{2} & \text{if } a = b \\[3mm] \min\left\{V - b^2t,\, V - \left(\dfrac{b-a}{2}\right)^2 t, V - (1-a)^2 t\right\}\dfrac{a+b}{2} & \text{if } a > b. \end{cases}$$

We now proceed to chracterize the equilibrium conditions in this location game.

Lemma 4. For $V > 5t$, in any equilibrium of the location game $(\tilde{a}, \tilde{b})$, we necessarily have $\tilde{a} = \tilde{b}$.

Proof: Suppose, to the contrary, there exists an equilibrium where $\tilde{a} \neq \tilde{b}$. Then, either $\tilde{a} < \tilde{b}$ or $\tilde{a} > \tilde{b}$. In the former case, we have:.

---

[9] For a general discussion on the choice of roles of leader and follower in the context of duopoly, see Dowrick [1986].

$$\pi_A(\tilde{a}, \tilde{b}) = \min\left\{V - \tilde{a}^2 t, V - \left(\frac{\tilde{b} - \tilde{a}}{2}\right)^2 t, V - (1 - \tilde{b})^2 t\right\} \frac{\tilde{a} + \tilde{b}}{2}.$$

Consider an arbitrarily small deviation by firm A, $a^d = \tilde{a} + \varepsilon$, where $\varepsilon > 0$, so that $a^d < \tilde{b}$ holds. Then, we have:

$$\pi_A(a^d, \tilde{b}) = \min\left\{V - (a^d)^2 t, V - \left(\frac{\tilde{b} - a^d}{2}\right)^2 t, V - (1 - \tilde{b})^2 t\right\}$$

$$\left(\frac{a^d + \tilde{b}}{2}\right) > \pi_A(\tilde{a}, \tilde{b}).$$

Thus, $(\tilde{a}, \tilde{b})$ cannot be an equilibrium. Similarly, in the case $\tilde{a} > \tilde{b}$, firm B will have incentives to relocate. Q.E.D.

Lemma 4 is intuitive. Since tacit collusion prevails in the market as a result of both firms' adopting the price-matching policy, price competition has been suppressed to become a secondary factor in location decisions. Thus competition for consumers through product locations is intensified. Each firm will locate as close to the other firm as possible, given the location of the latter firm, to create more hinterland customers and to secure a maximum market share. This is, of course, necessarily the case whichever side a firm decides to locate relative to its rival.

Theorem 1. For $V > 5t$, the unique Nash equilibrium in the location game is for both firms to locate at $\frac{1}{2}$ — i.e., to follow the principle of minimum differentiation.

Proof: Since $\tilde{a} = \tilde{b}$ in any equilibrium by Lemma 4, we have:

$$\pi_A^* = \min\{V - \tilde{a}^2 t, V - (1 - \tilde{b})^2 t\}\tfrac{1}{2}$$

$$\pi_B^* = \min\{V - \tilde{a}^2 t, V - (1 - \tilde{b})^2 t\}\tfrac{1}{2}.$$

Then, the equilibrium in the location stage is fully characterized by:

(1) $\lim\limits_{\varepsilon \to 0_+} \pi_A(\tilde{a} - \varepsilon, \tilde{b}) \leqslant \pi_A^*$

(2) $\lim\limits_{\varepsilon \to 0_+} \pi_A(\tilde{a} + \varepsilon, \tilde{b}) \leqslant \pi_A^*$

(3) $\lim\limits_{\varepsilon \to 0_+} \pi_B(\tilde{a}, \tilde{b} - \varepsilon) \leqslant \pi_B^*$

(4) $\lim\limits_{\varepsilon \to 0_+} \pi_B(\tilde{a}, \tilde{b} + \varepsilon) \leqslant \pi_B^*.$

That is, each firm lacks any incentive to relocate slightly to the other side of the rival firm's equilibrium location. From inequality (1), we have $\dfrac{\tilde{a} + \tilde{b}}{2} \leqslant \frac{1}{2}$.

From inequality (4), we have $1 - \dfrac{\tilde{a} + \tilde{b}}{2} \leqslant \frac{1}{2}$. These two inequalities imply

$\bar{a} + \bar{b} = 1$. Since $\bar{a} = \bar{b}$ in any equilibrium, we must have $\bar{a} = \bar{b} = \frac{1}{2}$. It is easy to check that inequalities (2) and (3) are both satisfied.   Q.E.D.

The equilibrium outcome is natural. Not anticipating any significant price competition, a firm is at a disadvantage if it locates on the either side of one-half, since the other firm is assured of the maximum market share by leapfrogging and locating arbitrarily close to the former on the long side. The only location where a firm is guaranteed at least one-half of the market is at the middle point. Thus minimum differentiation arises from independent location decisions by both firms.

V. CONCLUSION

This paper has shown that, when each firm promises to meet or beat the prices of its rival, collusive outcomes ensue in the sense that the market price is increased. The suppression of pricing rivalry does not stifle all competition, but instead diverts the firms' competition for market shares to their choices of product locations. Because of the price-matching practice, the firms reduce the extent of their product differentiation.

This paper has also shown that the validity of the principle of minimum differentiation does not depend on any exogenous difference in supply or demand attributes, or any specific conjectural variations, or the complete suppression of price competition. The key to the principle of minimum differentiation is the moderation of price competition. This is true in De Palma, et al [1985], where firms' "inherent attributes" and consumer heterogeneity dampen price competition, and in Rhee, et al [1992], where some unobservable product attribute suppresses pricing as a competitive instrument. It is also true in the case where firms collude on price through either bargaining (Jehiel [1992]) or punishment (Friedman and Thisse [1993]). Minimum differentiation arises here from the firms' strategic interactions in the marketplace: price competition is relegated to a secondary effect by both firms' independent decisions to adopt the price-matching policy, and market expansion thereby becomes a predominant concern for the competing firms in their location decisions. From this vantage point, one can expect minimum differentiation to occur in diverse institutional settings.

Z. JOHN ZHANG,   ACCEPTED DECEMBER 1994
John M. Olin School of Business,
Washington University in St. Louis,
St. Louis, MO 63130-4899,
USA

APPENDIX

(1) Since the effect of market expansion is the same for both firms and market expansion at one margin is less profitable than at two margins, it suffices to show

that firm A, as the price setter in the market, will lower its price if its left margin is uncovered—i.e., if $P_A > V - a^2 t$. Since the proofs for $a < b$ and $a = b$ are essentially the same, I only consider $a < b$ here.

Given $P_A > V - a^2 t$, one can find $X_A = a - \sqrt{\dfrac{V - P_A}{t}} > 0$ so that the consumers located at X_A are indifferent between buying and not buying from firm A. Then,

$$\pi_A = P_A \left(\min \left\{ \frac{a+b}{2}, a + \sqrt{\frac{V - P_A}{t}} \right\} - a + \sqrt{\frac{V - P_A}{t}} \right) \quad \text{if } 0 < a < b \leqslant 1.$$

Since the right margin is assumed to be covered, we must have $\dfrac{a+b}{2} \leqslant a + \sqrt{\dfrac{V - P_A}{t}}$. Therefore,

$$\pi_A = P_A \left(\frac{b-a}{2} + \sqrt{\frac{V - P_A}{t}} \right).$$

By simple manipulations, we obtain the left derivative of the firm's profit function below:

$$\lim_{\varepsilon \to 0_+} \frac{\pi_A(P_A) - \pi_A(P_A - \varepsilon)}{\varepsilon} = \frac{b-a}{2} + \sqrt{\frac{V - P_A}{t}} \left(1 - \frac{P_A}{2(V - P_A)} \right)$$

$$\leqslant \sqrt{\frac{V - P_A}{t}} \left(2 - \frac{P_A}{2(V - P_A)} \right) < 0.$$

The first inequality comes from $\dfrac{a+b}{2} \leqslant a + \sqrt{\dfrac{V - P_A}{t}}$. The second inequality comes from the assumption $P_A > V - a^2 t$ and given assumption $V > 5t$. This means $P_A \leqslant V - a^2 t$ regardless of firm B's price. The same reasoning applies to all other margins for both firms.   Q.E.D.

(2) For any $P_A \in [0 \quad H_A]$ and $P_B \in [0 \quad H_B]$, the market is covered. In the case where $a = b$, the market shares for both firms are assumed to be $\frac{1}{2}$. The proof here is based on the case $a < b$, but the case for $a = b$ can obviously be handled in the same way. We have for firm A:

$$\pi_A(P_A, P_B) = \min \{P_A, P_B\} \frac{a+b}{2}.$$

Since $\pi_A(H_A, P_B) = \min \{H_A, P_B\} \dfrac{a+b}{2} \geqslant \min \{P_A, P_B\} \dfrac{a+b}{2}$ for all $P_A \in [0 \quad H_A]$, H_A is a weakly dominating strategy for firm A. Similarly, H_B is a weakly dominating strategy for firm B.   Q.E.D.

(3) The equilibria where $\tilde{P}_A = \tilde{P}_B$ are fully characterized by the following conditions:

$$(5) \qquad (\tilde{P}_A - c)\frac{a+b}{2} \geqslant (\tilde{P}_A - c - \varepsilon)\left(\frac{\varepsilon + (b^2 - a^2)t}{2(b-a)t} \right)$$

$$(6) \qquad (\tilde{P}_B - c)\left(1 - \frac{a+b}{2} \right) \geqslant (\tilde{P}_B - c - \varepsilon)\left(1 - \frac{a+b}{2} \right)$$

$$(7) \qquad (\tilde{P}_B - c)\left(1 - \frac{a+b}{2} \right) \geqslant (\tilde{P}_B - c + \varepsilon)\left(1 - \frac{\varepsilon + (b^2 - a^2)t}{2(b-a)t} \right)$$

where $\varepsilon > 0$ is arbitrarily small. Inequality (5) is the condition under which firm A has no incentive to deviate by lowering its price. Given $\bar{P}_A = \bar{P}_B$, firm A has no incentive to raise its price since doing so is inconsequential for firm A. Inequality (6) and (7) are the conditions under which firm B has no incentive to deviate by either lowering or raising its price. For any $\varepsilon > 0$, inequality (6) is satisfied since firm B has no incentive to lower its price once the market is covered. For an arbitrarily small ε, inequality (5) implies $\bar{P}_A = \bar{P}_B \leqslant (b^2 - a^2)t$. Inequality (7) implies $\bar{P}_A = \bar{P}_B \geqslant (b - a)(2 - b - a)t$. For $a + b \geqslant 1$, the set defined by these last two inequalities are not empty.   Q.E.D.

REFERENCES

BECKMANN, M.J., 1976, 'Spatial Price Policies Revisited', *The Bell Journal of Economics and Management Science*, 7, pp. 619–630.

BELTON, T. M., 1987, 'A Model of Duopoly and Meeting or Beating Competition', *International Journal of Industrial Organization*, 5, pp. 399–417.

D'ASPREMONT, C., GABSZEWICZ, J. J. and THISSE, J. F., 1979, 'On Hotelling's "Stability in Competition"', *Econometrica*, 47, pp. 1145–1150.

DE PALMA, A., GINSBURGH, V., PAPAGEORGIOU, Y. Y. and THISSE, J. F., 1985, 'The Principle of Minimum Differentiation Holds Under Sufficient Heterogeneity', *Econometrica*, 53, pp. 767–781.

DIXIT, A. K. and STIGLITZ, J., 1977, 'Monopolistic Competition and Optimum Product Diversity', *The American Economic Review*, 67, pp. 297–308.

DOWRICK, S., 1986, 'von Stackelberg and Cournot Duopoly: Choosing Roles', *Rand Journal of Economics*, 17, pp. 251–260.

DOYLE, C., 1988, 'Different Selling Strategies in Bertrand Oligopoly', *Economics Letters*, 28, pp. 387–390.

ECONOMIDES, N., 1986, 'Minimal and Maximal Product Differentiation in Hotelling's Duopoly', *Economics Letters*, 21, pp. 121–126.

FRIEDMAN, J. W. and THISSE, J. F., 1993, 'Partial Collusion Fosters Minimum Product Differentiation', *Rand Journal of Economics*, 24, pp. 631–645.

HAUSER, J. R., 1988, 'Competitive Price and Positioning Strategies', *Marketing Science*, 7, pp. 76–91.

HESS, J. D. and GERSTNER., E., 1991, 'Price–Matching Policies: An Empirical Case', *Managerial and Decision Economics*, 12, pp. 305–315.

HOTELLING, H., 1929, 'Stability in Competition', *Economic Journal*, 39, pp. 41–57.

JEHIEL, P., 1992, 'Product Differentiation and Price Collusion', *International Journal of Industrial Organization*, 10, pp. 633–641.

LIN, Y. J., 1988, 'Price–matching in a Model of Equilibrium Price Dispersion', *Southern Economic Journal*, 55, pp. 57–69.

LOGAN, J. W. and LUTTER, R. W., 1989, 'Guaranteed Lowest Prices: Do They Facilitate Collusion?' *Economics Letters*, 31, pp. 189–192.

NEVEN, D., 1985, 'Two Stage (Perfect) Equilibrium in Hotelling's Model', *The Journal of Industrial Economics*, 33, pp. 317–325.

NEVEN, D., 1986, 'On Hotelling's Competition with Non–Uniform Customer Distributions', *Economics Letters*, 21, pp. 121–126.

PNG, I. P. L. and HIRSHLEIFER, D., 1987, 'Price Discrimination Through Offers to Match Price', *Journal of Business*, 60, pp. 365–383.

RHEE, B., DE PALMA, A., FORNELL, C. and THISSE, J. F., 1992, 'Restoring the Principle of Minimum Differentiation in Product Positioning', *Journal of Economics and Management Strategy*, 1, pp. 475–505.

SALOP, S. C., 1986, 'Practices that (Credibly) Facilitate Oligopoly Co-Ordination', in STIGLITZ, J. E. and MATHEWSON, G. F. (eds.), *New Developments in the Analysis of Market Structure* (MIT Press).

SPENCE, M., 1976, 'Product Selection, Fixed Costs, and Monopolistic Competition', *Review of Economic Studies*, 43, pp. 217–235.

STAHL, K., 1982, 'Location and Spatial Pricing Theory with Nonconvex Transportation Cost Schedules', *The Bell Journal of Economics and Management Science*, 13, pp. 575–582.

Pricing Access Services

Skander Essegaier • Sunil Gupta • Z. John Zhang

The Stern School of Business, New York University, 44 West Fourth Street, Room 8-85,
New York, New York 10012
Columbia Business School, Columbia University, Uris Hall, Room 508, 3022 Broadway,
New York, New York 10027
University of Pennsylvania, Wharton School, 3620 Locust Walk, Suite 1400,
Philadelphia, Pennsylvania 19104-6371
sessegai@stern.nyu.edu • sg37@columbia.edu • zz25@columbia.edu

Abstract

Many established industries, such as the online service industry, the telecommunication industry, or the fitness club industry, are access service industries. When using services in these industries, consumers pay for the privilege of accessing the firm's facilities but do not acquire any right to the facility itself. A firm's pricing decisions in access industries frequently come down to a simple choice among *flat fee* pricing, *usage* pricing, or *two-part tariff* pricing. However, it is not so simple for firms in those industries to make this choice. Access service firms typically face a mix of consumers who have intrinsically different usage rates. A key characteristic of access service firms, however, is that the cost of providing an additional minute of usage is typically negligible, as long as the firm has the necessary capacity to serve its customers. Service capacity, which corresponds to the total available time on a firm's system, is often limited.

In this paper, we show that service capacity and consumer usage heterogeneity are two important factors that determine a firm's optimal choice. We develop a model that incorporates these two salient characteristics shared by access industries and study what determines a firm's choice among the three alternative pricing structures (*flat fee* pricing, *usage* pricing, or *two-part tariff* pricing). Our analysis shows that, in the presence of consumer usage heterogeneity, service capacity mediates a firm's optimal choice in a complex, yet predictable way. A firm's choice also hinges on whether heavy or light users are more valuable in terms of their willingness-to-pay on a per-unit-capacity basis. The presence of both consumer usage heterogeneity and capacity constraints prompts a firm to choose its pricing structure to attract a desired customer mix and to price discriminate. As a result, two-part tariff pricing is not always optimal in access industries, and a firm's pricing structure can vary in a complex way with the interaction of those two factors.

Specifically, we show that when light users are more valuable, a firm may use a two-part tariff or a flat fee, depending on whether the firm is constrained by its service capacity, but never charge a usage price alone or offer any signing bonus (a negative flat fee or a flat payment to customers). When heavy users are more valuable, a firm may choose to set a usage price, a signing bonus plus a usage price, or a flat fee. Interestingly, regardless of whether heavy or light users are more valuable in an access service industry, only flat rate pricing is a sustainable pricing structure once the industry has developed sufficient excess capacity.

We also show that the optimal pricing strategy in access industries can have some intriguing, nonintuitive implications that have not been explored elsewhere. For instance, when the industry capacity is unevenly distributed between competing firms, the large-capacity firm may well be advised to increase, rather than to decrease, its price to accommodate the small firm. It would be too costly and too tactless for the large firm to do otherwise. In fact, the strategy of accommodation calls on the larger firm to retreat in both light and heavy user markets and leave more of its capacity idle and more of the market demand unmet when the small firm's capacity (hence, the industry capacity) increases. This implies that incremental policy measures that encourage the growth of smaller companies in the presence of a large company can be welfare-decreasing because the growth of a smaller firm can force the retreat of a large company at the expense of market coverage.

Today, services account for two-thirds to three-quarters of the GNP, not only in the United States but also in many industrial countries. Access industries are growing rapidly to exert profound impact on today's economy. However, service pricing in general and pricing access services in particular have not received adequate attention in the literature. In this paper, we take the first step in understanding how capacity constraints and consumer usage heterogeneity mediate the choice of pricing structures in both monopolistic and competitive contexts.

(*Pricing Strategy; Service Pricing; Competitive Strategies; Access Services; Capacity; Equilibrium Models*)

0732-2399/02/2102/0139/$05.00
1526-548X electronic ISSN

1. Introduction

"Access industries" are industries in which consumers pay for the privilege to access a facility but do not acquire any right to, or "use up," the facility itself. Companies such as Bloomberg, Reuters, Associated Press, and LexisNexis, for instance, sell access to information content. Internet service providers such as America Online and AT&T WorldNet Service sell access to the World Wide Web as well as to proprietary content. In addition to the information and media industries, firms offer access services in many other industries such as communications, entertainment, and health clubs. In pricing their access services, firms in these diverse industries frequently choose a simple pricing structure of either *flat fee* pricing, *usage* pricing, or a combination of the two, commonly referred to as *two-part tariff* pricing. In this paper, we investigate what a firm in access industries ought to consider in making such a choice.

Access industries share four salient characteristics:

- Capacity constraint: Firms can allow only a limited number of consumers to access the service simultaneously at any time, and this capacity constraint is fairly rigid in the short run.
- Usage heterogeneity: Consumers have different usage rates for the service. For instance, 97% of AT&T Worldnet customers are *light users*. Under the current flat fee pricing schedule, they average 25 hours of online usage per month. The remaining 3% are *heavy users*, or "campers" in Internet parlance, averaging 400 hours and tying up 30% of WorldNet network resources (*Investor's Business Daily* 1998). A similar usage pattern holds for other Internet access service providers.
- Low marginal cost: Provided that capacity is available, the marginal cost of serving a customer is very low and, to a large extent, independent of the consumer's usage rate. For instance, in the telecom industry, PCS carriers' operating costs are essentially unrelated to minutes of usage because of their large empty networks (*PCS Week* 1997).
- Competition: These industries are also competitive and offer differentiated products and services (Stroh 1998).

Despite these common structural characteristics, the choice of pricing structure in access industries is by no means common. Sports clubs, ski resorts, and cable TV companies, for instance, tend to use a flat rate pricing scheme. Long distance phone companies typically adopt usage pricing, charging by the minute of usage. Many Internet service providers and local telephone companies use two-part tariff pricing. In fact, the pricing structure may even vary across firms and over time in the same industry as firms frequently experiment with different pricing schemes at great cost (*PCS Week* 1997). AT&T WorldNet Service, for instance, started out with two-part tariff pricing and then switched to a flat fee, thus initiating the industry-wide move to unlimited Internet access for $19.95 per month. It then reverted back again to its more usage-based pricing strategy (*Investor's Business Daily* 1998). All these variations are rather puzzling in the context of the existing literature, suggesting that a firm's choice of its pricing structure is by no means simple.

The existing literature in economics strongly advocates two-part tariffs as the pricing structure of choice for a profit-maximizing firm with market power. In a classical article, Oi (1971) shows that a nondiscriminating two-part tariff scheme allows a monopolist to be both allocatively efficient, setting its usage price at the marginal cost or close to it, and profit-maximizing, using a flat fee to extract all or most consumer surplus. A number of follow-up studies explore the determinants of the optimal two-part tariff and its welfare implications in different demand and supply conditions (Schmalensee 1981, Calem and Spulber 1984, Hayes 1987, Stole 1995, Armstrong and Vickers 1999). More recently, in the context of nonlinear pricing with random participation constraints, Rochet and Stole (1999) show that the optimal nonlinear pricing schedule takes the simple form of cost-plus-fee schedules, once again affirming the optimality of two-part tariff pricing. However, none of these studies considers capacity constraints and consumer usage heterogeneity. As a result, neither sanctions the choice of usage pricing or flat fee pricing. Access industries need to look elsewhere for guidance in making their choices.

Research on the pricing implications of capacity constraints dates back at least to Edgeworth (1897), when he noted that a firm's pricing strategy is "indeterminant" in a price competition game with capacity constraints. Many economists have subsequently studied this game under different institutional assumptions and establish that capacity constraints underlie strategic interactions among competing firms in the marketplace (Kreps and Scheinkman 1983, Peters 1984, Davidson and Deneckere 1986, Benoit and Krishna 1987, Maggi 1996). However, this line of inquiry does not consider nonlinear pricing or consumer usage heterogeneity and once again cannot address the issue of choosing a pricing structure in access industries. One study that does consider nonlinear pricing and capacity related issues is Scotchmer (1985). She shows that when facilities can be shared and consumers care about the number of sharers, two-tier pricing, e.g., the membership fee plus a usage price, can arise in a symmetrical Nash equilibrium where all competing firms have an identical, fixed size. In our study, two-tier pricing is not motivated by congestion but by a firm's desire to exact the maximum return on its limited capacity when consumer usage intensity differs. As we will show shortly, capacity constraints are entirely different from congestion as a determinant of a firm's optimal pricing structure both in terms of modeling and strategy prescriptions, especially when firms are asymmetrical.

In this paper, we develop a model that incorporates the four salient characteristics shared by access industries and study what determines a firm's choice among the three alternative pricing structures.[1] Our analysis shows that service capacity mediates a firm's optimal choice in a complex yet predictable way. In addition, a firm's choice also hinges on whether heavy or light users are more valuable in terms of their willingness to pay on a per-unit-capacity basis. The presence of both consumer usage heterogeneity

and capacity constraints prompts a firm to choose its pricing structure in order to attract a desired customer mix and to price discriminate. As a result, two-part tariff pricing is not always optimal in access industries. Specifically, when light users are more valuable, a firm may use a two-part tariff or a flat fee, depending on whether the firm is constrained by its service capacity, but never charge a usage price alone or offer any signing bonus (a negative flat fee or a flat payment to customers). When heavy users are more valuable, a firm may choose to set a usage price, or a signing bonus plus a usage price, or a flat fee. Interestingly, regardless of whether heavy or light users are more valuable in an access industry, only flat fee pricing is a sustainable pricing structure once the industry has developed sufficient *excess* capacity.

In the following sections, we first analyze a monopolist's choice in a market where light users are more attractive to develop the basic intuition. Then, we incorporate competition into this basic model and extend our analysis to the case where heavy users are more valuable. Finally, we conclude with suggestions for future research.

2. Pricing Monopolistic Access Service

Consider the case of a monopolist service provider. We assume that the firm is located at the left extremity of the Hotelling line bounded between 0 and 1. For its service, the firm can charge an access fee f and a usage price p per capacity unit (e.g., rides at an amusement park or access time). Because the marginal cost of providing access service is, in general, negligible, we set it to zero. The capacity of the firm at a given point in time is fixed at K and the costs for the capacity are sunk. With this setup, we can focus on a firm's short-term pricing decisions.

There are two types of consumers in the market: *heavy users* (h) and *light users* (l). Heavy users, accounting for a fraction α of the market, use d_h units of capacity when accessing the service, while light users, accounting for the rest of the market, use d_l units of capacity with $d_l < d_h$. Both d_h and d_l are as-

---

[1] We limit our attention to the three pricing schemes not because they are more profitable than some more complex multipart pricing schemes, but because firms frequently focus on these three options for the sake of simplicity, flexibility, and ease of administration (Curle 1998, Wilson 1993, p. 136).

sumed to be inelastic to the changes in price. Although this assumption is made to simplify our analysis, evidence seems to suggest that it is a good first-order approximation of reality in many industries, at least in the short run. In the Internet service industry—where flat fee pricing is common, for instance, despite zero marginal price—an overwhelming majority of users spend an average of only 25 hours online per month. This suggests that consumer usage rate is more a function of individual usage propensity than a function of price. In the concluding section, we will discuss how our conclusions may change if we relax this assumption.

In our basic model, we assume that heavy and light users have the same reservation price V for their ideal access service. We can easily extend this analysis to the case where light users have a higher reservation price with our conclusions essentially intact.[2] Thus, the analysis of our basic model is applicable to those service industries where heavy users are mostly the consumers with a low opportunity cost of time. For instance, a senior citizen who reads *The Wall Street Journal* from cover to cover may not be willing to pay a higher price than an academic scholar who only scans the headlines and browses occasional articles. A college student who spends over five hours a day on the Internet everyday chatting or playing games may not be willing to pay more for the access than a business professional who spends less than an hour a day online.[3] However, when an access service, such as the cellular phone service, is used predominantly for business, heavy users may have a higher willingness to pay for the service. In §4, we will explore a firm's pricing decisions in that case.

Without loss of generality, we normalize the total number of customers in the market to 1. Then, the maximum usage rate in the market is $\bar{d} = \alpha d_h + (1 - \alpha)d_l$, which is also the total capacity required to

service the market. To introduce consumer heterogeneity in preference, we follow a well-established modeling convention, assuming that both heavy and light users are located uniformly along the Hotelling line. A consumer located at $0 \le x \le 1$ incurs the transportation cost of tx to access the monopolist's service. This cost measures the disutility that the consumer suffers when the service is away from the consumer's ideal point so that the further away the consumer is from the monopolist, the lower is the consumer's preference for the monopolist's service. Since consumers have a reservation price of V, the monopolist can never charge a positive price for its service and still attract a consumer located at a distance greater than. $\gamma = V/t$. We assume $\gamma \ge 3$ to ensure that the monopolist covers the whole market if it is not capacity constrained.

2.1. Monopolist Without Capacity Constraint

Our assumptions about two types of consumers in the market and the firm's ability to use a two-part tariff effectively allow the monopolist to price discriminate between these two segments. For any given f (fee) and p (usage price), light users pay $P_l = f + pd_l$ and heavy users pay $P_h = f + pd_h$. At first blush, one might expect that a segmented pricing based on the usage rate, charging a different type of consumer a different total price, is always optimal for the monopolist. However, this is not the case when the monopolist is not capacity constrained, as the following proposition makes clear.

PROPOSITION 1. *When the monopolist is not capacity constrained ($K > \bar{d}$), it charges only a flat fee and all consumers who purchase the access service pay the same amount, irrespective of their usage rate.*

Proposition 1 is true because in the absence of any capacity constraint, the monopolist is only concerned with penetrating the market profitably, which means in this case covering the entire market since $\gamma \ge 3$. The optimal price for the monopolist is the maximum price it can charge while still attracting all consumers to buy, or $f = P_l = P_h = V - t$. Indeed, Proposition 1 seems hardly surprising, given that both types of consumers have the same reservation price for their

---

[2]Let $v_h d_h$ and $v_l d_l$ be the reservation prices for heavy and light users, respectively. We can show that our conclusions are not altered, given that $v_h d_h \le v_h d_h(2 - d_l/d_h)$. The details of analysis are available from the website for *Marketing Science* at http://mktsci.pubs.informs.org.

[3]AT&T classifies those Internet users who spend an average of 150 hours per month online as heavy users. See *Investor's Business Daily* (1998).

ideal service. Intuition would suggest that segmented pricing exploits the difference in consumer willingness to pay at the segment level. Absent of this difference, one would expect that the monopolist has no motivation to use segmented pricing and is inclined to use a flat fee to attract the consumers who are most willing to pay, regardless of their usage rates. However, this intuition is misleading, as it ignores the mediation of capacity and consumer usage heterogeneity in a firm's pricing decision. As we show now, capacity constraint turns on the need for price discrimination: The monopolist will use segmented pricing even when there is no difference in consumer willingness to pay at the segment level, provided that it is capacity constrained.

2.2. Monopolist With Capacity Constraint

For any given capacity $0 \leq K \leq \bar{d}$, the monopolist must decide what pricing structure to use to engage its limited capacity optimally. For any given (f, p), all light users located to the left of x_l who gain positive surplus will make a purchase, where $x_l = (V - f - pd_l)/t$ is the location of the marginal light users who are just indifferent between buying and not buying. Similarly, all heavy users to the left of $x_h = (V - f - pd_h)/t$ will also make a purchase. Given that the total capacity engaged to service these purchases cannot exceed the total capacity available, the monopolist's optimization problem is given below:

$$\max_{(f,p)} (1 - \alpha)x_l(f + pd_l) + \alpha x_h(f + pd_h), \quad (1)$$

$$\text{s.t.} \quad 0 \leq x_l \leq 1, \quad (2)$$

$$0 \leq x_h \leq 1, \quad (3)$$

$$(1 - \alpha)x_l d_l + \alpha x_h d_h \leq K. \quad (4)$$

The analysis of the monopolist's optimization problem is fully detailed in Appendix 1. The solution is illustrated in Figure 1. There we see that when the monopolist's capacity is sufficiently small, or $K \leq \bar{K}^a = \gamma(d_h - d_l)(1 - \alpha)d_l/2d_h$, it draws only the light users located nearby because they are the least resource-demanding and the most profitable customers. The parameter $\bar{K}^a$ is determined by making sure that the constraint $x_h \geq 0$ is binding. To sell all avail-

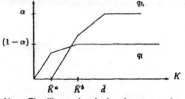

Figure 1   Monopolist's Optimal Customer Mix Under Capacity Constraint

Note: The illustration is for the case where $\gamma \leq 2d_h/(d_h - d_l)$. When $\gamma > 2d_h/(d_h - d_l)$, the only difference is that the monopolist exhausts light users in the market first before it taps into the heavy user segment.

able capacity to light users, the monopolist simply sets (f, p) so that there are just enough light users to exhaust the capacity, or $(1 - \alpha)x_l d_l = K$. This yields $f + pd_l = V - [K/(1 - \alpha)d_l]t$. To screen out heavy users, the monopolist makes sure $f + pd_h = V$, or $x_h = 0$. The two-part tariff that implements this pricing structure is given by

$$f = V - \frac{Kd_h}{(d_h - d_l)(1 - \alpha)d_l}t \quad \text{and}$$

$$p = \frac{K}{(d_h - d_l)(1 - \alpha)d_l}t, \quad (5)$$

where $f > 0$ and $p > 0$.

The fact that the monopolist sets $p > 0$ in this case indicates that it tends to charge heavy users more than it does light users. However, price discrimination arises here not because it allows the monopolist's profit from each segment to rise (the monopolist's profit from the heavy user segment is zero), but because it allows the firm to engage *all* of its capacity in the light user segment to maximize its overall profit. This indicates that the primary motivation for the monopolist to use two-part tariff pricing in this case is not to price discriminate but to attract a desired customer mix to engage its limited capacity. Indeed, this primary motivation prevails throughout our basic model where there exists no difference in willingness to pay for access service at the segment level. This explains why, as illustrated in Figure 2, the monopolist lowers the fixed-fee component of its price as its capacity expands ($K \leq \bar{K}^a$), while simultaneously increasing the usage price. The monopolist simply wants to attract more light users while sifting out

Figure 2   Monopolist's Optimal Pricing Structure

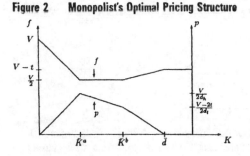

heavy users. This adjustment has the intended effect because a higher usage price hits heavy users harder than it does light users. The combination of these two changes enables the monopolist to deliver more incentives to light users without offering any to heavy users.

As the monopolist's capacity continues to increase beyond $\bar{K}^a$, it pulls in light users who are located further away. Eventually, attracting the heavy users located close to the firm becomes more profitable than attracting additional light users located far away, despite the fact that the former use up more capacity. This is when the monopolist adjusts its pricing structure to serve both light and heavy users, as illustrated in Figure 1 for $\bar{K}^a \leq K \leq \bar{K}^b$, where $\bar{K}^b = [2\hat{d} - \gamma(d_h - d_l)\alpha d_h]/2d_l$ and $\hat{d} = (1 - \alpha)d_l^2 + \alpha d_h^2$. The optimal mix of light and heavy users, as shown in Appendix 1, is given by the optimal sales in each segment below:

$$q_l = \frac{(1 - \alpha)}{2}\left(\frac{2Kd_l + \gamma(d_h - d_l)\alpha d_h}{\hat{d}}\right), \quad (6)$$

$$q_h = \frac{\alpha}{2}\left(\frac{2Kd_h - \gamma(d_h - d_l)(1 - \alpha)d_l}{\hat{d}}\right). \quad (7)$$

In this case, the monopolist prices its service such that any additional capacity yields the same return whether this incremental capacity is engaged by light users or by heavy users. The two-part tariff that achieves the optimal customer mix is given by

$$f = \frac{V}{2} \quad \text{and} \quad p = \frac{\gamma\hat{d} - 2K}{2\hat{d}}t. \quad (8)$$

By maintaining the level of its fixed fee but decreasing its usage price when it has a larger capacity, the

monopolist offers a larger incremental incentive to heavy users to secure more of them.

At an even greater capacity ($\bar{K}^b \leq K < \hat{d}$), all light users have already become the monopolist's customers. The incremental units of capacity above and beyond $\bar{K}^b$ are all used to attract additional heavy users that remain unserved. The optimal tariff schedule, as shown in Appendix 1, is given by

$$f = V - \frac{\hat{d} - Kd_l}{(d_h - d_l)\alpha d_h}t \quad \text{and} \quad p = \frac{\hat{d} - K}{(d_h - d_l)\alpha d_h}t. \quad (9)$$

In this case, the monopolist continues to lower its usage price all the way to zero (its marginal cost) as its capacity expands to attract more heavy users. In the meantime, it raises the fixed fee so that light users are not getting a free ride.

Thus, when consumers have different usage rates and preferences, customer mix becomes an important strategic consideration for a firm because of its capacity constraint. Capacity constraint motivates the monopolist to focus on the customer mix it attracts, rather than on the total number of customers, in order to reap the maximum return on its scarce resource. To generate the desired customer mix at a given level of capacity, the monopolist must rely on a two-part tariff because this pricing structure offers the flexibility for the monopolist to deliver differential incentives to heavy and light users. This allocative role of two-part tariff pricing is primarily motivated by the supply factor—capacity. Figure 2 shows that the flat fee component need not be flat because it decreases and then increases with a firm's capacity level. The usage price is also not constant. It increases and then decreases with the firm's capacity. These two components of the pricing structure are negatively correlated to ensure that the desired customer mix is obtained in the most remunerative fashion.

As a managerial insight, this analysis shows that a firm must not only pay customary attention to demand factors but also heed its capacity constraint in using a two-part tariff. When a firm faces capacity constraint, it should not have a limited resource priced in an unlimited fashion and it should use a two-part tariff to pull in the desired mix of customers to optimally engage its limited capacity. An oversight of capacity constraint and the allocative role of two-part tariff pricing can prove costly, as AOL and many other Internet companies have found out not long ago. Our analysis also suggests that the two components of a two-part tariff should be negatively correlated. The flat fee is a relatively more effective way to deliver incentives to, or extract surplus from, light users, whereas heavy users are more sensitive to the changes in the usage price. To prepare for the elimination of usage price, a firm should gradually raise its flat fee. Our analysis further points out that when capacity is plentiful, market penetration should be a firm's main strategic focus and a flat fee is the most efficient way to penetrate a market populated by both light and heavy users indiscriminately.

3. Pricing Competitive Access Service

Our analysis of pricing strategies for a monopolist service provider establishes that with no capacity constraint, the monopolist should simply use a flat fee to pursue market penetration. When capacity constrained, it should use a two-part tariff primarily as an allocative device to attract the desired customer mix in order to maximize its overall profit from the limited capacity. However, this analysis falls short of suggesting whether capacity plays the same role in determining a firm's pricing structure in a competitive context. Competition is, after all, the norm in many access industries.

Many questions arise in the presence of competition. Is a flat fee or two-part tariff sustainable? It is not obvious that either pricing scheme can survive competition. A firm that uses a flat fee pricing effectively subsidizes heavy users at the expense of light users and, hence, opens itself up to a rival's attack on light users. A firm that adopts a two-part tariff may be vulnerable to the rival's efforts to peel off either light or heavy users. When a pricing scheme is sustainable, we can ask some further questions. In what ways may service capacity in an industry mediate the optimal pricing structure? Should a firm still pursue either market penetration or the customer mix, de-

pending on whether it faces capacity constraint? If there is a mediating role for capacity, what matters more, the industry capacity or the distribution of industry capacity across firms? How should a firm with a given level of capacity choose its pricing scheme in a competitive context? Our answers to these questions will not only help us understand how to price access services in a competitive environment but also will provide a normative guide for practitioners in setting their prices.

To address these questions, we incorporate competition into our model by introducing a second access service provider at the right extremity of the Hotelling line while maintaining the rest of the assumptions we made in our monopolist model. We refer to the firm located at the left extremity as Firm 1 and at the right as Firm 2. We denote their capacity respectively by K_1 and K_2. Because these two competing firms are symmetric except in capacity, we can focus our analysis on the case where $K_2 \geq K_1$. In addition, we assume that heavy users are sufficiently different from light users in terms of their usage rate, or $d_h \geq 4d_l$.[4]

Competitive strategies for pricing access services are quite complex to analyze. There are a large number of potential equilibria because of competitive interactions with different levels of capacity constraints for both firms. In the light user market, both firms may be local monopolists (the market is uncovered), or secret handshakers (the market is covered but does not overlap), or competitors (they compete for a common subset of light users). When both firms are local monopolists in the light user market, the heavy user market may be uncovered, served by neither, or by a single firm, or by both firms. Moreover, firms may engage in a secret handshake or competition in the heavy user market. The same permutations of the heavy user market also apply to the cases where firms are secret handshakers and competitors in the light user market. Thus, there are altogether 15 potential equilibria. However, all but five of these potential equilibria are ruled out by the six lemmas in

---

[4]This assumption is sufficient, but not necessary, for our proofs. It greatly simplifies our derivations.

Figure 3   Equilibrium with Two Competing Firms

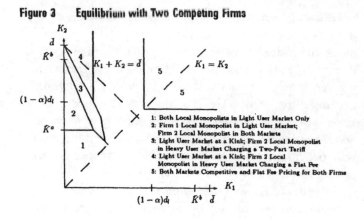

Appendix 2, so that we only need to focus on the remaining five.

3.1.   Local Monopolists
Competition is immaterial if none of the firms has sufficient capacity. Thus, it comes as no surprise that when the industry does not have sufficient capacity to service even the light users, or $K_1 + K_2 < (1 - \alpha)d_l$, and each individual firm's capacity is also small, $K_i \leq \bar{K}^a$ for $i = 1, 2$, a pure strategy equilibrium exists where both firms mimic the monopolist behavior in the previous section, serving only light users. We can find each firm's two-part tariff schedule by substituting into Equation (5) the appropriate capacity constraint. This equilibrium is shown in Region 1 of Figure 3.

A pure strategy equilibrium can also exist where both firms are local monopolists in the light user market, but Firm 2, the larger capacity firm, also attracts heavy users when its capacity is larger than $\bar{K}^a$. To see this, note that if $K_2 > \bar{K}^a$, Firm 2 will want to sell to both light and heavy users if it is the monopolist in both markets. In that case, the optimal sales to each segment are given by Equations (6) and (7), substituting in K_2 for K. Similarly, the optimal two-part tariff schedule is given by Equation (8). Then, the sufficient condition for such an equilibrium to exist is that both Firm 1 and Firm 2 are local monopolists in the light user market or that the sum of both firms' capacities engaged in that market is not sufficient to cover the market. This condition is given by

$$K_1 < (1 - \alpha)d_l\left(1 - \frac{2K_2 d_l + \gamma(d_h - d_l)\alpha d_h}{2\hat{d}}\right). \quad (10)$$

We show this equilibrium in Region 2 of Figure 3.

When the latter condition is not satisfied, a similar equilibrium exists where Firm 1 still sells all its capacity to light users, only Firm 2 serves heavy users exhausting all of its capacity, and both firms use a two-part tariff. The difference is that the light user market now becomes just covered. The necessary and sufficient conditions for such an equilibrium are given by

$$K_1 < (1 - \alpha)d_l\left(1 - \frac{K_2}{\hat{d}}\right), \quad (11)$$

$$K_1 \geq (1 - \alpha)d_l\left(1 - \frac{2K_2 d_l + \gamma(d_h - d_l)\alpha d_h}{2\hat{d}}\right), \quad (12)$$

$$K_1 \leq (1 - \alpha)d_l\left(1 - \frac{2K_2 d_l + \gamma(d_h - d_l)\alpha d_h}{2\hat{d} + \alpha d_h^2}\right). \quad (13)$$

Condition (11) ensures that the larger capacity firm has a smaller coverage in the heavy user segment than in the light user segment and therefore charges a two-part tariff. Conditions (12) and (13) ensure that Firm 2 will neither raise nor lower its price to light users, while simultaneously reducing or increasing its price to heavy users to keep its capacity fully engaged.[5] We show this equilibrium in Region 3 of Figure 3.

In all three equilibria, two-part tariff pricing is the optimal pricing structure for both firms regardless of their own capacity level. This pricing scheme plays the same role, as in the monopoly case, of attracting the optimal mix of light and heavy users so that each firm gets the most bang for its limited capacity. As we can see from Figure 3, these three equilibria all take place below the line $K_1 + K_2 \leq \hat{d}$, or when the industry capacity is inadequate to cover the whole market.

3.2.   Secret Handshake and Flat Fee Pricing
When the industry capacity is inadequate to cover the market, the optimal pricing structure for a firm

---

[5]The derivations for Condition (13) are available from the website for *Marketing Science* at http://mktsci.pubs.informs.org.

varies, depending on the distribution of the industry capacity.

PROPOSITION 2. *In a competitive context, even if the industry capacity is insufficient to cover the whole market $(K_1 + K_2 < d)$, flat fee pricing can be optimal for a large capacity firm. When the industry has excess capacity $(K_1 + K_2 \geq d)$, two-part tariff pricing can be optimal for a small capacity firm.*

Proposition 2 arises from the equilibrium where Firm 1 serves light users to its full capacity; Firm 2 pulls in, with a flat fee, the rest of light users and some heavy users without exhausting its capacity. As we show in Appendix 2, as long as $K_1 > (1 - \alpha)d_l(1 - K_2/d)$ and $K_1 \leq (1 - \alpha)d_l\{1 - [(1 + \alpha)/(3 + \alpha)]\gamma\}$, such an equilibrium exists where

$$f_1 = V - \frac{d_h K_1 t}{(1 - \alpha)(d_h - d_l)d_l},$$

$$p_1 = \frac{K_1 t}{(1 - \alpha)(d_h - d_l)d_l}, \qquad (14)$$

$$f_2 = V - t + \frac{K_1 t}{(1 - \alpha)d_l}, \qquad p_2 = 0. \qquad (15)$$

This equilibrium is shown in Region 4 of Figure 3.

Proposition 2 is true as Region 4 in Figure 3 spans across the dotted line $K_1 + K_2 = d$. In this equilibrium, the small capacity firm plays a niche strategy. Such a niche strategy is viable, even when excess capacity exists in the industry, because the firm with the lion's share of the market has too much to lose if it competes with a nonthreatening, small capacity firm for more light users. Indeed, light users are the most valuable customers from the perspective of the small capacity firm and it can most efficiently deploy its capacity if it concentrates on serving only light users. Furthermore, because of its small capacity and market share, the small firm is also best positioned to compete for light users. As a result, the optimal strategy for the large firm is to accommodate the small firm with a secret handshake: conceding just enough light users to the small firm to keep its capacity fully engaged and leaving some of its own capacity idle even when the market is not fully covered. In this equilibrium, a two-part tariff scheme allows

the niche player to choke off the demand from heavy users, while bringing in just enough light users, so that it can most profitably engage its capacity. For the large capacity firm, a flat-fee allows it to expand most effectively in the heavy user segment, and it also helps sustain the secret handshake because any further decrease in the flat fee will generate a large inframarginal loss in both light and heavy user markets. Thus, capacity constraints also inject a strategic motivation into a firm's pricing decision.

In this equilibrium of secret handshake, the total numbers of consumers each firm and the industry as a whole serve are given by

$$N_1 = \frac{K_1}{d_l}, \qquad N_2 = 1 - \frac{K_1}{(1 - \alpha)d_l},$$

$$N_I = 1 - \frac{\alpha K_1}{(1 - \alpha)d_l}.$$

A simple comparative statics analysis on these numbers will lead us to the following proposition:

PROPOSITION 3. *In the equilibrium of secret handshake, the strategy of accommodation calls on the larger firm to retreat in both light and heavy user markets and leave more of its capacity idle and more of the market demand unmet when the small firm's capacity (hence, the industry capacity) increases.*

Proposition 3 has an intriguing, nonintuitive policy implication for access industries, which has not been explored elsewhere. It suggests that incremental policy measures that encourage the growth of smaller companies in the presence of a large company can be welfare-decreasing. This is because the growth of a smaller firm can force the retreat of a large company at the expense of market coverage.

Both Proposition 2 and Proposition 3 have some important managerial implications for pricing access services. Proposition 2 suggests that if the industry capacity is unevenly distributed, it is the large capacity firm, the firm that has excess capacity, that should use the flat fee pricing in an industry. A small capacity firm, the firm that must make every unit of its capacity count, should not follow suit, even when the industry as a whole has excess capacity. Proposition 3 suggests that in response to a small firm's encroachment on its market share, the large capacity firm may well be advised to increase, rather than decrease, its flat fee to accommodate the small firm because it may be too costly and too tactless for the large firm to do otherwise.

3.3. Competitive Flat Fee Pricing

Interestingly, whether or not a firm should use a flat fee pricing does not depend on whether or not it is capacity-constrained or whether or not the opportunity cost of its capacity is zero. This can be shown by analyzing the equilibrium where two firms without capacity constraints compete for both light and heavy users in the market and all use flat fee pricing. The equilibrium is fully characterised in Appendix 3. We show that there exists a pure strategy equilibrium only when both competing firms have sufficient excess capacity relative to the market demand they each serve: specifically, when $K_i \geq \bar{K}^c = (\bar{d}/2)[\sqrt{\gamma^2 - 2} - (\gamma - 2)]$, where $\bar{d}/2 < \bar{K}^c < \bar{d}$, for $i = 1, 2$. In this case, the equilibrium entails the use of a flat fee $f_1 = f_2 = t$ by both competing firms. We summarize the results in the following proposition.

PROPOSITION 4. *Flat fee pricing is optimal for competing firms only when they all have sufficient excess capacity relative to the market demand they each serve.*

Proposition 4 thus suggests that the optimal pricing structure also depends on the excess capacity each firm possesses. When $\gamma = 4$, for instance, each firm must have 74% more capacity than it needs to cover its share of the market to sustain competitive flat fee pricing.[6] Sufficient excess capacity serves two functions in a competitive context. First, it motivates a firm to focus on the number of customers it attracts, rather than the customer mix so that both types of consumers are equally attractive to the firm. A flat fee allows a firm to tap into both light and heavy user markets with equal efficiency, so it is the best choice for the firm.

Second, a firm's excess capacity deters any opportunistic behavior on the part of its rival. A firm can always take advantage of its rival's low price by raising its own price if the rival firm does not have suf-

ficient excess capacity to meet the surge in demand. Then the rival firm wants to set a high price in the first place, which can then be taken advantage of by the firm's setting a low price to expand its market. This opportunistic behavior, along with the possibility that a firm can always redirect its capacity between the two markets through pricing, explains why there exists no pure strategy equilibrium when two large capacity firms do not have sufficient excess capacity, or when two capacity-constrained firms have a similar level of capacity.

Proposition 4 provides an alternative explanation for the popularity of flat fee pricing. Major amusement parks in this country, for instance, all use flat fee pricing (*The New York Times* 1999). One rationale for this pricing scheme is provided by Oi (1971): The firm with market power uses a flat fee to extract as much surplus as possible from those consumers who use a service that can essentially be provided at zero marginal cost. Scotchmer (1985) shows that the membership fee, in addition to a usage price, can arise in a symmetric Nash equilibrium because of congestion, but flat fee pricing *per se* is never optimal for a firm. Our analysis shows that flat fee pricing can be motivated by competitive pressure for market expansion. Such pressure is generated by the firm-level excess capacity. To expand its market, a firm must seek to attract both light and heavy users with a flat fee.

The managerial implication from this analysis is that two-part tariff pricing cannot be sustained in a competitive context when competing firms have developed sufficient excess capacity, but flat fee pricing can. However, only with *sufficient* excess capacity should a firm charge a flat fee for its access service. Thus, a firm is cautioned not to embrace a flat fee pricing when it has only *some* excess capacity. The fee that a firm can charge depends on consumer preference t, indicating the advisability of brand building and service differentiation in an industry where service capacity increases rapidly.

4. Extension

Our analysis thus far identifies three driving forces in a firm's pricing decision when capacity plays an

[6] As γ approaches $+\infty$, $\bar{K}^c$ approaches $\bar{d}$.

important mediating role. A firm's primary motivation may be to draw a desired mix of customers to deploy its limited capacity optimally, or to engage the rival in a secret handshake, or to pursue market penetration, depending on whether or not all competing firms are capacity-constrained and how industry capacity is distributed. However, these pricing insights are drawn in the context where light users are more "valuable" than heavy users because the former have a higher willingness to pay on a per-unit-of-capacity basis. This begs the question of whether these insights carry over to the situation where heavy users are more valuable, and if they are, in what form? In this section, we extend our basic model to address those questions.[7]

4.1. Usage Pricing and Signing Bonus for the Monopolist

We start with the monopoly case to gain some intuition. Consider the case where the reservation prices for heavy and light users are respectively given by vd_h and vd_l, instead of the common V as in our basic model. Analogously, we assume $vd_l/t > 3$ to ensure that the market is always covered when the monopolist does not face any capacity constraint. We also maintain the rest of the assumptions in our basic model. Therefore, at any given $(f + pd_h, f + pd_l)$, all heavy users located to the left of x_h, where $x_h = (vd_h - f - pd_h)/t$, will make a purchase. Similarly, all light users to the left of $x_l = (vd_l - f - pd_l)/t$ will also make a purchase. The monopolist's optimization problem is identical, in form, to that of our basic model as defined by Equations (1)–(4). However, the pricing structure that emerges is quite different.

Figure 4 illustrates the solution to this optimization problem. In this market, the monopolist wants to attract more heavy users than light users and charge heavy users more, too. This is because at any given location $x > 0$, the willingness to pay for one unit of capacity is higher for heavy users ($v - tx/d_h > v - tx/d_l$). The monopolist does so by starting with a high unit price and zero fee and gradually lowers the unit price as its capacity increases. This process continues as long as the monopolist's capacity is not large enough to service all heavy users ($K < K_{b3} = \hat{d}/d_h$). By charging a unit price alone and lowering it with a larger capacity, the monopolist delivers more incentives to heavy users as its capacity increases, thus engaging more of its limited capacity with the more valuable consumers in the market. Once all heavy users are pulled in ($K \geq K_{b3}$), the monopolist must find a way to attract more light users without giving heavy users a free ride. The monopolist does so by simultaneously raising its unit price and offering a "signing bonus," a negative flat fee, to target its incentives at light users. Here, a two-part tariff plays the dual role of helping a firm to attract a desired customer mix and to price discriminate.

In comparison to our basic model, the surprising insight from this analysis is that a flat fee is no longer optimal, even at a high level of capacity when heavy users in a market are more valuable. In its place, the monopolist uses a "signing bonus" and a unit price to penetrate the light user market while still taking relatively more surplus away from heavy users.

4.2. Competitive Flat Fee Pricing

In the competitive context, as we show in Appendix 4, when industry capacity is sufficiently small ($K_1 + K_2 < \hat{d}/d_h$), and hence, competition is immaterial, a unit price is all that a firm needs to set, as in the case of monopoly. When $\hat{d}/d_h \leq K_1 + K_2 \leq \hat{d}/d_h + (1 - \alpha)(d_1^2/2d_h)$, both firms will use a two-part tariff that consists of a signing bonus and a unit price. This pricing structure, as in the monopoly case, allows a firm to penetrate the light user segment to fully engage its capacity while taking advantage of the higher willingness to pay on the part of heavy users. Further-

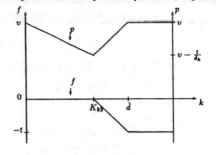

Figure 4   Monopolist's Optimal Pricing Structure

[7]The authors thank an anonymous reviewer for suggesting this analysis.

Table 1   Market Conditions and Optimal Pricing Structure

Optimal Pricing Structure	Market Condition	
	Heavy Users More Valuable	Light Users More Valuable
Flat fee	Sufficient firm excess capacity $(K_i \geq \bar{K}^c, i = 1, 2)$	• Sufficient industry excess capacity $(K_i \geq \bar{K}^c, i = 1, 2)$ • Noncapacity constrained (competing with a capacity constrained)
Usage price	Industry capacity sufficiently small* $(K_1 + K_2 \leq \partial/d_h)$	Never
Flat fee plus usage price	Never	Capacity constrained firm
Signing bonus plus usage price	Medium industry capacity† $(\partial/d_h < K_1 + K_2 \leq \partial/d_h + (1 - \alpha)\, d_l^2/2d_h)$	Never

*The larger capacity firm charges a smaller usage price.
†The larger capacity firm offers a larger signing bonus and charges a smaller usage price.

more, because of the fact that heavy users are both more valuable and resource consuming, both firms price strategically not to compete for more heavy users at the expense of light users such that the heavy user market is just covered. As each firm's capacity becomes sufficiently large, i.e., $K_i > \bar{K}^c$ ($d/2 < \bar{K}^c < d$), both firms will, surprisingly, charge a flat fee. This is because excess capacity unleashes intense price competition, which in turn drives the prices each firm charges in both segments of the market to be the same.

Thus, the analysis of this extended model offers three interesting new insights, as summarized in Table 1. First, when capacity is a mediating factor, a firm's pricing structure also depends on whether heavy or light users are more valuable in terms of their willingness to pay on a per-unit-capacity basis. When light users are more valuable, a firm may use a flat fee or a flat fee plus a unit price, but never charge a unit price alone or offer any signing bonus. However, when heavy users are valuable, a firm may use a unit price, or a signing bonus plus a unit price, or a flat fee. This perhaps explains why the pricing structure varies across different access industries. Second, regardless of whether heavy or light users are more valuable in an access industry, only flat fee pricing is a sustainable pricing structure once the industry has developed sufficient excess capacity. This may provide useful insights about the future pricing implications in cellular phone or broadband indus-

tries as industry capacity continues to increase rapidly. Third, in a market where heavy users are more valuable, the larger capacity firm will charge a lower usage price and offer a larger signing bonus whenever such bonus is required. This is because a larger capacity motivates the firm to pursue heavy users more aggressively.

5.   Conclusion

Today, services account for two-thirds to three-quarters of the GNP, not only in the United States but also in many industrial countries (Lovelock 1996). Access industries are growing rapidly to exert profound impact on today's economy (Rifkin 2000). However, service pricing in general and pricing access services in particular have not received adequate attention in the literature. In this paper, we take the first step in understanding how capacity constraints and consumer usage heterogeneity mediate the choice of pricing structures in both monopolistic and competitive contexts.

We show that capacity constraints, along with consumer usage heterogeneity, are an important determinant for pricing access services. Because of these two interacting factors, pricing access services is a delicate decision that requires a firm to balance two frequently conflicting incentives. On one hand, once a firm acquires a certain level of capacity, the firm has incentives to use it to the full extent and in the most efficient way. These incentives can tempt a firm to become as aggressive in pricing as it is consistent with the efficient use of its limited resource. On the other hand, a firm's aggressiveness in pricing is tempered by its desire to price discriminate based on consumer usage heterogeneity and by its strategic motivation to accommodate a capacity-constrained rival. A profit-maximizing firm responds to all these incentives by focusing on customer mix, a driving force in a firm's choice of its pricing structure.

However, there is no simple rule for designing the optimal pricing structure in a competitive context. The past research on nonlinear pricing suggests that two-part tariff pricing is always the pricing structure of a profit-maximizing firm's choice whenever a positive marginal cost is involved, and flat fee pricing is the choice whenever it is not. It is tempting to extend this rule to access industries by replacing the marginal cost with the opportunity cost of capacity: Whenever there exists a positive opportunity cost for a firm's capacity or a firm is capacity-constrained, it should choose a two-part tariff, and otherwise a flat fee. However, such a rule would be misleading. As we have shown in our basic model, competitive flat fee pricing occurs only when there exists sufficient *excess* capacity in an industry. This means that even if the opportunity cost of a firm's capacity is zero, i.e., the shadow price of capacity is zero, it may not be advisable for a firm to use flat fee pricing. In our extended model, usage pricing, rather than two-part tariff pricing, is the pricing structure of a firm's choice even when the opportunity cost of capacity is positive. Choosing a pricing structure is far more complex in access industries because with capacity constraints and hence uncovered market, price discrimination, and surplus extraction are no longer the only motives for a firm.

Nevertheless, aside from the detailed strategic prescriptions uncovered in this study, our analysis does provide a general, managerial guide to narrow down a firm's choice. We show that when light users are more valuable, a firm may use a two-part tariff or a flat fee depending on whether the firm is constrained by its service capacity, but never charge a usage price

alone or offer any signing bonus (a negative flat fee or a flat payment to customers). When heavy users are more valuable, a firm may change from a usage price to a signing bonus plus a usage price and then to a flat fee as its capacity increases. Interestingly, regardless of whether heavy or light users are more valuable in an access industry, only flat fee pricing is a sustainable pricing structure once the industry has developed sufficient *excess* capacity.

Our conclusions are based on some important assumptions that warrant further discussion. In our model, the consumer usage rate is inelastic to price changes. Implicitly, what we are saying here is that the consumer usage rate depends largely on individual propensity rather than price. This assumption may seem extreme. However, in the context of service industries, we believe this is a good first-order approximation of reality. Unlike physical goods for which "free disposal" is always an option and more is, in general, always better, service delivery is intrinsically participatory. Participation requires time commitment and physical effort on the part of consumers. Thus, there is no free disposal for service, and time cost and physical efforts limit the effectiveness of price incentives in altering consumer usage habit. This perhaps explains why a vast majority of consumers spend only an average of 25 online hours per month even when they face zero marginal price. However, we acknowledge that this assumption limits the applicability of our conclusions to the service industries where consumer usage propensity is relatively inelastic to price changes.

Implicitly, we also assume that a firm has little room to adjust its "service quality" such that it cannot provide different versions of the same service targeted at consumers of different quality sensitivity with different prices. This assumption rules out any possibility for a firm to offer different versions of access services along with a menu of two-part tariffs to induce consumer self-selection. We make this assumption for two reasons. First, for many access services such as access to ski lift, to Internet, to movie theaters, to sports facilities, or to amusement parks, consumers may care much more about access than about service. In those industries, it is either not feasible or not desirable for firms to offer exclusive services with an elaborate pricing menu. In that case, firms can only tap into usage heterogeneity to charge differential prices. A two-part tariff has the sufficient degree of pricing freedom to allow a firm to do just that. This perhaps explains why we frequently observe the three simple choices we have discussed in the introduction. Thus, our conclusions are applicable to those industries. Of course, our conclusions are also applicable to the industries where the "service" dimension is important under a restrictive but plausible condition. The condition is that the distribution of consumer service sensitivity is lumpy, such that the incentive compatibility constraint for each consumer segment is not likely to distort a firm's pricing choice for any specific segment.

Second, as a modeling choice, this assumption allows us to explore how the interactions between capacity constraints and consumer usage heterogeneity determine a firm's choice of its pricing structure. Adding a quality dimension in the context of incomplete market coverage, which the literature has so far deliberately avoided, would have made our analysis much less tractable and transparent without any apparent promise for new insights. The same can be said about extending our model to incorporate more than two usage segments where consumer willingness to pay depends on usage rates.

Future research can extend our analysis in a number of promising directions. For instance, the long-term impact of pricing structures on consumer usage rates and the issue of capacity investment can be discussed in conjunction with pricing decisions. The model can also be extended to include multiple firms with varying sizes to examine the relationship between the market structure and the pricing structure. We hope that this first step we have taken will spark further interest in pricing access services.

Acknowledgments

The authors thank the editor, the area editor, and two anonymous reviewers for their detailed feedback and constructive suggestions. Thanks are due to Don Lehman, Kyle Bagwell, Jagmohan Raju, Paolo Siconolfi, and the participants of the 1999 Marketing Science Conference for their helpful comments. The authors are solely responsible for any error in the paper.

Appendix 1. Analysis of the Capacity Constrained Monopolist

We assume $\gamma \geq 3$ henceforth, so that the monopolist always chooses to cover the market if it has sufficient capacity. Then, for any given capacity $0 \leq K \leq d$, the monopolist must decide what pricing structure to use to engage its limited capacity optimally. For any given pricing structure (f, p), all light users located to the left of x_l who gain positive surplus will make a purchase, where

$$x_l = \frac{V - f - pd_l}{t} \qquad (A.1)$$

is the location of the marginal light users who are just indifferent between buying and not buying. Similarly, all heavy users to the left of

$$x_h = \frac{V - f - pd_h}{t} \qquad (A.2)$$

will also make a purchase. Of course, the total capacity needed to service these purchases cannot exceed the total capacity available. As noted in §2.2, the monopolist optimization problem is therefore

$$\max_{(f,p)} (1 - \alpha)x_l(f + pd_l) + \alpha x_h(f + pd_h), \qquad (A.3)$$

$$\text{s.t.} \quad 0 \leq x_l, \qquad (A.4)$$

$$x_l \leq 1, \qquad (A.5)$$

$$0 \leq x_h, \qquad (A.6)$$

$$x_h \leq 1, \qquad (A.7)$$

$$(1 - \alpha)x_l d_l + \alpha x_h d_h \leq K, \qquad (A.8)$$

This optimization problem is considerably simpler to solve if we note that:

• The monopolist capacity will always be fully engaged, given $\gamma \geq 3$, if $K \leq d$, i.e., that Constraint (A.8) is always binding.

• As long as $K > 0$, we must have $x_l > 0$, as the monopolist always taps into the light user segment first, i.e., that Constraint (A.4) is never binding.

• When the monopolist capacity is infinitely small, it draws only the light users located nearby because they are the least resource-demanding and the most profitable customers. So for small levels of capacity, Constraint (A.6) is always binding (and therefore (A.7) is not). Also, for small levels of capacity, not all of the light users are served by the monopolist, and therefore Constraint (A.5) is not binding. To determine the boundary conditions of this case, as well as derive the monopolist's optimal pricing structure in this case, we need to solve for the following Lagrangian function:

$$L_1(f, p, u_1, w) = (1 - \alpha)x_l(f + pd_l) + \alpha x_h(f + pd_h) + u_1 x_h$$

$$- w(K - (1 - \alpha)x_l d_l - \alpha x_h d_h).$$

We use the Mathematica software to maximize the Lagrangian $L_1(f, p, u_1, w)$ (as well as all subsequent Lagrangian functions in this appendix), and solve for f, p, u_1, and w. The optimal pricing structure (f, p) that we obtain in this case is reported in Equations (5) of the paper. The boundary condition of this case (that $x_h = 0$) is given by the condition that the Lagrangian parameter u_1 is positive: We find that constraint (A.6) is binding (i.e., $x_h = 0$) as long as the firm capacity is sufficiently small, i.e., $K \leq \bar{K}^a = [\gamma(d_h - d_l)(1 - \alpha)d_l/2d_h$.

- We focus on the case where $\bar{K}^a$ is smaller than $(1 - \alpha)d_l$. This is the case (a) of Figure 1, where $\gamma \leq 2d_h/(d_h - d_l)$. In this case, the monopolist will start attracting heavy users before having served all the light users in the market (i.e., $x_l < 1$). So when Constraint (A.6) stops to bind (i.e., $x_h > 0$), Constraint (A.5) does not bind as yet (as $x_l < 1$), nor does Constraint (A.7). The first boundary condition of this case is therefore $\bar{K}^a \leq K$, which ensures that $x_h > 0$ (i.e., Constraint (A.6) stops to bind). To determine the other boundary condition of this case, as well as derive the monopolist's optimal pricing structure in this case, we need to solve for the following Lagrangian function:

$$L_2(f, p, w) = (1 - \alpha)x_l(f + pd_l) + \alpha x_h(f + pd_h)$$
$$- w(K - (1 - \alpha)x_l d_l - \alpha x_h d_h).$$

We maximize $L_2(f, p, w)$ and solve for f, p, and w. The optimal pricing structure (f, p) that we obtain in this case is reported in Equation (8) of the paper. Using this optimal pricing structure and Equations (A.1) and (A.2), we derive the optimal penetration levels x_l and x_h in each of the light and the heavy user segments, respectively. We obtain that $x_l = [2Kd_l + \gamma(d_h - d_l)\alpha d_h]/\hat{d}$ and $x_h = [2Kd_h - \gamma(d_h - d_l)(1 - \alpha)d_l]/\hat{d}$. It is straightforward to check that $x_h < x_l$. We can therefore derive the number of light and heavy users served by the monopolist $q_l = (1 - \alpha)x_l$ and $q_h = \alpha x_h$, respectively. The results are reported in Equations (6) and (7) of the paper. The second boundary condition for this case is given by $x_l < 1$ (i.e., that Constraint (A.5) does not bind, and hence neither does Constraint (A.7): Using the expression for the optimal penetration level $x_l = [2Kd_l + \gamma(d_h - d_l)\alpha d_h]/\hat{d}$ derived above, we find that the condition $x_l < 1$ implies that the firm capacity needs to be lower than the threshold $\bar{K}^b$, where $\bar{K}^b = [2\hat{d} - \gamma(d_h - d_l)\alpha d_h]/2d_l$, and hence the boundary conditions of this case are $\bar{K}^a \leq K \leq \bar{K}^b$.

- When the monopolist capacity increases beyond $\bar{K}^b$, Constraint (A.5) starts to bind (i.e., $x_l = 1$). As long as the monopolist capacity remains below $\hat{d}$, Constraint (A.7) does not bind (i.e., $x_h < 1$). The boundary conditions of this case are $\bar{K}^b \leq K < \hat{d}$, which ensure that $x_h > 0$ (i.e., Constraint (A.6) stops to bind). To derive the monopolist's optimal pricing structure in this case, we need to solve for the following Lagrangian function:

$$L_3(f, p, u_3, w) = (1 - \alpha)(f + pd_l) + \alpha x_h(f + pd_h) - u_3(x_l - 1)$$
$$- w(K - (1 - \alpha)x_l d_l - \alpha x_h d_h).$$

We maximize $L_3(f, p, u_3, w)$ and solve for f, p, u_3, and w. The optimal pricing structure (f, p) that we obtain in this case is reported in Equation (9) of the paper. We check that the boundary conditions

of this case are indeed $\bar{K}^b \leq K < \hat{d}$. First, the boundary condition that $x_l = 1$ (i.e., that Constraint (A.5) is binding) is given by the condition that the Lagrangian parameter u_3 is positive, which is equivalent to the firm's capacity being greater than $\bar{K}^b$. Second, using the optimal pricing structure for this case (as reported in Equation (9)) and Equation (A.2), we derive the optimal penetration level x_h in the heavy user segment, and we check that $x_h < 1$ is equivalent to $K < \hat{d}$.

Appendix 2. Equilibrium Analysis of Basic Model

In §3, we noted that there are possibly as many as 15 potential equilibria. We can classify these potential equilibria into three general classes, depending on how light users are served: both firms are local monopolists (the market is uncovered), secret handshakers (the market is covered but does not overlap), or competitors (firms compete for a common subset of light users).

Observe that when the total equilibrium prices in the light user segment are P_{1l} and P_{2l}, the last light user who is willing to buy from firm i is located at a distance $(V - P_{il})/t$ from the firm. One can therefore characterize the three general classes of equilibria in terms of the relative locations of the firms' marginal light users. This yields conditions on the equilibrium prices in the light user market:

Class 1: Equilibria. The light user segment is uncovered (both firms are local monopolists) if and only if $P_{1l} + P_{2l} > 2V - t$.

Class 2: Equilibria. The light user segment is just covered (firms are secret handshakers) if and only if $P_{1l} + P_{2l} = 2V - t$.

Class 3: Equilibria. The light user segment is competitive (firms compete for a common subset of light users) if and only if $P_{1l} + P_{2l} < 2V - t$.

In this appendix, we rule out all but the five equilibria identified in the main text.

Note that the unit price p must be nonnegative for a two-part tariff. This implies that firms must set a light user price $P_l = f + pd_l$ no greater than the heavy user price $P_h = f + pd_h$. However, it is always a *permissible deviation* for a firm to lower its price to light users. In what follows, whenever rationing needs to be invoked for our proofs, we use the efficient rationing rule.

Class 1: Equilibria—Light User Segment Uncovered

If $P_{1l} + P_{2l} > 2V - t$, we must also have $P_{1h} + P_{2h} > 2V - t$, as $P_{ih} \geq P_{il}$ for $i = 1, 2$ under a two-part tariff. This means that in any equilibrium where the light user market is uncovered, the heavy user market must also be uncovered. This, in turn, implies that both firms are capacity constrained. Otherwise, both firms would have incentives to expand their market coverage given $\gamma > 3$.

We can also rule out the case where both firms are local monopolists in the heavy user market when the light user market is uncovered. Note that if an equilibrium exists where both firms are local monopolists in the heavy user market, it must mean that one of the firms, say Firm 1, serves less than half of the light users (i.e., less than $1 - \alpha/2$ users). Otherwise, the light user market would be covered. Then, Firm 1 is a local monopolist in both light and heavy user markets with less than $(1 - \alpha)d_l/2 < \bar{K}^a$ units of capacity engaged in the light user market. However, from our analysis of the monopolist case, we know that this is not possible, as the optimal strategy for a monopolist is to engage its capacity up to $\bar{K}^a$ in the light user market before it attracts any heavy user. Regions 1 and 2 of Figure 3 illustrate the remaining equilibria of this class.

Class 2: Equilibria—Light User Segment Just Covered

In any equilibrium where the light user market is at a kink, we must have $P_{1l} + P_{2l} = 2V - t$. The following five lemmas will establish that the only Class 2 equilibria are those identified in Regions 3 and 4 of Figure 3.

LEMMA 1. *If none of the firms is capacity constrained, the light user market cannot be just covered.*

PROOF. Suppose, to the contrary, that there exists an equilibrium where the light user market is just covered, but none of the firms is capacity constrained. Then, we must have $q_{1l} > (1 - \alpha)(\gamma/3)$, i.e., Firm 1's sales to light users must be sufficiently large that Firm 1 has no incentive to lower its price to light users further to attract more of them. Similarly, we must have $q_{2l} > (1 - \alpha)(\gamma/3)$, so that Firm 2 does not deviate. As $q_{2l} = (1 - \alpha) - q_{1l}$ when the light user market is at a kink, the previous two inequalities then imply $\gamma < 3/2$, a contradiction ($\gamma > 3$ by assumption). $\square$

LEMMA 2. *If only one firm is capacity constrained, there exists no equilibrium in which the light user segment is just covered, both firms are present in the heavy user market and the heavy user market is either uncovered or just covered.*

PROOF. Suppose, to the contrary, that there exists an equilibrium where only one firm is capacity constrained, say Firm 1, the light user segment is just covered, both firms are present in the heavy user market, and the heavy user market is either uncovered or just covered. Firm 2 will not attract new light users (with its unused capacity) only if $q_{1l} < (1 - \alpha)(1 - \gamma/3)$ because the light user market is at a kink. Firm 1 will not release capacity from the heavy user segment and engage the same capacity in the light user segment if

$$q_{1l} \geq \frac{1 - \alpha}{2\hat{d} + \alpha d_h^2}(2K_1 d_l + \gamma(d_h - d_l)\alpha d_h). \quad (A.9)$$

Because $K_1 \geq q_{1l}d_l$, the above inequality implies $q_{1l} > (1 - \alpha)[(d_h - d_l)/d_h](\gamma/3)$. This and the inequality $q_{1l} < (1 - \alpha)(1 - \gamma/3)$ imply $\gamma < 3d_h/(2d_h - d_l)$. Because $d_h > 4d_l$, we must have $3d_h/2(d_h - d_l) < 2$. A contradiction. $\square$

LEMMA 3. *If both firms are capacity constrained, there exists no equilibrium in which both segments are just covered.*

PROOF. Suppose, to the contrary, that there exists an equilibrium

where both firms are capacity constrained and both segments are just covered. We then necessarily have $K_1 + K_2 = d$.

Firm 1 will not attract additional light users and disconnect the heavy user segment as long as Inequality (A.9) holds. Neither does Firm 2 if

$$q_{2l} > \frac{1 - \alpha}{2\hat{d} + \alpha d_h^2}(2K_2 d_l + \gamma(d_h - d_l)\alpha d_h). \quad (A.10)$$

Because $q_{2l} = (1 - \alpha) - q_{1l}$ and $K_2 = \hat{d} - K_1$, we have from Inequality (A.10)

$$q_{1l} < \frac{1 - \alpha}{2\hat{d} + \alpha d_h^2}(2K_1 d_l - (\gamma - 2)(d_h - d_l)\alpha d_h + \alpha d_h^2). \quad (A.11)$$

Then inequalities (A.9) and (A.11) imply $\gamma < 1 + d_h/2(d_h - d_l)$. As $d_h > 4d_l$ (by assumption), we have $d_h/2(d_h - d_l) < 1$. This implies that $\gamma < 2$, a contradiction. $\square$

LEMMA 4. *If both firms are capacity constrained, there is no equilibrium in which the light user segment is just covered, and both firms serve the heavy user segment as local monopolists.*

PROOF. In any such equilibrium, Firm 1 will not deviate by attracting additional light users and release some heavy users if Inequality (A.9) holds. Neither does Firm 2 if Inequality (A.10) holds. Because $q_{2l} = (1 - \alpha) - q_{1l}$ when the light user market is at a kink, we must have from Inequality (A.10),

$$q_{1l} < (1 - \alpha) - \frac{1 - \alpha}{2\hat{d} + \alpha d_h^2}(2K_2 d_l + \gamma(d_h - d_l)\alpha d_h). \quad (A.12)$$

In this equilibrium, we necessarily have $K_1 + K_2 > (1 - \alpha)d_l$. This, along with Inequality (A.12), implies

$$q_{1l} < (1 - \alpha)$$

$$- \frac{1 - \alpha}{2\hat{d} + \alpha d_h^2}(2((1 - \alpha)d_l - K_1)d_l + \gamma(d_h - d_l)\alpha d_h), \quad (A.13)$$

which we can simplify as

$$q_{1l} < \frac{1 - \alpha}{2\hat{d} + \alpha d_h^2}(2K_1 d_l + 3\alpha d_h^2 - \gamma(d_h - d_l)\alpha d_h). \quad (A.14)$$

Then, Inequalities (A.9) and (A.14) imply $\gamma < 3d_h/2(d_h - d_l)$. However, because $d_h > 4d_l$, we must have $3d_h/2(d_h - d_l) < 2$. This implies $\gamma < 2$, a contradiction. $\square$

LEMMA 5. *Whenever a firm is not capacity constrained and serves the light user segment in an equilibrium, the firm must also serve the heavy user segment.*

PROOF. Suppose, to the contrary, that an equilibrium exists where the firm serves only the light users. Then, by lowering its price in the heavy user segment to $v - \epsilon$, the firm will use some of its unused capacity to attract some heavy users and increase its profit. A contradiction. $\square$

We can now establish that the only Class 2 equilibria are those identified in Regions 3 and 4. Because the light user market is just covered, at least one of the firms is capacity constrained (Lemma

1), and hence the heavy user segment cannot be just covered as well (Lemma 3). Moreover, the heavy user segment cannot be competitive since $P_{1l} + P_{2l} = 2V - t$, which implies that $P_{1h} + P_{2l} \geq 2V - t$. The heavy users segment is therefore uncovered.

If both firms are capacity constrained, then only one firm can serve the heavy users segment (Lemma 4). This is the local monopolist case discussed in the text and illustrated in Region 3 of Figure 3.

If one firm, say Firm 1, is capacity constrained and Firm 2 is not, Firm 2 must be present in the heavy user segment (Lemma 5), and hence Firm 1 cannot be present in the heavy user segment as well (Lemma 2). Firm 2 is the unique local monopolist in the heavy user market. Therefore, Firm 2 must be charging a flat fee. To see that, note that if Firm 2 were charging a two-part tariff ($p_l^2 < p_h^2$), it would be able to lower its heavy user price and expand in the heavy user market (which is always profitable as $\gamma > 3$). This implies that any Class 2 equilibrium entails that Firm 1 serves only light users to its full capacity, and Firm 2 is not capacity constrained and serves both light and heavy users with a flat fee. This is the case that we now discuss and that is illustrated in Region 4 of Figure 3.

We first derive the necessary conditions for the existence of an equilibrium where Firm 1 serves light users to its full capacity and Firm 2 serves both light users and heavy users with a flat fee. Firm 1, in this proposed equilibrium, serves all light users to the left of x such that its capacity K_1 is exhausted, or $x = K_1/(1 - \alpha)d_l$. In this equilibrium, the light user located at x must be indifferent between buying from Firm 1 and from Firm 2 and has zero surplus. Otherwise, Firm 2 can always raise its flat fee without losing any customer. This necessarily implies $f_1 + p_1d_l = V - tx$ and $f_2 = V - t(1 - x)$. Because Firm 1 does not sell to any heavy user, we must also have $f_1 + p_1d_h = V$. Thus, we have

$$f_1 = V - \frac{d_h K_1 t}{(1 - \alpha)(d_h - d_l)d_l}, \qquad p_1 = \frac{K_1 t}{(1 - \alpha)(d_h - d_l)d_l}, \qquad (A.15)$$

$$f_2 = V - t + \frac{K_1 t}{(1 - \alpha)d_l}, \qquad p_2 = 0. \qquad (A.16)$$

Because Firm 2 does not exhaust its capacity, we must also have in this proposed equilibrium $(1 - \alpha)(1 - x)d_l + \alpha(1 - x)d_h < K_2$, or

$$K_1 > (1 - \alpha)d_l\left(1 - \frac{K_2}{d}\right). \qquad (A.17)$$

To check the sufficient conditions for this equilibrium, note that Firm 1 will never lower its price to attract more light users because it is already capacity constrained. Neither will it raise its price charged to light users to make room for some heavy users, as $K_1 \leq (1 - \gamma/3)(1 - \alpha)d_l < \bar{K}^a$. Thus, Firm 1 has no incentive to deviate from the proposed equilibrium.

Firm 2, on the other hand, has no incentive to raise its price because it desires to serve the whole market as a monopolist, but it may want to lower its price to either light users or both light and heavy users to gain a larger market share. The most profitable way for Firm 2 to lower its price is to lower its price to both segments

of consumers by the same amount, i.e., reducing its flat fee.[8] In that case, if Firm 2 lowers its flat fee by $\epsilon > 0$, it gains $(1 - \alpha)\epsilon/2t$ light users, each of whom pays $(f_2 - \epsilon)$. In addition, it gains $\alpha\epsilon/t$ heavy users, each of whom also pays $(f_2 - \epsilon)$. However, Firm 2 incurs the total loss of $(1 - x)\epsilon$, because it charges a lower price to all those light and heavy users who are currently buying from it. The gain is smaller than the loss if

$$K_1 \leq (1 - \alpha)d_l\left(1 - \frac{1 + \alpha}{3 + \alpha}\gamma\right). \qquad (A.18)$$

As long as Condition (A.18) is satisfied, Firm 2 has no incentive to deviate from the proposed equilibrium, either. Thus, the proposed equilibrium is indeed an equilibrium, which we show in Region 4 of Figure 3.

Class 3: Equilibria—The Light Users Segment Competitive

In this case, $P_{1l} + P_{2l} < 2V - t$. We first develop two lemmas (Lemmas 6 and 7) that will help us establish that the only Class 3 equilibria is the competitive equilibrium in Region 5.

LEMMA 6. *In any equilibrium where the light user segment is competitive, if the heavy user segment is not, one of the firms must be capacity constrained while the other is not. The unconstrained firm charges a flat fee only.*

PROOF. In any equilibrium where the light user segment is competitive but not the heavy user segment, we necessarily have $P_{1h} + P_{2h} \geq 2V - t > P_{1l} + P_{2l}$. Therefore, one of the firms' light user price must be *strictly* smaller than its heavy user price, say Firm 2's or $P_{2l} < P_{2h}$. Then, Firm 1 cannot be capacity constrained. Otherwise, Firm 2 can raise its price to light users slightly to $P_{2l} + \epsilon < P_{2h}$ and extract some additional surplus from its light users without losing anyone of them. Given that Firm 1 is not capacity constrained, Firm 2 must be. Otherwise, none of the firms is capacity constrained and the standard Hotelling no-deviation conditions yield $P_{il} = P_{ih} = t$ for both firms ($i = 1, 2$), which then implies $P_{1h} + P_{2h} = 2t < 2V - t$ (the heavy user segment is competitive). A contradiction. If the unconstrained Firm 1 does not charge a flat fee, its light user price would be strictly smaller than its heavy user price ($P_{1l} < P_{1h}$). However, this cannot be an equilibrium because Firm 1 can raise its light user price slightly to $P_{1l} + \epsilon < P_{1h}$ and extract some additional surplus from its light users without losing anyone of them because Firm 2 is capacity constrained. A contradiction again. $\square$

LEMMA 7. *There exists no equilibrium where the light user segment is competitive and the heavy user segment is not.*

PROOF. Suppose, to the contrary, that an equilibrium exists where the light user segment is competitive and the heavy user segment

---

[8] The alternative is for the firm to use a two-part tariff to deliver a lower price to light users than to heavy users. However, such a deviation can be shown to be less profitable, given that the demand in the light user market is at a kink.

is not. Then, by Lemma 6 we know that in the equilibrium one of the firm must be capacity constrained, say Firm 2, while Firm 1 is not. Moreover, Firm 1 must charge a flat fee only. In this equilibrium, there are only two possibilities in the heavy user market: Either Firm 1 is a local monopolist in the heavy user market, or its demand in the heavy user market is at a kink. We now consider the first case.

Suppose that Firm 1 increases its price by $\epsilon > 0$ in both markets and deviates to $P_{1l} = P_{1h} = f_1 + \epsilon$. Firm 1 will lose $\alpha(\epsilon/t)$ heavy users. Firm 1 does not lose any light users since the light user market is competitive and Firm 2 is capacity constrained. Firm 1's first order gain is $(2q_{1h} + q_{1l} - \alpha\gamma)\epsilon$. Such a deviation is not profitable if

$$\gamma \geq \frac{q_{1l} + q_{1h}}{\alpha} + \frac{q_{1h}}{\alpha}. \tag{A.19}$$

Suppose that Firm 1 lowers its price by $\epsilon > 0$ in both markets and deviates to $P_{1l} = P_{1h} = f_1 - \epsilon$. Firm 1 will attract $(1 - \alpha)(\epsilon/2t)$ light users in the light user market and $\alpha(\epsilon/t)$ in the heavy user market. The first-order gain from the deviation is negative if and only if

$$\gamma \leq \frac{2(q_{1l} + q_{1h})}{1 + \alpha} + \frac{q_{1h}}{\alpha}. \tag{A.20}$$

Inequalities (A.19) and (A.20) imply

$$(1 - \alpha)(q_{1l} + q_{1h}) \leq 0, \tag{A.21}$$

which is not possible. Thus, Firm 1 always has an incentive to deviate.

We now consider the second case, where Firm 1's demand in the heavy user market is at a kink, and show that this equilibrium is also impossible. Suppose, to the contrary, that such an equilibrium exists. Once again, by Lemma 6, one of the firms, say Firm 2, must be capacity-constrained, while Firm 1 is not. In addition, Firm 1 must charge a flat fee. Firm 2 has no incentive to lower its price to light users, while simultaneously increasing its price to heavy users so that all its capacity is still engaged, if

$$\frac{P_{2l}}{t} \leq \frac{2\hat{d}\left(1 - \frac{q_{1l}}{1 - \alpha}\right) - 2K_2 d_l + \gamma\alpha d_h d_l}{\alpha d_h^2}. \tag{A.22}$$

Note also that in this equilibrium, we have $P_{1l} + P_{2l} < 2V - t$ (the light user market is competitive) and $P_{1h} + P_{2h} = 2V - t$ (the heavy user market at a kink) so that $P_{1l} + P_{2l} < P_{1h} + P_{2h}$. Because $P_{1l} = P_{1h}$ in this equilibrium, we must have $P_{2l} < P_{2h}$. This means that Firm 2 can also deviate by raising its price to light users, while simultaneously lowering its price to heavy users so that all of its capacity is still engaged. This deviation is not profitable if

$$\frac{P_{2l}}{t} \geq \frac{(4\hat{d} - 2\alpha d_h^2)\left(1 - \frac{q_{1l}}{1 - \alpha}\right) - 4K_2 d_l + 2\gamma\alpha d_h d_l}{\alpha d_h^2}. \tag{A.23}$$

Note that in this equilibrium, we have $(1 - \alpha) - q_{1l} = q_{2l}$ and $q_{2h}d_l + q_{2h}d_h = K_2$. Using these two equalities, we have from Inequalities (A.22) and (A.23)

$$\gamma \leq \frac{2q_{2h}}{\alpha}. \tag{A.24}$$

However, Inequality (A.24) and the assumption $\gamma > 3$ imply $q_{2h} > \alpha$, i.e., that Firm 2's sales to heavy users are larger than the heavy user segment. A contradiction. This means that Firm 2 always has an incentive to deviate. $\square$

Appendix 3. Competitive Flat Fee Pricing

To derive the equilibrium of competitive flat fee pricing, we note that if none of the firms is constrained by its capacity, the no-infinitesimal-deviation conditions yield the standard Hotelling result for the price competition game, or $f_1 + p_1 d_l = f_1 + p_1 d_h = f_2 + p_2 d_l = f_2 + p_2 d_h = t$. This means that in this equilibrium we must have $f_1 = f_2 = t$, while $p_1 = p_2 = 0$. We then have the standard Hotelling payoff for each firm, or $\pi_1^* = \pi_2^* = t/2$. Notice that in such an equilibrium, firms must share the market equally, and each firm uses $\hat{d}/2$ units of its capacity. The condition that none of the firms is capacity constrained therefore implies that both K_1 and K_2 are greater than $\hat{d}/2$.

We now check the sufficiency conditions for such an equilibrium. The no infinitesimal deviation conditions rule out any unilateral deviation by a firm that leaves its competitor with some unused capacity. The only potentially profitable deviation for a firm is to raise its price unilaterally such that its competitor becomes capacity constrained. Firm i's unused capacity under our proposed equilibrium is $K_i - \hat{d}/2$. If each firm's capacity is greater than $\hat{d}$, each has at least $\hat{d}/2$ units of unused capacity under our proposed equilibrium. In this case, there is no deviation by a firm that can leave its competitor capacity constrained, and hence none of the firms wants to deviate unilaterally. Thus, a firm may deviate only if the competitor's capacity is between $\hat{d}/2$ and $\hat{d}$.

Suppose Firm 1's capacity is between $\hat{d}/2$ and $\hat{d}$. Firm 2 deviates by raising its price so much that all of Firm 1's capacity becomes engaged. Here, we assume for simplicity that Firm 1 always sells first to the consumers who value its service the most until it exhausts its capacity. In other words, we use the efficient rationing rule whenever excess demand arises because of capacity constraint. Once Firm 1 becomes capacity constrained, Firm 2 can charge a monopoly price to the remaining customers in the market.

At the point where Firm 1 becomes capacity constrained because of Firm 2's deviation, Firm 1 must be selling at the price t to both light and heavy users to the left of $\hat{x}$ such that it just exhausts its capacity K_1, where $\hat{x} = K_1/\hat{d}$. Then, the optimal deviation for Firm 2 is to sell to the rest of the consumers at a price that leaves zero surplus to the marginal consumers located at $\hat{x}$, or $P_h = P_l = V - (1 - \hat{x})t$. Thus, the optimal deviation profit is given by $\hat{\pi}_2 = [V - (1 - \hat{x})t](1 - \hat{x})$. This deviation payoff is smaller than $\pi_2^* = t/2$ if

$$K_1 \geq \tilde{K}^c = \frac{d}{2}[\sqrt{\gamma^2 - 2} - (\gamma - 2)], \qquad (A.25)$$

where $d/2 < \tilde{K}^c < d$. This means that only when $K_1 \geq \tilde{K}^c$, Firm 2 has no incentive to deviate from the proposed equilibrium. Symmetrically, Firm 1 has no incentive to deviate if $K_2 \geq \tilde{K}^c$. $\square$

Appendix 4. Equilibrium Analysis of Extended Model

To analyze the competitive case, note that at any given prices (p_h^2, p_h^1) charged respectively by the two competing firms, the heavy users who are indifferent between purchasing from either firm must be located at $\tilde{x}_h = (p_h^2 - p_h^1 + t)/2t$. These indifferent heavy users may derive negative surplus at those prices. In that case, they do not purchase from any firm and the heavy user segment is uncovered, i.e., $p_h^1 + p_h^2 > 2vd_h - t$; or they derive zero surplus from their purchase such that the heavy user segment is just covered (just covered), i.e., $p_h^1 + p_h^2 = 2vd_h - t$; or they enjoy positive surplus such that the heavy user segment is not only covered, but also competitive, i.e., $p_h^1 + p_h^2 < 2vd_h - t$. We now take up each possibility in turn to look for an equilibrium.

Heavy User Segment Uncovered

When the heavy user segment is uncovered, both firms are local monopolies in the heavy user segment. From our analysis of the monopolist case, we know that in any such equilibrium $x_h^i = (d_h/\hat{d})k^i$ is strictly greater than $x_l^i = (d_l/\hat{d})k^i$. Therefore, if the heavy user segment is uncovered, so must be the light user segment. Thus, both firms will price their access services as if they are a monopolist, charging only a per-unit price $p^i = v - (k^i/\hat{d})t$. In this equilibrium, we must have $x_h^1 + x_h^2 < 1$, i.e., $K_1 + K_2 < \hat{d}/d_h$.

Heavy User Segment Just Covered

In any equilibrium where the heavy segment is just covered, the light user segment can be either uncovered, just covered, or competitive. We will first show that there exists no equilibrium where the light user segment is either just covered or competitive and then derive the equilibrium where the light user segment is uncovered. We proceed first by proving a useful lemma.

LEMMA 8. *In any equilibrium where the heavy segment is just covered and the light segment is either just covered or uncovered, if Firm i is present in both markets charging a two-part tariff, we must have* $(2/3)x_h^i d_h \leq x_l^i d_l$.

PROOF. Firm i charging a two-part tariff ($p_l^i < p_h^i$) in equilibrium can always deviate by raising its price to light users by ϵ and lowering its price to heavy users by ϵ'. Because the light user segment is not competitive, such price changes will drop $(1 - \alpha)\epsilon/t$ light users and free $(1 - \alpha)(\epsilon/t)d_l$ units of capacity. Because the heavy user segment is just covered, the decrease in price to heavy users will attract $\alpha\epsilon'/2t$ heavy users and engage $\alpha(\epsilon'/2t)d_h$ units of additional capacity in that segment. Such simultaneous price changes are always feasible, irrespective of whether or not the firm is capacity constrained, because it can

always set $(1 - \alpha)(\epsilon/t)d_l = \alpha(\epsilon'/2t)d_h$. The net gain from these price changes is $(1 - \alpha)(x_l^i - \epsilon/t)\epsilon - (1 - \alpha)(\epsilon/t)p_l^i + \alpha(\epsilon'/2t)(p_h^i - \epsilon') - \alpha x_h^i \epsilon'$. Because none of the user segments are competitive, we must have $p_h^i = vd_h - x_h^i t$ and $p_l^i = vd_l - x_l^i t$. Then, the first-order net gain can be simplified to $\alpha(\epsilon/td_h)(2x_l^i td_h - 3x_h^i td_l)$. To sustain the equilibrium, the first order gain is necessarily negative, which implies $(2/3)x_h^i d_h \leq x_l^i d_l$. $\square$

We now show that there exists no equilibrium where both the heavy and light segments are just covered. Suppose, to the contrary, that such an equilibrium exists. Then, there must exist a firm, say Firm i, such that $x_l^i \geq x_l^j$, as if otherwise the inequality must apply to the rival firm ($x_l^i < x_l^j$). Given that $x_l^i \geq x_l^j$, Firm i cannot charge a flat fee in this equilibrium. Otherwise, we must have $p_h^i = p_l^i$, which in turn implies, by the fact that both heavy and light user markets are just covered, $x_l^i < x_l^j$, which contradicts $x_l^i \geq x_l^j$. Therefore, Firm i must be charging a two-part tariff, i.e., $p_h^i > p_l^i$. Then, by Lemma 8, we must have $(2/3)x_h^i d_h \leq x_l^i d_l$ or $x_l^i > 2x_l^i$, because $d_h > 4d_l$ by assumption. A contradiction. $\square$

Now we show that there exists no equilibrium where the heavy user segment is just covered and the light user segment is competitive. Suppose, to the contrary, that such an equilibrium exists. In any such equilibrium, at least one firm is capacity constrained. Otherwise, the standard Hotelling conditions (no-infinitesimal deviations) would yield a flat fee pricing structure for both firms with $f^1 = f^2 = t$. This would further mean that the indifferent heavy user would enjoy positive surplus, which is not possible. Now, let Firm 2 be capacity constrained. Then, Firm 1 must charge a flat fee f^1 in this equilibrium. Otherwise, it can profitably deviate by raising its light user price, extracting additional surplus from its light users without losing any of them to Firm 2 (which is unable to serve them because of its capacity constraint). Furthermore, the capacity constrained Firm 2 necessarily charges a two-part tariff ($p_l^2 < p_h^2$). Otherwise, if it were to charge a flat fee f^2, the fact that the heavy market is just covered and the light market is competitive implies $2vd_h - t = f^1 + f^2 < 2vd_h - t$, which is impossible because $d_h > d_l$ by assumption.

Firm 1 cannot be capacity constrained in this equilibrium. Or Firm 2 can always profitably deviate by raising its price to light users, extracting additional surplus from its light users without losing any of them to Firm 1 because of the firm's capacity constraint. As the heavy user segment is just covered, we have in equilibrium $p_h^2 = vd_h - (1 - x_h^1)t$ and $f^1 = vd_h - x_h^1 t$. Furthermore, as the light user segment is competitive, we must have $p_l^2 = 2x_l^1 t + f^1 - t$. These three equalities imply $p_h^2 = p_l^2 + 2(x_h^1 - x_l^1)t$. Now, as $p_l^2 < p_h^2$, we must have in equilibrium

$$x_h^1 > x_l^1. \qquad (A.26)$$

In the hypothesized equilibrium, Firm 2 has no incentive to drop some light users while simultaneously picking up some heavy users if

$$vd_h(d_h - d_l) > tx_l^2 4d_h - tx_h^2(d_h + 3d_l). \qquad (A.27)$$

Given $d_h > d_l$, this inequality implies $vd_h(d_h - d_l) > tx_l^2 4d_h - tx_h^2 4d_h$, which can be simplified to $v(d_h - d_l) > 4t(x_l^2 - x_h^2)$. This inequality, along with $x_l^2 - x_h^2 = x_h^1 - x_l^1$, yields

$$v(d_h - d_l) > 4t(x_h^i - x_l^i). \tag{A.28}$$

Once again, because the heavy user segment is just covered in the hypothesized equilibrium, Firm 1's marginal heavy users must have zero surplus, i.e., $s_h^1 = vd_h - tx_h^1 - f^1 = 0$. Because the light user segment is competitive, Firm 1's marginal light users must derive a positive surplus, i.e., $s_l^1 = vd_l - tx_l^1 - f^1 > 0$. These two inequalities imply

$$v(d_h - d_l) < t(x_h^1 - x_l^1). \tag{A.29}$$

From Inequalities (A.26), (A.28), and (A.29), we get $0 < 4t(x_h^1 - x_l^1) < t(x_h^1 - x_l^1)$. Because $(x_h^1 - x_l^1) > 0$ from Inequality (A.26), we must have $4t < t$. A contradiction. $\square$

Therefore, the only possible equilibrium we can find is the one where the heavy segment is just covered and the light segment is uncovered. In such an equilibrium, we must have $vd_h - p_h^i - tx_h^i = 0$ for $i = 1, 2$ by definition. Furthermore, both firms' capacity must be binding. Otherwise, the firm whose capacity is not binding can always lower its price to light users to gain more profit, as $\gamma_l \geq 3$ by assumption.

In this equilibrium, we have either $p_h^i = p_l^i$ or $p_h^i > p_l^i$ for any Firm i. However, we cannot have $p_h^i = p_l^i$ in equilibrium. This can be shown as follows. Suppose, to the contrary, that in equilibrium we have $p_h^i = p_l^i$ for Firm i. Then, the fact that the marginal heavy users derive zero surplus at Firm i and the marginal light users gain nonnegative surplus implies

$$\frac{x_h^i - x_l^i}{x_l^i} \geq \frac{(d_h - d_l)v}{tx_l^i}. \tag{A.30}$$

Furthermore, in this equilibrium, Firm i should not have any incentive to deviate by lowering its price to light users and increasing its price to heavy users simultaneously, while keeping its capacity full engaged. This implies $x_l^i d_l \geq x_l^i d_h$, or

$$\frac{x_h^i - x_l^i}{x_l^i} \leq \frac{d_h - d_l}{d_l}. \tag{A.31}$$

Inequalities (A.30) and (A.31), together with $\gamma_l \geq 2$, imply $x_l^i \geq 2$, a contradiction. $\square$

Because we must have $p_h^i > p_l^i$ in equilibrium, we must also have $vd_l - p_l^i - tx_l^i = 0$, i.e., that Firm i's marginal light users derive zero surplus. Otherwise, Firm i can always raise its price to light users slightly to increase its profit. Thus, the necessary conditions for this equilibrium are characterized by the following equalities:

$$vd_h - p_h^i - tx_h^i = 0, \tag{A.32}$$

$$vd_l - p_l^i - tx_l^i = 0, \tag{A.33}$$

$$\alpha x_h^i d_h + (1 - \alpha)x_l^i d_l = K_i, \tag{A.34}$$

$$x_h^1 + x_h^2 = 1, \tag{A.35}$$

where $i = 1, 2$. The sufficient conditions are given by the following two inequalities:

$$\frac{2}{3}x_l^i d_h \leq x_h^i d_l, \tag{A.36}$$

$$x_l^i d_h \geq x_h^i d_l. \tag{A.37}$$

Inequality (A.36) comes from Lemma 8, which ensures that neither firm has an incentive to deviate by simultaneously raising its price to light users and lowering its price to heavy users while still engaging its capacity fully. Inequality (A.37) ensures that neither firm has incentive to make the simultaneous price changes the other way around.

Conditions (A.32)–(A.37) define multiple equilibria. The multiplicity arises from the fact that both firms desire to engage their capacities in the heavy user segment first and they have no incentive to initiate price competition in that market as long as they engage a sufficient amount of capacity in that segment. However, if we impose the condition that the heavy user segment is "equitably" shared, i.e., $x_h^i = K_i/(K_1 + K_2)$, we have a unique equilibrium as long as $\hat{d}/d_h \leq K_1 + K_2 \leq \hat{d}/d_h + (1 - \alpha)d_l^2/2d_h$, where

$$f^1 = \frac{K_1 t[\hat{d} - (K_1 + K_2)d_h]}{(1 - \alpha)(d_h - d_l)d_l(K_1 + K_2)} \leq 0,$$

$$f^2 = \frac{K_2 t[\hat{d} - (K_1 + K_2)d_h]}{(1 - \alpha)(d_h - d_l)d_l(K_1 + K_2)} \leq 0,$$

$$p^1 = v - \frac{[\hat{d} - (K_1 + K_2)]K_1 t}{(1 - \alpha)(d_h - d_l)d_l(K_1 + K_2)} > 0,$$

$$p^2 = v - \frac{[\hat{d} - (K_1 + K_2)]K_2 t}{(1 - \alpha)(d_h - d_l)d_l(K_1 + K_2)} > 0.$$

Heavy User Segment Competitive

In any equilibrium where the heavy user segment is competitive, none of the firms can be capacity constrained. This is because if one of the firms is constrained by its capacity, the rival firm can always profitably deviate by raising its price to heavy users, extracting additional surplus from its heavy users without losing any of them to the capacity-constrained firm. This, in turn, means that the light user segment cannot be uncovered or just covered in equilibrium. The standard Hotelling conditions (no infinitesimal deviations) then yield, as the necessary conditions for a competitive equilibrium, a flat fee pricing structure for both firms with $f^1 = f^2 = t$ and a profit of $t/2$ for each firm. In this equilibrium, each firm's capacity must be large enough to cover half of the market, i.e., $K_i > \hat{d}/2$. We now derive the sufficient conditions for this equilibrium.

The optimal deviation for any firm in this hypothesized equilibrium is to raise its prices such that the rival, charging the flat fee t, becomes capacity constrained. Without the rival being capacity constrained, a firm's best response to the rival's charging the flat fee t is to charge the flat fee t itself. This implies that a firm may deviate only when the rival's capacity is not large enough to cover the whole market, i.e., $K_i < \hat{d}$. Otherwise, the optimal deviation can never make a firm better off. Now, consider, say, Firm 2 unilaterally takes the optimal deviation, given that

$d/2 < K_1 < d$. In that case, Firm 2's prices will be such that the marginal light and heavy users to Firm 2 will all have zero surplus. As Firm 1's price in both segments is fixed at t, we need to specify a rationing rule to allocate Firm 1's capacity at that low price. For simplicity, we assume that Firm 1's capacity is allocated on the basis of location such that we always have $x_l^1 = x_h^1 = x^1$. This means $x^1 = K_1/d$. Here we can also use the efficient rationing rule. Such a rule will not qualitatively alter our conclusion but will yield a far more complex cutoff point in capacity for the competitive equilibrium to be sustained.

Firm 2's optimal deviation prices can be determined from $vd_h - p_h^2 - t(1 - x^1) = 0$ and $vd_l - p_l^2 - t(1 - x^1) = 0$. Then, the optimal deviation profit for Firm 2 is given by $\alpha x^1 p_h^2 + (1 - \alpha)x^1 p_l^2$. Let

$$\tilde{K}^c = \frac{d}{2}(\sqrt{\bar{\gamma}^2 - 2} - (\bar{\gamma} - 2)),$$

where $\bar{\gamma} = dv/t > 2$ and $d/2 < \tilde{K}^c < d$. It is straightforward to show that as long as $K_1 > \tilde{K}^c$, Firm 2's optimal deviation profit is strictly less than $t/2$, its profit in the hypothesized equilibrium, so that Firm 2 has no incentive to deviate. The same analysis also applies to Firm 1. □

References

Armstrong, Mark, John Vickers. 2001. Competitive price discrimination. *Rand J. Econom.* 32(4) 579–605.

Benoit, Jean-Pierre, Vijay Krishna. 1987. Dynamic duopolies: Prices and quantities. *Rev. Econom. Stud.* LIV 23–35.

Calem, P. S., D. F. Spulber. 1984. Multiproduct two-part tariffs. *Internat. J. Indust. Organ.* 2 339–357.

Curle, David. 1998. There's no value if it's not relevant. *Inform. Today* 15 (8) 10–15.

Davidson, Carl, Raymond Deneckere. 1986. Long-run competition in capacity, short run competition in price, and the Cournot model. *Rand J. Econom.* 17(3) 402–415.

Edgeworth, F. 1897. La Teoria Pura del Monopolio. *Giornali degli Economisti* 40 13–31. Reprinted in English as "The Pure Theory of Monopoly." F. Edgeworth, ed. *Papers Relating to Political Economy.* MacMillan & C., Ltd., London, UK. 1925. Vol. 1, 111–142.

Hayes, Beth. 1987. Competition and two-part tariffs. *J. Bus.* 60(1) 41–54.

Investor's Business Daily. 1998. "End internet's free lunch." April 9, A6.

Kanell, Michael E. 1999. "BellSouth tries flat-rate plan competitive move called a gamble. *Atlanta J.,* April 17, D 1.

Kreps, David M., Jose A. Sheinkman. 1983. Quantity precommitment and Bertrand competition yield Cournot outcomes. *Bell J. Econom.* 14(2) 326–337.

Lovelock, Christopher H. 1996. *Services Marketing,* 3rd ed. Prentice Hall, Upper Saddle River, NJ. 3.

Maggi, Giovanni. 1996. Strategic trade policies with endogenous mode of competition. *Amer. Econom. Rev.* 237–258.

Oi, Walter Y. 1971. A Disneyland dilemma: Two-part tariffs for a Mickey Mouse monopoly. *Quart. J. Econom.* 85 77–96.

Peters, Michael. 1984. Bertrand equilibrium with capacity constraints and restricted mobility. *Econometrica* 52(5) 1117–1127.

PCS Week. 1997. "Market worries as PCS carriers experiment with pricing." February 7, 8(6).

Rifkin, Jeremy. 2000. *The Age of Access.* Tarcher-Putnam, New York.

Rochet, Jean-Charles, Lars A. Stole. 2002. Nonlinear pricing with random participation constraints. *Rev. Econom. Stud.* 69(1).

Schmalensee, R. 1981. Monopolistic two-part pricing arrangements. *Bell J. Econom.* 12 445–466.

Scotchmer, Suzanne. 1985. Two-tier pricing of shared facilities in a free-entry equilibrium. *Rand J. Econom.* 16 456–472.

Stole, Lars A. 1995. Nonlinear pricing and oligopoly. *J. Econom. Management Strategy* 4(4) 529–562.

Stroh, Michael. 1998. AT&T is dropping unlimited internet plan. *Sacramento Bee,* April 1.

The New York Times. 1996. "What price fun?" Sunday, May 9, section TR, 12.

Wilson, Robert B. 1993. *Nonlinear Pricing.* Oxford University Press, New York.

This paper was received June 4, 1999, and was with the authors 22 months for 2 revisions; processed by Rajiv Lal.

The Costly Bargain of Trade Promotion

Robert D. Buzzell, John A. Quelch, and Walter J. Salmon

ne of the most significant phenomena in retailing in recent years has been the shift in power from manufacturers to the trade. In frequently purchased, heavily advertised goods, the dominant players have become the big chains like Safeway, Wal-Mart, Kroger, K mart, Toys "R" Us, Walgreen, CVS, Home Depot, and Circuit City.

Partly as a result of manufacturers' relative loss of clout, they have been reducing their commitment to advertising—especially national advertising—and spending much more on consumer and trade promotion. But systemic inefficiencies resulting from these short-term incentives have blossomed into huge problems: the high costs involved in paying slotting allowances, in forward buying, in diversion of goods, and in running promotion programs. These are problems for the trade and for manufacturers, but especially for manufacturers.

Manufacturers pay dearly for burgeoning promotional programs; for example, managers at Procter & Gamble estimate that 25% of salesperson time and about 30% of brand management time are spent in designing, implementing, and overseeing promotions. The costs are high for others too. In this promotion-intensive environment, consumers pay more for the goods they buy as distributors pass along the higher costs. In the food industry, for instance, increases in manufacturer and distributor costs from trade promotion alone amount to an estimated 2.5% or more of retail sales, including the costs of administering promotional programs.

The game playing and power playing inherent in

promotions and related activities, like slotting allowances, have generated an enormous amount of mistrust in channels of distribution—manufacturers, wholesalers, and retailers have big bones to pick with one another. The mistrust has dominated the headlines in *Supermarket News* for two years or more. Here are sample news stories:

☐ Some consumer-goods producers have had to set up large reserves on their accounts receivable to handle expected retailer claims for damaged or spoiled merchandise and for promotion allowances for which they allegedly have not received full credit. These claims are not speculative; in 1988, for example, Kraft took a $35 million write-off. Such instances cause great friction because retailers have been known to file claims on merchandise as a way of getting discounts they could not have gotten otherwise. The number of contested claims has risen to an all-time high.

☐ Last year, two of the largest grocery chains,

The authors, senior faculty at the Harvard Business School, concentrate on consumer marketing. Robert D. Buzzell is the Sebastian S. Kresge Professor of Marketing, John A. Quelch is professor of business administration, and Walter J. Salmon is the Stanley Roth, Sr., Professor of Retailing.

Author's note: The material on forward buying in this article is taken from a study sponsored by the Food Marketing Foundation, which we thank. Associate Professor Marie-Therese Flaherty and Professor Ramchandran Jaikumar of the Harvard Business School and Marci Dew of the consulting firm IAMCO were coauthors of the study.

Winn-Dixie and Kroger, boycotted some products of Pillsbury, Procter & Gamble, and other vendors after those companies refused to charge uniform prices for their goods throughout the chains' trading areas. Winn-Dixie started the imbroglio by telling the big suppliers, "Everything we buy from you will be at the lowest promotion price offered throughout our entire system." The asserted motive: to smooth operations and save consumers money. Manufacturers took Winn-Dixie's demands as an infringement on their ability to engage in regional pricing. Winn-Dixie deleted from its shelves several hundred items of Pillsbury, P&G, Quaker Oats, and others. Negotiation eventually ended the standoff.

□ For years, Kellogg has refused to pay slotting allowances—the fees mass merchandisers, mostly food chains, charge packaged-goods producers to allow new products into their stores—to Stop & Shop and other companies. These fees commonly amount to four- or five-figure numbers per item per chain. Countering Kellogg's stance, Stop & Shop for a time refused to carry its new cereal varieties.

Battles like these are a common occurrence today now that retailers hold sway over manufacturers. Routinely, for example, department stores and other retailers demand from vendors cooperative advertising allowances, guaranteed gross margins, return privileges, reimbursement for the cost of fixtures, and in-store selling and stockkeeping help to promote their merchandise.

Deep-seated feelings about unfairness in today's promotion-laden atmosphere go hand in hand with the rising costs of promotions and the inefficiencies they produce. Mistrust inhibits industry cooperation on key issues like data exchange. The promotion practices also appear to be dispelling Washington's prolonged lack of interest in violation of laws upholding fair competition.

Here we will examine the by-products of the promotion explosion by putting under a microscope one widespread practice, forward buying, in key product lines sold in supermarkets: dry grocery products, health and beauty aids, and general merchandise. We examine the effects of forward buying and then of trade promotion in general on the entire distribution chain—manufacturers, wholesalers, retailers, and consumers. We suggest one pricing policy that not only helps get costs under control but also builds cooperation and trust among the parties.

Analysis of the costly inefficiencies that spill out of forward buying in food supermarkets may help manufacturers and distributors in other fields put the spotlight on practices in their own backyards. Although promotion practices are probably most widespread in the supermarket business, forward buying and diversion are also common in, say, athletic foot-

wear, and slotting allowances are not unknown in the chain drugstores.

HIGH TIDE OF PROMOTION

At the expense of advertising, promotion has received a big lift in recent years. Just how much a lift can be seen in the responses to an annual survey of marketing managers in consumer packaged-goods companies showing the breakdowns of their marketing budgets. In 1978, advertising accounted for 42% of those budgets and consumer and trade promotion, 58%. By 1988, ad spending had slipped to 31% against 69% for promotion.[1] Trade promotion accounted for three-quarters of the shift.

There are some powerful forces in motion that explain the intensifying stress on sales promotion:

□ The U.S. population is growing at only 0.8% annually, and growth in per-capita consumption of most mature products is modest. This situation, combined with excess production capacity, has aggravated competition for market share and the use of price promotions to secure it.

□ Today's consumer is less interested in shopping, more likely to hold a job, under greater time pressure, and less inclined to prepare a shopping list ahead of a store visit. Hence today's consumer is more susceptible to prominent displays in the store and more likely to buy whichever of several acceptable brands happens to be on deal.

□ As the technologies underpinning established products mature, the opportunities for product and quality differentiation shrink. That fact, combined with the weaker involvement of the consumer, makes development of creative advertising copy more difficult. The result: emphasis on price competition.

□ While there is no shortage of new products, most are line extensions and me-too imitations. Given the proliferation of new products clamoring for finite shelf space and retailers' limited promotion capacity, distributors try to ration their resources. They turn to slotting allowances and press for more and better deals on all products in their stores.

□ Many factors influence manufacturers and retailers in the direction of a short-term outlook. On the manufacturers' side, for example, top management's concern for meeting quarterly earnings targets, plus the fast career advancement that young managers expect, reinforces this orientation. A result is a preference for boosting sales through promotion instead of taking the time to strengthen the consumer franchise through advertising.

Of course, there are many good reasons for undertaking a serious promotion program. The insert "Why Sales Promotions?" lists several of them.

Why Sales Promotions?

They are useful in securing trial for new products and in defending shelf space against anticipated and existing competition.

☐ The funds manufacturers dedicate to them lower the distributor's risk in stocking new brands.

☐ They add excitement at the point-of-sale to the merchandising of mature and mundane products. They can instill a sense of urgency among consumers to buy while a deal is available.

☐ Since sales promotion costs are incurred on a pay-as-you-go basis, they can spell survival for smaller, regional brands that cannot afford big advertising programs.

☐ Sales promotions allow manufacturers to use idle capacity and to adjust to demand and supply imbalances or softness in raw material prices and other input costs—while maintaining the same list prices.

They allow manufacturers to price-discriminate among consumer segments that vary in price sensitivity. Most manufacturers believe that a high-list, high-deal policy is more profitable than offering a single price to all consumers. A portion of sales promotion expenditures, therefore, consists of reductions in list prices that are set for the least price-sensitive segment of the market.

A CASE: FORWARD BUYING

In our study of the important food distribution sector of the economy—accounting for supermarket sales of $240 billion in 1988—we sought to discover how much trade promotion raises certain expenses. While our estimates of such cost effects apply only to food distributors and manufacturers, we believe that they will give a useful perspective on sales promotion broadly throughout the U.S. consumer-marketing system.

During the 1980s, marketers of food, household, and personal-care products offered more frequent and more attractive trade deals to food chains and wholesalers. These are inducements used to influence a distributor to stock or display more of a product or cut its price to consumers. The distributors responded by:

☐ Adding to their "forward-buy" inventories. These stocks—merchandise bought at cut prices in addition to quantities needed to sell at reduced prices or to sell through retailer advertising or end displays during the deal period—are held for later sale, usually at regular prices.

☐ Diverting goods from regions in which manufacturers offer especially deep discounts to higher priced areas when different deals are offered in different areas. The means of doing it include (1) transfer from one division of a multiregional or national retailer or wholesaler to another division, (2) sale and direct shipment from one distributor to another, and (3) consignment via "diverters" who make this their business.

Both practices add to the distributors' costs. Forward buying inflates inventories and thereby boosts interest expense, storage charges, and insurance costs. Forward buying also means extra transportation and handling outlays because forward-buy stocks are almost always kept separate from the "regular" inventories. Diversion of merchandise involves trans-shipment and double-handling, which of course cost money.

To estimate the added costs from diversion would have meant determining the normal paths followed by a sample shipment from suppliers to distributors. A comparison of actual shipping and handling expenses, including diversions, with normal costs would have yielded the desired numbers. But this would have been a monumental task given the large number of shipping points and warehouses in the United States, so we did not attempt it.

Even so, we believe that the added costs of diversion are substantial. Food-marketing consultant Willard Bishop, a long-time observer of the industry, estimates that the volume of merchandise involved amounts to at least $5 billion a year.

Impact on Distributor Inventories. We did estimate the impact of forward buying by comparing distributors' purchasing patterns with those that would have been expected if there had been no (or less) forward buying. ("Distributors" here means both retail chains and wholesalers.)

If trade deals did not exist, food chains and wholesalers customarily would order from their major suppliers about every two weeks. A company would order enough merchandise to cover the next two weeks plus a safety stock, typically about one week's supply, to accommodate unforseeable variations in sales patterns leading to above-average sales. A distributor following this pattern would have an average inventory of two weeks' supply, as shown in the chart "No-Trade-Deal Distributor Inventory."

Now let's look at reality: distributors take advan-

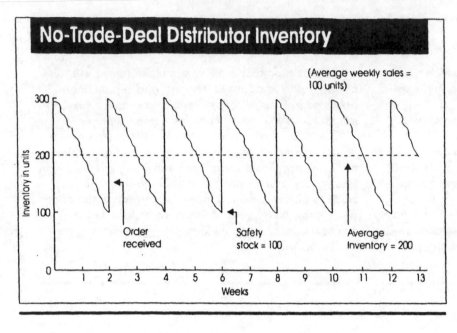

No-Trade-Deal Distributor Inventory

(Average weekly sales = 100 units)

Order received

Safety stock = 100

Average Inventory = 200

Inventory in units

Weeks

tage of periodic trade opportunities to forward-buy goods for later sale. Most well-run distributors use widely available computer programs to determine how much to buy on a given supplier's deal. The savings that distributors realize normally more than offset the extra costs of buying, double-handling, and stocking enough merchandise to last perhaps until the next deal. Distributors usually have a good idea when the next deal will be offered because most suppliers schedule their trade deals well ahead. So a rational distributor will make nearly all purchases during deal periods.

How would average inventories then be affected? The answer depends on how often the price reductions are offered and the extent to which consumer purchases shift to the deal periods. The chart "Distributor Inventory on Trade Deals" illustrates a typical situation in which deals are offered during four weeks of each quarter, and 50% of consumer purchases are made during those weeks because the retailer features the manufacturer's merchandise. The effect on distributor inventories is drastic: year-round average inventory is 80% greater.

While this estimate is based on just one set of assumptions about deal frequency and the size of deal discounts, this estimated increase agrees with information that food distributors gave us in our study. Their forward-buy inventories normally amounted to 40% to 50% of total stocks. If forward buying raised inventory by 80% over the level it would be under a no-dealing scenario, then 80/180 or 44% of total inventory is attributable to forward buying.

Most forward buying in the retail food sector is in dry grocery goods, household supplies, and personal-

care products. We estimate that supermarket sales of dry groceries, health and beauty aids, and general merchandise were $109 billion or about $87.5 billion at wholesale values. In the absence of any forward buying, distributors' inventories of these goods would have neared $4.4 billion. If actual inventories included 40% to 50% of forward-buy stocks, the *increase* in distributors' inventories attributable to forward buying ranged from $2.9 billion to $4.4 billion. If these forward-buy purchases were usually bought at 10% below "normal" prices, the amount invested in them ranges from $2.6 billion to $4 billion.

Moreover, some forward buying in high-volume frozen foods and dairy products also goes on. Forward-buy stocks of these products represent a distributor investment of about $500 million. This brings the total to $3.1 billion to $4.5 billion.

The carrying costs on distributors' inventories—including handling, storage, and capital charges—were about 30% per year. Applying this figure to the added inventories in the system from forward buying yields an added system cost of between $930 million and $1.35 billion a year. While this is obviously a substantial amount, it represents only between 0.65% and 0.9% of total retail sales of the products affected.

Costs to the Manufacturers. Forward buying is a chief cause of fluctuations in a supplier's rate of shipment to distributors. How much does it contribute to the total "cost of uncertainty" for manufacturers? Our study shows that the impact of forward buying on suppliers' costs depends on:

☐ The fraction of total sales accounted for by forward-buy purchases. Not surprisingly, the more important forward buying is, the more it contributes to total uncertainty costs.

☐ The interval between promotions. The longer the interval, the greater the uncertainty about demand. (At the other extreme, continuous promotions would make forward buying unnecessary and, obviously, generate no uncertainty about it. A few heavily promoted categories, like ground coffee, nearly fit this description.)

☐ The number of items, or stockkeeping units (SKUs), in a supplier's product line. The more SKUs, the greater the demand uncertainty for any particular item.

For a manufacturer, distributors' forward buying is a serious factor, but only one of several factors (some of them having nothing to do with sales promotion)

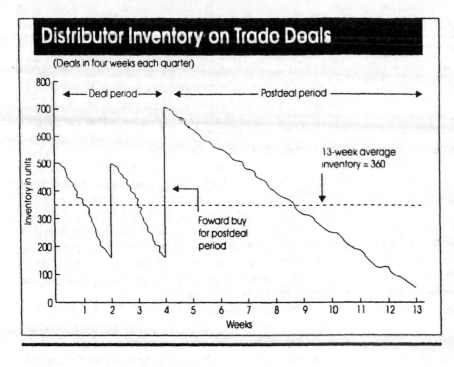

Distributor Inventory on Trade Deals

(Deals in four weeks each quarter)

Deal period — Postdeal period

13-week average inventory = 360

Foward buy for postdeal period

Inventory in units

Weeks

that generate uncertainty about demand and limit producers' ability to forecast sales accurately. So they maintain excess production capacity and carry safety stocks of finished goods, which cost money. Several leading food-industry suppliers are paying the price: they have undertaken large-scale plant closings. Among them are P&G, which in 1987 set up an $805 million reserve to "restructure" worldwide production operations, and Campbell Soup, which last summer scheduled a similar charge, to cost $343 million.

From discussions with several big food-industry suppliers, we estimate that for most food companies the incremental costs related to forward buying range between 1% and 2% of their costs of goods sold. If typical gross margins are around 33 1/3% for suppliers and 20% for distributors, this added cost represents 0.5% to 1.1% of retail prices of the products involved. Applying these figures to total 1988 retail sales of dry groceries and selected dairy and frozen products makes the incremental supplier costs from forward buying between $720 million and $1.58 billion.

Costs to the System. Adding the two figures yields the total of $1.6 billion to $2.9 billion shown in the table "Total Added Costs Resulting from Forward Buying." Nonperishable food-store products represent some 5% of all retail sales. Forward buying is of course impractical for perishable merchandise, like fruit and vegetables, or short life-cycle merchandise, like fashion apparel. But if all consumer goods are considered, forward-buying costs could total several times the $1.6 billion to $2.9 billion spread.

Moreover, these substantial amounts represent only a part of the true costs of trade promotion, let alone the total cost of all forms of sales promotion. Other expenses, which we have not tried to quantify, include.

☐ The added transportation and handling costs in diverting merchandise among regions.

☐ The higher administrative and selling costs that suppliers and distributors incur to operate increasingly complex selling and purchasing programs. We mentioned P&G's assertion that 30% of the brand management organization's time and 25% of field salespeople's time is absorbed by these tasks. The proportions are typical.

☐ The costs of the time that buyers and merchants spend evaluating deals, which would be better spent in competitive analyses and category management.

These hidden costs of promotion could easily equal or exceed the more tangible costs that we explored. The total cost is very high, both absolutely and relative to suppliers' and distributors' earnings. Reduction of these costs would produce savings that could greatly benefit consumers and retailers, wholesalers, and manufacturers.

SOME LIKE IT, SOME DON'T

In addition to impairing the efficiency of the distribution system, the explosion in sales promotion expense has other important, harmful effects on the distribution chain.

Our analysis of the food industry yields estimates that the increase in manufacturer and distributor costs from more trade promotion amounts to about 2 1/2% of retail sales. Since there has been no noticeable decline of manufacturer and distributor *profits,* the consumer has presumably absorbed these costs.

This cost burden has not affected all consumers equally. Those with the time and inclination to shop for bargains, termed "cherry pickers" by the trade, have probably enjoyed lower prices as a result of the higher proportion of items offered on sale. But most consumers, whose shopping time is often constrained by work and other responsibilities, have probably seen their prices on affected items rise by somewhat more than 2%.

Other consequences of higher sales promotion expenses have affected consumers too. Because it is harder to predict the rate of sale of merchandise offered at special prices, stock-outs of preferred brands may be more frequent. This phenomenon would apply more to risky, short life-cycle fashion merchandise offered at special prices than to staple items where forward-buy inventories probably offset the less predictable sales rate of merchandise that is sold on specials.

Another probable effect of the availability of more merchandise at special prices is a deterioration of in-store service. Special sales exaggerate the normal peaks and valleys of store traffic and thus impair service, whether it is the availability of a salesperson in a department store or the length of a checkout line in a discount store or supermarket.

The extra costs that trade promotions impose on distribution channels do not affect all classes of trade equally. Such distributors as deep-discount drugstores and warehouse clubs—which carry few items in each category and have no commitment to item continuity—favor heightened manufacturer sales-promotion activity.

Warehouse clubs especially have this attitude. The burgeoning volume of trade deals, in particular, means that more items (or the same items more often) are available to them at sharply reduced prices. Moreover, since they usually offer only a few brands and sizes in a category, they can quickly dispose of the promoted items with no effect on the movement of competing items. Competitors allege that the frequency of trade deals, combined with relaxed enforcement of the Robinson-Patman Act and manufacturers' hunger for more volume, allows these limited-line distributors to buy at more favorable prices than traditional channels or to obtain other concessions like direct store delivery of smaller quantities at no extra cost.

Food wholesalers are ambivalent about promotion practices. While they vigorously condemn the allegedly better treatment that nonfood channels receive, they do not advocate elimination of these practices. Because quasinational or multiregional operators dominate food wholesaling, they have established their own internal diversion networks. Moreover, the difference between forward-buying income and expense gives them added flexibility. While passing on some of these funds to customers in proportion to their purchases, they can use a portion of the income to subsidize weak areas, underwrite new operations, support added services for retailers, or boost their own profits.

The wholesalers' ambivalent attitude toward promotion practices contrasts sharply with the views of some food retailers. They argue that the labor and storage costs of forward-buy inventories and the extra transportation costs in diverting merchandise, while more than offset by lower purchase prices for merchandise, nevertheless add to their costs of goods sold. These expenses, many retailers assert, undercut

the advantages of just-in-time replenishment practices for their regular inventories. They fear that an overriding concern for buying at the lowest cost diverts their merchandising organizations from the primary goal of serving consumers better. What these retailers would prefer is a system that provides them with the lower purchase prices for merchandise *without* the added costs of forward buying and diversion.

Producers of health and beauty aids and food also take exception to these promotion practices. Apart from the incremental manufacturing or inventory costs they incur, they perceive serious, though non-quantifiable, consequences. Among them is a decline in brand loyalty arising from elevated consumer price sensitivity. Even consumers once faithful to certain brands may switch to other products that are on deal or time the purchase of their preferred products to coincide with available deals.

Food manufacturers also complain that retailers often fail to discharge their responsibility to provide temporary price reductions, special displays, or feature advertisements. Often retailers allegedly accept promotional allowances for more deals than they are able to fulfill. Manufacturers' attempts to enforce deal terms, however, may spur retailer retaliation, such as deducting unearned merchandise allowances from invoices, increasing claims for damaged merchandise, or delisting low turnover items.

The aforementioned trade-deal terms that favor limited-line distributors, like warehouse clubs, are another sore spot for manufacturers. Because the main goal of limited-line distributors is to sell merchandise at the lowest prices rather than have particular brands always in stock, their priorities inherently conflict with brand loyalty. Furthermore, limited-line distributors refuse to carry the slow movers in a manufacturer's line—but these are often the manufacturer's most profitable items.

The trade promotion climate has had two disturbing effects. First, as we have indicated, it has aroused mistrust between manufacturers and distributors. This could inhibit cooperation on matters that benefit the whole distribution chain, including electronic-data interchange, modular packaging, and more use of direct product-profit accounting.

Second, today's climate invites political intervention to rid the system of the wasteful expenses of forward buying and diversion. The Federal Trade Commission has been studying slotting allowances for some time. If the Bush Administration decides to renew enforcement of the Robinson-Patman Act, manufacturers and distributors would be endangered. Running afoul of this law in the past has resulted in prolonged and costly litigation, stiff fines, and government-imposed sanctions and reporting requirements that are competitively disadvantageous. Im-

Total Added Costs Resulting from Forward Buying

	Millions of Dollars	Percent of Retail Sales
Distributors	$ 930 to $1,350	0.65% to 0.9%
Manufacturers	$ 720 to $1,584	0.5% to 1.1%
Total	$1,650 to $2,934	1.15% to 2.0%*

*Excluding added administrative costs

proving sales promotion practices ethically and legally would reduce this threat.

Despite their concern about the situation, manufacturers have not acted in concert to change matters. Competitive rivalries and fear of being charged with illegal price fixing have inhibited them.

LIVING WITH PROMOTIONS

Forward buying, diversion, higher manufacturing expenses, and inflated selling and administrative expenses for manufacturers as well as distributors are costing consumers billions each year. And all indications are that the problem is becoming worse. Trade promotions cannot be wished away. But surely there must be a means to execute them at lower cost.

One way to smooth the expense peaks and valleys is a policy of everyday low purchase price (EDLPP). A retailer arranges to buy a particular product from a manufacturer on an as-needed basis at a weighted average price reflecting both the proportion of merchandise recently bought on a deal basis and the proportion bought at the regular price. In return, the retailer agrees to support the product with a certain number and type of promotional events or, more likely, a guarantee to "sell through" to consumers a given quantity of the particular item over a designated period. (Scanner tapes reveal whether the retailer has met the commitment.)

This arrangement has three great benefits. It avoids forward-buy inventory buildup for manufacturers and distributors. It reduces SG&A expenses for producers and sellers because they spend less time negotiating—the contracts run for six months to a year—or supervising performance—because the scanner tapes supply the evidence. Finally, it makes the relationship a collaborative, long-term effort and fosters a spirit of partnership that is seldom found in the monthly deal-buying frenzy.

True, wholesalers would lose some of the flexibility they now enjoy in the use of forward-buy income. In addition, since they have less influence over their retail customers than a chain store does, they could find it difficult to fulfill sell-through guarantees. EDLPP also violates tradition. Chain and wholesale buyers and suppliers' salespeople would have to be weaned away from deal-to-deal buying and selling. Moreover, performance evaluation and incentive systems geared to current practice would have to be changed.

Despite these obstacles, a number of distributors and manufacturers view EDLPP as a source of competitive advantage and are expanding their use of it. In New England, two leading supermarket chains, Hannaford Brothers and Shaw's, are doing business with suppliers on this basis. If EDLPP is superior to deal-to-deal transactions in executing trade promotions, it will gain greater acceptance. (Moreover, we believe, it leads to lower average prices for consumers because of pass-through of savings on handling costs and interest and transportation expenses, as well as administrative costs.)

Clearly, however, EDLPP does not constitute a panacea for all the problems associated with the current promotion climate. With EDLPP, friction among particular channel members will lessen but it will not disappear altogether. Manufacturers will therefore have to dedicate more resources than ever to evaluating their individual trade promotion policies.

While for the most part trade power is rising, the balance of power between manufacturers and distributors depends on the industry, product category, and market shares. Formulation of a trade-promotion program should begin with an examination of what is practical and profitable for a particular manufacturer to do in lieu of trade promotion to market its products effectively.

We say "in lieu of" because trade promotion should be a last resort in the marketing mix. Product improvement, more effective advertising, and better packaging that more favorably differentiates the manufacturer's offering to the targeted consumer segments (that is, better marketing) are the best avenues for reducing promotion spending and its attendant costs. Investment in R&D is the best way to differentiate and to avoid the necessity of promotions. Even if the payoff is not immediate, discretionary funds can be invested in activities that strengthen a product's consumer franchise unless the present value of the resulting earnings stream is lower than the returns from comparable outlays on promotions.

If the manufacturer nevertheless concludes that it must continue to invest at least some funds in promotions, we recommend adherence to the following guidelines:

☐ Focus on the particular support needed from the trade. What these are depends on an understanding of consumer buying behavior. In stimulating sales on impulse-oriented products—cookies, for example—displays are more effective than extra feature ads in retailers' circulars.

☐ Think through the ways that your trade-support needs differ by distributor. From one distributor, a manufacturer may want authorization for additional sizes and flavors; from a second, more shelf space for existing items; and from a third, better pricing on advertised items.

☐ Productivity improves when promotions complement distributors' merchandising thrusts. Money for a feature ad may work more effectively if it ties into a distributor's special-event promotion, while funds for a special display may spark more cooperation than a feature ad from a distributor committed to everyday low pricing. Provide a menu of promotions that distributors with different merchandising strategies can choose from.

☐ Look for ways to reduce the administrative burden imposed on distributors as well as on yourself. For example, there is much to be said for using scanner tapes to verify sell-through objectives instead of using hard-to-track measures like number of incremental end-aisle displays.

☐ Spread trade-promotion funds fairly among distributors. Fairness should take into account differences in the services they demand from you. A distributor that, say, wants a lot of help from your salespeople to do shelf resets will ordinarily be entitled to less trade-promotion support than a distributor that takes on this task itself. Therefore, be familiar with the components of your cost structure to know how many dollars to give an account in trade-promotion funds.

Effective use of trade-promotion funds means allocating them quantitatively and qualitatively on an account-by-account basis. A field sales organization that is close to the distributors is obviously better positioned to take on this burden than headquarters marketing personnel. Sales force upgrading, training, and performance criteria that recognize trade-promotion profit as well as volume are therefore a necessity.

Of course, there are often ways to cut costs even in a full-scale promotion program. P&G has established product-supply managers for each of its products. They are charged with supervising the procurement and smoothing the logistics of getting Procter goods to market. The company has also eliminated special packs after discovering that the cost of running these promotions was far greater for distributors as well as for themselves than the cost of regular price promotions of equivalent value. For distributors, using special packs means removing regularly priced goods from the shelf and replacing them with the special packs, and then reversing the procedure at the end of the deal period. For P&G, the necessity of adding SKUs, for which demand had to be forecast, and the increased chances of residuals after the promotion ended were the villains in the cost structure of special packs.

The elimination of special packs has been a major factor in the dramatic improvement of P&G's relationships with wholesalers and retailers. We believe that P&G's success in taking this action is compelling evidence of what can be accomplished by a more rational approach to pricing and sales-promotion management. Many manufacturers are experimenting with EDLPP sales programs; we are confident that the resulting improvements in efficiency and trade relations can be even greater than those achieved by P&G via eliminating special packs.

Obviously, the responsibility for a more rational sales-promotion climate does not lie entirely with manufacturers. Retailers and wholesalers have to take advantage of their enhanced power in ways that do not encumber the distribution system with additional costs.

One way is through a switch in accounting systems so they can distinguish between "the most deal money" and acquiring merchandise at the lowest net cost, including their own expenses for storing and handling inventory. Accounting systems, however, are only as good as the people who use them. Therefore, reorientation and incentive programs that encourage their merchants and buyers to think in this manner are also necessary.

The balance of power in marketing is changing. Companies will best preserve and enhance their positions if they adjust their sales-promotion programs to reflect this reality without burdening the distribution system—and ultimately consumers—with additional costs.

---

1. Donnelley Marketing, *Eleventh Annual Survey of Promotional Practices* (Stamford, Conn., 1989).

Competitive One-to-One Promotions

Greg Shaffer • Z. John Zhang

William E. Simon Graduate School of Business, University of Rochester, Rochester, New York 14627
The Wharton School of Business, University of Pennsylvania, Philadelphia, Pennsylvania 19104
shaffer@simon.rochester.edu • zjzhang@wharton.upenn.edu

One-to-one promotions are possible when consumers are individually addressable and firms know something about each customer's preferences. We explore the competitive effects of one-to-one promotions in a model with two competing firms where the firms differ in size and consumers have heterogeneous brand loyalty. We find that one-to-one promotions always lead to an increase in price competition (average prices in the market decrease). However, we also find that one-to-one promotions affect market shares. This market-share effect may outweigh the effect of lower prices, benefiting the firm whose market share increases. Our results suggest that of two firms, the firm with the higher-quality product may gain from one-to-one promotions. Our model also has implications for the phenomenon of customer churn, where consumers switch to a less preferred brand due to targeted promotional incentives. We show that churning can arise optimally from firms pursuing a profit-maximizing strategy. Instead of trying to minimize it, the optimal way to manage customer churn is to engage in both offensive and defensive promotions with the relative mix depending on the marginal cost of targeting.

(*Database Marketing; Game Theory; Strategy; Price Discrimination*)

Somewhere, a network has more personal data about you than you probably ever imagined.

—*Business Week*, April 5, 1999

1. Introduction

Advances in information technologies and the Internet today allow firms to identify individual consumers with greater accuracy and cost-effectiveness than ever before, which, in turn, allows firms to tailor their promotional prices to consumers on a one-to-one basis. Many firms are already taking advantage of this new-found ability to customize their prices. AT&T, for instance, has successfully lured many MCI customers to switch carriers by offering them personalized checks in the amounts of $25 to $100 depending on each consumer's long-distance calling history and experience with AT&T (Turco 1993). Other examples include mail-order companies, like LL Bean, which often insert into their catalogs "special offers" that

vary across households, and the online data provider Lexis-Nexis, which "sells to virtually every user at a different price" (Shapiro and Varian 1999).

One-to-one promotions are facilitated by many information-intensive marketing approaches such as database marketing, target marketing, micromarketing, and one-to-one marketing.[1] One-to-one promotions are often seen as beneficial to practicing firms because they allow a firm to charge lower prices to new consumers (for the purpose of inducing trial or

[1] Practitioners sometimes use these terms interchangeably. Database marketing refers to any marketing activity that is aided by a consumer database. Target marketing refers to the process by which a firm offers promotional incentives tailored to individual consumers or small group of consumers. Micromarketing goes one step further in that a firm also customizes its service, products, or product assortments to satisfy the needs of targeted consumers. One-to-one marketing, a term coined by Peppers and Rogers (1993), focuses on establishing long-term relationships with individual consumers through customized production, individually addressable media, and personalized marketing.

0025-1909/02/0000/0001$5.00
1526-5501 electronic ISSN

MANAGEMENT SCIENCE © 2002 INFORMS
Vol. 00, No. 00, Xxxxx 2002 pp. 1–18

brand switching) without giving discounts to those who do not need any inducement to buy from the firm (Hof 1998, McCollum 1998, Mills 1999).

The view that one-to-one promotions (and other forms of customized pricing) ultimately benefit firms by allowing them to generate incremental sales without sacrificing on the profit margins they receive from their loyal customers has been challenged in several recent game-theoretic articles (Shaffer and Zhang 1995, Bester and Petrakis 1996, Chen 1997, Taylor 1999, Fudenberg and Tirole 2000). These articles find that when promotions can be targeted, a prisoner's dilemma invariably results. Prices decrease as the distinction between marginal and inframarginal consumers becomes blurred, and the alleged gain in incremental sales that the practicing firms are going after never materialize, as the competing firms simply neutralize each other's promotional efforts.

However, these articles all bias their results in favor of a prisoner's dilemma because they start with the assumption that firms are symmetric ex ante. Thus, it is not surprising that the firms remain symmetric after all pricing and promotional decisions have been made. In essence, these articles have identified a deleterious *price-competition* effect from one-to-one promotions, but they have implicitly ruled out the possibility of one of the firms gaining from a *market-share effect*.

In this article, we consider a game-theoretic model that allows for the possibility of both effects. When competing firms differ in size, and consumers have heterogeneous brand loyalty, we find that one-to-one promotions can affect market shares, even when the targeting technology is available to all firms at the same cost. We also find that this market-share effect may outweigh the adverse effect of lower prices, benefiting the firm whose market share increases. Thus, unlike in the previous literature, we find that one-to-one promotions do not invariably lead to a prisoner's dilemma.

This has important managerial implications. We incorporate the four main features of one-to-one promotions: *individual addressability, personalized incentives, competition,* and *costs of targeting* (Blattberg and Deighton 1991, Schultz 1994). We ask (i) which firms are more likely to benefit from one-to-one promotions, and hence have more incentive to acquire the capability to target; (ii) how might firms best position themselves to take advantage of the new targeting technologies; and (iii) when competing firms are also targeting, which consumers should a firm target, what incentives should these consumers be offered, and how does this depend on firm size and consumer loyalty.

We find that one-to-one promotions tend to favor firms that command stronger brand loyalties and have larger market shares. The smaller market-share firm always loses, but the larger firm may win or lose depending on the magnitude of the market-share effect *vis à vis* the price competition effect. This is most easily seen when two firms sell vertically differentiated products and compete in prices. In the absence of one-to-one promotions, the higher-quality firm charges a price in excess of its marginal cost, allowing the lower-quality firm to capture some of the market. With one-to-one promotions, the higher-quality firm can outbid the lower-quality firm on each consumer. Although many (but not all) consumers end up paying lower prices, the higher-quality firm can gain because of the resulting increase in its market share. That the lower-quality firm always loses in this case (its market share falls and prices are lower) suggests that positioning one's brand as the higher-quality product may be even more important in the information age than previously thought.

Our model also provides insights on how to manage customer churn, a phenomenon that arises when consumers are induced to switch to a less preferred product because of having received a targeted promotion. We show that it is not advisable for a firm to eliminate customer churn even if it were possible to do so. Instead, it is optimal for firms to engage in both offensive promotions (targeting consumers who prefer the rival firm's product) and defensive promotions (targeting consumers who prefer one's own product) with the relative mix depending on the marginal cost of targeting.

We differ from the above-cited literature on one-to-one promotions in that we are the first to introduce asymmetry in a model in which there are costs of targeting. The asymmetry allows us to see how qualitatively different competitive implications may arise from one-to-one promotions when there are market-share effects. The targeting costs give rise to the possibility that firms will randomize their promotions, which allows us to discuss the phenomenon of customer churn.

Shaffer and Zhang (1995) consider a model where firms choose regular prices and coupon face values and then choose how to distribute the coupons. Although they allow for targeting costs, the firms in their model are symmetric and offer at most one promotional price. In this article, we do not restrict the firms' promotional strategies to just one price (each consumer can potentially be offered a different price) and we allow the firms to be asymmetric. Lederer and Hurter (1986) also allow for asymmetric firms, but they do not incorporate targeting costs nor do they explore the implications of their findings on firm profits and market shares. Corts (1998) and Shaffer and Zhang (2000) were the first to find that targeted promotions need not lead to a prisoner's dilemma. However, these articles allow for at most one promotional price, and their conclusions arise because of a possible lessening of price competition and not, as in our model, from a market-share effect.

The rest of the paper proceeds as follows. In §2, we set up the model and discuss its properties. In §3, we solve for the second-stage equilibrium of a game in which firms simultaneously choose regular prices in the first stage, and then simultaneously choose which consumers to target and with what promotional incentives in the second stage. In §4, we solve for the mixed-strategy equilibrium and draw conclusions about the competitive effects of one-to-one promotions. In §5, we look at the phenomenon of customer churn and ask whether firms should predominantly focus on offensive or defensive targeting. Section 6 concludes.

2. Model

Suppose firms A and B sell competing brands of a consumer good that is produced at constant marginal cost, $c \geq 0$. Each consumer buys at most one unit of the good and all consumers are willing to pay at most $V \geq c$ for their more preferred brand. Consumers differ in how much they are willing to pay for their less

Figure 1 **Consumer Heterogeneity**

Consumers Loyal to Brand B	Consumers Loyal to Brand A
$-l_B$	l_A

(centered: 0)

preferred brand, which makes them heterogeneous in brand loyalty.

We define a consumer's brand loyalty as the minimum price differential necessary to induce her to purchase her less preferred brand. Thus, a consumer who prefers brand A by a loyalty of l will buy brand B, in the absence of any promotional incentives, if and only if firm A's regular price, P_A, exceeds firm B's regular price, P_B, by more than l. That is, the consumer will buy brand B if and only if $P_A - P_B > l$. We assume $l \in [-l_B, l_A]$ follows a uniform distribution, where $0 \leq l_i < V$, for $i \in \{A, B\}$.[2] Figure 1 illustrates the setup. Consumers with positive loyalty prefer brand A all else equal. Consumers with negative loyalty (toward brand A) prefer brand B all else equal. The consumer located at 0 is just indifferent between purchasing brands A and B at equal prices.

Without loss of generality, we assume $l_A \geq l_B$. If $l_A = l_B$, the setup is analogous to the standard model of horizontal differentiation with the loyalty parameter playing the same role as the transportation cost in other spatial models. If $l_B = 0$, the setup is analogous to the standard model of vertical differentiation in which all consumers agree that brand A is of higher quality than brand B. If $l_A > l_B > 0$, the setup has elements of both horizontal and vertical differentiation.

We assume also that firms know the locations of all consumers in the market and thus know their exact brand loyalties. In practice, of course, we would expect firms to be more or less certain about the loyalty of each consumer, depending on the quality and quantity of their data on individuals' past purchasing behavior. Thus, our results should be interpreted as the solution to an important limiting case—the case of perfect information. Nevertheless, it is an important

---

[2] Our assumption of a uniform distribution is made to obtain explicit solutions. This assumption is not as restrictive as it may seem at first because it turns out that firms' promotional strategies in equilibrium depend only on l—and not on the distribution of consumers—for any given pair of regular prices in the market.

case to consider because the effects we identify in this limiting case will also be present in a more general case.

The firms play a two-stage game of pricing and promotions in which regular prices are chosen in the first stage and promotional strategies are chosen in the second stage. This two-stage structure reflects a commonly held view that a firm's choice of regular price is a higher-level managerial decision and is relatively slower to adjust in practice than a firm's choice of promotions.[3] Later, in §6, we will discuss the implications of one-to-one promotions with no regular prices.

In choosing its promotional strategy, each firm must decide which consumers to target and with what discounts. Targeted promotions are not free; we assume the cost of targeting each consumer is given by $z \geq 0$ (this cost is incurred whether or not the consumer buys from the firm). Let $t_i(l)$ be an indicator variable that equals one if firm i promotes to consumers located at l and zero otherwise, and let $d_i(l)$ denote firm i's discount to these consumers. For example, if promotions take the form of targeted coupons, then $t_i(l)$ indicates whether consumers at l are targeted with a coupon and, if they are, $d_i(l)$ is the face value of the coupon. More generally, $d_i(l)$ is the monetary value of any individual-specific promotional incentives, including coupons, premiums, prizes, or alterations in the basic product that firm i offers to consumers to gain their patronage.

Consumers maximize their surplus given each firm's regular price and promotional incentives. Thus, a consumer located at l who receives $d_A(l)$ from firm A and $d_B(l)$ from firm B will purchase from firm A if and only if firm A's net price does not exceed firm B's net price by more than l. If a consumer located at l only receives promotional incentives from firm A, then she will purchase from firm A if and only if $P_A - d_A(l) - P_B \leq l$. If a consumer located at l only receives promotional incentives from firm B, then she will purchase from firm A if and only if $P_A - (P_B - d_B(l)) < l$.

[3] See, for example, Rao (1991), Shaffer and Zhang (1995), and Banks and Moorthy (1998).

3. One-to-One Promotions Given Regular Prices

We assume that the regular prices are observable to both firms when they choose their promotional strategies, and we use subgame perfection as our solution concept. Thus, we solve for the equilibrium strategy of each firm by solving first for the Nash equilibria of the second stage.

Our analysis in this stage is complicated in three important ways by the existence of a targeting cost ($z \geq 0$). First, it means that the profitability of one-to-one promotions depends on the relationship between z and $P_i - c$. This gives rise to four possible subgames. Second, it means that a firm may not want to target all consumers in the market even if it makes use of one-to-one promotions. This gives rise, for each subgame, to a firm's "targeting zone." Third, it means that pure-strategy equilibria may not exist. As we shall see, in one subgame, we will need to solve for a mixed-strategy equilibrium, jointly determining each firm's targeting zone and discount schedule.

Subgame 1: $P_A \leq c + z$ and $P_B \leq c + z$.

In this case, the cost of targeting is sufficiently high that neither firm can profitably promote. Thus, the solution is similar to what one gets from a standard spatial model of demand. Let $\hat{l} \equiv P_A - P_B$ denote the location of the marginal consumer. Then, firm A's demand is $(l_A - \hat{l})/(l_A + l_B)$, firm B's demand is $(\hat{l} + l_B)/(l_A + l_B)$, and the equilibrium payoffs for the two firms are[4]

$$\Pi_A^1 = \frac{(P_A - c)(l_A - \hat{l})}{l_A + l_B}, \qquad \Pi_B^1 = \frac{(P_B - c)(\hat{l} + l_B)}{l_A + l_B}. \quad (1)$$

Subgame 2: $P_A > c + z$ and $P_B \leq c + z$.

In this case, although firm A can profitably promote, it will never want to target consumers located at $l \geq \hat{l}$ because these consumers will buy from firm A even in the absence of any promotions. As for consumers located at $l < \hat{l}$, note that the largest discount firm A can offer any consumer and still earn nonnegative profit is $\bar{d}_A \equiv P_A - c - z$. For all consumers

[4] It should be noted that each firm's demand is bounded below by zero. That is, the demand for firm A is equal to $\max\{(l_A - \hat{l})/(l_A + l_B), 0\}$. However, for convenience, we suppress writing out the inequalities in the text.

Figure 2   The Targeting Zone: $\mathcal{T}^4$

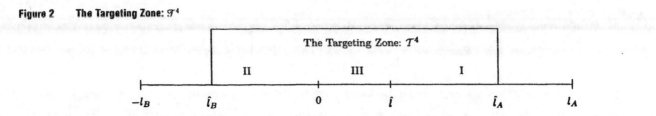

located at $l < \hat{l}_B$, where $\hat{l}_B \equiv c + z - P_B$, however, this discount is not large enough to induce them to switch brands, as they are so loyal to firm B that they will buy from firm B even if they receive $\bar{d}_A$ from firm A. Thus, it is not profitable for firm A to target them. The rest of firm B's customers, however, can profitably be induced to switch. Thus, in equilibrium, firm A will target consumers located between $\hat{l}_B$ and $\hat{l}$.

It remains to solve for firm A's optimal discount schedule inside the targeting area. Let $\mathcal{T}_A^2 \equiv \{l \mid \hat{l}_B \le l < \hat{l}\}$. Then consumers located at $l \in \mathcal{T}_A^2$ will purchase from firm A if and only if $P_A - d_A(l) - P_B \le l$. It follows that firm A will offer these consumers the smallest discount that satisfies this inequality, i.e., $d_A(l) = P_A - P_B - l$, yielding a profit margin for firm A of $P_A - d_A(l) - c - z = P_B + l - c - z$. Thus, the equilibrium payoffs for the two firms are

$$\Pi_A^2 = \frac{1}{l_A + l_B}\left((P_A - c)(l_A - \hat{l}) \right.$$
$$\left. + \int_{l \in \mathcal{T}_A^2} (P_B + l - c - z)\,dl \right),$$
$$\Pi_B^2 = \frac{1}{l_A + l_B}(P_B - c)(\hat{l}_B + l_B). \qquad (2)$$

Firm A's profit is the sum of the profit it earns from sales to consumers who buy at the regular price and the profit it earns from sales to consumers who otherwise would have bought from firm B. Its profit margin is lower on the latter consumers due to the cost of targeting and the promotional incentives it must offer them. Nevertheless, firm A's ability to target consumers with individual-specific incentives allows it to create incremental sales at the expense of its nontargeting rival.

Subgame 3: $P_A \le c + z$ and $P_B > c + z$.

Since this subgame is analogous to Subgame 2, with the role of each firm reversed, we simply list each

firm's equilibrium payoff. Let $\hat{l}_A \equiv P_A - c - z$ and $\mathcal{T}_B^3 \equiv \{l \mid \hat{l} < l \le \hat{l}_A\}$. Then

$$\Pi_B^3 = \frac{1}{l_A + l_B}\left((P_B - c)(\hat{l} + l_B) \right.$$
$$\left. + \int_{l \in \mathcal{T}_B^3} (P_A - c - z - l)\,dl \right),$$
$$\Pi_A^3 = \frac{1}{l_A + l_B}(P_A - c)(l_A - \hat{l}_A). \qquad (3)$$

Subgame 4: $P_A > c + z$ and $P_B > c + z$.

In this case, both firms can profitably promote and the targeting zone, $\mathcal{T}^4$, is simply the union of $\mathcal{T}_A^2$ and $\mathcal{T}_B^3$ as illustrated in Figure 2.[5] The targeting zone is the same for both firms because in the region where firm A is trying to induce consumers to switch brands, firm B is trying to defend its customer base, and vice versa. In equilibrium, neither firm targets outside $\mathcal{T}^4$, since these consumers are sufficiently loyal that the rival firm cannot profitably attract them.

As in the other subgames, the promotional decisions that each firm makes can be divided conceptually into two components. A firm must decide with what probability to target consumers at each location and, to those it targets, what depth of discount to offer. A major difference from the other subgames, however, is that, in equilibrium, each firm will randomize inside the targeting zone. The randomization will occur not only over whether or not to target consumers at a particular location but also over what discount to offer them. To see this, consider the consumers located in region I. Firm A will not want to target consumers in this region if firm B does not, since these consumers are already predisposed to purchasing from firm A. If firm A does not target these

---

[5] Figure 2 illustrates the case where $0 \le \hat{l} \le l_A$. There is also another case (not shown) where $-l_B \le \hat{l} < 0$. As we will show in Appendix A, however, the second-stage equilibrium does not depend on the relation between $\hat{l}$ and 0.

Figure 3   Payoffs from Contested Consumers

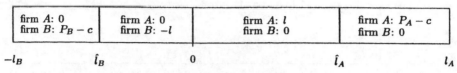

consumers, however, then firm B will. But if firm B targets these consumers firm A's optimal strategy is to do likewise, since it would rather outbid its rival and retain its customers than lose them altogether. Finally, if firm A targets these consumers, then firm B would rather not, and so on. Furthermore, given that both firms may target the same consumers, neither firm will use a pure strategy for its discount $d_i(l)$. This is because if the rival firm has provided sufficient incentives to win the patronage of a consumer, then a firm will either increase its own incentives to the consumer to outbid its rival or give up completely on targeting the consumer to save the targeting cost z.

Fortunately, the equilibrium payoffs of firms A and B in each region are easy to derive (the details can be found in Appendix A) and are illustrated in Figure 3. Since consumers located at $-l_B \le l < \hat{l}_B$ do not receive any promotions and are loyal to firm B, firm A earns zero and firm B earns $P_B - c$ from each consumer in this region. Similarly, since the consumers located at $\hat{l}_A < l \le l_A$ do not receive any promotions and are loyal to firm A, firm B earns zero and firm A earns $P_A - c$ from each consumer in this region. The contested consumers are the ones in the middle two regions. For consumers located at l to the left of 0, firm B has a preference advantage of $-l$. For consumers located at l to the right of 0, firm A has a preference advantage of l. Equilibrium payoffs in these regions then follow immediately as a direct consequence of mixed-strategy equilibria.

PROPOSITION 1. *With one-to-one promotions, a firm's equilibrium payoff from each consumer in the targeting zone depends only on the price premium the consumer is willing to pay for its brand.*

Proposition 1 implies that with one-to-one promotions, a firm's expected payoff from consumers in the targeting zone derives solely from the loyalty these consumers have for its brand. The reason is that although a firm is always able to outbid its

competitor for the consumers who prefer its own brand, one-to-one promotions dissipate all potential rents except for the premiums that contested consumers are willing to pay for a brand. This result highlights the vital importance of individual (rather than average) consumer loyalty in the information age and suggests that the increased interest in recent years among marketing practitioners in relationship marketing, customer satisfaction, customer life-time value, and one-to-one marketing can be viewed as a manifestation of firms' efforts to position themselves for the upcoming information-intensive marketing.

Summing up each firm's expected payoff in all four regions of Figure 3 yields:

$$\Pi_A^4 = \frac{(P_A - c)(l_A - \hat{l}_A)}{l_A + l_B} + \frac{\hat{l}_A^2}{2(l_A + l_B)}$$

$$\Pi_B^4 = \frac{(P_B - c)(l_B + \hat{l}_B)}{l_A + l_B} + \frac{\hat{l}_B^2}{2(l_A + l_B)}. \qquad (4)$$

4.   Equilibrium Pricing and Promotions

In this section we address several questions of interest. First, how do one-to-one promotions affect the average prices paid by consumers? Second, which firm has more incentive to initiate one-to-one promotions? Third, who will gain or lose from one-to-one promotions? Intuitively, one might expect that a firm's decision on whether or not to target will depend on the magnitude of the targeting costs relative to l_A and l_B. The next proposition summarizes this relationship.

PROPOSITION 2. *For all $z \ge 0$, there exists a unique subgame perfect equilibrium.*

(a) *If $z \ge (2l_A + l_B)/3$, then the equilibrium regular prices are $P_A = (2l_A + l_B)/3 + c$ and $P_B = (l_A + 2l_B)/3 + c$, and neither firm offers one-to-one promotions.*

(b) *If $l_B \le z < (2l_A + l_B)/3$ (note $l_A \ge l_B$ by assumption), then the equilibrium regular prices are*

Figure 4   One-to-One Promotions by Firm *A* Only

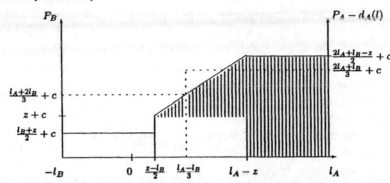

Note. Dotted lines illustrate the equilibrium in Part (a) and solid lines illustrate the equilibrium in Part (b). Vertical shaded area is firm *A*'s profit assuming $c = 0$ when it alone offers one-to-one promotions.

$P_A = (2l_A + l_B - z)/2 + c$ and $P_B = (l_B + z)/2 + c$, *and only firm A offers one-to-one promotions.*

(c) *If $z < l_B$, then the equilibrium regular prices are $P_A = l_A + c$ and $P_B = l_B + c$, and both firms offer one-to-one promotions.*

Neither Firm Offers One-to-One Promotions

The first thing to notice from Proposition 2 is that there exists a cutoff level of z such that if z is greater than or equal to this cutoff level, then neither firm offers one-to-one promotions. This has both an obvious and a less-than-obvious implication. The obvious implication is that if the cost of targeting is sufficiently high then no firm will promote. The less-than-obvious implication is that, at a given point in time, one-to-one promotions may be optimal in some industries but not others, even if the underlying targeting technology and its associated cost is the same across all industries. To see this, note that the cutoff level of z in this case is equal to firm A's regular-price markup, which depends on the degree of competition in the market. It follows that firms in less profitable industries (those that have low contribution margins) will be less inclined to offer one-to-one promotions. For example, in an industry where the products are homogeneous ($l_A = l_B = 0$), we have that $P_A = P_B = c$ and so one-to-one promotions will not occur for any $z \geq 0$.

Let $\widetilde{\Pi}_i$ denote firm i's payoff and $\widetilde{S}_i$ its market share. Then the firms' payoffs and market shares (the share

of total sales accounted for by a firm) when neither firm offers targeted promotions are

$$\widetilde{\Pi}_A = \frac{(2l_A + l_B)^2}{9(l_A + l_B)}, \qquad \widetilde{\Pi}_B = \frac{(l_A + 2l_B)^2}{9(l_A + l_B)},$$

$$\widetilde{S}_A = \frac{2l_A + l_B}{3(l_A + l_B)}, \qquad \widetilde{S}_B = \frac{l_A + 2l_B}{3(l_A + l_B)}. \qquad (5)$$

If $l_A = l_B$, then each firm earns the same profit and has the same market share. If $l_A > l_B$, then firm A earns more profit and has a larger market share than firm B. The dotted lines in Figure 4 illustrate an asymmetric equilibrium; firm B sells to all consumers with loyalties $-l_B$ to $\frac{l_A - l_B}{3}$ at price $(l_A + 2l_B)/3 + c$, and firm A sells to all consumers with loyalties $(l_A - l_B)/3$ to l_A at price $(2l_A + l_B)/3 + c$.

Only Firm *A* Offers One-to-One Promotions

The second thing to notice from Proposition 2 is that there exist intermediate values of z such that in equilibrium firm A will want to promote but firm B will not (it is never the case that only firm B will promote). The solid lines in Figure 4 illustrate the equilibrium. In Figure 4, firm B chooses a regular price of $(l_B + z)/2 + c$ and sells to all consumers with loyalties $-l_B$ to $(z - l_B)/2$. All consumers with loyalties to the right of $(z - l_B)/2$ buy from firm A. Of these consumers, consumers with loyalties $(z - l_B)/2$ to $l_A - z$ receive promotional incentives. These are the consumers in firm A's targeting zone. The consumers with loyalties $l_A - z$ to l_A are sufficiently loyal to firm A that they are not given any discounts. These consumers buy from firm A at firm A's regular price of $(2l_A + l_B - z)/2 + c$.

This case is interesting for three reasons. First, it is the case implicitly assumed by the non game-theoretic literature, which views one-to-one promotions as ultimately benefiting firms by allowing them to generate incremental sales without sacrificing on the profit margins they receive from their loyal customers. However, as we shall see, the implications of this case are much richer, and the conventional view that the promoting firm will be better off does not always hold. Second, this case is important because it has been missed by the previous game-theoretic literature, which assumes that firms are ex ante symmetric. Note that at $l_B = l_A$, the region of z such that only firm A promotes, $l_B \leq z < (2l_A + l_B)/3$, does not exist, and so our model predicts that in a market with two equally matched firms, we would not expect to see only one firm offering targeted promotions. Third, this case is the only relevant case when the firms' products are vertically differentiated. To see this, note that if firm B's product is of lower quality than firm A's product ($l_B = 0$), then the lower bound of z is never binding, which implies that firm B never promotes.

Notice that each firm responds differently to a decrease in the marginal cost of targeting; firm A responds by *raising* its regular price, while firm B responds by *lowering* its regular price. Both intuitions can be seen from the profit expressions in (2). In this case, we see that firm A's profit-maximizing regular price balances the marginal profit from selling to a consumer in the "regular-price market" with the marginal profit from selling to a consumer in the "one-to-one market." When the marginal cost of targeting decreases, the marginal profit of selling to a consumer in the one-to-one market increases, and so to equalize its marginal profits across markets, firm A will want to raise its regular price.[6] In contrast, the effect of a lower cost of targeting on firm B is much different. As it becomes more profitable for firm A to

[6] One can think of the two markets as analogous to substitute products in a product line. When the contribution margin of the first product exogenously increases, profit maximization requires that the firm raise the price of the other product, because the consumers who are induced to switch to the first product now bring in more profit.

promote, firm B will find it necessary to lower its regular price in an effort to offset firm A's encroachment into its regular-price market.

The equilibrium payoffs and market shares when only firm A promotes are:

$$\widetilde{\Pi}_A = \frac{(2l_A + l_B)^2 - z(4l_A + 2l_B - 5z)}{8(l_A + l_B)}, \qquad \widetilde{\Pi}_B = \frac{(l_B + z)^2}{4(l_A + l_B)}$$

$$\widetilde{S}_A = \frac{2l_A + l_B - z}{2(l_A + l_B)}, \qquad \widetilde{S}_B = \frac{l_B + z}{2(l_A + l_B)}. \tag{6}$$

Differentiating market shares $\widetilde{S}_A$ and $\widetilde{S}_B$ with respect to z, we see that firm A's market share increases, and firm B's market share decreases, with a lower z. Thus, it follows that when the marginal cost of targeting decreases, firm B will not be completely successful in stopping firm A's encroachment on its regular-price market. As illustrated in Figure 4, firm A's sales increase relative to the case of no promotions by the number of additional consumers with loyalties ($z - l_B)/2$ to $(l_A - l_B)/3$.

All else equal, this market-share effect harms firm B and benefits firm A. In fact, a smaller market share coupled with a lower regular price implies that firm B will necessarily be worse off when the cost of targeting falls, as can easily be seen by differentiating $\widetilde{\Pi}_B$ with respect to z. Surprisingly, however, it does not follow that firm A will necessarily be better off. Although firm A earns a higher contribution margin from its regular-price market and has a larger market share, the fraction of its consumers that buy on promotion increases when the cost of targeting falls. In fact, contrary to what the non-game-theoretic literature would predict, it is easy to construct examples in which firm A is worse off when z falls. For example, in Figure 4, firm A's profit when it promotes is given by the vertically shaded area (where we assume $c = 0$ for convenience). When z is sufficiently high that no firm promotes, firm A's profit is given by the rectangular region with base $l_A - (l_A - l_B)/3$ and height $(2l_A + l_B)/3 + c$. The difference in this example is a net loss for firm A.

More generally, although firm B's profit always decreases when the cost of targeting falls, firm A's profit may or may not decrease. Differentiating firm A's equilibrium profit in (6) with respect to z, and comparing its equilibrium profit in (5) and (6), yields the following proposition.

PROPOSITION 3. *There exists* $\bar{z} > 0$ *such that firm A's equilibrium profit when only firm A promotes is increasing in the cost of targeting for* $z > \bar{z}$, *and decreasing in the cost of targeting for* $z < \bar{z}$. *For* $z \geq \bar{z}$, *firm A is worse off relative to the case of no promotions. For* $z < \bar{z}$, *firm A may or may not be better off relative to the case of no promotions. When firm A's product is of higher quality than firm B's product, there exists a sufficiently small z such that firm A is always better off.*

Figure 5 illustrates the results in Proposition 3 for the case where firm A's product is of higher quality than firm B's product. At $z = 0$, firm A's profit is $l_A/2$ when it promotes, which exceeds $4l_A/9$, its profit when z is sufficiently high that neither firm promotes. As z decreases below the cut-off level for targeting, firm A's profit initially decreases and then increases. This is the result of two opposing effects. On the one hand, firm A benefits from an increase in its market share when z decreases. On the other hand, firm A loses from an increase in price competition caused by firm B's lower regular price. For small enough z, the beneficial market-share effect outweighs the adverse price-competition effect and firm A's profit increases as the cost of targeting further decreases.

These results differ from previous literature on targeted promotions. The non-game-theoretic literature fails to identify the adverse effect on firm A's profit

Figure 5 Firm *A*'s Profit When Its Product Is of Higher Quality

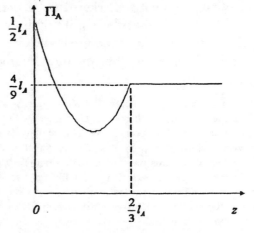

caused by firm B's lower regular price, and the previous game-theoretic literature, in assuming symmetry, fails to identify the beneficial market-share effect. Figure 5 shows that either of the two effects can dominate for firm A.

Both Firms Offer One-to-One Promotions
When both firms offer targeted promotions, each firm's regular price is increasing only in the loyalty of its own consumers (Part (c) in Proposition 2). Thus, an exogenous change in the maximum loyalty of firm B's consumers has no effect on firm A's regular price, and vice versa. This result suggests that one-to-one promotions lead to a much different form of competition than the competition that occurs when each firm is constrained to charge a single price. Intuitively, when both firms offer one-to-one promotions, there is a bandwidth of marginal consumers (where the width is determined by the size of the targeting zone) which buffer each firm's regular price from the other. As we shall see, this buffering, and what happens in the targeting zone, affects the two firms similarly.

The equilibrium expected payoffs and market shares when both firms promote are:

$$\tilde{\Pi}_A = \frac{l_A^2 + z^2}{2(l_A + l_B)}, \qquad \tilde{\Pi}_B = \frac{l_B^2 + z^2}{2(l_A + l_B)},$$

$$\tilde{S}_A = \frac{l_A}{l_A + l_B}, \qquad \tilde{S}_B = \frac{l_B}{l_A + l_B}. \qquad (7)$$

In the mixed-strategy equilibrium, firm A and B's expected market share is independent of the cost of targeting and converges, not surprisingly, to each firm's base of loyal consumers. This is because with one-to-one promotions each firm can always outbid its rival for the consumers who prefer its product. Thus, when both firms promote, changes in targeting costs operate on each firm's equilibrium profit only through the price-competition effect, and so it is also not surprising that each firm's profit is increasing in z (a higher z moderates the price competition effect).

However, it would be incorrect to assume that each firm's profit in this case is necessarily less than what its profit would be in the case in which no firm offered promotions. It follows by continuity from our results in the previous subsection that there exist parameters

Figure 6   Price-Competition Effect Under Symmetry

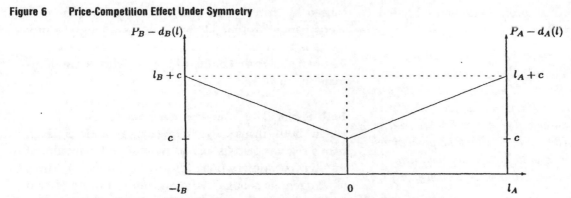

Note. Dotted lines illustrate the equilibrium in Part (a) and solid lines illustrate the equilibrium in Part (c).

such that firm A is better off with one-to-one promotions, even when both firms promote. To see this, note that for firm A to be better off (firm B is always worse off) when both firms promote, we require

$$l_A^2 - 8l_Al_B - 2l_B^2 + 9z^2 > 0. \qquad (8)$$

When the products are symmetrically differentiated ($l_A = l_B$), the condition in (8) is never satisfied. But when the products are vertically differentiated ($l_A > 0, l_B = 0$), (8) is always satisfied. More generally, the condition in (8) is satisfied when l_A is sufficiently large relative to l_B, which is more likely to be the case when the relationship between the firms' products is closer to vertical differentiation than to symmetric horizontal differentiation. This yields the following proposition.

PROPOSITION 4. *One-to-one promotions need not lead to a prisoner's dilemma situation in which all firms are worse off. The firm with the more loyal following and larger market share can be better off when both firms use one-to-one promotions than when neither firm uses one-to-one promotions.*

Proposition 4 lends some support to the intuition that one-to-one promotions can favor "large firms with strong brand identities" (Blattberg and Deighton 1991). However, it should be emphasized that in suggesting that one-to-one promotions need not lead to a prisoner's dilemma, we are comparing a case in which both firms offer one-to-one promotions at a particular marginal cost of targeting to a case in which the cost of targeting is sufficiently high that no firms offer

promotions. This comparison is relevant, for example, if the targeting technology and associated consumer data is available for purchase and firms A and B are deciding whether or not to purchase it. If the comparison is instead between two levels of z conditional on both firms offering promotions, then the profits in (7) imply that both firms are worse off when the marginal cost of targeting decreases.

To understand why earlier game-theoretic literature concludes that targeted promotions lead to a prisoner's dilemma, and to understand why it need not, it is useful to examine through some polar cases how the two effects of one-to-one promotions manifest themselves in a competitive context.

Figure 6 illustrates equilibrium prices and expected market shares under symmetry for the cases in Parts (a) and (c) of Proposition 2 (we assume $z = 0$ for convenience). From Proposition 2, we see that the equilibrium regular prices remain unchanged with one-to-one promotions. From the market-share expressions in (5) and (7), we see that the equilibrium expected market shares also remain unchanged with one-to-one promotions.[7] Thus, when the loyalties for the two

---

[7] In fact, when $z = 0$, it can be shown that all consumers with loyalties $-l_B$ to 0 buy from firm B and all consumers with loyalties 0 to l_A buy from firm A in both cases. This should be clear in the case where neither firm promotes. The reason it is also true in the case where both firms promote is that, when $z = 0$, there is no cost of targeting and so each firm's equilibrium strategy calls for it to distribute defensive promotions with probability one. In other words, the equilibrium mixed strategies in the case where both firms promote become degenerate when $z = 0$.

Figure 7   Market-Share Effect Under Asymmetry

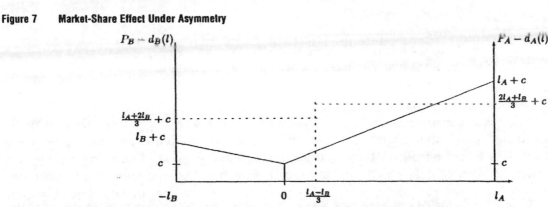

Note. Dotted lines illustrate the equilibrium in Part (a) and solid lines illustrate the equilibrium in Part (c).

firms are identical ($l_A = l_B$), the only effect of one-to-one promotions is to intensify price competition.

Figure 7 illustrates the fact that if the firms are asymmetric, there will also be a market-share effect. In the absence of targeted promotions, it is not optimal for the firm with a larger loyal following to sell to all consumers who prefer its product. This is because to capture more consumers with weaker preferences for its product, it must lower its price to all consumers, including those with strong preferences who do not need any additional inducement to purchase from it. Although all firms face this tradeoff between incremental sales and inframarginal losses in their pricing decisions, the fact that firm A has a larger loyal following than firm B tilts the balance of the tradeoff in favor of firm B setting a lower price than firm A. As a result, firm B sells to consumers with loyalties 0 to $(l_A - l_B)/3$ even though these consumers would have bought from firm A at equal prices.

One-to-one promotions allow a firm to generate incremental sales from consumers with weaker preferences without sacrificing margins from consumers with strong preferences. An obvious consequence of this increase in pricing flexibility is more intense price competition (each firm is now free of any inframarginal loss when lowering its price). A more subtle consequence is that the increase in pricing flexibility levels the playing field (the ability to offer one-to-one promotions allows each firm to avoid the aforementioned tradeoff). This accentuates any advantage that a firm may have in customer loyalty. As a result, firm A can take advantage of its pricing flexibility to

increase its market share at the expense of firm B by capturing those consumers that prefer its product.

It is this tradeoff between market share and price competition that determines whether firm A will be better or worse off with one-to-one promotions. As we have seen, it can go either way.

5. Customer Churn and Optimal Targeted Promotions

Customer churn arises when consumers who would otherwise prefer a firm's product switch to a rival firm's product because of the promotional incentives they receive.[8] So, for example, in Figure 2, those consumers in Region II who buy from firm A represent positive customer churn for firm B, and those consumers in Regions I and III who buy from firm B represent positive customer churn for firm A. There are two reasons why a firm might lose customers to its rival even though the consumer prefers the firm's product given each firm's regular price. One reason is that the consumer does not receive any promotional incentives from its more preferred firm but does receive promotional incentives from the rival firm, where the incentives are such that $P_i - (P_{-i} -$

---

[8] Our definition of customer churn is necessarily a static one, given the limitations of our static model. The practicing manager's definition of churn is a more dynamic concept that considers churn to be a proportion of customers lost in a given period of time. To relate the two definitions, one can think of the consumers who comprise customer churn in our model as having bought their preferred brand sometime prior to the start of the game.

Figure 8 **Targeting Zone Under Symmetry**

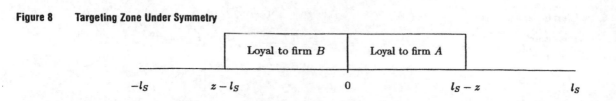

$$-l_S \qquad z - l_S \qquad\qquad 0 \qquad\qquad l_S - z \qquad\qquad l_S$$

$d_{-i}(l)) > l$, with firm i being the consumer's more preferred firm. Another reason is that the consumer receives promotional incentives from both firms, but the rival firm's inducement is such that $P_i - d_i(l) - (P_{-i} - d_{-i}(l)) > l$.

Customer churn has become a source of concern in many industries. For example, it is a concern in long-distance telephone service, wireless communications, and banking, where targeted promotions have induced a large number of consumers to switch.[9] It is thus important for any manager to address the following two questions in an information-intensive marketing environment. First, does customer churn become worse as targeted promotions become increasingly feasible and accurate due to lower costs of targeting? If so, how pervasive will it become? Second, what should a firm do to manage customer churn in an information-intensive marketing environment?

Our analysis can shed light on both questions. Figure 8 illustrates the targeting zone for the case of symmetry when both firms promote and loyalties are $l_A = l_B = l_S$. In this case, we see that the targeting zone expands when z decreases until at $z = 0$, all consumers in the market receive promotions. One might think, therefore, that as the marginal cost of targeting decreases, the number of consumers that churn will inevitably rise. Surprisingly, this turns out to be incorrect.

PROPOSITION 5. *When both firms offer one-to-one promotions, the number of consumers that churn first increases and then decreases as the marginal cost of targeting decreases. In the limit, when the marginal cost of targeting is zero, the phenomenon of customer churn disappears.*

[9] In long-distance service, one in four residential subscribers switched long-distance carriers in 1997 (Lawyer 1998). Even worse, it has been alleged that some 30% of the 55 million wireless customers in the U.S. churn (Cane 1999).

Intuitively, there are two opposing effects at work that give rise to the inverted-U relationship between customer churn and the cost of targeting. On the one hand, each firm has a greater incentive to offer targeted promotions as the cost of targeting decreases. All else equal, this tends to increase customer churn. On the other hand, each firm also has a greater incentive to retain consumers who are more loyal to its own product as the cost of targeting decreases. All else equal, this tends to reduce customer churn. In the special case where $z = 0$, all consumers receive a targeted promotion on the product they most prefer and customer churn is eliminated.[10]

To gain a more complete sense of each firm's overall strategic orientation, we define an offensive promotion as a promotion that is given to consumers who prefer the rival's product, and a defensive promotion as a promotion that is given to consumers who prefer one's own product. Then the number of offensive and defensive promotions that are distributed by each firm is given by:

$$\mathcal{N}_D = \int_0^{l_S - z} \tilde{q}_A(l)\, \frac{dl}{2l_S} = \frac{l_S - z + z \log \frac{z}{l_S}}{2l_S},$$

$$\mathcal{N}_O = \int_0^{l_S - z} \tilde{q}_B(l)\, \frac{dl}{2l_S} = \frac{l_S^2 - z^2}{4l_S^2},$$

where $\tilde{q}_i(l)$ is the equilibrium probability that consumers with loyalty l receive a promotion from firm i (see Appendix C). By setting $z = \beta l_S$ where $0 \le \beta \le 1$, we can plot $\mathcal{N}_D$ and $\mathcal{N}_O$ on the vertical axis against β on the horizontal axis in Figure 9. This yields the following proposition.

[10] When $z = 0$, there is no cost of targeting and so each firm's equilibrium strategy calls for it to distribute defensive promotions (a promotion that is given to consumers who prefer one's own product) with probability one. In other words, the equilibrium mixed strategies in the case where both firms promote become degenerate when $z = 0$.

Figure 9   Defensive and Offensive Promotions*

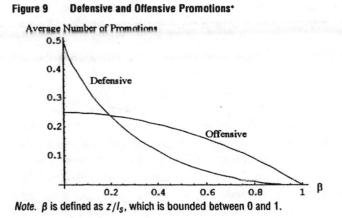

Note. β is defined as z/l_s, which is bounded between 0 and 1.

PROPOSITION 6. *When both firms offer one-to-one promotions, the relative mix of offensive to defensive promotions increases as the cost of targeting increases. A firm's targeting is predominantly offensive when the targeting cost is high and predominantly defensive when the targeting cost is low.*

As the cost of targeting decreases, the targeting zone expands on both sides, encompassing consumers with increasingly stronger loyalties. This implies two things. First, it implies that the total number of offensive and defensive promotions is decreasing in z. This can be seen from the fact that both curves decrease from left to right in Figure 9. Second, it implies that offensive promotions must be given with increasingly larger discounts to be effective, while defensive promotions can be effective with increasingly smaller discounts. As a result, the attractiveness of an additional consumer captured with offensive promotions decreases with lower z, while the attractiveness of an additional consumer retained with defensive promotions increases with lower z. This can be seen from the concavity of the offensive promotion curve, which achieves a maximum of 0.25 at z = 0, and the convexity of the defensive promotion curve, which achieves a maximum of 0.5 at z = 0.[11]

Propositions 5 and 6 imply that customer churn results from firms optimally taking chances with their

[11] In the limit, when z = 0, every consumer receives a defensive promotion and a random half of all consumers receive an offensive promotion. Offensive promotions in this special case fail to attract any switchers.

loyal customers in order to capture as much consumer surplus from them as possible. Consequently, customer churn will occur in equilibrium as long as the marginal cost of targeting is positive. This suggests that the optimal way to manage customer churn is not to eliminate it, but to engage in more defensive promotions (e.g., loyalty programs) as the cost of targeting decreases.

6. Conclusion

The addressability of individual consumers, along with personalized promotional incentives, fundamentally changes a firm's pricing decision. The parsimonious model we have developed here allows us to investigate this phenomenon. We show that one-to-one promotions allow a firm the flexibility to generate incremental sales without offering any unnecessary discount. But it also tends to intensify competition since all consumers, including loyal consumers, are potentially contestable.

In assuming symmetry, previous studies conclude that one-to-one promotions invariably lead to a prisoner's dilemma in which all firms are worse off. However, when firms are asymmetric, there will also be a market-share effect. We show that the firms that are best positioned to gain from this additional effect are those that have a larger loyal following. One-to-one promotions gives these firms the flexibility they need to capitalize on their customer loyalty. Thus, one-to-one promotions may be a boon for large firms in today's market environment, as it allows large companies to compete with small firms for niche markets in an ever more fragmented marketplace (Bessen 1993).

One striking message from our analysis is that building customer brand loyalty is of paramount importance. In an information-intensive marketing environment, all consumers, not just "marginal consumers," are potentially exposed to competitive bidding, and customer loyalty is the only line of defense for a firm. This is reflected in the fact that a firm's payoffs from contested consumers can only be as large as the premiums they are willing to pay for the firm's brand. It is also reflected in the fact that a firm with a large loyal following can best take advantage of one-to-one promotions, while a small firm with a weak brand will simply bear the brunt of intensified competition.

Our analysis also sheds light on the subject of customer churn, which is increasingly occupying the attention of management in many industries. To our knowledge, it is the first rigorous analysis of this widely publicized phenomenon arising from targeted promotions. We show that customer churn can result from firms optimally taking chances with their loyal customers. Therefore, it is not advisable to eliminate or even to minimize customer churn. While increasing customer loyalty in a cost-effective manner may always be beneficial to a firm, it should not be the focus of any churn reduction program. Indeed, it follows from our results that the optimality of a firm's pricing strategy may be suspect if customer churn reduces as customer loyalty increases, unless there is already a high level of customer loyalty. We show that the optimal way to manage customer churn is to engage in relatively more and more defensive promotions as the cost of targeting decreases.

Our conclusions are based on a two-stage game where each firm commits to a regular price. The reader may wonder whether our conclusions would hold if firms do not have regular prices. Could it be the case that the regular price serves no useful function in the age of one-to-one marketing? We can address this question by amending our game to allow each firm to choose whether or not to set a regular price prior to its targeting decisions. Our analysis shows that the regular price plays a strategic role in the game of one-to-one promotions.[12] This strategic role arises from the fact that the regular price places an upper bound on the transaction price that any consumer would have to pay and hence discourages each firm from pursuing its rival's most loyal customers. Without a regular price to shelter a firm's loyal consumers from the rival's targeting, the targeting zone in Figure 3 would expand to cover the entire line and each firm's payoff would be reduced.

Because of its strategic role, we can show that competing firms all have incentives to choose a regular price in the amended game. This means that

the regular price is not passé but instead performs an indispensable function of sheltering its loyal customers from competitive poaching. This also means that our two-stage setup is an innocuous simplification, as it prunes off-equilibrium subgames without affecting any substantive conclusions. In the unlikely case where regular prices cannot arise for institutional reasons (or if firms play a simultaneous game of one-to-one pricing), each firm's payoff will be the same as its payoff in the two-stage game we consider here when $z = 0$, and our main conclusions will not be qualitatively altered.

One intriguing question that our analysis does not answer directly is what role would nontargeted promotions play in the context of targeted promotions?[13] In our model, we implicitly assume that all consumers avail themselves of any promotions offered to them, and so nontargeted promotions if offered would serve the same purpose as the regular price. On the other hand, if not all consumers make use of promotions offered to them, and if these consumers have different aggregate elasticities of demand than consumers who do use promotions, then we conjecture that nontargeted promotions could serve a price-discrimination role and be used by firms even if targeted promotions are also used. In addition, we conjecture that nontargeted promotions could benefit a firm in an environment of one-to-one promotions by discouraging a competing firm from targeting its consumers aggressively. We leave it to future research to confirm these intuitions. We hope that our analysis sparks further interest from both academics and practitioners in this pricing tactic.

Acknowledgments
The authors thank two anonymous referees, the co-editor, and seminar participants at Carnegie-Mellon University, Columbia University, Duke University, University of California at Los Angeles, University of Chicago, University of Southern California, University of Texas at Dallas, and Washington University in St Louis for helpful comments.

Appendix A
In this appendix, we derive the mixed-strategy equilibrium in each of the regions of Subgame 4. To start, we partition consumers in $\mathcal{T}^4$ into three regions, as illustrated in Figure 2. For each region, we

---

[12] We thank an anonymous referee for raising these questions and for suggesting the analysis. The details of this analysis are available from the authors upon request.

[13] We thank an anonymous reviewer for raising this question.

show that a mixed-strategy equilibrium exists and we derive for each firm a probability distribution defined over the set of feasible (undominated) pure strategies $\mathfrak{D}_i(l)$.

Region I. Since all consumers located in Region I will purchase from firm A if they do not receive any promotional incentives from firm B, and any sales that firm B generates through targeted promotions are incremental, the maximum discount that firm B will be willing to distribute to the consumers located at l in Region I must satisfy $P_B - d_B(l) - c - z \geq 0$ (this is the maximum discount that firm B can offer and still earn nonnegative profit). This implies that $d_B(l) \leq P_B - c - z$. Furthermore, firm B's discount in this region must be sufficiently large to overcome consumers' loyalty to brand A. Otherwise, firm B would incur the targeting cost without affecting consumers' purchasing decisions. This means that, for the consumers located at l in Region I, $d_B(l)$ is bounded from below such that $P_A - P_B + d_B(l) \geq l$. This implies that $d_B(l) \geq P_B - P_A + l$. Thus, firm B's feasible strategy set is given by $\mathfrak{D}_B(l) \equiv \{d_B(l) \mid d_B(l) \in [(P_B - P_A + l), (P_B - c - z)]\}$.

Firm A's maximum discount is determined by insuring that the targeted consumers will buy from firm A and derive minimum surplus even if they get the maximum discount from firm B. Since consumers who receive discounts from both firms will buy from firm A if and only if $P_A - d_A - (P_B - d_B) \leq l$, and since firm B's maximum discount is $d_B(l) = P_B - c - z$, it follows that firm A's maximum discount must satisfy $P_A - d_A - c - z = l$. Firm A's minimum discount is $d_A \geq 0$. Thus, firm A's feasible strategy set is given by $\mathfrak{D}_A(l) \equiv \{d_A(l) \mid d_A(l) \in [0, (P_A - c - z - l)]\}$.

Using the same arguments as in Varian (1985) and Narasimhan (1988), we can show that, in any mixed-strategy equilibrium, there can only be one mass point. This mass point occurs at $d_B(l) = P_B - P_A + l$, and we denote it by m_B. We can also show that, conditional on its targeting consumers located at $l \in \mathcal{T}_B^3$, each firm's distribution function is continuous. We now proceed to show by construction that a unique mixed-strategy equilibrium exists for all l in Region I.

Let $F_A(d; l)$ be the probability that firm A targets consumers located at l with a discount depth less than d, conditional on it targeting those consumers, and let $m_B + (1 - m_B)F_B(d; l)$ be the probability that firm B targets consumers located at l with a discount depth less than d, conditional on it targeting those consumers. Then, if $q_i(l) \in (0, 1]$ denotes the probability that firm i will target a consumer located at l, the probability that firm A targets these consumers with a discount less than d is given by $q_A(l)F_A(d; l)$, and the probability that firm B targets these consumers with a discount less than d is given by $q_B(l)(m_B + (1 - m_B)F_B(d; l))$.

In any mixed-strategy equilibrium, a firm's strategy must make its rival indifferent among all of its feasible strategy choices. In particular, firm B's strategy must be such that

$$(1 - q_B(l))(P_A - c) + q_B(l)0 = l, \tag{A1}$$

where the left side of (A1) is firm A's expected payoff from a consumer located at l if it does not target, and the right side of (A1) is firm A's expected payoff from the consumer if it targets with its maximum discount depth of $(P_A - c - z - l)$, thereby always insuring itself a payoff of l.

Furthermore, firm B's strategy must also make firm A indifferent between targeting with any $d_A(l) \in \mathfrak{D}_A(l)$, and targeting with its maximum discount depth of $P_A - c - z - l$. We thus have:

$$[1 - q_B(l)][P_A - d_A(l) - c - z]$$
$$+ q_B(l)[m_B + (1 - m_B)F_B(P_B - P_A + d_A(l) + l)](P_A - d_A(l) - c - z)$$
$$+ q_B(l)(1 - m_B)[1 - F_B(P_B - P_A + d_A(l) + l)](-z) = l. \tag{A2}$$

The first term in (A2) is firm A's expected gain from a consumer located at l when firm B happens not to target the same consumer. The second term is firm A's expected gain when it wins the competitive bid for the consumer and the third term is its expected gain when it loses the bid. Using (A1), (A2), and the regularity conditions $0 \leq F_B(d) \leq 1$, we can solve for m_B, $q_B(l)$ and $F_B(d; l)$. By setting $P_B - P_A + d_A(l) + l = d$, we have:

$$\tilde{q}_B(l) = \frac{P_A - c - l}{P_A - c}, \qquad \tilde{m}_B = \frac{z}{P_A - l - c}, \tag{A3}$$

$$\tilde{F}_B(d; l) = \frac{(l + z)(P_A - P_B - l + d)}{(P_A - l - c - z)(P_B + l - d - c)}, \tag{A4}$$

where tildes denote equilibrium values and $0 \leq \tilde{F}_B(d) \leq 1$ is right continuous and monotonically increasing as are required of a distribution function. Thus, the probability that a consumer located at l will receive a promotional incentive from firm B with a discount value less than d is given by

$$\mathcal{F}_B(d) = \begin{cases} 0 & \text{if } d < P_B - P_A + l \\ \tilde{q}_B(l)[\tilde{m}_B + (1 - \tilde{m}_B)\tilde{F}_B(d)] & \text{if } d \in \mathfrak{D}_B(l) \\ \tilde{q}_B(l) & \text{if } d \geq P_B - c - z \end{cases}. \tag{A5}$$

Similarly, firm A's strategy must make firm B indifferent among all of its feasible strategy choices. In particular, firm A's strategy must be such that

$$[1 - q_A(l)](P_A - l - c - z) + q_A(l)(-z) = 0, \tag{A6}$$

where the left side of (A6) is firm B's expected payoff from a consumer located at l if it targets with its minimum discount depth of $P_B - P_A + l$, and the right side of (A6) is firm B's expected payoff from the consumer if does not target, thereby insuring itself a payoff of 0. In addition, firm B must also be indifferent between targeting with any $d_B(l) \in \mathfrak{D}_B(l)$ and not targeting at all, i.e.,

$$[1 - q_A(l)](P_B - d_B(l) - c - z)$$
$$+ q_A(l)F_A(P_A - P_B + d_B(l) - l)(P_B - d_B(l) - c - z)$$
$$+ q_A(l)[1 - F_A(P_A - P_B + d_B(l) - l)](-z) = 0. \tag{A7}$$

Solving (A6) and (A7), and setting $P_A - P_B + d_B(l) - l = d$, we have:

$$\tilde{q}_A(l) = \frac{P_A - c - l - z}{P_A - c - l}, \tag{A8}$$

$$\widetilde{F}_A(d) = \frac{dz}{(P_A - c - d - l)(P_A - c - z - l)}. \qquad (A9)$$

Thus, the probability that a consumer located at l will receive a promotional incentive from firm A with a discount value less than d is given by

$$\mathcal{F}_A(d) = \begin{cases} 0 & \text{if } d \leq 0 \\ \tilde{q}_A(l)\widetilde{F}_A(d) & \text{if } d \in \mathcal{D}_A(l) \\ \tilde{q}_A(l) & \text{if } d \geq P_A - c - z - l \end{cases} \qquad (A10)$$

It follows from these derivations that the expected payoff from any consumer located at l in Region I is given by $\pi_A(\tilde{q}_A, \tilde{q}_B, \widetilde{F}_A, \widetilde{F}_B) = l$ for firm A and $\pi_B(\tilde{q}_A, \tilde{q}_B, \widetilde{F}_A, \widetilde{F}_B) = 0$ for firm B. It also follows that neither firm can do better by deviating unilaterally to some other possible strategy.[14]

Region II. The equilibrium in Region II is symmetric to that in Region I and can be derived by substituting A for B, B for A, and l for $-l$ in Equations (A5) and (A10). Thus, in Region II, firm A's expected payoff is zero and firm B's expected payoff from a consumer located at l is l.

Region III. In Region III, a consumer will purchase from firm B absent any promotion and the consumer is loyal to firm A. We can show, following the same process as we did for Region I, that in equilibrium, we must have $d_A(l) \in [P_A - P_B - l, P_A - c - z - l]$ and $d_B(l) \in (0, P_B - c - z]$. Furthermore, firm A always promotes with a ~ass point, m_A, at the minimum value, and firm B promotes with ⌐bability $q_B \leq 1$. In equilibrium, the following three conditions must be satisfied:

$$(1 - q_B)(P_B + l - c - z) + q_B(-z) = l, \qquad (A11)$$

$$(1 - q_B)(P_A - d_A - c - z) + q_B F_B(P_B - P_A + d_A + l)(P_A - d_A - c - z)$$
$$+ q_B(1 - F_B(P_B - P_A + d_A + l))(-z) = l, \qquad (A12)$$

$$m_A(P_B - d_B - c - z) + (1 - m_A)F_A(P_A - P_B + d_B - l)(P_B - d_B - c - z)$$
$$+ (1 - m_A)(1 - F_A(P_A - P_B + d_B - l))(-z) = 0. \qquad (A13)$$

Equation (A11) insures that firm A is indifferent between $d_A = P_A - P_B - l$ and $d_A = P_A - c - z - l$ given firm B's strategy. Equation (A12) insures that firm A is indifferent between any $d_A \in (P_A - P_B - l, P_A - c - z - l)$ and $d_A = P_A - c - z - l$ given firm B's strategy. Equation (A13) insures that firm B is indifferent between any $d_B(l) \in (0, P_B - c - z)$ and the maximum value $P_B - c - z$. Solving A1, A2, and A3, along with the regularity conditions, we have:

$$\mathcal{F}_A(d) = \begin{cases} \tilde{m}_A + (1 - \tilde{m}_A)\widetilde{F}_A(d) & \text{if } d \in [P_A - P_B - l, P_A - c - z - l] \\ 1 & \text{if } d \geq P_A - c - z - l \end{cases} \qquad (A14)$$

[14] If firm A unilaterally deviates to any other strategy $(q_A, F_A(d))$, firm A can only do worse if $d \notin \mathcal{D}_A(l)$. If $d \in \mathcal{D}_A(l)$, then firm A's expected payoff is l given any strategy of firm B. The same logic also applies to firm B. Thus, the singular distributions in (A5) and (A10) are the Nash equilibrium strategies for both firms.

$$\mathcal{F}_B(d) = \begin{cases} 0 & \text{if } d \leq 0 \\ \tilde{q}_B(l)\widetilde{F}_B(d) & \text{if } d \in (0, P_B - c - z] \\ \tilde{q}_B(l) & \text{if } d \geq P_B - c - z, \end{cases} \qquad (A15)$$

where

$$\tilde{m}_A = \frac{z}{P_B - c}, \qquad \widetilde{F}_A(d) = \frac{(d + l + P_B - P_A)z}{(P_B - c - z)(P_A - l - d - c)}, \qquad (A16)$$

$$\tilde{q}_B(l) = \frac{P_B - c - z}{P_B - c + l}, \qquad \widetilde{F}_B(d) = \frac{d(l + z)}{(P_B + l - c - d)(P_B - c - z)}. \qquad (A17)$$

In this region, only firm A has positive profit. Firm A's payoff from a consumer is simply equal to the premium the consumer is willing to pay for firm A's brand.

Thus, we can conclude that a firm's payoff from a contested consumer is equal to the premium the consumer is willing to pay for the firm's brand. Q.E.D.

Appendix B

PROOF OF PROPOSITION 2. The steps we take to prove Parts (a), (b), and (c) are the same. In each case, we derive the necessary conditions for an equilibrium. We then show that in the proposed equilibrium, neither firm has an incentive to deviate unilaterally. We will first take up Part (a).

Neither Firm Offers One-to-One Promotions. Note that in any equilibrium where $P_A \leq c + z$ and $P_B \leq c + z$ hold, both firms must have positive market shares. Otherwise, a monopolist firm should set its price at $V > c + z$. This means that in any such equilibrium we must have $l_A - \hat{l} > 0$ and $l_B + \hat{l} > 0$. The equilibrium regular prices $(\widetilde{P}_A, \widetilde{P}_B)$ then necessarily satisfy the following conditions for all P_A and P_B

$$\widetilde{P}_A = \arg\max_{P_A} \frac{1}{l_A + l_B}(P_A - c)(l_A - \hat{l})$$
$$\text{s.t. } P_A \leq c + z$$

$$\widetilde{P}_B = \arg\max_{P_A} \frac{1}{l_A + l_B}(P_B - c)(l_B + \hat{l})$$
$$\text{s.t. } P_B \leq c + z.$$

In other words, in equilibrium, $(\widetilde{P}_A, \widetilde{P}_B)$ must solve the following system of first-order conditions

$$\frac{1}{l_A + l_B}(l_A - \hat{l} - P_A + c) - \mu_A = 0$$

$$\frac{1}{l_A + l_B}(l_B + \hat{l} + P_B - c) - \mu_B = 0$$

$$\mu_A(P_A - c - z) = 0, \quad \mu_A \geq 0, \quad P_A \leq c + z$$

$$\mu_B(P_B - c - z) = 0, \quad \mu_B \geq 0, \quad P_B \leq c + z,$$

where μ_A and μ_B are Lagrange multipliers.

If $\mu_A = \mu_B = 0$, i.e., none of the constraints bind, a unique solution to the above first-order conditions exists if $z \geq (2l_A + l_B)/3$, and we have the following candidate equilibrium

$$\widetilde{P}_A = \frac{2l_A + l_B}{3} + c, \qquad \widetilde{P}_B = \frac{l_A + 2l_B}{3} + c$$

$$\widetilde{\Pi}_A^1 = \frac{(2l_A + l_B)^2}{9(l_A + l_B)}, \qquad \widetilde{\Pi}_B^1 = \frac{(l_A + 2l_B)^2}{9(l_A + l_B)}.$$

We now show that the strategies in this candidate equilibrium indeed constitute a Nash equilibrium since none of the firms can do better by deviating unilaterally from its strategy above.

Given $\widetilde{P}_B$, the first-order conditions already insure that firm A never wants to deviate from $\widetilde{P}_A$ by choosing some $P_A \leq c+z$. However, firm A may want to deviate by choosing some $P_A > c+z$ so that targeted promotions then become profitable. This gives a deviation profit of

$$\Pi_A^d = \frac{1}{l_A + l_B}\left\{(P_A - c)\max\{l_A - \hat{l}, 0\} + \int_{l \in \mathcal{I}_A}(\widetilde{P}_B - c - z + l)\,dl\right\}.$$

We now show that any deviation $P_A > c+z$ by firm A can only make firm A worse off. First, firm A can deviate by choosing some $P_A > l_A + \widetilde{P}_B$. In that case, firm A's profit is nonzero only if $l_A - c - z + \widetilde{P}_B > 0$ holds, or equivalently the following condition holds

$$2l_A + l_B > \frac{3}{2}z. \tag{B1}$$

Given Condition (B1), we have

$$\Pi_A^d = \frac{1}{l_A + l_B}\int_{c+z-\widetilde{P}_B}^{l_A}(\widetilde{P}_B - c - z + l)\,dl.$$

However, in that case, we have

$$\begin{aligned}\widetilde{\Pi}_A - \Pi_A^d &= \frac{-2(2l_A + l_B)^2 + 3z(8l_A + 4l_B - 3z)}{18(l_A + l_B)}\\ &\geq \frac{-2(2l_A + l_B)^2 + (2l_A + l_B)(8l_A + 4l_B - 3z)}{18(l_A + l_B)}\\ &= \frac{(2l_A + l_B)[2(2l_A + l_B) - 3z]}{18(l_A + l_B)}\\ &> 0.\end{aligned}$$

The first inequality follows from the fact that we have $z \geq (2l_A + l_B)/3$, and the second inequality follows from Condition (B1). Thus, firm A never deviates by setting some $P_A > l_A + \widetilde{P}_B$.

Firm A may, however, deviate by choosing some $P_A \in (c+z, l_A + \widetilde{P}_B]$. In that case, we have

$$\Pi_A^d = \frac{1}{l_A + l_B}\left[(P_A - c)(l_A - \hat{l}) + \int_{c+z-\widetilde{P}_B}^{\hat{l}}(\widetilde{P}_B - c - z + l)\,dl\right]. \tag{B2}$$

By differentiating Equation (B2), we have

$$\begin{aligned}\frac{\partial \Pi_A^d}{\partial P_A} &= \frac{1}{l_A + l_B}(l_A - P_A - z + \widetilde{P}_B)\\ &< \frac{2}{l_A + l_B}\left[\frac{2l_A + l_B}{3} - z\right]\\ &\leq 0.\end{aligned}$$

The first inequality follows from $P_A > c+z$, and the second follows from $z \geq (2l_A + l_B)/3$. The above derivation implies that firm A's optimal deviation is to set P_A arbitrarily close to $c+z$, and not to use targeted promotions. Thus, the optimal deviation will make the

second part of Equation (B2) drop out. Obviously, $\widetilde{\Pi}_A^1 > \Pi_A^d$ in this case since $\widetilde{P}_A$ maximizes the first part of Equation (B2).

Thus, we have shown that firm A will not unilaterally deviate from $\widetilde{P}_A$. Using the same steps, we can also show that firm B will not unilaterally deviate from $\widetilde{P}_B$ so that $(\widetilde{P}_A, \widetilde{P}_B)$ is an equilibrium given $z \geq (2l_A + l_B)/3$. Furthermore, we can show, by going through the same steps, that no other equilibrium exists where $P_A \leq c+z$ and $P_B \leq c+z$. Q.E.D.

Only Firm A Offers One-to-One Promotions. To prove Part (b) of Proposition 2, we first show that it is impossible for an equilibrium to exist where $\widetilde{P}_A \leq c+z$ and $\widetilde{P}_B > c+z$ such that firm B targets while firm A does not. In this were not true, we must have in this equilibrium either $\widetilde{P}_A = c+z$ or $\widetilde{P}_A < c+z$. In the former case, the payoffs for each firm are given by

$$\begin{aligned}\widetilde{\Pi}_A &= \frac{zl_A}{l_A + l_B},\\ \widetilde{\Pi}_B &= \frac{1}{l_A + l_B}\left[(\widetilde{P}_B - c)(c + z - \widetilde{P}_B + l_B) + \int_0^{c+z-\widetilde{P}_B}l\,dl\right].\end{aligned}$$

As $\widetilde{P}_B$ must maximize firm B's payoff, we necessarily have $\widetilde{P}_B = l_B + c$ in this equilibrium.

We now consider firm A's deviation by setting $P_A^d = l_A + c > c+z$ so that we are in the subgame of competitive targeting. In that case, firm A's payoff becomes $\Pi_A^d = (l_A^2 + z^2)/(2(l_A + l_B)) > \widetilde{\Pi}_A$. Therefore, if an equilibrium exists where $\widetilde{P}_A \leq c+z$ and $\widetilde{P}_B > c+z$, we must have $\widetilde{P}_A < c+z$. In this case, both firms' payoffs are given by

$$\begin{aligned}\widetilde{\Pi}_A &= \frac{1}{l_A + l_B}(\widetilde{P}_A - c)(l_A - \widetilde{P}_A + c + z),\\ \widetilde{\Pi}_B &= \frac{1}{l_A + l_B}\left[(\widetilde{P}_B - c)(\widetilde{P}_A - \widetilde{P}_B + l_B) + \int_{\widetilde{P}_A - \widetilde{P}_B}^{\widetilde{P}_A - c - z}(\widetilde{P}_A - c - z - l)\,dl\right].\end{aligned}$$

By examining the first order necessary conditions for an equilibrium with these payoff functions, we must have $\widetilde{P}_A = (l_A + z)/2 + c$ and $\widetilde{P}_B = (l_A + 2l_B - z)/2 + c$. However, $\widetilde{P}_A < c+z$ and $\widetilde{P}_B > c+z$ must imply $l_A < z < (l_A + 2l_B)/3$, which is not possible given $l_A \geq l_B$.

We can then go through the same steps to show that the equilibrium exists where firm A targets unilaterally under the conditions specified in Proposition 2. Q.E.D.

Both Firms Offer One-to-One Promotions. We now prove Part (c) of Proposition 2. In any equilibrium where $\widetilde{P}_A > c+z$ and $\widetilde{P}_B > c+z$ such that competitive targeting ensues, the firms' payoff functions are given by

$$\begin{aligned}\widetilde{\Pi}_A &= \frac{1}{2(l_A + l_B)}\hat{l}_A^2 + \frac{(\widetilde{P}_A - c)(l_A - \hat{l}_A)}{l_A + l_B},\\ \widetilde{\Pi}_B &= \frac{1}{2(l_A + l_B)}\hat{l}_B^2 + \frac{(\widetilde{P}_B - c)(\hat{l}_B + l_B)}{l_A + l_B},\end{aligned}$$

where, as we recall, $\hat{l}_A = \widetilde{P}_A - c - z$ and $\hat{l}_B = c + z - \widetilde{P}_B$. Through first-order conditions, we necessarily have $\widetilde{P}_A = l_A + c$ and $\widetilde{P}_B = l_B + c$. Then, to insure $\widetilde{P}_A > c+z$ and $\widetilde{P}_B > c+z$, we need to have $z < l_B$. We now check if any firm have any incentive to deviate from this candidate equilibrium.

Given $\widetilde{P}_B = l_B + c > c + z$, firm A may deviate by setting $P_A^d \le c + z$ and thus giving up on targeting. In that case, firm A's payoff is given by

$$\Pi_A^d = \frac{1}{l_A + l_B}(P_A^d - c)(l_A - P_A^d + c + z).$$

The best firm A can do through this deviation is to set $P_A^d = c + z$ and obtain the payoff $\Pi_A^d = zl_A/(l_A + l_B)$. However, we have

$$\widetilde{\Pi}_A - \Pi_A^d = \frac{(z - l_A)^2}{2(l_A + l_B)} > 0.$$

Thus, firm A has no incentive to deviate.

Similarly, the optimal deviation for firm B is to set $P_B^d = c + z$, which yields $\Pi_B^d = zl_B/(l_A + l_B)$. However, we have

$$\widetilde{\Pi}_B - \Pi_B^d = \frac{(z - l_B)^2}{2(l_A + l_B)} > 0.$$

Therefore, firm B has no incentive to deviate.   Q.E.D.

Appendix C

PROOF OF PROPOSITION 5. Note that from Proposition 2 and Equations (A5) through (A10), the expected number of consumers who, all else being equal, prefer firm A's product but purchase from firm B due to targeted promotions is

$$\mathscr{C} = \frac{1}{2l_S} \int_0^{l_S - z} \left\{ \bar{q}_B(l)(1 - \bar{q}_A(l)) + \int_{d_B \in \mathscr{D}_B(l)} \mathscr{F}_A(d_B - l) \, d\mathscr{F}_B(d_B) \right\} dl,$$
(C1)

where $\mathscr{C}$ is concave in z and approaches 0 as z approaches l_S or 0. A similar expression holds for the expected number of consumers who are, all else being equal, loyal to firm B but purchase from firm A due to targeted promotions. Proposition 5 then follows after substituting the equilibrium values into (C1) and conducting comparative statics with respect to z.   Q.E.D.

References

Banks, J., S. Moorthy. 1999. A model of price promotions with consumer search. *Internat. J. Indust. Organ.* 17 371–398.

Bessen, J. 1993. Riding the marketing information wave. *Harvard Bus. Rev.* (September–October) 150.

Bester, H., E. Petrakis. 1996. Coupons and oligopolistic price discrimination. *Internat. J. Indust. Organ.* 14 227–242.

Blattberg, R., J. Deighton. 1991. Interactive marketing: Exploiting the age of addressability. *Sloan Management Rev.* 22(September) 5.

Business Week. 1999. Privacy: Special report. (April 5) 84–88.

Cane, A. 1999. Industry frets over its fickle friends: CHURN RATES. *Financial Times* (June 9) 14.

Chen, Y. 1997. Paying customers to switch. *J. Econom. Management Strategy* 6 877–897.

Corts, K. 1998. Third-degree price discrimination in oligopoly: All-out competition and strategic commitment. *Rand J. Econom.* 29 306–323.

Fudenberg, D., J. Tirole. 2000. Customer poaching and brand switching. *Rand J. Econom.* 31 634–657.

Hof, R. D. 1998. Now it's your web. *Business Week* (October 5) 164.

Lawyer, Gail. 1998. Rate games exact a price. *Telecom* 3(3) 19.

Lederer, P., A. P. Hurter, Jr. 1986. Competition of firms: Discriminatory pricing and location. *Econometrica* 54(3) 623–640.

MaCollum, T. 1998. Tools for targeting customer service. *Nation's Bus.* (November) 49.

Mills, L. 1999. The main front: Direct marketing is the key battleground in the phone wars as the telcos shift decisively away from mass marketing. *Marketing Magazine* 104(17) MD2.

Narasimhan, C. 1988. Competitive promotional strategies. *J. Bus.* 61 427–449.

Peppers, D., M. Rogers. 1993. *The One to One Future.* Currency/Doubleday.

Rao, R. 1991. Pricing and promotions in asymmetric duopolies. *Marketing Sci.* 10 131–144.

Schultz, D. 1994. Driving integration is what IT is all about. *Marketing News* (October 10) 12.

Taylor, C. 1999. Supplier surfing: Competition and consumer behavior in subscription markets. Mimeo, Duke University, Durham, NC.

Shapiro, C., H. Varian. 1999. *Information Rules.* HBS Press, Boston, MA, 40–43.

Shaffer, G., Z. John Zhang. 1995. Competitive coupon targeting. *Marketing Sci.* 14 395–416.

——, ——. 2000. Pay to switch or pay to stay: Preference-based price discrimination in markets with switching costs. *J. Econom. Management Strategy* 9 397–424.

Turco, F. 1993. Call is on to switch long-distance firms: Pennies, $100 checks among lures. *Arizona Republic* (April 7) A1.

Accepted by Depak Jain; received February 18, 2000. This paper was with the authors for 3 revisions.

Southwest Airlines (A)

"Y'all buckle that seat belt," said the hostess over the public address system, "because we're fixin' to take off right now. Soon as we get up in the air, we want you to kick off your shoes, loosen your tie, an' let Southwest put a little love in your life on our way from Big D to Houston." The passengers settled back comfortably in their seats as the brightly-colored Boeing 737 taxied toward the takeoff point at Dallas's Love Field airport. Moments later, it was accelerating down the runway and then climbing steeply into the Texas sky on the 240-mile flight to Houston.

On the other side of Love Field across from the airport terminal, Southwest Airlines executives ignored the departing aircraft's noise, clearly audible in the company's modest but comfortable second-floor offices next to the North American–Rockwell hangar. They were about to begin an important meeting with representatives from their advertising agency to discuss alternative strategies in response to an announcement by their chief competitor, Braniff International Airways, that it was introducing a 60-day, half-price sale on Southwest's major route effective that same day, February 1, 1973.

Company Background

Southwest Airlines Co., a Texas corporation, was organized in March 1967. The founder, Rollin W. King, had graduated from the Harvard Business School in 1962 and was previously an investment counselor with a San Antonio firm. Since 1964, King, who held an airline transport pilot's license, had also been president of an air taxi service operating from San Antonio to various smaller south Texas communities.

During the mid-1960s, King and his associates became increasingly convinced that a need existed for improved air service between Houston, Dallas-Fort Worth, and San Antonio. These four cities were among the fastest growing in the nation. By 1968 Houston's standard metropolitan statistical area had a population of 1,867,000. Dallas's population was 1,459,000, San Antonio's 850,000, and Fort Worth's 680,000. Located 30 miles apart in northeastern Texas, Dallas and Fort Worth were frequently thought of as a single market area. Although each had its own airport—with Dallas's Love Field the busier of the two and the only one served by the airlines—construction had recently begun on the huge, new Dallas-Fort Worth Regional Airport, located midway between the two cities and intended to serve both.

Assistant Professor Christopher H. Lovelock prepared this case as a basis for class discussion and not to illustrate either effective or ineffective handling of an administrative situation.

Braniff International Airways and Texas International Airlines (TI) provided most of the air service between these markets. In 1967 Braniff operated a fleet of 69 jet and turboprop aircraft on an extensive route network, with a predominantly north-south emphasis, serving major U.S. cities, Mexico, and South America. Total Braniff revenues that year were $256 million, and the airline carried 5.6 million passengers. Texas International Airlines (then known as Trans-Texas Airways) was a regional carrier, serving southern and southwestern states and Mexico. In 1967 it operated a fleet of 45 jet, turboprop and piston-engined aircraft on mostly short-haul routes, carrying 1.5 million passengers and generating total revenues of $32 million. Both Braniff and Tl were headquartered in Texas.

Service by these two carriers within Texas represented legs of much longer, interstate flights; travelers flying from Dallas to San Antonio, for example, might find themselves boarding a Braniff flight that had just arrived from New York and was calling at Dallas on its way to San Antonio. In 1967 local travel between Dallas and Houston (the most important route) averaged 483 passengers daily in each direction, with Braniff holding 86% of this traffic (see **Exhibit 1**).[1] Looking back at the factors that had first stimulated his interest in developing a new airline to serve these markets, King recalled:

> The more we talked to people, the more we looked at figures of how big the market was and the more we realized the degree of consumer dissatisfaction with the services of existing carriers, the more apparent the opportunities became to us. We thought that these were substantial markets, and while they weren't nearly as large as the Los Angeles-San Francisco market, they had a lot in common with it. We knew the history of what PSA [Pacific Southwest Airlines] had been able to do in California with the same kind of service we were contemplating.[2]

On February 20, 1968, the Texas Aeronautics Commission granted a Certificate of Public Convenience and Necessity to Southwest, permitting it to provide intrastate air service between Dallas-Fort Worth, Houston, and San Antonio, a triangular route with each leg ranging in length from roughly 190 to 250 miles (see **Figure A**). Since the new airline proposed to confine its operations to Texas, its executives maintained that it did not need certification from the federal Civil Aeronautics Board (CAB).[3]

The next day, Braniff and TI asked the Texas courts to enjoin issuance of the Texas certificate. These two airlines already served the proposed routes and considered market demand insufficient to support another airline. The resulting litigation proved costly and time consuming, eventually reaching the U.S. Supreme Court. However, the suit was finally decided in Southwest's favor.

During the summer of 1970 M. Lamar Muse, an independent financial consultant, approached King. Muse had resigned the previous fall as president of Universal Airlines—a Detroit-based supplemental carrier—over a disagreement with the major stockholders on their planned purchase of Boeing 747 jumbo jets. Muse had read of Southwest's legal battles and told King and his fellow directors that he would like to help them transform the company from a piece of paper into an operating airline.

---

[1] Local travel figures excluded passengers traveling between these cities as part of a longer journey.

[2] PSA had built up a substantial market share on the lucrative Los Angeles-San Francisco route, as well as on other operations within California. Southwest executives subsequently carefully studied PSA when designing their operations.

[3] The Civil Aeronautics Board regulated all interstate airlines in matters such as fares and routes, but had no authority over airlines operating exclusively within a single state. (The CAB should not be confused with the Federal Aviation Administration [FAA], which regulated safety procedures and flight operations for all passenger airlines, including intrastate carriers.)

Figure A   Southwest Airlines Route Map

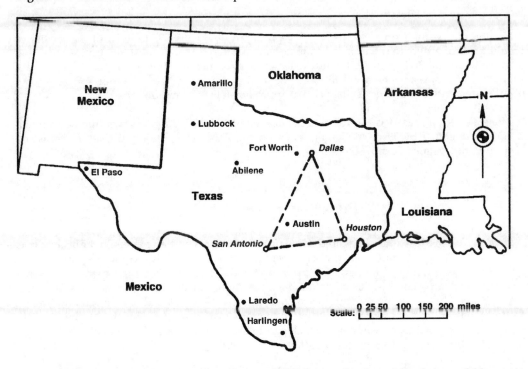

The wealth of experience that Muse could bring to the new airline was quickly recognized. Before assuming the presidency of Universal in September 1967, he had served for three years as president of Central Airlines, a Dallas-based regional carrier. Before 1965 he had been secretary-treasurer of Trans-Texas Airways, assistant vice president–corporate planning of American Airlines, and vice president–finance of Southern Airways. After working informally with Southwest for a couple of months, Muse became a company employee in October 1970 and was elected president, treasurer, and a director on January 26, 1971. King was simultaneously named executive vice president of operations.

Muse explained one reason why he was attracted to Southwest:

> I felt the interstate carriers just weren't doing the job in this market. Every one of their flights was completely full—it was very difficult to get reservations. There were a lot of canceled flights; Dallas being Braniff's base and Houston TI's base, every time they had a mechanical problem it seemed like they always took it out on the Dallas-Houston service. From Dallas south to San Antonio and Houston is the tag end of Braniff's system, everything was turning around and going back north to Chicago or New York or wherever. There was so much interline traffic that most of the seats were occupied by those people. While Braniff had hourly service, there really weren't many seats available for local passengers. People just avoided flying in this market—they only went when they had to.

Muse added that Braniff's reputation for punctuality was so poor that many travelers popularly referred to it as the "World's Largest Unscheduled Airline."

Optimistic over the outcome of Southwest's legal battles, Muse and King spent many weeks on the West Coast in late 1970 and early 1971, prospecting for new aircraft. The airline industry was then in a recession, and aircraft purchasers were courted assiduously. Southwest initiated high-pressure negotiations with McDonnell-Douglas, Boeing, and several other airlines for the purchase of new or used jets.

Finally, the Boeing Company, having overproduced its Boeing 737 twin jet (in a speculative assessment of future orders that had failed to materialize), offered both a substantial price reduction and favorable financing. In March 1971 Southwest signed a contract for three Boeing 737-200 aircraft, some months later increasing the order to four. The total purchase price for the four 737s was $16.2 million, compared with a previous asking price of approximately $4.6 million each.

Muse and King regarded the 737 as a better aircraft for their purposes than the McDonnell-Douglas DC-9s operated by TI or the larger, tri-jet Boeing 727s, which required a larger crew and were flown by Braniff on its Texas routes.

Preparing for Takeoff

Back in Texas, Muse and King faced some urgent problems and an extremely tight deadline. Scheduled operations had been tentatively set to begin on June 18, slightly over four months away. During this time, Southwest had to raise additional capital to finance both startup expenses and what might prove to be a prolonged period of deficit operations. The existing skeleton management team had to be expanded by recruiting several specialist executives. Personnel had to be hired and trained for both flight and ground operations. Meantime numerous marketing problems had to be resolved and an introductory advertising campaign developed to launch the new airline. Finally, Braniff and TI were pressing their legal battles to stifle Southwest.

The company's lawyers handled the legal matters while the Southwest executives moved quickly to confront financial, personnel, and marketing problems. The airline's financial position demanded immediate attention, since at year's end 1970 the company had a mere $183 in its bank account (see **Exhibit 2**). Between March and June 1971, Southwest raised almost 58 million selling convertible promissory notes and common stock.

Four executives with many years' airline experience soon filled vacancies on the management team. Three had previously worked for either Braniff or TI and had recently been fired by those carriers—a fact that Muse considered one of their strongest recommendations for employment with Southwest.

Decisions on route structure and schedules had already been made. Initially two of the three Boeing 737s would be placed in service on the busy Dallas-Houston run, and the third would fly between Dallas and San Antonio. Meanwhile, Southwest did not plan to exercise its rights to operate service on the third leg of the triangle between Houston and San Antonio. Flight frequency depended on aircraft availability. Allowing time for turning around the aircraft at each end, management concluded that flights could be offered in each direction between Dallas and Houston at 75-minute intervals, and between Dallas and San Antonio at 2 1/2-hour intervals. Both services were scheduled for 50 minutes. The Monday-Friday schedule called for 12 daily round trips between Dallas and Houston and 6 daily round trips between Dallas and San Antonio. Saturday and Sunday schedules were more limited, reflecting both the lower travel demand on weekends and the need for downtime to service the aircraft.

The pricing decision, meantime, had been arrived at following talks with PSA executives in California. King recalled:

> What Andy Andrews [president of PSA] said to Lamar and me one day was the key to our initial pricing decision. Andy told us that the way you ought to figure your price is not on how much you can get or what the other carriers were charging.

He said, "Pick a price at which you can break even with a reasonable load factor, and a load factor that you have a reasonable expectation of being able to get within a given period of time, and that ought to be your price. It ought to be as low as you can get it without leading yourself down the primrose path and running out of money."

After estimating the money required for preoperating expenses and then carefully assessing both operating costs and market potential, Muse and King settled on a $20 fare for both routes, with a break-even point of 39 passengers per flight. In comparison, Braniff and TI coach fares were $27 on the Dallas-Houston run and $28 on the Dallas-San Antonio service. The two executives believed that an average of 39 passengers per flight was a reasonable expectation considering the market's growth potential and the frequency of flights Southwest planned to offer, although they projected a period of deficit operations before this break-even point would be reached. They anticipated that while Braniff and TI might eventually reduce their fares, Southwest could expect an initial price advantage.

Early in 1971 Muse met with the vice president of marketing, Dick Elliott, to select an advertising agency. (The airline already employed a public relations agency to handle publicity.) The Bloom Agency, a large regional advertising agency conveniently headquartered in Dallas, was awarded the account. The assignment was to come up with a complete communications program—other than publicity—within four months. "We've got no hostesses and no uniforms and no airplanes and no design and no money," Muse told the agency people, "but we're going to have an airline flying in 120 days!"

Bloom approached Southwest Airlines "as though it were a packaged goods account." The first task was to evaluate the characteristics of all U.S. carriers competing in the Texas markets. To simplify comparisons, a two-dimensional positioning diagram was prepared, rating each airline's image on conservative-fun and obvious-subtle scales (see **Figure B**). These judgments were based primarily on an analysis of recent airline advertising, to determine each carrier's image.

TI was immediately dismissed as dull and conservative, with a bland image. (**Exhibit 3** shows typical TI advertisements at that time.) Braniff's advertising, however, presented an interesting stylistic contrast. From 1965 to 1968 Braniff had employed Wells, Rich, Greene, a New York agency that had developed an innovative marketing and advertising strategy for its client, with a budget exceeding $10 million in 1967. Braniff's aircraft were painted in various brilliant colors covering the entire fuselage and tailfin. Hostesses wore couture costumes created by an Italian fashion designer, and the advertising sought to make flying with Braniff seem glamorous and exciting. This approach proved extremely successful and was believed by many observers to have prompted Braniff's rapid growth during the second half of the 1960s. Bloom's executives, however, concluded that by 1971 Braniff's image was changing from a fun image to a subtler, more conservative style (see **Exhibit 4**), with an advertising budget reduced to approximately $4 million. This left a vacuum for Southwest Airlines to fill. So the agency decided to position Southwest beyond the fun-obvious side of the old Braniff image.

Accordingly, the account group developed "an entire personality description model" for the new airline. The objective was to provide the agency's creative specialists with a dear understanding of the image that Southwest should project, so that this might be consistently reflected in every facet of the communications campaign they had to design. This personality statement, also used as a guideline in staff recruiting, described Southwest as "young and vital . . . exciting . . . friendly . . . efficient. . . dynamic."

One constraint on marketing activities in the months before passenger operations was the planned issue of over $6 million of Southwest stock on June 8. The company's lawyers had advised that a media campaign promoting the airline before the stock issue might violate Securities and Exchange Commission regulations against promoting stock. Virtually the only advertising conducted before June 8, therefore, was for personnel.

Figure B   Positioning Diagram of U.S. Airlines Advertising and Competing in Texas

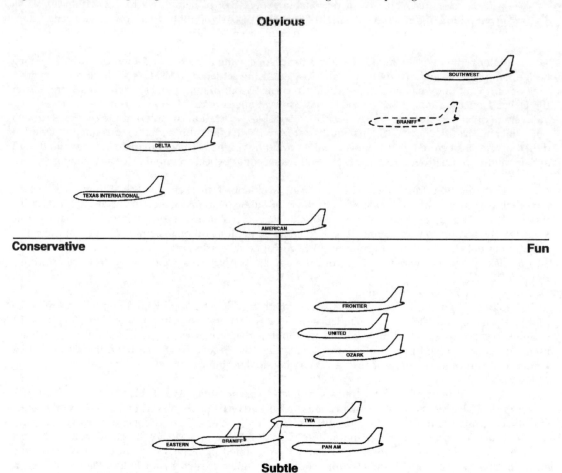

Source: The Bloom Agency (February 11, 1971)
[a] Former advertising by Wells, Rich, Greene ("The End of the Plain Plane," "The Air Strip").
[b] Clinton E. Frank advertising, 1971.

Recruitment advertising in one area proved outstandingly effective, with over 1,200 young women responding to advertisements placed in national media for positions as Southwest air hostesses. Forty applicants were selected for training and although airline officials made no secret of the attractive looks of the successful candidates, it was also pointed out that their average scores on the required FAA proficiency test ranked among the highest of all U.S. carriers.

The advertising prohibition did not entirely keep Southwest out of the news. The airline's continuing legal battles with Braniff and TI received extensive publicity from the mass media, and Southwest's public relations agency put out several press releases that subsequently appeared as news or feature stories.

Service Begins: The First Six Months

On June 10, 1971, The Bloom Agency's advertising campaign for Southwest finally broke. It began modestly with small teaser ads in the newspapers, containing provocative headlines such as

"The 48-Minute Love Affair," "At Last a $20 Ticket You Won't Mind Getting," "Love Can Change Your Ways," and "A Fare to Remember." The unsigned ads contained a telephone number for the reader to call. On phoning, a caller in Dallas would hear a taped message.

> Hi. It's us. Southwest Airlines. Us with our brand-new, candy-colored, rainbow-powered Boeing 737 jets. The most reliable plane flying today. And we start flying June 18, to Houston or San Antonio. You choose—only 45 minutes nonstop. In that time, we'll be sharing a lot of big little things with you that mean a lot. Like love potions, a lot of attention and a new low fare. Just $20. Join us June 18. Southwest Airlines. The somebody else up there who loves you.

Approximately 25,000 telephone calls resulted from these ads.

On Sunday, June 13, all newspapers in the three market areas ran a four-color double-truck[4] ad for Southwest (see centerspread). Daily, full-page newspaper ads appeared for the next two weeks in all markets highlighting the advantages Southwest Airlines offered the traveler—new aircraft, attractive hostesses, low fares, fast ticketing, and inexpensive, exotically-named drinks. TV advertising was also heavy and included 30-second spots featuring the Boeing 737, the hostesses, and what was referred to as the "Love Machine" (see **Exhibit 5**). Whereas the competition used traditional, handwritten airline tickets, Southwest counter staff shortened ticket purchases, using a machine to print out tickets and a pedal-operated tape recorder to enter names on the passenger list as they checked in—both ideas were copied from PSA. Rounding out the advertising campaign were prominently displayed billboards at entrances to all three airports served by Southwest. Nearly half the year's promotional budget was spent in the first month of operations (see **Table A**).

Table A   Southwest Advertising and Promotional Expenditures, 1971 and 1972

	1971			1972
	Preoperating	**Operating**	**Total**	**(budgeted)**
Advertising				
Newspaper	$139,831	$131,675	$271,506	$60,518
Television	36,340	761	37,101	127,005
Radio	5,021	60,080	65,101	95,758
Billboards	26,537	11,670	38,207	90,376
Other publications	710	20,446	21,156	28,139
Production costs	52,484	43,483	95,967	83,272
Other promotion and publicity	29,694	27,200	56,894	48,366
	$290,617	$295,315	$585,932	$533,434

Source: Company records

Scheduled revenue operations were inaugurated in a blaze of publicity on Friday, June 18, but evidently the competition was not about to take matters lying down. In half-truck and full-page newspaper ads, Braniff and TI announced $20 fares on both routes. The CAB had disclaimed authority over intrastate fares and Texas law barred jurisdiction by TAC over carriers holding Federal Certificates of Public Convenience and Necessity; thus, the CAB carriers could charge any fare they wanted. Braniff's advertising stressed frequent, convenient service "every hour on the hour," hot and cold towels "to freshen up with," beverage discount coupons and "peace of mind" phone calls at the boarding gate; it also announced increased service between Dallas and San Antonio, effective July 1 (see **Exhibit 6**). TI, meantime, announced that on July 1 hourly service would begin on the Dallas-Houston route, leaving Dallas at 30 minutes past each hour. TI also introduced extras such as free beer, free newpapers, and $1 drinks on routes competing with Southwest (see **Exhibit 7**). Southwest

---

[4] "Double-truck" is a printer's term that describes material printed across two full pages. A "half-truck" ad is printed across two half pages.

countered with advertising headlined "The Other Airlines May Have Met Our Price But You Can't Buy Love."

Advertising and promotion continued regularly both on television and with frequent publicity events, usually featuring Southwest hostesses. A direct-mail campaign targeted 36,000 influential business executives in Southwest's service areas. Each received a personalized letter from Muse describing Southwest's service and enclosing a voucher worth half the cost of a round-trip ticket; about 1,700 vouchers were redeemed.

Surveys of Southwest's passengers departing from Houston revealed that a substantial percentage would have preferred using the William P. Hobby Airport, 12 miles southeast of downtown Houston, rather than the new Houston Intercontinental Airport, 26 miles north of the city. Accordingly, in mid-November, 7 of Southwest's 14 round-trip flights between Dallas and Houston were transferred to Hobby Airport, thus reopening this old airport to scheduled commercial passenger traffic. Additional schedule revisions made simultaneously included a reduction to four round-trips each weekday of the Dallas-San Antonio flights, inauguration of three daily round-trips on the third leg of the route triangle between Houston (Hobby) and San Antonio, and elimination of the extremely unprofitable Saturday flights on all routes. These actions contributed to increased transportation revenues in the final quarter of 1971 over those of the third quarter, but Southwest's operating losses in the fourth quarter fell only slightly, from $1,006,000 to $921,000 (see **Exhibit 8**). At year's end 1971, Southwest's accumulated deficit stood at $3.75 million (see **Exhibit 2**).

The Second Six Months

In February 1972, Southwest initiated a second phase of the advertising campaign, hired a new vice president of marketing, and scrapped its public relations agency. Meanwhile, the company recruited the agency's publicity director to fill a newly created position as public relations director at Southwest.

The objective was to sustain Southwest's presence in the marketplace after eight months of service. Frequent advertising, with a wide variety of messages, was directed at the regular business commuter. Surveys had shown that such travelers represented 89% of Southwest's traffic. The campaign made extensive use of TV advertising, featuring many of Southwest's hostesses.

Dick Elliott, whom the President described as having performed a herculean task in getting Southwest off the ground, had resigned to join a national advertising agency. The new vice president of marketing, Jess R. Coker, had spent 10 years in the outdoor advertising business after graduating from the University of Texas. His assignment before joining the airline had been as vice president of Southern Outdoor Markets, a company representing 85% of all outdoor advertising, in the 14 southern and southeastern states. Coker assumed responsibility for all marketing functions of the airline, including advertising, sales, and public relations (see **Figure C**). He often met weekly with the account executive from The Bloom Agency to discuss not only media advertising, but also numerous other details handled by the agency, including the preparation and execution of pocket timetables, point-of-sales materials for travel agents, and promotional brochures.

Although the majority of tickets were sold over the counter at the airport, sales were also made to travel agents and corporate accounts. Travel agents received a 7% commission on credit card sales and 10% on cash sales. Corporate accounts—companies whose personnel regularly used Southwest—received no discount, but benefited from the conveniences of a private supply of ticket stock that they issued themselves and a single monthly billing. Coker commanded a force of six sales representatives, whose job was to develop and service both travel agents and corporate accounts, encouraging maximum use of Southwest through distribution of point-of-sales materials, development of package arrangements, distribution of pocket timetables, and so forth. Sales representatives also promoted Southwest's air freight business, which featured a special rush delivery service for packages. Each representative, as well as most company officers, drove an AMC Gremlin car, strikingly painted in the color scheme of Southwest's aircraft.

Southwest's new public relations director, Camille Keith, also reported to Coker. Keith was a former publicity director of Read-Poland, Inc., the public relations agency that had previously handled the airline's account. Keith's responsibilities focused on obtaining media coverage for the airline, and also included publication of Southwest's in-flight magazine and joint development of certain promotions with the advertising agency.

Between October 1971 and April 1972, average passenger loads systemwide increased from 18.4 passengers per flight to 26.7 passengers, still below the number necessary to cover the rising total costs per trip. The volume of traffic during the late morning and early afternoon could not support flights at hourly intervals. Conforming to Houston passenger preference, Southwest gradually shifted its operations to Hobby Airport and abandoned Houston Intercontinental.

On May 14, a new schedule reduced daily flights between Dallas and Houston from 29 to 22, primarily by curtailing service between 9:30 A.M. and 3:30 P.M. from once an hour to once every two hours. Eleven daily flights were still offered on the Dallas-San Antonio route and six between San Antonio and Houston, with some minor schedule changes. Hobby Airport was to be used exclusively for all flights to and from Houston. Braniff quickly retaliated by introducing service from Dallas to Hobby and undertaking an extensive publicity program promoting this move.

Financially, the new schedule allowed the company to sell its fourth Boeing 737. Experience had shown that the 737s could be turned around (i.e., loaded and unloaded) at the gate within 10 minutes. This meant that an hourly schedule on the Dallas-Houston run could be maintained with only two aircraft, instead of three. With the slack provided by the reduced midday frequencies and a schedule that involved periodically flying an aircraft around all three legs of the triangular routes, management concluded that three aircraft would suffice. By mid-1972, the airline industry had recovered from its 1970-1971 slump, and aircraft manufacturers had waiting lists for the popular models. Southwest found a ready buyer for its surplus 737 and made a profit of $533,000 on the sale. With this capital gain, lower operating costs, and a continued increase in revenues, net loss fell from $804,000 to $131,000 between the first and second quarters of 1972 (see **Exhibit 3**).

For some months Southwest had been experimenting with a $10 fare on Friday flights after 9:00 P.M. In May this reduced fare was extended to post-9:00 P.M. daily flights. These discount flights attracted more business than the standard-priced flights (see **Exhibit 9**).

In June 1972 Southwest Airlines celebrated its first birthday, giving Camille Keith an opportunity for more of the publicity stunts for which the airline was already famous. Posters were hung inside the aircraft and in the waiting lounges, the aircraft cabins were decorated, and an on-board party was held every day for a week, with birthday cake for the passengers and balloons for the children. This hoopla, promoted by newspaper advertising, generated considerable publicity for the airline and, in management's view, reinforced Southwest's image as the plucky, friendly little underdog that had survived an entire year against powerful, entrenched competition.

Not all public relations was just hoopla, Keith stressed, mentioning that she worked closely with the advertising agency to coordinate the airline's mass communication plan.

One example of a specialized promotional campaign involving inputs from both Keith and The Bloom Agency was the Southwest Sweetheart's Club. Using a mailing list, a direct-mail piece was sent to executive secretaries in Southwest's market area, offering them membership in this club. For each reservation on Southwest made for the boss, the secretary received a "sweetheart stamp," and for each 15 stamps, obtained a free ride on Southwest. Other bonuses for members included a twice-yearly drawing for a Mexico City vacation.

Figure C Southwest Partial Organization Chart, 1972–1973

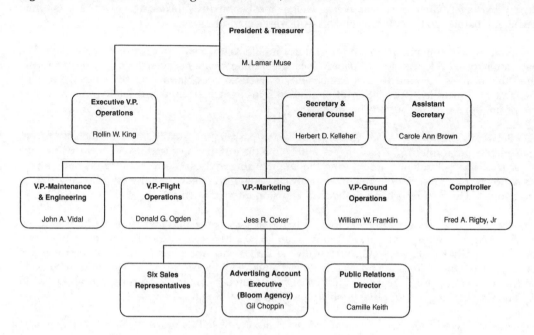

Introduction of New Pricing Policies

After operating a year, Southwest management decided to scrutinize the fare structure and its relationship to costs and revenues. They concluded that the airline could no longer afford a $20 fare on daytime flights. New tariffs were therefore filed with the Texas Aeronautics Commission, effective July 9, 1972; these raised Southwest's basic one-way fare from $20 to $26, established a round-trip fare of $50, and offered a $225 Commuter Club Card, providing unlimited transportation on all routes for 30 days.

One problem was how to break the news of the increased fares to the public. Talking with representatives of The Bloom Agency, Keith suggested that Southwest announce a new Executive Class service on all full-fare flights, offering passengers new amenities. The idea was quickly refined: two rows of seats would be removed from the aircraft, reducing capacity from 112 to 104 seats but increasing legroom; also, passengers would be offered free drinks. (The hostesses would probably not have time to serve more than two drinks per passenger on such short flights.) Full-page newspaper ads appeared proclaiming Southwest Airlines' new Executive Class service, with first-class legroom and free cocktails. The $26 fare also provided free security check charges that had been introduced the previous month.

The key consideration was the competition's reaction. "For a few days," admitted Coker, "we were really sweating." Braniff initially added another aircraft to its Dallas-Hobby Airport flights on July 11, thus offering on-the-hour service most of the business day. However, on July 17, TI increased its fares to match Southwest's; then on July 21 Braniff met all aspects of the fare and on-board service charges, also adding a $10 "Sundowner" flight to Hobby at 7:30 P.M. Braniff's increased service and the higher fares, as well as cutbacks in the number of Southwest flights, caused Southwest's July passenger count to fall on all three routes (see **Exhibit 10**). Overall, Southwest's patronage fell 2% in the third quarter of 1972, compared with the second quarter, but transportation revenues increased.

During September a third phase of the advertising campaign was launched, based on the slogan "Remember What It Was Like Before Southwest Airlines?" The agency considered this a war cry to rally consumers. The principal media used were television (see **Exhibit 11**) and billboards.

At the end of October another major pricing change occurred. The $10 discount fares, which had never been advertised, were replaced by half-fare flights ($13 one-way, $25 round-trip) in both directions on the two major routes each weekday after 8 P.M. Saturday flights were reintroduced and *all* weekend flights were offered at half-fare. A three-week advertising blitz accompanied the new schedule and prices, using one-minute radio commercials on such stations as country and western, and Top 40.[5] The response was immediate: November 1972 traffic levels were 12% higher than those in October—historically the best month in Southwest's commuter markets.

In the new year management turned its attention to the remaining problem. The company was actually making money on its Dallas-Houston flights, but incurring substantial losses in the Dallas-San Antonio market, where passenger volume was much lower (see **Exhibit 10**). Southwest offered only 8 flights a day on this route, versus 33 by its major competitor, and was averaging a mere 17 passengers on each full-fare flight. Southwest management concluded that unless patronage dramatically improved, this route would be discontinued. In a last attempt to obtain the needed increase, Southwest announced on January 22, 1973, a "60-Day-Half-Price-Sale" on *all* flights between Dallas and San Antonio. This sale was advertised on television and radio (see **Exhibit 12**). If successful, Muse intended to make this reduced fare permanent, but he believed that announcing it as a limited time offer would stimulate consumer interest more effectively and reduce the likelihood of competitive response.

The impact of these half-price fares was faster and more dramatic than the results of the evening and weekend half-price fares introduced the previous fall. As the first week ended, average loads on Southwest's Dallas-San Antonio service rose to 48 passengers per flight and continued to rise sharply as the next week began.

On Thursday, February 1, however, Braniff employed full-page newspaper ads to announce a half-price "Get Acquainted Sale" between Dallas and Hobby on all flights, until April 1 (see **Exhibit 13**).[6]

Muse called an urgent meeting of the management team, including King, the marketing vice president, the public relations director, the company's attorneys, and the account people from The Bloom Agency. Southwest had to decide how to respond to Braniff's move.

---

[5] A "Top 40" station plays currently popular rock music recordings.

[6] Braniff flights to Houston intercontinental continued at the higher fare.

Exhibit 1   Southwest Airlines and Competitors: Average Daily Local Passengers Carried in Each Direction, Dallas-Houston Market

	Braniff[a]		TI[a]		Southwest		Total Market—
	Passengers	% of Market	Passengers	% of Market	Passengers	% of Market	Passengers
1967	416	86.1%	67	13.9%	–	–	483
1968	381	70.2	162	29.8	–	–	543
				24.6			
1969	427	75.4	139		–	–	566
1970							
1st half	449	79.0	119	21.0	–	–	568
2nd half	380	76.0	120	24.0	–	–	500
Year	414	77.5	120	22.5	–	–	534
1971							
1st half	402	74.7	126	23.4	10	1.9%	538
2nd half	338	50.7	120	18.0	209	31.3	667
Year	370	61.4	123	20.4	110	18.2	603
1972							
January	341	48.3	105	14.9	260	36.8	706
February	343	47.6	100	13.9	277	38.5	720
March	357	47.5	100	13.3	295	39.2	752
April	367	48.3	97	12.8	296	38.9	760
May	362	48.5	84	11.3	300	40.2	746
June	362	46.8	81	10.5	330	42.7	773
1st half	356	48.0	93	12.5	293	39.5	742
July	332	48.1	74	10.7	284	41.2	690
August	432	53.7	56	6.9	317	39.4	805
September	422	54.9	55	7.2	291	37.9	768
October	443	53.1	56	6.7	335	40.2	834
November	439	50.6	55	6.3	374	43.1	868
December	396	52.1	56	7.4	308	40.5	760
2nd half	411	52.1	59	7.5	318	40.4	788
Year	384	50.1	77	10.0	306	39.9	767
1973							
January[b]	443	51.5	62	7.3	354	41.2	859

Source: Company records

Note: Passenger figures should be doubled to yield market statistics for travel in both directions.

[a] These figures were calculated by Muse from passenger data that Braniff and TI were required to supply to the Civil Aeronautics Board. He multiplied the original figures by a correction factor to eliminate interline traffic and arrive at net totals for local traffic.
[b] Projected figures from terminal counts by Southwest personnel.

Exhibit 2 Southwest Airlines: Balance Sheet at December 31, 1972, 1971, and 1970

	1972	1971	1970
Assets			
Current assets	$133,839	$231,530	$183
Cash	1,250,000	2,850,000	–
Certificates of deposit			
Accounts receivable			
Trade	397,664	300,545	–
Interest	14,691	35,013	–
Other	67,086	32,569	100
Total accounts receivable	479,441	368,127	100
Less allowance for doubtful accounts	86,363	30,283	–
	393,078	337,844	100
Inventories of parts and supplies, at cost	154,121	171,665	–
Prepaid insurance and other	75,625	156,494	31
Total current assets	2,006,663	3,747,533	314
Property and equipment, at cost			
Boeing 737-200 jet aircraft	12,409,772	16,263,250	–
Support flight equipment	2,423,480	2,378,581	–
Ground equipment	346,377	313,072	9,249
	15,179,629	18,954,903	9,249
Less accumulated depreciation and overhaul allowance	2,521,646	1,096,177	–
	12,657,983	17,858,726	9,249
Deferred certification costs less amortization	371,095	477,122	530,136
Total assets	$15,035,741	$22,083,381	$539,699
Liabilities and Stockholders' Equity			
Current liabilities			
Notes payable to banks (secured)	$950,000	–	–
Accounts payable	124,890	$355,539	$30,819
Accrued salaries and wages	55,293	54,713	79,000
Other accrued liabilities	136,437	301,244	–
Long term debt due within one year	1,226,457	1,500,000	–
Total current liabilities	2,493,077	2,211,496	109,819
Long-term debt due after one year			
7% convertible promissory notes	–	1,250,000	–
Conditional purchase agreements— Boeing Financial Corporation (11/2% over prime rate)	11,942,056	16,803,645	–
	11,942,056	18,053,645	–
Less amounts due within one year	1,226,457	1,500,000	–
	10,715,599	16,553,645	–
Contingencies			
Stockholders' equity			
Common stock, $1.00 par value, 2,000,000 shares authorized, 1,108,758 issued (1,058,758 at 12/31/71)	1,108,758	1,058,758	372,404
Capital in excess of par value	6,062,105	6,012,105	57,476
Deficit	(5,343,798)	(3,752,623)	–
	1,827,065	3,318,240	429,880
Total liabilities	$15,035,741	$22,083,381	$539,699

Source: Southwest Airlines Co. annual reports 1971, 1972
Note: Notes to financial statement not shown here.

At last, there's somebody el

se up there who loves you.

By paying attention to you, giving efficient service, and getting you there on time.

And, if for some reason, you don't get all the love we've got to give, we'll make it up by giving you a Love Stamp. Why are we doing all this? Because we need your love, too. And we know we won't get it unless we give it.

She will not plee-aze you. Plee-aze is stiff, formal and very affected English for please. It is usually accompanied by a gleaming toothpaste smile. People who say plee-aze are trying very, very hard to be nice to you. Too hard. And it isn't real. It's like plastic flowers vs. real flowers. You can feel the difference. That's why in our hostess school we haven't taught our girls how to be nice to you. We figure if they didn't already know, they weren't for us. In our school we teach other things. Mostly how to take care of you. Then we dress them in our exciting new hot pants designed for Southwest Airlines by Lorch of Dallas. That really ought to please you.

$20

Save from $14 to $16 per round trip. Eventually, the other airlines may meet our price, but remember, you can't buy love.

Love Potions for the very weary. Order by numbers 1-10, and they're only $1.00 each, not $1.50. That's what happens when you have somebody else up there who loves you.

A love machine which issues you tickets in under 10 seconds. Another way we prove our love: love machines in two great locations — at the ticket counter and at the departure gate, take your pick. Then you give your $20 (or any one of five charge cards) to our people stationed behind the love machines and you're on your way.

DALLAS 826-8840 • HOUSTON 228-8791
SAN ANTONIO 224-2011 • FORT WORTH 283-4661

This is another Southwest Airlines exclusive — our phone number. Keep it on file in your head or elsewhere because it's not in the phone book yet! Use this number to call ahead for reservations if you want to. If you don't want to, that's o.k. too. You don't need reservations to board the plane. Just come, plunk down $20 and out pops your ticket from our Love Machine. We plan to make waiting in line a thing of the past.

SOUTHWEST AIRLINES
The somebody else up there who loves you.

185

Exhibit 3   Examples of TI Newspaper Advertising, 1970–1971

Note: Reproductions same size as originals

Exhibit 4   Example of Clinton E. Frank Press Advertising for Braniff International, 1970

Exhibit 5   Southwest Airlines' Introductory TV Advertising, June 1971

SOUTHWEST AIRLINES   CODE NO: SWA-3-30-71   TELEVISION STORYBOARD
                            TITLE: "TV Love Machine"   THE BLOOM AGENCY

1. (Natural sfx, people talking up and under)...

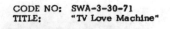

2. ...

3. ...

4. ...

5. (Wm Anncr VO) If you're standing in line...

6. ...you're not flying...

7. ...Southwest Airlines.

8. Because our Love Machine gives you a ticket...

9. ...in under ten seconds.

10. HOSTESS: Have a nice flight.

11. (Sfx: music and jet engine) 12 flights each day to Houston...

12. ...6 to San Antonio, for a loveable $20...

13. ...on Southwest Airlines.

14. "The somebody else up there...

15. ...who loves you."

Source: Company Records

Exhibit 6   Braniff's Response to Southwest Introduction: Advertising in Dallas Newspaper, June 1971

Prepared by: Clinton E. Frank, Inc.

Note: The original of this advertisement extended across the bottom half or two full newspaper pages.

Exhibit 7   TI Response to Southwest Introduction: Advertising in Dallas Newspapers, June 1971

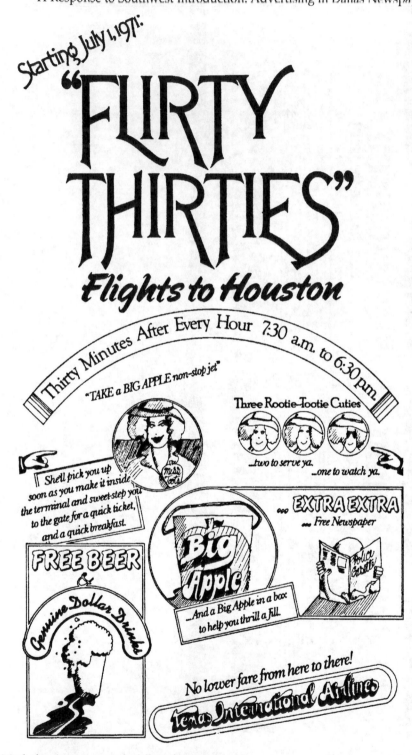

Note: The original advertisement covered a full-sized newspaper page.

Exhibit 8   Southwest Airlines: Quarterly Income Statements

	1971		1972			
Income Statements ($000s)	Q3	Q4	Q1	Q2	Q3	Q4
Transportation revenues[a]	$887	$1,138	$1,273	$1,401	$1,493	$1,745
Operating expenses						
Operations and maintenance[b]	1,211	1,280	1,192	1,145	1,153	1,156
Marketing and general administration	371	368	334	366	313	351
Depreciation and amortization	311	411	333	334	335	335
Total	1,893	2,059	1,859	1,845	1,801	1,842
Operating profit (loss)	(1,006)	(921)	(586)	(444)	(308)	(97)
Net interest revenues (costs)	(254)	(253)	(218)	(220)	(194)	(204)
Net income (loss) before extraordinary items	(1,260)	(1,174)	(804)	(664)	(502)	(301)
Extraordinary items	(571)[c]	(469)[c]	–	533[d]	–	–
Net income (loss)	$(1,831)	$(1,643)	$(804)	$(131)	$(502)	$(301)

Source: Company records

[a] Included both passenger and freight business.

[b] Incremental costs per flight were $226 during the second half of 1971, $231 in the first half of 1972, and $244 in the second half of 1972. Management estimated that variable costs per passenger carried amounted to $2.53 during the first half of 1972 and to $2.80 during the second half of the year. These variable costs per passenger included $.13 for passenger beverages and supplies in the first half and $.43 in the second half of 1972.

[c] Write-off of preoperating costs.

[d] Capital gain on sale of one aircraft.

Exhibit 9   Southwest: Discount vs. Regular Fare Flights

	All Routes				
	Regular Flights		Discount Flights[a]		
Month	Passengers	Flights	Passengers	Flights	Price Changes
1971					
June[b]	5,530	424	–	–	
July	15,459	988	–	–	
August	16,121	1,026	–	–	
September	16,440	939	–	–	
October	21,044	1,146	–	–	
November	19,042	963	73	3	$10 fares on some evening weekend flights
December	20,178	981	198	5	
1971 total	113,814	6,467	271	8	
1972					
January	20,694	899	170	4	
February	20,696	912	216	4	
March	24,656	1,014	702	10	
April	24,077	916	573	8	
May	23,112	869	2,189	51	$10 fare on all flights after 9 P.M.
June	22,972	784	4,636	78	
July	18,994	740	5,720	78	Basic fare raised to $26
August	21,257	819	5,739	81	
September	19,020	717	5,358	83	
October	21,894	786	6,599	98	
November	19,825	648	12,141	197	Half-price fares weekdays after 8 P.M. and on all weekend flights
December	17,142	604	10,617	176	
1972 total	254,339	9,708	54,660	868	
1973					
January[c]	18,893	599	13,635	239	Half-price fares on all Dallas-San Antonio flights

Source: Company records

[a] Included flights on which gifts were offered.

[b] Part-month only.

[c] Estimated figures.

Exhibit 10 Southwest: Number of Flights and Passengers on Each Route

Month	Dallas-Houston		Dallas-San Antonio		San Antonio-Houston	
	Passengers	Flights	Passengers	Flights	Passengers	Flights
1971						
June[a]	3,620	276	1,910	148	–	–
July	10,301	642	5,158	346	–	–
August	11,316	672	4,805	354	–	–
September	11,674	612	4,766	327	–	–
October	14,552	764	6,492	382	–	–
November	14,060	654	4,167	240	888	72
December	14,665	687	4,004	165	1,707	134
1971 total	80,188	4,307	31,302	1,962	2,595	206
1972						
January	16,122	634	2,788	141	1,954	128
February	16,069	640	2,755	142	2,088	134
March	18,285	669	4,270	209	2,803	146
April	17,732	605	4,617	189	2,301	130
May	18,586	584	4,254	198	2,461	138
June	19,782	521	5,198	201	2,628	140
July	17,596	494	5,011	193	2,107	131
August	19,620	546	4,978	208	2,398	146
September	17,472	489	4,734	184	2,172	127
October	20,776	545	5,197	200	2,520	139
November	22,461	507	6,640	199	2,865	139
December	19,080	468	6,211	186	2,468	126
1972 total	223,581	6,702	56,653	2,250	28,765	1,624
1973						
January[b]	21,948	505	7,710	197	2,870	136

Source: Company records

[a] Part-month only.

[b] Estimated figures.

Exhibit 11   "Remember What It Was Like Before Southwest Airlines," TV Advertising,
              September 1972

SOUTHWEST AIRLINES	CODE NO: SWA-34-30-72 TITLE: "Executive Class"	TELEVISION STORYBOARD THE BLOOM AGENCY

1. HOSTESS: Remember what it was like...

2. ...before there was somebody else up there who loved you?

3. There was no such thing as executive class service to Dallas, Houston and San Antonio.

4. With first class leg room, free cocktails for everyone,...

5. ...and a schedule you could depend on.

6. (Sfx: jet taking off)...

7. ...

8. ...

9. Remember?

10. (Natural sfx up and out)

Exhibit 12   Southwest: Radio Advertising for Half-Fare Flights—All San Antonio Flights, January 1973

Number	I I8-23-2	Length: 00 seconds	Date: 12/21/72, revised 12/00/72
Music:	*Clinky piano*		
Announcer:	It's time for Captain Moneysaver, the man who knows how to save your dough!		
Captain Moneysaver:	Hello, moneysavers! Since Southwest Airlines introduced its half-price sale on all flights every day between Dallas and San Antonio, many listeners have asked that age-old question: Can I get there cheaper? Cheaper than $13? Sure! You can strap 5,000 pigeons to your arms and fly yourself. Or propel your body with a giant rubber band. Put a small motor on a ten-speed bike . . .		
Music:	*Light, happy*		
Hostess:	Southwest Airlines announces the 60-day half-price sale between Dallas and San Antonio. It's good on all flights every day. Just $13 one way. 25 round trip. So what are you waiting for?		
Cowboy:	You mean I kin fly between San Antonio and Dallas on a real jet airplane fer only $13?		
Announcer:	That's right! On any Southwest Airlines flight, every day.		
Cowboy	They still gonna have them pretty girls and all?		
Announcer:	Same Southwest Airlines love service. And it's cheaper than the best bus service.		
Cowboy:	Howzit compare to my pickup?		
Music:	*Light, happy*		
Hostess:	Fly now while it's half fare on every Southwest Airlines flight every day between Dallas and San Antonio. All our love at half the price.		
Voice:	Half price? Can they do that?		
Second voice:	They did it!		

Prepared by: The Bloom Agency

Exhibit 13   Braniff's Ad for Dallas-Hobby Half-Price Sale, February 1973

Braniff's 'Get Acquainted Sale'

Half-price to Houston's Hobby Airport.

$13 Coach $17 First Class

To Hobby			Back to Dallas-Fort Worth		
Leave		**Arrive**	**Leave**		**Arrive**
7:30 a.m.	Non-stop	8:20 a.m.	8:00 a.m. (Ex. Sun.)	Non-stop	8:50 a.m.
9:30 a.m.	Non-stop	10:20 a.m.	9:00 a.m. (Ex. Sun.)	Non-stop	9:50 a.m.
11:30 a.m.	Non-stop	12:20 p.m.	11:00 a.m.	Non-stop	11:50 a.m.
2:30 p.m.	Non-stop	3:20 p.m.	1:00 p.m.	Non-stop	1:50 p.m.
3:30 p.m. (Ex. Sat.)	Non-stop	4:20 p.m.	4:00 p.m.	Non-stop	4:50 p.m.
5:30 p.m.	Non-stop	6:20 p.m.	5:00 p.m. (Ex. Sat.)	Non-stop	5:50 p.m.
6:30 p.m. (Ex. Sat.)	Non-stop	7:20 p.m.	7:00 p.m. (Ex. Sat.)	Non-stop	7:50 p.m.
			9:00 p.m.	Non-stop	9:50 p.m.

Sale lasts 'til April 1

From now until April 1, all Braniff International flights to Houston's Hobby Airport are priced to go. Half price to be exact. 50% off.

A one-way ticket in coach is $13.00. Round-trip is an even better bargain at $25.00. And in first class, $17.00 one-way, $34.00 round-trip.

We believe we have the best service to Hobby Airport. But not enough people know about it. So, we're offering you a chance to sample our big 727 Wide-Body jets to Houston's Hobby at half the regular price. We call it our "Get Acquainted Sale."

Half price and a reserved seat, too. Call Braniff International at 357-9511 in Dallas; 335-5811 in Fort Worth.

You'll like flying Braniff Style.

BRANIFF
US MAINLAND   HAWAII   MEXICO   SOUTH AMERICA

Source: Dallas newspaper

Justifying profitable pricing
Joel E Urbany
The Journal of Product and Brand Management; 2001; 10, 3; ABI/INFORM Global
pg. 141

An executive summary for managers and executive readers can be found at the end of this article

Justifying profitable pricing

Joel E. Urbany
University of Notre Dame, Indiana, USA

Keywords Keywords *Decision making, Economic theory, Competitive strategy*

Abstract *Economic theory depicts a price-setter who is cognizant of both the incremental profit implications of changing price and likely competitive reactions. Marketplace observations suggest otherwise; several studies and anecdotal evidence find a tendency for pricing to be driven by cost and market share rather than marginal profit. Further, recent evidence suggests that competitive reactions are often overlooked. This paper develops an explanation of these observations via decision accountability. The literature on accountability is based on the premise that in any social or organizational context, people are compelled to make decisions that can be justified. This justification involves searching for criteria on which those decisions will be judged by others and decision making which can be rationalized on those criteria. New evidence reviewed here suggests that people tend to justify decisions on the basis of more familiar and less ambiguous criteria, giving too little weight to more ambiguous but important considerations. The omission of future profit projections and competitive behavior in decision making, then, can be explained by ambiguity surrounding the estimation of these factors (relative to more concretely measured and familiar internal criteria). I examine three case studies that illustrate how firms have changed information strategy, culture, and competitive thinking in the interest of making profitability and competitive information more justifiable inputs for pricing decisions.*

Experimental shift

If there is any element in the marketing mix that would seem amenable to rational decision making, it is pricing. Pricing decisions are quantitative, generally visible across competitors, and are linked more easily to revenues than other marketing decisions. Considering their characteristics, it is surprising that several studies have identified suboptimal pricing behavior. For example, Hoch *et al.* (1994) find positive profit effects of an experimental shift to higher regular prices for a retail grocer. Little and Shapiro (1980) observe that retailers set prices as if they believe the market is much more price-sensitive than it actually is. While Little and Shapiro's model suggests that there may be a longer-term logic to suboptimal pricing in the short-term, Kopalle *et al.* (1999) find pricing behavior to be substantially suboptimal in an individual product category over an eight-year period. Further, experimental studies on hundreds of managers over the last several years have revealed a consistent tendency to price below optimal levels (Keil *et al.*, 1999; Reibstein 1999).

As noted, there are some reasonable explanations why prices – which might be optimal in the longer term – may often appear suboptimal in the short term (see Table I). Yet, even those explanations cannot account for the tendencies considered in this paper. The objective here is to explore two

The author thanks Terry Shimp, Aradhna Krishna, and Peter Dickson for comments on an earlier draft, as well as participants in seminars at the Conference on Competition and Marketing in Weisbaden (June 1999), MIT, the University of South Carolina, Southern Methodist University, the University of Wollongong, New South Wales and the Australian Graduate School of Management.

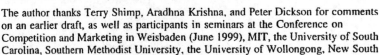

The research register for this journal is available at
http://www.mcbup.com/research_registers
The current issue and full text archive of this journal is available at
http://www.emerald-library.com/ft

Explanation	Source
1. *Maintain customer loyalty/limit search.* Retailers lower nonfeatured prices by an extra margin to maintain the patronage of current customers; seek to limit their experimentation with other stores	Little and Shapiro (1980)
2. *Fairness.* Consumers react negatively when they perceive the firm is violating an implicit agreement to maintain the existing reference profit (suboptimal prices maintain current custom)	Kahneman, Knetsch, and Thaler (1986) Okun (1981) Shipley (1981)
3. *Rational assessment of costs and returns of changing price.* Prices may not adjust to changes in supply and demand; possibly because the costs of experimentation or changing price are high, the demand curve is kinked, or some threshold level of motivation to change has not been reached. Alternatively, adjustments may be made to nonprice strategy dimensions (e.g. product or service features) instead of price	Carlton (1986) Blinder (1991) Rothschild (1974) Hall and Hitch (1939) Sweezy (1939) DeSarbo *et al.* (1987)
4. *Cross-elasticities/price image.* The prices of certain products may be below optimal levels to encourage their purchase as well as the purchase of other related products. Retailer price image may also be enhanced by such pricing	Walters and MacKenzie (1988)

Table I. Rational explanations of short-term suboptional pricing

apparent deficiencies or flaws in price-setting that are so contrary to conventional wisdom that they have largely escaped attention by academic researchers. The first flaw is that managers do not always apply basic marginal profit analysis in pricing decisions. The second flaw is managers do not regularly account for the likely behavior and reactions of competitors in price-setting. Based upon early reports from several studies examining these issues and the literature on accountability, an explanation of why such tendencies exist is offered.

Potential ambiguity and profit

The paper is not intended to suggest that firms do not attempt to price profitably or never consider competitive reactions. Instead, it suggests that often basic economic concepts that could make pricing more profitable may not be among the criteria on which pricing decisions are typically justified within organizations. Because of potential ambiguity in estimating demand at alternative prices and predicting competitive reactions, pricing practice in many firms systematically may ignore these two important fundamentals. Over time, managers may "lock out" evaluation of such factors from their information search as decisions tend to focus on more accessible and less ambiguous inputs. We explore the reasons underlying this and suggest resolutions.

Fundamentals
MR=MC
The standard economic model provides a basis for rational thinking and is extremely useful for structuring thinking about how a price-setter ought to behave. In the neoclassical model, the economic agent is assumed to be fully informed about costs and demand and to have "the mental ability to effortlessly calculate the behavioral choice that maximizes utility" (profit) (Kaufman, 1999; Monroe, 1990). The optimal policy is to raise or lower price over time only to the point where the incremental revenue equals the marginal cost. In short, managers should be attentive to the changes in profits of potential price changes. In the marketing literature, more complex pricing problems have been modeled in a normative sense (e.g. Dolan and Jeuland,

1981; Monroe and Mazumdar 1988), but the core principle of any complex normative model is the same: the optimum price for the last unit sold is where MR=MC.

Anticipate competitor reactions

When competitors are added to the game as in traditional oligopoly theory, the model gets more complex, but the MR=MC principle continues to provide guidance. The difference, though, is that decision makers should recognize that their own pricing decisions may prompt changes in how their rivals set prices. Given this recognition, the optimal strategy is to anticipate how future marginal revenues/costs from changing price today is a function of competitors' reactions to any price moves. Hence, thinking of pricing within the context of a game suggests that a critical aspect of pricing strategy for the manager in oligopoly is "understanding (the) opponent's point of view and (assuming your opponent is rational) deducing how he or she is likely to respond to your actions" (Pindyck and Rubinfeld, 1989, p. 459; see also Kreps, 1990; Urban and Star, 1990).

It has long been recognized that managers do not literally seek to maximize profits in their decision making generally (cf. Kaufman, 1999; Cyert and March, 1992; Simon, 1997) and specifically with respect to price (Bonoma *et al.*, 1988; Lanzillotti, 1958; Morgenroth, 1964). The cost and complexity of such rational behavior are simply too high given the time and resource constraints that firms face. Yet, this difficulty does not diminish the relevance of the basic principles derived from the normative theory; they should be applied in simpler contexts. The following sections suggest instead that they are frequently violated.

Consider the following scenario, which was given to 60 managers, all of whom were involved in pricing decisions at manufacturing firms (Urbany and Dickson, 1994):

Your firm currently sells product _____ at $10.00 and your unit cost is $7.00. You are considering cutting price. The best estimates of the likely outcomes are as follows:

A. Hold price – 100 per cent chance that you will sell 1,000 units ($3,000)

B. Cut price to $9.50 – 80 per cent chance that you will sell 1,250 units ($3,125)
20 per cent chance that you will sell 1,000 units ($2,500)

Choice A is a "sure thing" and Choice B is a risky choice. The profits from each choice (in parentheses, but not given to respondents), produce identical expected values for A and B ($3,000). The problem is based upon the classic prospect theory problem in which subjects, evaluating outcomes in the domain of gains, predominantly take the safe choice (A). When the problem is dressed in pricing clothes, however, the majority of the managers choose the uncertain choice (B), to cut price. The most straightforward explanation of the difference would be that the profit outcomes for the risky choice reveal little downside risk to taking the price cut – in that the worst case outcome for cutting price is still a profit of $2,500, perhaps worth the risk of increasing sales by 25 percent. Remarkably, though, only about half made general reference to profit in explaining why they cut price (e.g. "still make a profit even if sales go down") and less than 10 per cent provided specific calculations in justifying their answers.

Competitive information

In addition, a follow-up problem asked them to re-make their pricing decision with new information. Respondents were told explicitly that a competitor was very likely to match the price cut if they chose to drop price to $9.50. They were again asked to choose either cutting or holding price. This competitive information did dissuade several respondents from cutting price, but the majority continued to recommend cutting price.

The responses to this problem illustrated that:

- many respondents were concerned less with the profit consequences of their pricing actions than other objectives (particularly sales volume); and

- that competitor reactions were either ignored in the first problem, or were considered but given little weight in the decision.

We elaborate on these two findings below.

Profit consequences

It would seem a sign of author irrationality to claim that managers may not consider the incremental profit consequences of pricing decisions. After all – although profit *maximization* is generally not a useful or achievable target – clearly it would be grounds for demotion for any manager who was not profit-driven. Yet, consider the following quotes which describe current pricing practice:

> In our observations of the industry, it has been surprising to see how infrequently mortgage bankers go beyond their intuition and rigorously analyze the profitability implications of their own pricing decisions ... (Rigsbee *et al.*, 1992).

> ... companies often make major pricing moves that substantially reduce their profitability ... Few companies go so far as to measure their returns on promotions. If they did, many would find they are negative (Davey *et al.*, 1998).

> A lot of companies just throw up their hands and say pricing isn't manageable. Those companies take the classic but simplistic approach of "pricing to the market" – pegging their prices to competitors' prices – or they simply add up their production costs and tack on a standard markup" (Michael Marn, director of pricing services, McKinsey and Company, quoted in Anthes, 1998).

"Lunk-headed pricing strategies"

Interestingly, concerns like the above are not isolated. Similar comments range from *Business Week*'s recent general contention that "few (companies) have figured out how much money they are giving up by using lunk-headed pricing strategies" (Coy, 2000) to industry-specific concerns about how pricing decisions seem to ignore basic economic principles (Schuster, 1987; Scott, 1995). Popular books on pricing strategy (Monroe, 1990; Nagle and Holdren, 1995) give extensive coverage of financial analysis, in part because such analysis is "often overlooked" in practice (Mondello, 1992). In a recent experimental program (Krishna *et al.*, 2000), we consistently observe suboptimal pricing among business student subjects in a simple pricing exercise in which they are given complete information about past prices and unit sales, as well as cost information. These subjects appear to apply predominantly intuitive pricing rules which are heavily influenced by the firm's past prices. In this research program, experienced managers are more likely to price optimally than are students, but still evidence errors in pricing, particularly in setting sale prices.

Competitor reactions

Sports and military analogies are used widely in business (Kotler and Singh, 1981; Rao *et al.*, 2000). Both traditions make strong assumptions about the participant's knowledge of her or his rival's likely behavior, as does classic oligopoly theory and game theory (Kreps, 1990; Scherer and Ross, 1990). In the same way that professional football teams and attacking armies anticipate their foes' strengths, weaknesses, and likely reactions to every move, it seems ludicrous to think that business people would not do the same thing. Yet, many have observed otherwise:

> Given a chance to take its decision back, American [Airlines] would in all likelihood do so (Rao and Steckel 1998, p. 145, referring to a decision that ignited a mileage war).

> ... all too often a retailer will decide to cut prices to overcome his troubles. He does so with no evident consideration for the reaction of his competitors (O'Conner, 1986).

> ... many moves to increase share or sales/profit never would be made if one were aware of the immediate countermove (Ramaswamy et al., 1994).

Potential competitive reactions

Urbany et al. (2000) assess whether these concerns extend beyond the anecdotal, examining the decision-accounts (both retrospective and prospective) of nearly 150 managers. We find consideration of expected future competitive reactions to play a very small role in decision making. Consideration of potential competitive reactions is more frequent for pricing decisions than for other types of marketing decisions, but still has an incidence below 20 percent. Given our surprise at these results and the incredulity of some to whom we presented them, we surveyed a sample of 98 experienced managers, asking them to indicate on several scales how well the results matched their experience. Averaging the 10-point scales produced an aggregate mean of 7.31 (standard deviation = 1.94), with nearly half of the sample averaging 8 or higher. A two-group cluster analysis revealed that three-quarters would be classified as expressing "high agreement." In short, the majority of these executives found the results to be unsurprising and consistent with their own experience. Some of their explanations provide the basis for the following sections.

Potential explanations: belief in hysteresis and decision accountability

What would explain lack of attention to marginal profit considerations of alternative price points and limited consideration of competitive reactions pricing decisions? Two alternative explanations are offered below. The first addresses the well-known focus on market share. The second provides the larger basis of the paper and is based upon more recent work on accountability in decision making.

Pursuit of market share: intuitive visions of hysteresis?

The pursuit of sales volume and market share as primary strategic objectives has been roundly criticized (Armstrong and Collopy, 1995; Anterasian et al., 1996). However, recent evidence suggests a built-in bias toward attempting to obtain market share at the expense of profit. Keil et al. (1999) find that when executives are allowed to self-select their own objective in a competitive pricing simulation, they behave much more in line with a market share objective than when they are explicitly asked to maximize profit (in the former condition, managers price more aggressively, react more intensely to competitive price changes, have higher market shares but lower profits).

Sales volume

Two explanations for this tendency might be offered. First, as Keil et al. note, feedback on marketing decisions may predominantly appear in the form of sales volume or market share. Second, and potentially as a result, there may exist a natural devotion to an intuitive model of what has been labeled hysteresis (Simon, 1997; DeKimpe and Hanssens, 1999). Hysteresis is a term used to describe a scenario in which a firm engages in some short-term aggressive behavior to gain (usually) volume and market share that is retained and eventually produces favorable longer term profits[1]. (Many dot.com companies are holding on today only by the thread of this promise.) Hysteresis is a real phenomenon and belief in it may be due to highly memorable (even if infrequent) instances in which firms have experienced longer term gains attributable to aggressive behavior in the short-term. Yet, very often visions of long-term payoffs from buying market share through aggressive pricing fail to come true. Such pricing is usually imitated by competitors with three effects:

(1) any gain in market share is short-lived;

(2) price-sensitive customers become even more price-sensitive; and

(3) margin is given away to less price-sensitive customers *and they* become more price-sensitive.

The fact that this profit-wrecking alternative scenario – labeled *escalation* by DeKimpe and Hanssens (1999) – has played out in so many industries over the last 20 years (e.g. O'Conner, 1986; Rao *et al.*, 2000) suggests that much decision-making is based upon a *short-sighted* belief in hysteresis.

Plausible account

The concept of hysteresis (and managers' own intuitive theories of the payoffs of aggressive short-term investment in the marketing mix) provides a plausible account of the two managerial tendencies described earlier. The larger issue, however, may be that visions of market share and long-term profit make aggressive action justifiable in the short-term. When coupled with concerns over accountability, the *ex ante* logic of the above choice behavior (that *ex post* appears irrational) can be compelling.

Accountability

For a variety of reasons (e.g. uncertainty-reduction, impression management, regret reduction), people seek to make decisions based upon good reasons. This tendency is especially strong in social settings in which others will be evaluating those decisions (Curley *et al.*, 1986; Simonson, 1989); i.e. in settings in which they will be held accountable for their choices. Accountability refers to the degree to which one feels responsible for rationalizing or defencing dcisisons. In his seminal piece, Tetlock (1985) argues persuasively that the nature of both individuals (who seek approval, status, and control of resources) and organizations (which represent organized social systems in need of order) points to accountability as a fundamental force in organizational life:

> Organized social life cannot exist without some degree of regularity ... Accountability is a critical rule and norm enforcement mechanism: the social psychological link between individual decision-makers on the one hand and the social systems to which they belong on the other (Tetlock, 1985, p. 307).

"Cognitive miser" premise

Beginning with the "cognitive miser" premise adopted from the cognitive research stream, Tetlock suggests that the decision maker will seek in most circumstances not to pursue an optimal decision, but to pursue a decision which is acceptable or *justifiable* within the organization's or supervisor's value system. Experimental research suggests that when the evaluator's value system is less known, people will work harder in justifying their decisions; will think more analytically, rely more on data than intuitive theory, be less susceptible to peripheral decision cues, and will use more complex decision strategies (Bazerman *et al.*, 1998; Chaiken, 1980; Tetlock,

1983) Yet, when the value system or criteria of the evaluator are known, decision makers will fall back on an "acceptability heuristic", seeking decisions that they believe will meet some minium standard of acceptability on key criteria on which they expect to be evaluated (as opposed to "best" on a particular criterion; Tetlock 1985).

What types of pricing decisions are most defensible? One way to consider how accountability works in pricing decisions is to examine what sorts of decisions appear to be the most defensible:

Pricing decisions

(1) *Decisions consistent with previous practice.* A pervasive tendency observed and discussed in many contexts is the status quo bias, which illustrates that decision makers have a strong preference for maintaining current decision states (Kahneman and Knetsch, 1991; Samuelson and Zeckhauser, 1988; Silver and Mitchell, 1990; see also Bacharach *et al.*, 1995). In the pricing experiments conducted by Krishna *et al.* (2000), the characteristics of the company's past price distribution (e.g. the range of past prices charged, or the frequency of individual past prices) are found to significantly influence prices recommended by experimental price-setters, when in fact the distribution is irrelevant to determining the profit-maximizing price. Inertia continues to be a major problem in business, as change in firms often lags change in the marketplace (Bonoma, 1981; Day, 1991; Hamel and Prahalad, 1994; Sull, 1999). In fact, the pricing arena may be historically one of the strongest illustrations of status quo effects. Price inertia or rigidity (even in the face of changing conditions of supply and demand) is one of the most common empirical anomalies in economics (cf. Blinder, 1991; Carlton, 1986).

Easily justified

(2) *Decisions made relative to competitor reference points.* Decisions made to match competitors or beat competitors or shadow competitors' current prices tend to be easily justified. The competitor's current behavior is likely to be a highly concrete and unambiguous reference point for most firms. Further, in so much as the competitors' actions are believed to provide information about market conditions, a "herd" mentality can be very powerful. This is so since managers generally "seek to enhance their reputations as decision-makers" (Scharfstein and Stein 1990, p. 478) and may believe that being a contrarian signals dumb rather than smart behavior. Note again that, even though competitors' current behavior is frequently considered when firms make such competitor-oriented decisions (nearly 60 percent of the Urbany *et al.* (2000) protocols mentioned competitors' past or current behavior), there still appears to be limited attention to the explicit marginal profit implications of the decision or competitors' future reactions.

(3) *Decisions based upon unambiguous or familiar data/criteria.* This third point reinforces the above two points. Criteria or data that everyone understands and uses regularly are more defensible when one must justify a decision. For example, if unit sales or market share are the primary measures of performance, pricing will be judged according to whether unit sales or market share objectives are achieved (not profit). More objective, easily accessible, and unambiguous data are more influential in decision making than are less accessible data (Culnan, 1983; Day and Wensley, 1988; O'Reilly, 1982). This influence creates a bias *against* incorporating uncertain information or inferences (e.g. about price-demand relationships or projected competitor behavior) into decision making. Pricing managers often lack good information about

the relationship between price and demand (Shipley, 1981; Coy, 2000; Anthes, 1998), as it requires either careful experimentation or tracking of prices and sales over time, which many information systems are not set up to do. Regarding competitor reactions, managers often appear to believe that predicting such future behavior is the equivalent of fortune-telling, and they give it as much credence. Of the 98 experienced executives who provided reactions to the Urbany *et al.* (2000) results, we found concerns about the ambiguity of predicting competitor reactions to be a common refrain:

> While past competitive pricing, product offerings can be obtained, the future gets murky. I've found that many managers are extremely quantitative but are totally at sea when presented with soft information, even if it has a high degree of probability. They tend to go into denial rather than risk being wrong (Director, Research and Competitive Intelligence).

In fact, the research suggested that internal factors (e.g. capacity concerns, costs, human resource issues) tended to dominate new product, pricing, and advertising decisions, precisely because these factors are often *unambiguous*:

> More often than not the decision variables which are easiest to quantify also tend to be the easiest to justify (particularly to the board or executive level staff). The easiest variables to "confidently" quantify are almost exclusively limited to internal factors (Product manager).

Cost-plus heuristics

The results of this study are consistent with the often-cited notion that people tend to avoid ambiguity or uncertainty in decision making (Cyert and March 1992; Adams *et al.*, 1998). Hence, the reliable finding that cost-plus heuristics dominate pricing decisions (cf. Bonoma *et al.*, 1988; Lanzillotti 1958) should not be surprising. When measured carefully, cost information may be perceived as concrete, vivid, and unambiguous (certainly relative to other fuzzier factors in the equation like demand response, marginal profit, and competitive reactions).

Protecting rigid routines
Accountability is a good thing. Yet, making decisions largely in the interest of being able to defend them can be problematic for two reasons. First, people may choose to maximize or minimize criteria which are more easily assessed or leads to more socially comfortable outcomes, rather than one that defines a truly optimal outcome. For example, Adelberg and Batson (1978) had subjects role-play the part of a social agency administrator with the responsibility of making student loan allocations. Subjects accountable for their decisions were more likely to give insufficient loans to large numbers of students rather than making harder-to-justify decisions about who should and should not get loans.

Familiar process or criteria

Second, and at least partly as a function of the forces described above, organizations can get caught in a cycle of routine-reinforced decision making. In such a cycle, the "correctness" of last period's pricing decisions is always reinforced by the application of familiar process or criteria. Decision routines that are based upon familiar, objective feedback will apply the same criteria for subsequent decisions and may get "stuck in place" for several reasons:

- the traditional evaluative feedback reinforces the existing behavior (e.g. Repenning and Sterman, 1997);

- there is little incentive to gather new information which might call the routines into question and, even if such information is obtained;

• such routines may be resistant to new information, especially new criteria which may be less objective or require more speculation to apply.

Conventional wisdom

Decision making may become routinized (cf. Starbuck, 1983; Meyer and Rown, 1977) to a point in which new information which is contrary to existing beliefs or decisions is either discounted or reinterpreted in a manner consistent with conventional wisdom (cf. Alloy and Tabachnik, 1984; Day, 1991; Nisbett and Ross, 1980). Note that it is easiest to discount or attack information that is unfamiliar, ambiguous, and/or does not fit into the current decision paradigm[2]. In short, pricing decisions are traditionally explained or justified on the basis of achieving market share objectives, current competitive reference points, current costs, and/or other quantifiable inputs. As a result, other potentially important criteria or data may not be accounted for in decision making.

Justifying profitable pricing

How then can a firm deal with rigidity and inertia that is bogging down its current pricing practice? More generally, how can people be encouraged to introduce new criteria in their decision making? These questions are addressed in this section by examining firms who have made such changes or who have been innovative in treating pricing decisions strategically. A brief review of three such cases and a discussion of the commonalities among them suggest several important principles which are emerging from current practice.

• *Case 1: Revamping price-setting.* In his recent account of the trend toward "smart" pricing, Coy (2000) tells the tale of the Ford Motor company's effort over the past five years to better inform its pricing. Beginning in 1995, the company has experimented with using margins and value-added rather than strictly unit sales as metrics in assessing the effectiveness of its pricing. In addition, much new research was conducted to identify "features that 'the customer was willing to pay for but the industry was slow to deliver'". The strategy largely involved better equipping its decision makers with research that provided understanding of both demand at different price points and consumer perception of value-added features. The company slightly reduced prices on higher margin cars (e.g. Crown Victorias and Explorers) motivating an increase in unit sales of 600,000. At the same time, they raised prices on lower-end cars (e.g. Escorts and Aspires) increasing margins although selling 420,000 fewer units. Ford lost nearly 2 percentage points of market share between 1995 and 1999, but had earnings of $7.2 billion in 1999, setting a new auto industry record. The five regions in which its new pricing strategy was tested beat profit targets by a collective $1 billion.

Cost-cutting campaign

• *Case 2: Responding to commoditization.* After many years of success following innovation in the slow-moving paper-binding industry, Booklet Binding, Inc. (BBI) found its sales force increasingly coming back to headquarters asking for permission to give in on customer price concession requests. The financial crisis was further uncovered at the firm's year end review when management found that although sales revenue had increased 30 percent over the previous year, profits had not changed. Considering either raising prices across-the-board or going on a major cost-cutting campaign (including layoffs), company management instead pursued a third option: sales force training to change its price-driven selling culture. A training and new sales information program implemented new procedures for tracking sales and background information about customers. Processes were put in place (e.g. customer history, calendar log, pending project log, customer report cards) that encouraged salespeople to think ahead about a customer's business sales patterns and help them plan purchases several months in advance. In addition, emphasis was placed on promoting the higher margin, value-added items in the product line, and cross-selling. Through more in-depth education on the company's processes and products, the sales force gained the knowledge to counterargue customer price concerns and to be proactive in managing price. The actions were highly successful as BBI's revenues soared to $23 million in 1996 (up from just $9 million in the two years prior) and pretax margins were double the industry average (Hyatt 1996).

- *Case 3: Thwarting competitive entry.* Nagle (1993) describes the case of an industrial products firm which had competed cooperatively in a market with three segments, limiting production capacity until a time when the market was threatened by a new foreign competitor. This new competitor could not be persuaded to withdraw and began building capacity. In similar situations, firms often cut prices aggressively in an effort to protect market share. Anticipating severe reactions to an aggressive price defense, however, this firm raised its prices in the low-growth "commodity" segment (to create a higher price umbrella for the new entrant), and developed strong quality appeals for the other two segments (e.g. faster service, guaranteed supply) to offset concerns about price. In doing this, the firm found it was able to minimize the new entrant's impact in the commodity segment (providing it no incentive for aggressive pricing), and was able to block it from the more quality-driven segments.

Common threads

There is clearly not one correct competitive pricing strategy for all occasions. The recent work on fighting price wars provides a good sense of the contingencies which can be accounted for as well as the variety of different moves which might be considered (Nagle, 1993; Rao *et al.*, 2000). Yet, there are several common threads in how the firms above reoriented price-setters' attention to managing and maintaining profitability rather than pursuing strictly sales and market share objectives.

Data/feedback

As Peter Lewis, CEO of Progressive Insurance and architect of its innovative business model, has wisely noted: "If you want to change something, measure it". In firms that are improving their pricing profitability, efforts are made to turn seemingly soft decision inputs into "hard" quantities. The most obvious point about improving the profitability of pricing decisions is linking price, cost, and demand data within the same system. In addition, Ford and BBI each substantially improved what they knew about both customers' price sensitivity and what customers' valued in their products. The first stage of BBI's transition in their sales program required salespeople to interview customers to identify some basic facts, including BBI share of customer and competitive binderies used (which provided significant insight into price sensitivity). In addition, they gathered information about the historic timing of customer jobs, which allowed sales people to assist customers in their planning. Translating information about price response into pricing decisions is itself not obvious, as reflected in Davey *et al.*'s (1998) assessment in the *McKinsey Quarterly* that "even leading package goods companies are confused about the correct interpretation and use of price elasticity". A fundamental start would involve gearing the information system to provide key price decision makers with information about relative margins and profit results, focusing attention on those results via the incentive system (see below), and creating an environment where experimentation outside of the usual price bands is encouraged.

Reaction profile

Increasing the emphasis on competitive conjecture in decision making (beyond simply matching competitive moves) requires information not only about competitors' current prices but also a sense of the competitors' reaction profile (Chen et al., 1992; Porter 1980). The point is not to watch competitors to simply to imitate their past moves or attempt to infer information about the market from their actions, but to anticipate their moves and countermoves.

Segmentation logic and the courage to let customers go
Each case above, and many others which describe how to successfully navigate competitive pricing situations (e.g. Scott, 1995) reflect the recognition that all markets have heterogeneity in demand; i.e. some consumer segments are willing to pay higher prices for quality trade-offs. The impact of competitors' pricing moves can be offset by allowing an aggressive competitor to take some sales of the more price-sensitive segment (allowing this to happen requires a special kind of courage!) while targeting less price-sensitive customers. In fact, the logic of giving up unit sales is patently *unjustifiable* by historic standards in most businesses and requires a significant reorientation in the logic of decision making. In the end, though, more profitable pricing (and business in general) often requires a firm to be more selective in who it does business with, even if some existing customers have to be "fired".

Enhance understanding

A focus on the sales force
Implicit in at least two of the case studies above is the now-obvious point that an organization's sales force often plays a significant role in pricing success or failure. As a result, the sales force may have the greatest need for training, and tools that enhance understanding of both the profit effects of pricing decisions and likely competitive reactions (Davey et al., 1998). If the organization is attempting to change the way it makes decisions (and subsequently, the information used to support decisions), it will ultimately have to work through its salespeople. Prior to 1995, Ford compensated its sales force on the number of units sold, independent of profit margins. With the new experimental pricing program described above, Ford "set up its sales units as businesses and told them which vehicles and option packages made Ford the most money" (Coy 2000) – so attention and compensation (and results) shifted to profitability.

Longer-term profitability

Higher order thinking skills
Forcing consideration of new decision criteria will produce limited results if managers fail to account for potential difficulty that people have in applying them. A great deal of research has demonstrated that people tend to have difficulty: putting themselves into other's shoes (e.g. customers, competitors; Fiske and Taylor, 1991; Moore and Urbany, 1994) or; thinking ahead about dynamic, or longer-term effects of a decision (cf. Hutchinson and Meyer, 1994). Each of these skills is important in anticipating customer and competitor reactions to pricing decisions more than just one period ahead. Making longer-term profitability (which is driven by longer-term competitor

and customer response) a more justifiable basis for decision making requires helping to make such consequences vivid and giving managers the courage to move ahead even based on partially complete or ambiguous beliefs about the future.

Simulation. To address this, there is increasing interest in training via simulation techniques in which participants make decisions and are allowed to evaluate the longer-term implications of those decisions (and possibly replay them; Carbonara, 1997; Reibstein and Chussil, 1997). Such simulations would allow participants see, for example, the effect of a price cut on the behavior of customers and competitors not only next quarter, but several quarters down the road[3].

Discomfort zone

Allowing for "vaguely right" decisions. Lodish (1986) argues that many firms make budgeting decisions quite confidently, but based very precisely on the *wrong* criteria (e.g. matching competitors, percentage of sales). In contrast, Lodish recommends allowing for decision making which is "vaguely right" – that is, accounts for costs and likely market response to changes in spending in an approximate way, allowing for uncertainty. This recommendation is even more compelling today. There is an increasing premium on being able to make "vaguely right" decisions in the current business environment, as nearly all firms compete in rapidly changing, hypercompetitive markets (D'Aveni, 1994). This environment requires a new paradigm for managers: making decisions within a discomfort zone involving some degree of uncertainty (e.g. about customer response to a price change, technology requirements, competitive reactions), implementing those decisions quickly, obtaining feedback on critical performance metrics, learning, and continually adapting (cf. Brown and Eisenhardt, 1998). Such decision making would be facilitated by simple decision aids that focus attention on critical breakeven fundamentals (see, for example, Dickson's [1997] ELASTIC spreadsheet), with which managers can explore multiple uncertain scenarios.

Commitment and confirmation
The most powerful means of providing support for a particular decision rationale is if top management gets behind it. Especially in the BBI case above, the rationale for sales training and selling based upon profit margin was strongly led by top management. The most justifiable types of decisions are those that address particular criteria laid out by company leaders.

Two generic strategies

Justifying higher prices to customers
The primary premise of our discussion above (based upon research on accountability and reason-based choice) is that, within the organization, decisions are likely to be more acceptable when they are based upon good reasons. Similarly, customers who are being asked to bear the brunt of ostensibly higher prices certainly will likely expect justification. There are two generic strategies which can be pursued.

(1) *Offer good reasons for competitively higher or rising prices.* Kahneman *et al.* (1986) have demonstrated convincingly that cost-justified price increases are generally perceived to be fair (and certainly fairer than price increases which are not justified or are justified by increased demand). It is likely that arguments about current cost increases or past cost increases which the firm chose not to pass on (but have accumulated over time) offer an effective foundation for a defensive explanation of higher prices.

An issue

(2) *Control the conversation.* In contrast, going on the offense involves directing the conversation away from price. A frequently ignored reality is that marketers *shape* the behavior of the marketplace in addition to adapting to it. Once the vendor makes price an issue, it is an issue. Prior to the sales training that occurred at BBI, one salesperson described his approach in the following way: "I'd give customers the quote, and then I'd ask 'How does the price look?'". After training, he devised a different approach: meet with the customer to learn about a new business opportunity, listen carefully, head back to the office and quickly prepare and fax a list of the customer's needs as he interpreted them. Only after he had received feedback on this letter did he prepare a more formal proposal which included price. Sales proposals were more likely to focus on knowledge of the customer's unique needs and BBI's value-added following the company's new initiatives (Hyatt, 1996). The same logic is reflected in Ford's research on identifying customer value-added features and in our third case above as this industrial products firm survived competitive entry by firming up its relationships with more quality-sensitive segments.

Conclusion

It is true that, under certain circumstances, the errors discussed here may not be fatal. They may wash themselves out of the manager's system with enough learning and therefore may "self-correct over time". In short, I acknowledge that the world is complex enough that very often the marginal costs of learning or thinking deeply about decisions may not exceed the marginal return. Yet, there are too many observations of missed opportunities and laments from practitioners who observe such errors day-in and day-out to conclude that they are simply the exception rather than the rule. The implication is fairly clear; there may often be room to improve the profitability of pricing. Senior management should legitimate and encourage the discussion of incremental profit (rather than market share) and competitor reactions in pricing decisions and foster the development of feedback systems to support these critera.

Interesting challenges

The area poses many interesting challenges for researchers as well, especially in improving understanding of managers' information environment and how uncertainty is and should be dealt with. In particular, there is a need to examine the incidence of errors in pricing, what explains this incidence, and the consequences of such errors. In addition, the study of feedback is important, with issues including what metrics should be used to guide pricing and how managers interpret evidence about measures like market share and sales response. Finally, little is known about how and how much particular cues or factors are discounted by uncertainty. While research in psychology has addressed the issue of ambiguity in decision making (cf. Curley *et al.*, 1986; Einhorn and Hogarth, 1985), the concern identified here is whether or not (and how) people discount different decision cues based upon their confidence in information about those cues. As with the issues above, the largest concern is how to make the truly diagnostic criteria justifiable in the eyes of price-setters and those who evaluate their decisions.

Notes

1. In the commodity pricing study with manufacturers discussed earlier, the most common answer as to why respondents chose to cut price was the belief that customers gained in the short-run could be retained in the longer term. This answer effectively reflects a belief in hysteresis.

2. This tendency may run to farcical extremes as illustrated by a true story about a young marketing manager for a manufacturer of personal computer peripherals firm. After a meeting in which a new price promotion for one of the firm's product lines was announced, this manager privately approached his boss to show him a breakeven analysis which demonstrated that the promotion would potentially be very unprofitable. His boss responded by asking "what is this math BS?" (a slightly altered but nonetheless direct quote) and by roundly rejecting the analysis. The example illustrates not only how pricing decisions may not account for basic economic concepts, but also how managers may be very protective of the firm's existing decision calculus. Schuster (1987) similarly criticizes retailers for their lack of attention to the breakeven implications of price promotion decisions.

3. A vivid illustration of the longer-term path-dependent effects of early pricing decisions occurred in two recent simulations conducted in an MBA course. Substantially different average prices emerged in one simulated industry relative to another, in spite of the fact that each industry's game was: played at the same time with similar groups of students; had essentially the same patterns of customer preference weights; and had identical price response functions. Industry A (composed of five teams, about 25 players) had prices which were, on average, over $100 higher than Industry B and was substantially more profitable. It turned out that in Industry A, one team had been especially diligent early on in conducting research on consumer price sensitivity. As a result, this team had decided upon substantially higher price points than did teams in the other industry. As the diligent team became the industry leader, their pricing provided an umbrella in most markets that others followed. On average, Industry A was much more profitable than Industry B, in spite of very similar conditions.

References

Adams, M.E., Day, G.S. and Dougherty, D. (1998), "Enhancing new product development performance: an organizational learning perspective", *Journal of Product Innovation Management*, Vol. 15, pp. 403-22.

Adelberg, S. and Batson, C.D. (1978), "Accountability and helping: when needs exceed resources", *Journal of Personality and Social Psychology*, Vol. 36, April, pp. 343-50.

Alloy, L.B. and Tabachnik, N. (1984), "Assessment of covariation by humans and animals: the joint influence of prior expectations and current situational information", *Psychological Review*, Vol. 91, January, pp. 112-49.

Anterasian, C., Graham, J.L. and Money, B.R. (1996), "Are US managers superstitious about market share?", *Sloan Management Review*, Vol. 37, Summer, pp. 67-77.

Anthes, G.H. (1998), "The price had better be right", *Computerworld*, 21 December.

Armstrong, J.S. and Collopy, F. (1996), "Competitor orientation: effects of objectives and information on managerial decisions and profitability", *Journal of Marketing Research*, Vol. 33, May, pp. 188-99.

Bacharach, S.B., Bamberger, P. and Mundell, B. (1995), "Strategic and tactical logics of decision justification: power and decision criteria in organizations", *Human Relations*, Vol. 48, May, pp. 467-88.

Bazerman, M.H., Tensbrunsel, A.E. and Wade-Benzoni, K. (1998), "Negotiating with yourself and losing: making decisions with competing internal preferences", *Academy of Management Review*, Vol. 23, April, pp. 225-41.

Blinder, A. (1991), "Why are prices sticky? preliminary results from an interview study", *American Economic Review (AEA Proceedings)*, Vol. 81, May, pp. 89-96.

Bonoma, T. (1981), "Marketing success can breed 'marketing inertia'", *Harvard Business Review*, Vol. 59 No. 5, September/October, pp. 337-60.

Bonoma, T.V., Crittenden, V.L. and Dolan, R.J. (1988), "Can we have rigor and relevance in pricing research?", in DeVinney, T. (Ed.), *Issues in Pricing: Theory and Research*, Lexington Books, Lexington, MA, pp. 115-21.

Brown, S.L. and Eisenhardt, K. (1998), *Competing on the Edge*, Harvard Business School Press, Boston, MA.

Carbonara, P. (1997), "Game over", *Fast Company*, December-January, pp. 128-36.

Carlton, D. (1986), "The rigidity of prices", *American Economic Review*, Vol. 76, September, pp. 637-58.

Chaiken, S.S. (1980), "Heuristic versus systematic information processing and the use of source versus message cues in persuasion", *Journal of Personality and Social Psychology*, Vol. 39, November, pp. 752-66.

Chen, M.-J., Smith, K.G. and Grimm, C.M. (1992), "Action characteristics as predictors of competitive responses", *Management Science*, Vol. 38, March, pp. 439- 55.

Coy, P. (2000), "The power of smart pricing", *Business Week*, 10 April, p. 160.

Culnan, M.J. (1983), "Environmental scanning: the effects of task complexity and source accessibility on information gathering behavior", *Decision Sciences*, Vol. 14, April, pp. 194-206.

Curley, S.P., Yates, J.F. and Abrams, R.A. (1986), "Psychological sources of ambiguity avoidance", *Organizational Behavior and Human Decision Processes*, Vol. 38, April, pp. 230-56.

Cyert, R.M. and March, J.G. (1992), *A Behavioral Theory of the Firm*, 2nd ed., Blackwell Publishers, Oxford.

D'Aveni, R.A. (1994), *Hypercompetition*, The Free Press, New York, NY.

Davey, K.K.S., Childs, A. and Carolotti, S.J. Jr. (1998), "Why your price band is wider than it should be", *McKinsey Quarterly*, Vol. 1, Summer, pp. 116-27.

Day, G.S. (1991), "Learning about markets", Marketing Science Institute Report No. 91-117.

Day, G.S. and Wensley, R. (1988), "Assessing advantage: a framework for diagnosing competitive superiority", *Journal of Marketing*, Vol. 52, April, pp. 1-20.

DeKimpe, M.G. and Hanssens, D.M. (1999), "Sustained spending and persistent response: a new look at long-term marketing profitability", *Journal of Marketing Research*, Vol. 36, November, pp. 397-410.

DeSarbo, W. S., Rao, V.R., Steckel, J.H., Wind, J. and Colombo, R. (1987), "A friction model for describing and forecasting price changes", *Marketing Science*, Vol. 6, Fall, pp. 299-319.

Dickson, P.R. (1997), *Marketing Management*, 2nd ed., Dryden, Fort Worth, TX.

Dolan, R.J. and Jeuland, A.P. (1981), "Experience curves and dynamic demand models: implementation for optimal pricing strategies", *Journal of Marketing*, Vol. 45, Winter, pp. 52-73.

Einhorn, H.J. and Hogarth, R.M. (1985), "Ambiguity and uncertainty in probabilistic inference", *Psychological Review*, Vol. 92, pp. 433-61.

Fiske, S.T. and Taylor, S.E. (1991), *Social Cognition*, 2nd ed., McGraw-Hill, New York, NY.

Hall, R.L. and Hitch, C.J. (1939), "Price theory and business behavior", *Oxford Economic Papers*, Vol. 2, pp. 12-45.

Hamel, G. and Prahalad, C.K. (1994), *Competing for the Future*, Harvard Business School Press, Boston, MA.

Hoch, S.J., Dreze, X. and Purk, M.E. (1994), "EDLP, hi-lo, and margin arithmetic", *Journal of Marketing*, Vol. 58, October, pp. 16-27.

Hyatt, J. (1996), "Hot commodity", *Inc.*, 1 February, pp. 50-8.

Kahneman, D. and Knetsch, J.L. (1991), "Anomalies: the endownment effect, loss aversion and status quo biases", *Journal of Economic Perspectives*, Vol. 5, Winter, pp. 193-206.

Kahneman, D., Knetsch, J.L. and Thaler, R.H. (1986), "Fairness as a constraint on profit seeking: entitlements in the market", *American Economic Review*, Vol. 76, September, pp. 728-41.

Kaufman, B.E. (1999), "Expanding the behavioral foundations of labor economics", *Industrial and Labor Relations Review*, Vol. 52, April, pp. 361-4.

Keil, S., Reibstein, D.J. and Wittink, D.R. (1999), "The impact of time horizon and objectives on the competitiveness of management behavior", Working Paper, School of Management, Yale University, New Haven, CT.

Kopalle, P., Mela, C.F. and Marsh, L. (1999), "The dynamic effect of discounting on sales: empirical analysis and normative pricing implications", *Marketing Science*, pp. 317-33.

Kotler, P. and Singh, R. (1981), "Marketing warfare in the 1980s", *Journal of Business Strategy*, Winter, pp. 30-41.

Kreps, D.M. (1990), *A Course in Microeconomic Theory*, Princeton University Press, Princeton, NJ.

211

Krishna, A., Mela, C.F. and Urbany, J.E. (2000), "Inertia in pricing", working paper, Duke University, Durham, NC.

Lanzillotti, R.F. (1958), "Pricing objectives in large companies", *American Economic Review*, Vol. 48, December, pp. 921-40.

Little, J.D.C. and Shapiro, J.F. (1980), "A theory of pricing nonfeatured products in supermarkets", *Journal of Business*, Vol. 53, July, pp. s199-s209.

Lodish, L.M. (1986), *The Advertising and Promotion Challenge*, Oxford University Press, Oxford.

Meyer, J.W. and Rowan, B. (1977), "Institutionalized organizations: formal structure as myth and ceremony", *American Journal of Sociology*, Vol. 83, September, pp. 340-63.

Mondello, M. D. (1992), "Naming your price", *Inc.*, Vol. 14, July, pp. 80-3.

Monroe, K.B. (1990), *Pricing: Making Profitable Decisions*, 2nd ed., McGraw-Hill, New York, NY.

Monroe, K.B. and Mazumdar, T. (1988), "Pricing-decision models: recent developments and research opportunities", in DeVinney, T. (Ed.), *Issues in Pricing: Theory and Research*, Lexington Books, Lexington, MA, pp. 361-88.

Moore, M.C. and Urbany, J.E. (1994), "Blinders, fuzzy lenses, and the wrong shoes: pitfalls in competitive conjecture", *Marketing Letters*, Vol. 5 No. 3, pp. 247-58.

Morgenroth, W. (1964), "A method for understanding price determinants", *Journal of Marketing Research*, Vol. 1, August, pp. 17-26.

Nagle, T.T. (1993), "Managing price competition", *Marketing Management*, Vol. 2 No. 1, pp. 36-45.

Nagle, T. T. and Holdren, R.K. (1995), *The Strategy and Tactics of Pricing*, 2nd ed., Prentice-Hall, Englewood Cliffs, NJ.

Nisbett, R. and Ross, L. (1980), *Human Inference: Strategies and Shortcomings of Social Judgment*, Prentice-Hall, Englewood Cliffs, NJ.

O'Conner, M.J. (1986), "What is the logic of a price war?", *International Trends in Retailing*, Vol. 3, Spring, pp. 15-21.

Okun, A.M. (1981), *Prices and Quantities: A Macroeconomic Analysis*, The Brookings Institute, Washington, D.C.

O'Reilly, C. (1982), "Variations in use of decision makers' use of information sources: the impact of quality versus accessibility of information", *Academy of Management Journal*, Vol. 25, December, pp. 756-71.

Pindyck, R.S. and Rubinfeld, D.L. (1989), *Microeconomics*, Macmillan, New York, NY.

Porter, M. (1980), *Competitive Strategy*, Free Press, New York, NY.

Ramaswamy, V., Gatignon, H. and Reibstein, D.J. (1994), "Competitive marketing behavior in industrial markets", *Journal of Marketing*, Vol. 58, April, pp. 45-55.

Rao, A.R., Bergen, M.E. and Davis, S. (2000), "How to fight a price war", *Harvard Business Review*, Vol. 78, March-April, pp. 107-15.

Rao, V.R. and Steckel, J.H. (1998), *Analysis for Strategic Marketing*, Addison-Wesley, Reading, MA.

Reibstein, D.J. (1999), "The impact of time horizon and objectives on the competitiveness of management behavior and related studies", University of Notre Dame, Notre Dame, IN, November.

Reibstein, D.J. and Chussil, M.J. (1997), "Putting the lesson before the test: using simulation to analyze and develop competitive strategies", in Day, G.S. and Reibstein, D.J. (Eds), *Wharton on Dynamic Competitive Strategy*, John Wiley, New York, NY, pp. 395-423.

Repenning, N.P. and Sterman, J.D. (1997), "Getting quality the old-fashioned way: self-confirming attributions in the dynamics of process improvement", working paper, Sloan School of Management, MIT, Cambridge, MA.

Rigsbee, S.R., Ayaydin, S.S. and Richard, C.A. (1992), "Pricing for profits", *Mortgage Banking*, Vol. 52, February, pp. 65-71.

Rothschild, M. (1974), "A two-armed bandit theory of market pricing", *Journal of Economic Theory*, Vol. 9, October, pp. 185-202.

Samuelson, W. and Zeckhauser, R. (1988), "Status quo bias in decision making", *Journal of Risk and Uncertainty*, Vol. 1, March, pp. 7-59.

Scharfstein, D.S. and Stein, J.C. (1990) "Herd behavior and investment", *American Economic Review*, Vol. 80, June, pp. 465-79.

Scherer, F.M. and Ross, D. (1990), *Industrial Market Structure and Economic Performance*, 3rd ed., Houghton Mifflin, Boston, MA.

Schuster, T.F. (1987), "A breeze in the face", *Harvard Business Review*, Vol. 65 No. 6, November-December, pp. 36-41.

Scott, I. (1995), "Pricing for profitability", *Foundry Management and Technology*, Vol. 123, August, pp. 51-2.

Shipley, D.D. (1981), "Pricing objectives in British manufacturing industry", *Journal of Industrial Economics*, Vol. 29, June, pp. 429-43.

Silver, W.S. and Mitchell, T.R. (1990), "The status quo tendency in decision making", *Organizational Dynamics*, Vol. 18, Spring, pp. 34-46.

Simon, H. (1997), "Hysteresis in marketing – a new phenomenon?", *Sloan Management Review*, Vol. 38, Spring, pp. 39-49.

Simon, H.A. (1997), *Administrative Behavior*, 4th ed., The Free Press, New York, NY.

Simonson, I. (1989), "Choice based on reasons: the case of attraction and compromise effects", *Journal of Consumer Research*, Vol. 16, September, pp. 158-74.

Starbuck, W.H. (1983), "Organizations as action generators", *American Sociological Review*, Vol. 48, February, pp. 91-102.

Sull, D.N. (1999), "Why good companies go bad", *Harvard Business Review*, Vol. 77 No. 4, July-August, pp. 42-6.

Sweezy, P.M. (1939), "Demand under conditions of uncertainty", *Journal of Political Economy*, Vol. 47, August, pp. 568-73.

Tetlock, P.E. (1983), "Accountability and the complexity of thought", *Journal of Personality and Social Psychology*, Vol. 45, pp. 74-83.

Tetlock, P.E. (1985), "Accountability: the neglected social context of judgment and choice", in Cummings, L.L. and Staw, B.M. (Eds), *Research in Organizational Behavior*, Vol. 7, pp. 297-332.

Urban, G. and Star, S.H. (1990), *Advanced Marketing Strategy*, Prentice-Hall, Englewood Cliffs, NJ.

Urbany, J.E. and Dickson, P.R. (1994), "Evidence on the risk-taking of price-setters", *Journal of Economic Psychology*, Vol. 15 No. 1, pp. 127-48.

Urbany, J. E., Montgomery, D.B. and Moore, M.C. (2000), "Competitive reactions and modes of competitive reasoning", working paper, Mendoza College of Business, University of Notre Dame, Notre Dame, IN.

Walters, R.G. and MacKenzie, S. (1988), "A structural equations analysis of the impact of price promotions on store performance", *Journal of Marketing Research*, Vol. 25, February, pp. 51-63.

213

This summary has been provided to allow managers and executives a rapid appreciation of the content of this article. Those with a particular interest in the topic covered may then read the article in toto to take advantage of the more comprehensive description of the research undertaken and its results to get the full benefit of the material present

Executive summary and implications for managers and executives

Being in business is about making a profit

A while ago, one of the big banks undertook a study into the profitability of its retail customers. The bank discovered that a large number of customers were unprofitable and acted as a drag on business development and expansion. The fact that the bank was highly profitable matters little at this point – the bank needed to charge these customers for the services they received.

In the end, the bank decided not to charge, to accept the cost of these unprofitable customers while, at the same time, reducing the services given for nothing. But, until the point of undertaking a profitability study, the bank had no idea that large numbers of its customers were losing the business money.

Urbany presents us with an exposé of the inadequacy of many managers and businesses when it comes to pricing. Faced with what is a largely rational decision, managers time and again make the wrong decision – selecting prices that are sub-optimal.

The tyranny of market share

Urbany sees part of the problem with sub-optimal pricing as lying in the encouragement of managers to seek greater market share rather than better levels of profitability. The car company that shifts its market share up a couple of points is seen as more successful than the car company that drops its market share but increases its profits.

Market share objectives are complemented by the ways in which sales people are rewarded. Instead of rewarding profitability we tend to reward sales volume – a sales person could be losing us money at the same time as that person receives the sales person of the year award! Even in fast moving goods markets where the sales force is less significant – we see pricing decisions being driven by the need to build or protect market share rather than on profit motives.

There may be good reasons (or at least it seems that way) to increase your product's market share but doing this at the expense of profits is usually mistaken. It is far better for us to set targets that generate profits over the long-term. And this means understanding the market we serve and the essential rules of microeconomics.

Economic illiteracy

Most of us pretend we know something about economics – especially if we have done our MBA. Yet, in our actions, we display a degree of economic illiteracy only matched by politicians. Since we are talking about pricing here, we should understand the basis of price effects in micro-economic theory. But we do not understand relying instead on a load of urban myths, what other folk have done before us and what our boss says.

The "rules" of pricing – higher prices mean fewer sales and vice versa – are appreciated but we do not recognise the other part of the equation. Higher prices mean higher margins and vice versa. And the marginal price increase is 100 per cent profit. As Urbany's example from Ford shows, you can raise prices and increase profits.

The second part of pricing theory we do not understand or use is price elasticity. We know that sales for some things drop more quickly in response *to higher prices. But we never try to understand what that means for our product or our market.*

These are simple economic ideas. We do not need to use complicated maths (or at least Adam Smith did not need to) to get an appreciation of what the proven rules of pricing mean for our business and our products.

Macho management let us crush the opposition
Why do managers respond to competition by aggressive actions? Why do we end up in price wars that destroy the profits of a whole industry? Mainly because we respond inappropriately to competitor actions. The firm down the road drops its prices and we respond the same. Why? It just costs both of us money.

Partly this is about market share. Fred has got more customers than me; therefore he is making more money. It ain't necessarily so. Fred could be losing money hand over fist. Urbany reports on the firm that lifted its sales revenue by 30 per cent without increasing profits – what a waste of time and effort.

Aggressive, short-term pricing seems not to achieve what we want. But many managers – even ones with expensive degrees that include economics – still fall back on hysteresis (aggressive short-term actions that result in long-term benefits). It is the blitzkrieg approach to business, pile in with all the tanks and big guns and crush the enemy. In the long run you get beat.

We are in business to make profits not sell widgets
I am forever hearing that business people are only motivated by profit and are grinding the faces of the poor worker or hard-pressed consumer to realise that profit. Let us at least give these folk the satisfaction of being right about the first part of their assertion – we are in this for profits.

Urbany's article is a sharp reminder of the inadequacies of management. Despite higher qualifications and endless short courses, managers are still getting it wrong, are still setting prices that reduce profitability, are still showing no real grasp of the basic maths needed to understand whether a particular pricing decision will improve or damage profits.

Price decisions should be informed by their effect of profit. Not their effect on market share or on the PR manager's stress levels. If doubling your prices triples your profits then do it. If it means you go bust don't do it. And the same goes for cutting prices – there are times when dropping the price will increase your profit. There are even times (I am sure there must be) when chasing market share will increase profits.

Basing prices on sentiment, past behaviour, competitor activity or simple cost-plus formulae indicates a lack of thought about securing the profits we want. Losing a customer is not always a problem nor is it wrong to insist to your sales people that there are no discounts or special deals. The price you see is the price you will pay.

Urbany's article is a must read for all of us involved in pricing decisions. It shows just how bad most of us have been at setting prices and gives a clear demonstration of how to go about setting justified prices that produce higher profits.

(A précis of the article "Justifying profitable pricing". Supplied by Marketing Consultants for MCB University Press.)